Neoclassical Realism, ɪ and Foreign Policy

Neoclassical realism is an important new approach to international relations. Focusing on the interaction of the international system and the internal dynamics of states, neoclassical realism seeks to explain the grand strategies of individual states as opposed to recurrent patterns of international outcomes. This book offers the first systematic survey of the neoclassical realist approach. The editors lead a group of senior and emerging scholars in presenting a variety of neoclassical realist approaches to states' grand strategies. They examine the central role of the "state" and seek to explain why, how, and under what conditions the internal characteristics of states intervene between their leaders' assessments of international threats and opportunities, and the actual diplomatic, military, and foreign economic policies those leaders are likely to pursue.

STEVEN E. LOBELL is Associate Professor in the Department of Political Science at the University of Utah.

NORRIN M. RIPSMAN is Associate Professor in the Department of Political Science at Concordia University.

JEFFREY W. TALIAFERRO is Associate Professor in the Department of Political Science at Tufts University.

Neoclassical Realism, the State, and Foreign Policy

Edited by

STEVEN E. LOBELL
NORRIN M. RIPSMAN
JEFFREY W. TALIAFERRO

CAMBRIDGE
UNIVERSITY PRESS

CAMBRIDGE UNIVERSITY PRESS
Cambridge, New York, Melbourne, Madrid, Cape Town, Singapore, São Paulo,
Delhi, Dubai, Tokyo, Mexico City

Cambridge University Press
The Edinburgh Building, Cambridge CB2 8RU, UK

Published in the United States of America by Cambridge University Press, New York

www.cambridge.org
Information on this title: www.cambridge.org/9780521731928

© Cambridge University Press 2009

First published 2009
Reprinted 2010

Printed in the United Kingdom at the University Press, Cambridge

A catalogue record for this publication is available from the British Library

ISBN 978-0-521-51705-8 Hardback
ISBN 978-0-521-73192-8 Paperback

Contents

Figures

Tables

Contributors

MARK R. BRAWLEY, Professor, Department of Political Science, McGill University

COLIN DUECK, Associate Professor, Department of Public and International Affairs, George Mason University

BENJAMIN O. FORDHAM, Associate Professor, Department of Political Science, Binghamton University (SUNY)

STEVEN E. LOBELL, Associate Professor, Department of Political Science, University of Utah

NORRIN M. RIPSMAN, Associate Professor, Department of Political Science, Concordia University

RANDALL L. SCHWELLER, Professor, Department of Political Science, The Ohio State University

JENNIFER STERLING-FOLKER, Associate Professor of Political Science, University of Connecticut

JEFFREY W. TALIAFERRO, Associate Professor, Department of Political Science, Tufts University

Acknowledgments

This volume began with a conference at Concordia University in May 2006. We gratefully acknowledge conference funding from the Canadian Department of National Defence, Security and Defence Forum, the Globalization and the State project (T. V. Paul, Michel A. Fortmann, John Hall, and Norrin M. Ripsman, co-investigators), Centre d'Études des Politiques Étrangères et de Sécurité (CEPES) in Montreal, the Faculty of Arts and Science at Concordia University (David Graham, Dean), the Department of Political Science at Concordia University (Peter Stoett, Chair), the Department of Political Science at the University of Utah (Ron Hrebenar, Chair), the College of Social and Behavioral Science at the University of Utah (Steven Ott, Dean), and the Department of Political Science at Tufts University (Rob Devigne, Chair). We thank Emilie Blais, Sébastien Mainville, Kathryn Rawlings, and Jeannie Krumel for their outstanding conference organization and support. The volume also benefited immensely from the input, comments, and feedback of the conference chairs and discussants, as well as the faculty and graduate student participants from Concordia University, McGill University, l'Université de Québec à Montréal, and l'Université de Montréal. We especially acknowledge feedback from Axel Huelsemeyer, Michael Lipson, Alex MacLeod, Nelson Michaud, Dan O'Meara, T. V. Paul, Brian Rathbun, Stéphane Roussel, Julian Schofield, and Marie-Joelle Zahar.

After the conference, the papers were revised and edited. We thank the contributors to the volume not only for their dedication and attention to detail, but also for their patience. We organized a special panel at the annual meeting of the American Political Science Association in Philadelphia in September 2006 and the annual meeting of the International Security Studies and International Security and Arms Control Session (ISSS-ISAC) in Montreal, Canada, in October 2007. The respective chairs and discussants, Karen Ruth Adams and Greg Kennedy, as well as the other participants on the panels helped us sharpen our arguments.

We would like to thank Ben Frankel, Patrick James, David A. Lake, Jack S. Levy, David McBride, Gideon Rose, and William C. Wohlforth for their advice and comments on this book manuscript. Andrew E. Title provided research assistance and edited an earlier version of the manuscript. Carrie Humphreys did a marvelous job assisting us in the preparation of the final manuscript. We are indebted to Cambridge University Press editor John Haslam for his enthusiastic support. We also acknowledge the extensive and useful comments by the anonymous reviewers for Cambridge University Press. We take full responsibility for the errors and omissions.

1 | Introduction: Neoclassical realism, the state, and foreign policy

JEFFREY W. TALIAFERRO, STEVEN E. LOBELL,
AND NORRIN M. RIPSMAN

How do states, or more specifically the decision-makers and institutions that act on their behalf, assess international threats and opportunities? What happens when there is disagreement about the nature of foreign threats? Who ultimately decides the range of acceptable and unacceptable foreign policy alternatives? To what extent, and under what conditions, can domestic actors bargain with state leaders and influence foreign or security policies? How and under what circumstances will domestic factors impede states from pursuing the types of strategies predicted by balance of power theory and balance of threat theory? Finally, how do states go about extracting and mobilizing resources necessary to implement foreign and security policies? These are important questions that cannot be answered by the dominant neorealist or liberal theories of international politics.

Consider the following: in 1945, and again in 1990, the United States emerged victorious from a major war or an enduring rivalry. In each postwar period, officials in Washington faced the daunting task of assessing and responding to new and unfamiliar international threats.[1] However, the resulting shifts in grand strategy were not predictable solely based upon an analysis of relative power distributions or the dynamics of American domestic politics at the time.[2]

---

[1] See William C. Wohlforth, "The Stability of a Unipolar World," *International Security* 21, no. 1 (summer 1999), pp. 1–36; Stephen G. Brooks and William C. Wohlforth, "American Primacy in Perspective," *Foreign Affairs* 81, no. 4 (July/August 2002), pp. 20–33; Wohlforth, "US Strategy in a Unipolar World," in G. John Ikenberry, ed., *America Unrivaled: The Future of the Balance of Power* (Ithaca: Cornell University Press, 2002), pp. 98–120.

[2] Kenneth N. Waltz repeatedly states that his is not a theory of foreign policy and that it only purports to explain broad patterns of systemic outcomes. See Waltz, *Theory of International Politics* (New York: McGraw-Hill, 1979), pp. 39, 48–9,

The bipolar distribution of power following the Second World War does not explain why the United States embarked upon a grand strategy of containment, which eventually mixed both realpolitik and liberal internationalist ends and means, over the alternative of competitive cooperation with the Soviet Union through a sphere-of-influence arrangement in Europe.[3] As others have noted, in an international system with only two first-tier great powers, some type of competition between them is likely. However, the system could not dictate how the superpowers would define their competitive relationship, let alone the nuances and evolution of their respective grand strategies.[4]

Neither a purely systemic theory of international outcomes, such as neorealist balance of power theory, nor a purely *Innenpolitik* theory of foreign policy, such as liberal or democratic peace theory, can explain why the George H. W. Bush and Clinton administrations sought to preserve and expand US influence in Europe and East Asia in the 1990s, despite the absence of a great power competitor (at least in the near term) and despite strong domestic pressure to reap the benefits of the so-called peace dividend following the Cold War.[5]

58–9, 72, 78, 87, and 121–3; Waltz, "Reflections on *Theory of International Politics*: A Response to My Critics," in Robert O. Keohane, ed., *Neorealism and its Critics* (New York: Columbia University Press, 1986), pp. 328, 339–40, and 343; and Waltz, "International Politics is Not Foreign Policy," *Security Studies* 6, no. 1 (autumn 1996), pp. 54–7.

[3] For two recent neoclassical realist examinations of US grand strategy and strategic adjustment over the past century, see Christopher Layne, *Peace of Illusions: American Grand Strategy from 1940 to the Present* (Ithaca: Cornell University Press, 2006); and Colin Dueck, *Reluctant Crusaders: Power, Culture, and Change in American Grand Strategy* (Princeton, NJ: Princeton University Press, 2006).

[4] See Deborah Welch Larson, *Origins of Containment: A Psychological Explanation* (Princeton, NJ: Princeton University, 1985), p. 3; Robert Jervis, *System Effects: Complexity in Political and Social Life* (Princeton, NJ: Princeton University Press, 1996), pp. 118–22; and Aaron L. Friedberg, *In the Shadow of the Garrison State: America's Anti-Statism and its Cold War Grand Strategy* (Princeton, NJ: Princeton University Press, 2000), esp. chap. 2.

[5] A structural realist exception would be offensive realism, which suggests that the international system provides strong incentives for all states to maximize their relative share of material power as the best route to security. The definitive statement of offensive realism is John J. Mearsheimer, *Tragedy of Great Power Politics* (New York: W. W. Norton, 2001). See also Mearsheimer, "Back to the Future: Instability in Europe after the Cold War," *International Security* 15, no. 1 (summer 1990), pp. 5–56; Mearsheimer, "The False Promise of

Instead, a combination of international opportunities, relatively low external threat levels, and domestic political constraints appear to account for the underlying continuities in US grand strategy during that decade.

Relative power and shifts in the level of external threat alone cannot explain the nuances of the George W. Bush administration's grand strategy after the September 11, 2001 terrorist attacks. Certainly, any presidential administration (Republican or Democratic) would have responded to the Al Qaeda attacks on New York City and Washington, DC by using American military might to topple the Taliban regime in Afghanistan and destroy Al Qaeda safe havens in that country. However, other aspects of the Bush administration's behavior defy simply systemic or domestic-level explanations. Instead, the so-called Bush doctrine, the March 2003 invasion of Iraq, and the administration's subsequent campaign to eliminate Islamist terrorism by fostering liberal democracy in the Middle East resulted from a veritable witches' brew of systemic and domestic-level factors. In other words, while external threats and preponderant American power set the parameters for a US military response, unit-level factors such as executive branch dominance in national security, policy entrepreneurship by neoconservatives within the administration and the think tank community, and the dominance of Wilsonian (or liberal) ideals in US foreign policy discourse determined both the character and the venue of that response.[6]

In each example, international imperatives filtered through the medium of state structure and affected how top officials assessed likely threats, identified viable strategies in response to those threats,

---

International Institutions," *International Security* 19, no. 3 (winter 1994/5), pp. 5–49; and Eric J. Labs, "Beyond Victory: Offensive Realism and the Expansion of War Aims," *Security Studies* 6, no. 4 (summer 1997), pp. 1–49. We consider the performance of neoclassical realism against offensive realism and rationalist approaches to foreign policy in our concluding chapter.

[6] Robert Jervis, "Understanding the Bush Doctrine," *Political Science Quarterly* 118, no. 3 (fall 2003), pp. 365–88; Chaim Kaufmann, "Threat Inflation and the Failure of the Marketplace for Ideas: The Selling of the Iraq War," *International Security* 29, no. 4 (summer 2004), pp. 5–48; Colin Dueck, "Ideas and Alternatives in US Grand Strategy, 2000–2004," *Review of International Studies* 30, no. 3 (October 2004), pp. 511–35; and Jonathan Monten, "The Roots of the Bush Doctrine: Power, Nationalism, and Democracy Promotion in Grand Strategy," *International Security* 29, no. 4 (spring 2005), pp. 112–56.

and ultimately extracted and mobilized the societal resources necessary to implement and sustain those strategies. Furthermore, complex relationships between systemic and unit-level variables in shaping foreign policy are not unique to the United States. Unit-level variables constrain or facilitate the ability of all types of states – great powers as well as lesser states – to respond to systemic imperatives.

This volume examines the intervening role of the "state" in neoclassical realism, an emerging school of foreign policy theories. Specifically, it seeks to explain why, how, and under what conditions the internal characteristics of states – the extractive and mobilization capacity of politico-military institutions, the influence of domestic societal actors and interest groups, the degree of state autonomy from society, and the level of elite or societal cohesion – intervene between the leaders' assessment of international threats and opportunities and the actual diplomatic, military, and foreign economic policies those leaders pursue. Neoclassical realism posits an imperfect "transmission belt" between systemic incentives and constraints, on the one hand, and the actual diplomatic, military, and foreign economic policies states select, on the other. Over the long term, international political outcomes generally mirror the actual distribution of power among states. In the shorter term, however, the policies states pursue are rarely objectively efficient or predictable based upon a purely systemic analysis.

Proponents of neoclassical realism draw upon the rigor and theoretical insights of the neorealism (or structural realism) of Kenneth N. Waltz, Robert Gilpin, and others without sacrificing the practical insights about foreign policy and the complexity of statecraft found in the classical realism of Hans J. Morgenthau, Henry Kissinger, Arnold Wolfers, and others. Like other variants of realism, neoclassical realism assumes that politics is a perpetual struggle among different states for material power and security in a world of scarce resources and pervasive uncertainty. Anarchy – the absence of a universal sovereign or worldwide government – is the permissive cause of international conflict. Systemic forces create incentives for all states to strive for greater efficiency in providing security for themselves. Relative power distributions and trends set broad parameters for states' external behavior. Thucydides' observation about state behavior still holds true: "The strong do what they have the power to do and the weak accept what they have to accept."[7] However, as Gideon Rose observes in the 1998 *World Politics* review article that coined the term "neoclassical realism":

Neoclassical realism argues that the scope and ambition of a country's foreign policy is driven first and foremost by the country's relative material power. Yet it contends that the impact of power capabilities on foreign policy is indirect and complex, because systemic pressures must be translated through intervening unit-level variables such as decision-makers' perceptions and state structure.[8]

The succeeding chapters examine different ways in which the state – that is, the central apparatus or institutions of government – inhibits or facilitates the ability to assess international threats and opportunities; to undertake grand strategic adjustments; and to implement specific military, diplomatic, and foreign economic policies.

The remainder of this chapter has five sections: the next one discusses the three overall objectives of this volume. A discussion of the relationship among classical realism, neorealism, and neoclassical realism follows in the second section. The third and fourth sections discuss the neoclassical realist conceptions of the state and the international system. The final section identifies questions that guide the rest of the volume and provides an overview of the following chapters.

Objectives of the volume

This volume has three overriding objectives. First, we seek to refine and systematize neoclassical realism and establish new avenues for research. Second, we seek to differentiate neoclassical realism from classical realism and neorealism, as well as from other schools of international relations theories. Finally, we seek to develop the concept of the state more fully as both an analytical concept in security studies and as an intervening variable in the study of foreign policy. Below, we discuss each of these goals in detail.

Rose coined the term "neoclassical realism" specifically in reference to books by Thomas Christensen, Randall Schweller, William Wohlforth,

---

[7] Thucydides, *History of the Peloponnesian War*, trans. Rex Warner (1954; reprint New York: Penguin, 1988), p. 402.

[8] Gideon Rose, "Neoclassical Realism and Theories of Foreign Policy," *World Politics* 51, no. 1 (October 1998), pp. 144–77.

and Fareed Zakaria, as well as an anthology of articles previously published in the journal *International Security*. These authors seek to explain the grand strategy of a particular modern great power at a specific time or place and not recurrent patterns of international political outcomes. Christensen argues that hostility between China and the United States in the early years of the Cold War was an unintended consequence of strategies Mao Zedong and the Truman administration used to mobilize societal resources for national security. Ultimately shifts in the international distribution of power drove Chinese and US foreign policies, but in both countries domestic politics led to the pursuit of overly competitive policies in secondary regions to secure broad support for necessary policies in primary regions. Soviet grand strategy during the Cold War, according to Wohlforth, was an outgrowth of disagreements between the Kremlin and Washington about the actual post-World War II distribution of power in Europe and the influence of Communist ideology on Soviet net assessments. Schweller argues that the tripolar international system of the late 1930s and early 1940s, as well as the distribution of revisionist and status quo interests among the three poles – Germany, the Soviet Union, and the United States – actually facilitated Adolf Hitler's expansionist grand strategy. Finally, Zakaria argues that the relatively weak extractive and mobilization capacity of the federal government (i.e. state power) delayed the United States' emergence as a great power in the late nineteenth century, despite a dramatic growth in population and economic capabilities (i.e. national power) in the decades following the American Civil War.[9]

---

[9] See Michael E. Brown et al., eds., *The Perils of Anarchy: Contemporary Realism and International Security* (Cambridge, MA: MIT Press, 1995); Thomas J. Christensen, *Useful Adversaries: Grand Strategy, Domestic Mobilization, and Sino-American Conflict, 1947–1958* (Princeton, NJ: Princeton University Press, 1996); Randall L. Schweller, *Deadly Imbalances: Tripolarity and Hitler's Strategy for World Conquest* (New York: Columbia University Press, 1998); William C. Wohlforth, *The Elusive Balance: Power and Perceptions during the Cold War* (Ithaca, NY: Cornell University Press, 1993); and Fareed Zakaria, *From Wealth to Power: The Unusual Origins of America's World Role* (Princeton, NJ: Princeton University Press, 1998). Rose identifies Aaron L. Friedberg, *The Weary Titan: Britain and the Experience of Relative Decline, 1895–1905* (Princeton, NJ: Princeton University Press, 1988) and Melvin P. Leffler, *A Preponderance of Power: National Security, the Truman Administration, and the Cold War* (Stanford, CA: Stanford University Press, 1992), as immediate precursors of neoclassical realism.

Rose argues that these books constitute a coherent school of foreign policy theories because they posit a single independent or explanatory variable (relative power), a common set of intervening variables (state structure and leaders' perceptions and calculations of relative power), have explicit scope conditions,[10] and share a distinct methodological perspective characterized by detailed historical analysis and attention to causal mechanisms. Drawing upon neorealism, they emphasize the importance of the anarchic international system, relative power distributions, and pervasive uncertainty. However, they see anarchy as a permissive condition, rather than an independent causal force. In this sense, these authors represent a return to the earlier views of Morgenthau, Kissinger, Wolfers, and other classical realists.[11]

In the short run, anarchy gives states considerable latitude in defining their security interests, and the relative distribution of power merely sets parameters for grand strategy. The actual task of assessing power and the intentions of other states is fraught with difficulty. The calculations and perceptions of leaders can inhibit a timely and objectively efficient response or policy adaptation to shifts in the external environment. In addition, leaders almost always face a two-level game in devising and implementing grand strategy: on the one hand, they must respond to the external environment, but, on the other, they must extract and mobilize resources from domestic society, work through existing domestic institutions, and maintain the support of key stakeholders. Over the long run, however, regimes or leaders who consistently fail to respond to systemic incentives put their state's very survival at risk.[12] Thus, while the international system may socialize states to respond properly to its constraints over time, as

[10] For a discussion of the importance of scope conditions for theories and competitive hypothesis testing, see Alexander L. George and Andrew Bennett, *Case Studies and Theory Development in the Social Sciences* (Cambridge, MA: MIT Press, 2005), pp. 113–20.

[11] For a critique of neorealism's reliance on anarchy as an implicit explanatory variable instead of a permissive condition for interstate conflict, see Marc I. Trachtenberg, "The Question of Realism: A Historian's View," *Security Studies* 13, no. 1 (autumn 2003), pp. 156–94.

[12] See Rose, "Neoclassical Realism and Theories of Foreign Policy," pp. 152–4 and 165–8. On two-level games, see Robert D. Putnam, "Diplomacy and Domestic Politics: The Logic of Two Level Games," *International Organization* 42, no. 3 (summer 1988), pp. 427–61.

Waltz contends, it cannot alone explain the shorter-term policy. choices that states make, which can have dramatic consequences for both national security and the structure of the international system.[13]

Since the publication of Rose's article, other scholars have employed neoclassical realist approaches to address an array of theoretical, historical, and policy debates, including: the politics of threat assessment and alliance formation in Britain and France before the two world wars and in Argentina, Brazil, and Paraguay before the 1870 War of the Triple Alliance;[14] the origins of Italy's revisionist grand strategy in the 1920s and 1930s;[15] the interventions of Wilhelmine Germany, Imperial Japan, and the United States in peripheral regions;[16] the dilemmas of assessing the intentions and capabilities of rising great powers;[17] the impact of individual leaders and ideology on grand strategy;[18] domestic constraints on great powers' ability to construct durable settlements after major wars;[19] the origins of containment and the evolution of the US military commitment to

---

[13] Waltz, *Theory of International Politics*, pp. 118–28.

[14] Randall L. Schweller, *Unanswered Threats: Political Constraints on the Balance of Power* (Princeton, NJ: University Press, 2006); and Steven E. Lobell, *The Challenge of Hegemony: Grand Strategy, Trade, and Domestic Politics* (Ann Arbor: University of Michigan Press, 2003).

[15] Jason W. Davidson, "The Roots of Revisionism: Fascist Italy, 1922–39," *Security Studies* 11, no. 4 (summer 2002), pp. 125–59, and Davidson, *The Origins of Revisionist and Status Quo States* (New York: Palgrave Macmillan, 2006).

[16] Jeffrey W. Taliaferro, *Balancing Risks: Great Power Intervention in the Periphery* (Ithaca, NY: Cornell University Press, 2004).

[17] David M. Edelstein, "Managing Uncertainty: Beliefs about Intentions and the Rise of Great Powers," *Security Studies* 12, no. 1 (autumn 2002), pp. 1–40; Randall L. Schweller, "Bandwagoning for Profit: Bringing the Revisionist State Back In," *International Security* 19, no. 1 (summer 1994), pp. 72–107; and Schweller, "The Twenty Years' Crisis, 1919–39: Why a Concert Didn't Arise," in Colin Elman and Miriam Fendius Elman, eds., *Bridges and Boundaries: Historians, Political Scientists, and the Study of International Relations* (Cambridge, MA: MIT Press, 2001), pp. 181–212.

[18] Daniel L. Byman and Kenneth M. Pollack, "Let Us Now Praise Great Men: Bringing the Statesman Back In," *International Security* 25, no. 4 (spring 2001), pp. 107–46.

[19] Norrin M. Ripsman, *Peacemaking by Democracies: The Effects of State Autonomy on the Post-World War Settlements* (University Park: Pennsylvania State University Press, 2002); and Ripsman, "The Curious Case of German Rearmament: Democracy and Foreign Security Policy," *Security Studies* 10, no. 2 (winter 2001), pp. 1–47.

western Europe between the 1940s and the 1960s;[20] the interaction of relative power shifts, the changing nature of global production, and domestic constraints on the Soviet leadership's response to deep relative decline in the 1980s;[21] US, South Korean, and Japanese strategies in the current North Korean nuclear crisis;[22] the evolution of US monetary policy after the demise of the Bretton Woods monetary regime in 1973;[23] the origins of the Bush doctrine and the 2003 US invasion of Iraq;[24] the possibility of ontological convergence between neoclassical realism and constructivism;[25] and debates over the usefulness of Imre Lakatos' methodology of scientific research programs (MSRP) in appraising theoretical progress in international relations.[26]

While there are numerous empirical applications and three frequently cited review or theoretical articles, we seek to develop

[20] James McAllister, *No Exit: America and the German Problem, 1943–1954* (Ithaca, NY: Cornell University, 2002); Aharon Barth, "American Military Commitments in Europe: Power, Perceptions, and Neoclassical Realism" (PhD dissertation, Georgetown University, 2005); Dueck, *Reluctant Crusader*, chap. 4; and Layne, *Peace of Illusions*, chaps. 3–5.

[21] Stephen G. Brooks and William C. Wohlforth "Power, Globalization, and the End of the Cold War: Re-Evaluating a Landmark Case for Ideas," *International Security* 25, no. 3 (winter 2000/1), pp. 5–53.

[22] Victor D. Cha, "Abandonment, Entrapment, and Neoclassical Realism in Asia: The United States, Japan, and Korea," *International Studies Quarterly* 44, no. 2 (June 2000), pp. 261–91; and Cha, "Hawk Engagement and Preventive Defense on the Korean Peninsula," *International Security* 27, no. 1 (summer 2002), pp. 40–78.

[23] Jennifer Sterling-Folker, *Theories of International Cooperation and the Primacy of Anarchy: Explaining US International Monetary Policy-Making after Bretton Woods* (New York: State University of New York Press, 2002).

[24] See Layne, *Peace of Illusions*, pp. 159–205; and Dueck, *Reluctant Crusader*, pp. 169–71.

[25] Jennifer Sterling-Folker, "Realism and the Constructivist Challenge: Rejecting, Reconstructing, or Rereading," *International Studies Review* 4, no. 1 (spring 2002), pp. 73–97; and Sterling-Folker, "Realist-Constructivism and Morality," *International Studies Review* 6, no. 2 (June 2004), pp. 341–43.

[26] Randall L. Schweller, "The Progressive Power of Neoclassical Realism," in Colin Elman and Miriam Fendius Elman, eds., *Progress in International Relations Theory: Appraising the Field* (Cambridge, MA: MIT Press, 2003), pp. 311–47; Schweller, "New Realist Research on Alliances: Refining, Not Refuting Waltz's Balancing Proposition," *American Political Science Review* 91, no. 4 (December 1997), pp. 927–30; Charles L. Glaser, "The Necessary and Natural Evolution of Structural Realism," and William C. Wohlforth, "Measuring Power – and the Power of Theories," in John A. Vasquez and Colin Elman, eds., *Realism and the Balancing of Power: A New Debate* (Upper Saddle River, NJ: Prentice Hall, 2003), pp. 250–79.

neoclassical realism theoretically, expand its empirical applications, and establish its limits as well.[27] As the following chapters illustrate, there is no single neoclassical realist theory of foreign policy, but rather a diversity of neoclassical realist *theories*. This volume, therefore, contains a mix of theoretical and empirical chapters dealing with the grand strategies of current and former great powers as well as second-tier states, such as Canada, Italy, and Taiwan, across different historical periods. Furthermore, several contributors address the theoretical and empirical limits of neoclassical realism, both from within this research program and from the perspective of *Innenpolitik* theories of foreign policy. In this way, we seek to highlight how the neoclassical realist conception of the state differs from those of non-realist schools of international relations theories.

The second objective is to differentiate neoclassical realism from classical realism and neorealism. (In this introduction, we focus particularly on the differences between neoclassical realism and its classical realist and neorealist antecedents. In the concluding chapter, we will further differentiate neoclassical realism from liberal and other approaches to foreign policy.) We believe there is considerable ambiguity over the empirical scope of neoclassical realism, the contingent nature of its hypotheses and policy prescriptions, and its exact relationship to other variants of realism. As a result, other international relations scholars criticize neoclassical realism on epistemological, methodological, and theoretical grounds. The following section addresses the relationship among neoclassical realism, neorealism, and classical realism in greater detail.

This volume's third goal is to fill a gap in the security studies literature about the role of the "state" and the interactions of systemic and unit-level variables in shaping foreign policies. For almost twenty years following the publication of Waltz's *Theory of International Politics*, much of the international relations literature focused on systemic or environmental constraints or inducements on actors' behavior, or on the outcomes of actors' interactions given certain background conditions. The emergence of constructivism and the

---

[27] See Rose, "Neoclassical Realism and Theories of Foreign Policy"; Schweller, "The Progressiveness of Neoclassical Realism"; and Jennifer Sterling-Folker, "Realist Environment, Liberal Process, and Domestic-Level Variables," *International Studies Quarterly* 41, no. 1 (March 1997), pp. 1–25.

democratic peace literature in the late 1980s and early 1990s shifted the focus of scholarly debates away from the rather static conception of the international system found in neorealism and neoliberal institutionalism. However, neither constructivism nor the democratic peace thesis and other variants of liberal international relations theory have managed to integrate systemic and unit-level variables in a deductively consistent manner.

Consider, for example, the democratic peace literature, which derives from the statistical observation that since 1815 pairs of liberal democracies have never waged war on each other.[28] Much of the quantitative literature treats democratic and non-democratic states as unitary actors: democratic states do not fight other democracies, democratic states tend to ally on the same side, democratic states tend to win the wars they fight, and democratic states are more trustworthy due to transparency. Only a few qualitative studies have attempted to disaggregate democracies and examine how the different institutional arrangements of different democratic states (such as presidential versus Westminster parliamentary systems) might constrain foreign policy choice.[29] Thus, democratic peace theorists have a very static and undifferentiated understanding of the democratic state.[30] Like other variants of liberal international relations theory, the democratic peace literature rests upon a "ground-up" or pluralist conception of the state. It assumes the state is a relatively passive set of institutions that merely serve as an arena for competition among different interest groups and that different

---

[28] See, for example, Michael Doyle, "Kant, Liberal Legacies, and Foreign Affairs, part 1," *Philosophy and Public Affairs* 12, no. 3 (1983), pp. 205–35; "Kant, Liberal Legacies, and Foreign Affairs, part 2," *Philosophy and Public Affairs* 12, no. 4 (1983), pp. 323–53; "Liberalism and World Politics," *American Political Science Review* 80, no. 4 (1986), pp. 1151–61; and Bruce M. Russett, *Grasping the Democratic Peace* (Princeton, NJ: Princeton University Press, 1993).

[29] Miriam Fendius Elman, "Presidentialism, Parliamentarism, and Theories of Democratic Peace," *Security Studies* 9, no. 4 (summer 2000), pp. 91–126; Susan Peterson, "How Democracies Differ: Public Opinion, State Structure, and the Lessons of the Fashoda Crisis," *Security Studies* 5, no. 1 (autumn 1995), pp. 3–37; and Ripsman, *Peacemaking by Democracies*.

[30] This critique of democratic peace theory is expanded in Norrin M. Ripsman, "Moving Beyond (or Beneath) the Democratic Peace Theory: Rediscovering Intermediate-Level Institutions in the Foreign Security Policy Literature," in Andre Lecours, ed., *New Institutionalism: Theory and Analysis* (Toronto: University of Toronto Press, 2005), pp. 301–18.

groups or coalitions occasionally capture it.[31] The quantitative and the qualitative work on the democratic peace thesis, therefore, focuses primarily on interest group preferences and bargaining, the institutional arrangements within states (such as executive account-ability to the legislature, separation of powers, and the recurrence of free elections), or ideational variables as constraints on leaders' ability to make foreign and security policies, with little regard for the inter-national environment.[32]

For their part, systemic liberal approaches, such as (neoliberal) institutionalist theory, have an even more problematic and truncated conception of the state. By encouraging certain behaviors while dis-couraging others, institutions or processes – whether operating at the domestic level or at the international level in the form of international organizations and regimes – become a primary causal determinant for actors' interests and behaviors as well as for bargaining outcomes. Systemic liberalism assumes that actors will strive toward the most objectively efficient course of action, which is generally synonymous with cooperative behavior. As Jennifer Sterling-Folker notes, there are at least two contradictions here. First, much of the early institution-alist literature assumed that states functioned as unitary rational actors. At the same time, institutionalist arguments rely on state officials as the vehicles through which international institutions or regimes teach states new behavior. Regardless of the fact that elected leaders, bureaucrats, and interest groups actually engage in very dif-ferent domestic processes or face different institutional constraints, and would therefore have very different interests and behaviors, according to institutionalist arguments they all reach the same con-clusion that more and more cooperation is the best – in fact, the *only* – solution to the problem facing them. Second, there can, however, be no "objective" most efficient course of action, since actors' interests, identities, and behaviors are grounded in process. Actors should then define efficiency according to ongoing processes

[31] Andrew Moravcsik, "Taking Preferences Seriously: A Liberal Theory of International Politics," *International Organization* 51, no. 4 (autumn 1997), pp. 513–53, esp. pp. 516–20.
[32] Miriam Fendius Elman, "The Need for a Qualitative Test of the Democratic Peace Theory," in Miriam Fendius Elman, ed., *Paths to Peace: Is Democracy the Answer?* (Cambridge, MA: MIT Press, 1997), pp. 1–57.

and would have no means of recognizing what was "objectively" in their own best interests.[33]

In contrast to the comparative politics subfield of political science and the political economy wing of international relations, the state – as both a political entity and an analytical concept – is arguably underdeveloped in the security studies literature.[34] This problem is especially endemic to realism. As many self-proclaimed realists acknowledge, realism in general, and neorealism in particular, lacks a well-articulated theory of the state.[35] Neoclassical realists have begun to fill that gap in the literature.

Classical realism, neorealism, and neoclassical realism

Neoclassical realism builds upon the complex relationship between the state and society found in classical realism without sacrificing the central insight of neorealism about the constraints of the international system. Nonetheless, several key questions about the relationship among classical realism, neoclassical realism, and neorealism must be answered: is neoclassical realism merely an attempt to supplement neorealism with unit-level variables – a move that Waltz clearly and repeatedly rejects? Alternatively, does neoclassical realism represent a new research program? By incorporating both systemic and unit-level variables, is neoclassical realism guilty of reductionism – the tendency to explain the whole with reference to

---

[33] Sterling-Folker, "Realist Environment, Liberal Processes, and Domestic Variables," esp. pp. 9–16.

[34] For summaries of the current comparative politics and political economy literature on the state, see Margaret Levi, "The State of the Study of the State," in Ira Katznelson and Helen V. Milner, eds., *Political Science: The State of the Discipline* (New York: W. W. Norton), pp. 33–55.

[35] See, for example, Barry Buzan, Charles Jones, and Richard Little, *The Logic of Anarchy: Neorealism to Structural Realism* (New York: Columbia University Press, 1993), pp. 114–31; Robert W. Cox, "Social Forces, States, and World Orders: Beyond International Relations Theory," in Keohane, *Neorealism and its Critics*, pp. 204–54; John Gerard Ruggie, "Continuity and Transformation in the World Polity: Toward a Neorealist Synthesis," in Keohane, *Neorealism and its Critics*, pp. 131–57; Hendrik Spruyt, *The Sovereign State and its Competitors: An Analysis of Systems Change* (Princeton, NJ: Princeton University Press, 1994); and Alexander Wendt, "Anarchy is What States Make of It," *International Organization* 42, no. 2 (spring 1992), pp. 391–426.

the internal attributes and the individual behavior of the units? By incorporating unit-level variables does neoclassical realism violate the structural logic of realism?

Realism, like Marxism and liberalism, is first and foremost a philosophical position, not a single theory subject to empirical confirmation or disconfirmation. Neoclassical realism, neorealism, and classical realism are heirs to a philosophical tradition dating to the writings of Thucydides and Sun Tzu in the fifth century BCE. What unites all self-described realists are the following: a profoundly pessimistic view of the human condition and the prospects for change in human behavior; a rejection of teleological conceptions of politics or notions of an "end of history";[36] a "skeptical attitude toward schemes for pacific international order";[37] and the recognition that ethics and morality are products of power and material interests, not the other way around.[38]

Scholars compile different lists of realism's first principles and core assumptions, but we identify three. First, human beings cannot survive as individuals, but rather as members of larger groups that command their loyalty and provide some measure of security from external enemies. Tribalism is an immutable fact of political and social life. Thus all variants of realism are inherently group-centric. Second, politics is a perpetual struggle among self-interested groups under conditions of general scarcity and uncertainty. The scarce commodities in question might be material capabilities, or they might be social resources, such as prestige and status. Groups face pervasive uncertainty about one another's present and future intentions.[39] Third, power is a necessary requirement for any group to

---

[36] By "teleology" we mean the notion that politics (whether within the state or among states) and history must ultimately result in some pre-ordained end or that they have some higher (and possibly divinely inspired) purpose.

[37] Michael W. Doyle, *Ways of War and Peace: Realism, Liberalism, and Socialism* (New York: W. W. Norton, 1997), p. 43.

[38] Edward Hallett Carr, *The Twenty Years' Crisis, 1919–1939: An Introduction to the Study of International Relations* (New York: Harper and Row, 1964), pp. 64–5.

[39] Randall L. Schweller, "Realism and the Present Great Power System: Growth and Positional Conflict over Scarce Resources," in Ethan B. Kapstein and Michael Mastanduno, eds., *Unipolar Politics: Realism and State Strategies after the Cold War* (New York: Columbia University Press, 1999), chap. 2; and Daniel Markey, "Prestige and the Origins of War: Returning to Realism's Roots," *Security Studies* 8, no. 4 (summer 1999), pp. 126–72.

secure its goals, whether those goals are universal domination or simply self-preservation.[40]

Certainly there are disagreements among classical realists about whether the permissive cause of conflict lies in the external environment or in human nature.[41] There are debates among neorealists over the amount of *unnecessary* or unintended conflict generated by the international system and the resulting implications for how states should assess one another's intentions and best promote security for themselves.[42] There are also disagreements among both classical realists and neorealists over the prevalence of international systems characterized by hierarchic (or hegemonic) or equilibria (balance of power) power distributions and the likelihood of major war across different types of systems.[43] Nonetheless, the above-mentioned first principles make it possible to speak of a coherent tradition that encompasses writings of philosophers, statesmen, historians, social scientists, and military strategists as diverse as Niccolò Machiavelli, Thomas Hobbes, Jean-Jacques Rousseau, Alexander Hamilton, Carl von Clausewitz, Max Weber, Raymond Aron, Winston S. Churchill,

---

[40] See Robert G. Gilpin, "No One Loves a Political Realist," in Benjamin Frankel, *Realism: Restatements and Renewal* (London: Frank Cass, 1996), pp. 3–26, esp. pp. 6–8; Gilpin, "The Richness of the Tradition of Political Realism," in Keohane, *Neorealism and its Critics*, pp. 304–8; Benjamin Frankel, "Introduction: Restating the Realist Case," ibid., pp. ix–xx; and Schweller, "Progressiveness of Neoclassical Realism," esp. pp. 322–9.

[41] See Michael Spirtas, "A House Divided: Tragedy and Evil in Realist Theory," in Frankel, *Realism: Restatements and Renewal*, pp. 385–423.

[42] This is the crux of the debate between offensive realism and defensive realism. See Jeffrey W. Taliaferro, "Security Seeking under Anarchy: Defensive Realism Revisited," *International Security* 25, no. 3 (winter 2000/1), pp. 128–61; and Robert Jervis, "Realism, Neoliberalism, and Cooperation: Understanding the Debate," *International Security* 24, no. 1 (summer 1999), pp. 42–63. For a slightly different conception of that debate, see Stephen G. Brooks, "Dueling Realisms," *International Organization* 51, no. 3 (summer 1997), pp. 445–77.

[43] See Robert Gilpin, *War and Change in World Politics* (Cambridge: Cambridge University Press, 1981); Gilpin, "Theory of Hegemonic War," in Robert I. Rotberg and Theodore K. Rabb, eds., *Origins and Prevention of Major War* (Cambridge: Cambridge University Press, 1988), pp. 15–37; A. F. K. Organski, *World Politics* (New York: Knopf, 1958); and Jacek Kugler and A. F. K. Organski, *The War Ledger* (Chicago: University of Chicago Press, 1980). For an overview and critical appraisal, see Jonathan M. DiCicco and Jack S. Levy, "The Power Transition Research Program: A Lakatosian Analysis," in Elman and Elman, *Progress in International Relations Theory*, pp. 109–57.

George F. Kennan, Reinhold Niebuhr, Kenneth Waltz, John Mearsheimer, and Robert Jervis.

The terms "classical realism" and "neorealism" did not come into widespread use in the international relations field until Richard Ashley drew a sharp distinction between Waltz's *Theory of International Politics* and the work of earlier realists.[44] Since numerous books and articles examine the areas of divergence and convergence between classical realism and neorealism, we present only a brief summary here.[45]

Classical realism is primarily concerned with the sources and uses of national power in international politics and the problems that leaders encounter in conducting foreign policy. These issues lead scholars to focus on power distributions among states, as well as the character of states and their relation to domestic society. Twentieth-century classical realists offer either philosophical reflections on the enduring principles of statesmanship or create inductive theories of foreign policy drawn largely from the experiences of European great powers from the sixteenth to the mid-twentieth century. Morgenthau, Kissinger, Wolfers, and others write extensively about the state and national power, but say little about the constraints of the international system. Finally, what we now call classical realism was never a coherent research program, but rather a vast repository of texts written by different authors for different purposes and in different contexts over the course of 2,500 years. Most classical realists were not social scientists; even the twentieth-century classical realists rarely adhered to what are now widely accepted standards of social science methodology.[46]

In contrast, the focus of neorealism is on explaining common patterns of international behavior over time. In particular, neorealists address many of the big questions of international politics, such as:

---

[44] Richard K. Ashley, "The Poverty of Neorealism," in Keohane, *Neorealism and its Critics*, pp. 255–300.

[45] Michael Joseph Smith, *Realist Thought from Weber to Kissinger* (Baton Rouge: Louisiana State University Press, 1986); Kenneth N. Waltz, "Realist Thought and Neorealist Theory," in Robert L. Rothstein, ed., *The Evolution of Theory in International Relations* (Columbia: University of South Carolina Press, 1992), pp. 31–8; Ashley J. Tellis, "Reconstructing Political Realism: The Long March Toward Scientific Theory," in Frankel, *Realism: Restatements and Renewal*, pp. 3–104; and Jack Donnelly, *Realism and International Relations* (Cambridge: University of Cambridge Press, 2000).

[46] Tellis, "Reconstructing Political Realism," pp. 49–51.

Why do wars occur? Why do states tend to balance against powerful states? Why is cooperation difficult and fleeting between states? They address these questions in a self-consciously scientific manner, with an attempt to harness the positivist methodological rigor that the classical realists lacked. They trace the recurring patterns of world politics to the structure of the international system and its defining characteristic, anarchy, which compels states to pursue similar strategies to secure themselves. Utilizing their most important variable, the relative distribution of capabilities, or the balance of power, they explain a vast array of great power behavior and systemic outcomes.

Waltz's balance of power theory is just one (albeit the most prominent) of the theories that fall under the rubric of neorealism.[47] Waltz creates a deductive theory to explain recurrent patterns of international outcomes, namely the recurrence of balances of power and the absence of sustained hegemonic international systems across history. He posits a single independent variable, the systemic distribution of power as measured by the number of great powers (or polarity). It makes two probabilistic predictions: (1) across different international systems, balances of power tend to form, and (2) states tend to emulate the successful practices of others.

Drawing upon analogies from microeconomics, Waltz focuses on the properties and constraints imposed by the international system on all states (especially the great powers) and abstracts from the internal characteristics of individual states. The state, in effect, becomes a "black box." What distinguishes international and domestic political systems are differences in ordering principle (anarchy versus hierarchy), the attributes of the units (functional similarity versus difference), and the distribution of material capabilities among those units (uneven). This has two implications for the present volume. First,

---

[47] In addition to Waltz's writings, other prominent books and articles that present neorealist theories include Gilpin, *War and Change in World Politics*; Robert Jervis, "Cooperation under the Security Dilemma," *World Politics* 30, no. 2 (January 1978), pp. 167–214; Glenn H. Snyder, *Alliance Politics* (Ithaca, NY: Cornell University, 1997); Snyder, "The Security Dilemma in Alliance Politics," *World Politics* 36, no. 4 (July 1984), pp. 461–95; Joseph Grieco, *Cooperation among Nations: Europe, America, and Non-Tariff Barriers to Trade* (Ithaca, NY: Cornell University, 1990); Benjamin Miller, *When Opponents Cooperate* (Ann Arbor: University of Michigan Press, 1995); and Charles L. Glaser, "Realists as Optimists: Cooperation as Self-Help," *International Security* 19, no. 3 (winter 1994/5), pp. 50–90.

balance of power theory assumes that, on average, most states correctly respond to systemic incentives and engage in balancing and emulation. This adaptive behavior, which states undertake to enhance their competitive advantage and probability of survival, has the unintended effect of perpetuating an anarchic international system. However, in an anarchic system, Waltz argues, "Those who do not help themselves, or who do so less effectively than others, will fail to prosper, will lay themselves open to danger, will suffer."[48] Second, balance of power theory assumes states have unlimited ability to extract and mobilize domestic resources, such that aggregate resources are equivalent to actual military and economic power and international influences.[49] Of course, these assumptions are simplifications of reality that are useful for constructing an elegant systemic theory.

Other versions of neorealist theory make similar simplifying assumptions. Offensive realism, for example, departs from Waltz's balance of power theory with its contention that states can never be certain how much power is necessary to achieve security for themselves now and in the future. Therefore, all states strive to maximize their relative share of material power as the only sure path to security. Great powers, in particular, engage in calculated bids of expansion and look for opportunities to weaken potential adversaries, with the ultimate goal of attaining regional or global hegemony.[50] Offensive realists, too, tend to treat the state as a black box and assume that all states will pursue similar strategies faced with similar systemic

---

[48] Waltz, *Theory of International Politics*, p. 118.

[49] John M. Hobson, *The State and International Relations* (Cambridge: University of Cambridge Press, 2000), pp. 17–63, and Christensen, *Useful Adversaries*, pp. 11–14.

[50] Mearsheimer, *Tragedy of Great Power Politics*, pp. 33–54. The question of whether great powers strive for regional hegemony (the status of being the only great power in its region of the globe) or global hegemony (the status of being the only great power in the international system) is one that divides offensive realists. Mearsheimer argues that great powers can only strive for regional hegemony because geography (namely large oceans) makes the attainment of global hegemony impossible. Others disagree. See, Christopher Layne, "The 'Poster Child for Offensive Realism': America as Global Hegemon," *Security Studies* 12, no. 2 (winter 2002/03), pp. 119–63; Layne, *Peace of Illusions*, chap. 1; and Gerald Geunwook Lee, "To Be Long or Not to Be Long: The Contradiction of Time Horizons in Offensive Realism," *Security Studies* 12, no. 2 (winter 2002/3), pp. 196–217.

incentives, regardless of domestic political arrangements.[51] The same is true of expected utility theory, which contends that states make foreign policy decisions fluidly on the basis of the expected utility of their actions, determined by calculations of systemic factors such as, inter alia, relative capability, the power of allies, and geographical distance.[52] None of these structural realist approaches considers that states may differ in their ability to control the policy agenda, select policy options, or mobilize resources to respond to systemic incentives.

Neoclassical realism shares classical realism's concern for the state and its relation to domestic society. It also defines its mission largely in terms of building theories of foreign policy, rather than theories of the system within which states interact. Nonetheless, neoclassical realists aspire to greater methodological sophistication than their classical realist predecessors. Moreover, they begin with the fundamental assumption of neorealists that the international system structures and constrains the policy choices of states.

What then is the relationship between neorealism and neoclassical realism? Both schools begin with assumptions about the conflictual nature of politics, the centrality of conflict groups, and the importance of relative power distributions. Both research programs assign causal primacy to systemic independent variables. Specific neorealist and neoclassical realist theories, in turn, generate testable and probabilistic hypotheses. It is clear, however, that neorealism and neoclassical realism differ from each other based on the range of phenomena each seeks to explain, or the dependent variable. The former seeks to explain recurring patterns of international outcomes, defined as the range of likely outcomes resulting from the interaction of two or more units in an anarchic environment. Examples would be the likelihood of major war across different types of international systems, the prevalence of hegemonic orders versus balances of power (defined in terms of state capabilities), and patterns of alliance behavior among states. Table 1.1 illustrates the areas of convergence and divergence among classical realism, neorealism, and neoclassical realism.

[51] See, for example, Steven E. Lobell, "War Is Politics: Offensive Realism, Domestic Politics, and Security Strategies," *Security Studies* 12, no. 2 (winter 2002/3), pp. 165–95.
[52] For example, Bruce Bueno de Mesquita, *The War Trap* (New Haven, CT: Yale University Press, 1981); and Bruce Bueno de Mesquita and David Lalman, *War and Reason* (New Haven, CT: Yale University Press, 1992).

Table 1.1. *Classical realism, neorealism, and neoclassical realism*

Research program	Epistemology and methodology	View of the international system	View of the units	Dependent variable	Underlying causal logic
CLASSICAL REALISM	Inductive theories; philosophical reflection on nature of politics or detailed historical analysis (generally drawn from W. European history)	Somewhat important	Differentiated	Foreign policies of states	Power distributions or distribution of interests (revisionist vs. status quo) → foreign policy
NEOREALISM	Deductive theories; competitive hypothesis testing using qualitative and sometimes quantitative methods	Very important; inherently competitive and uncertain	Undifferentiated	International political outcomes	Relative power distributions (independent variable) → international outcomes (dependent variable)
NEOCLASSICAL REALISM	Deductive theorizing; competitive hypothesis testing using qualitative methods	Important; implications of anarchy are variable and sometimes opaque to decision-makers	Differentiated	Foreign policies of states	Relative power distributions (independent variable) → domestic constraints and elite perceptions (intervening variables) → foreign policy (dependent variable)

Neoclassical realism is not simply a refinement of Waltz's balance of power theory nor an attempt to smuggle unit-level variables into the theory to explain anomalies. Nor is it correct to characterize realism as a tightly constructed Lakatosian research program whose "hard core" is synonymous with Waltz's theory, thus rendering any departure from that theory as evidence of a "degenerative problem shift."[53] Neoclassical realism seeks to explain variation in the foreign policies of the same state over time or across different states facing similar external constraints. It makes no pretense about explaining broad patterns of systemic or recurring outcomes. Thus, a neoclassical realist hypothesis might explain the likely diplomatic, economic, and military responses of particular states to systemic imperatives, but it cannot explain the systemic consequences of those responses.

A related question concerns reductionism – efforts to explain variation in the properties and characteristics of the system by only examining the behavior of the units and their relation to one another within that system. Waltz is highly critical of reductionist theories of international politics. The interaction of differently configured states produces similar as well as different international outcomes. Likewise, the interaction of similar states produces different as well as similar international outcomes. The same causes sometimes lead to different effects, and the same effects sometimes follow from different causes. Since neoclassical realism locates causal properties at both the structural and unit levels, the unit-level factors help to explain state external behavior. A critic might argue there is no way to avoid the reductionist trap, so long as unit-level factors have causal property. The charge that neoclassical realism is reductionist, though, is mistaken. Reductionist theories locate the causes of systemic outcomes – such as, the likelihood of interstate war or general patterns of alliance formation in the international system – in the internal attributes of states. Waltz is quite clear on this point: "One cannot infer the condition of international politics from the internal composition of states, nor can one arrive at an understanding of international politics by summing the foreign policies and the external behavior of states."[54]

---

[53] John Vasquez, "The Realist Paradigm and Degenerative versus Progressive Research Programs," *American Political Science Review* 91, no. 4 (December 1997), pp. 899–912.

[54] See Waltz, *Theory of International Politics*, p. 64. Waltz also notes that theories of foreign policy can and should include causal factors at the unit and systemic

Neoclassical realism does not do so. It uses the internal characteristics of states as a guide only to national responses to international constraints.

Some critics, such as John A. Vasquez, and Jeffrey Legro and Andrew Moravcsik, fault neoclassical realism for its alleged repudiation of core assumptions of realism in general, and Waltz's theory in particular. By positing an intervening role for elite perceptions of systemic variables, neoclassical realism allegedly violates the assumption that states act rationally in pursuit of their intended goals.[55] However, as many scholars note, while *some* realist theories make strong assumptions about state rationality, such assumptions are not essential to realism.[56] Both Waltz and Morgenthau reject the assumption that states act rationally. Waltz clearly states that his theory requires no rationality assumption and that over time the international system conditions states' behavior through socialization and competition.[57] Morgenthau's writings contain denunciations of both rationalist inquiry and the possibility of creating a so-called political science.[58]

levels. See Kenneth N. Waltz, *Foreign Policy and Domestic Politics: The American and British Experience* (1967; reprint, Berkeley: University of California, Institute of Governmental Studies, 1992).

[55] For the mistaken notion that rationality is a core assumption of realism, see Jeffrey W. Legro and Andrew Moravcsik, "Is Anybody Still a Realist?" *International Security* 24, no. 2 (fall 1999), pp. 5–55 at pp. 13–15; Andrew Moravcsik, "Liberal International Relations Theory: A Scientific Assessment," in Elman and Elman, *Progress in International Relations Theory*, pp. 190–3; and Keohane, "Theory of World Politics," in Keohane, *Neorealism and its Critics*, pp. 164–5.

[56] Examples of realist theories that do make strong assumptions about state rationality are Grieco, *Cooperation among Nations*; and Dale Copeland, *The Origins of Major War* (Ithaca, NY: Cornell University Press, 2000), chap. 2.

[57] See Waltz, *Theory of International Politics*, p. 118; and Waltz, "Reflections on Theory of International Politics: A Response to My Critics," pp. 330–1. For discussions of why rationality is not a core assumption, see Taliaferro, "Security Seeking under Anarchy," pp. 155–6, n. 105; Randall L. Schweller and William C. Wohlforth, "Power Test: Evaluating Realism in Response to the End of the Cold War," *Security Studies* 9, no. 3 (spring 2000), pp. 60–107, at p. 70; and Miles Kahler, "Rationality in International Relations," *International Organization* 52, no. 4 (autumn 1998), pp. 919–41, at pp. 924–5.

[58] Hans J. Morgenthau, *Scientific Man versus Power Politics* (Chicago: University of Chicago Press, 1946), p. 71. For a discussion of Morgenthau's rejection of rationalist inquiry and the possibility of a political science, see Tellis, "Reconstructing Political Realism," esp. pp. 39–51.

A third criticism is that neoclassical realism lacks theoretical rigor and predictive power because it eschews a mono-causal focus on either domestic or systemic variables.[59] We contend that parsimony must be balanced against explanatory power; on that score, neoclassical realism does quite well relative to other bodies of international relations theory.[60] Almost all of the extant applications of neoclassical realism entail conscious efforts to derive testable hypotheses, specify the predictions or observable implications of those hypotheses, and finally to test the relative explanatory power of neoclassical realist and alternative hypotheses against empirical evidence.[61] Furthermore, in this volume, we include several chapters that present new neoclassical realist hypotheses specifying the intervening role of unit-level variables, as well as circumstances under which such domestic constraints will likely have a major influence on foreign policy.

Finally, some critics might charge that by incorporating unit-level variables, neoclassical realism violates the structural logic of neorealism. By focusing on non-systemic variables, critics claim that neoclassical realists are really incorporating elements of liberal and institutionalist theories in an effort to salvage neorealism.[62] This criticism stems from a mistaken reading of the role of unit-level variables in realist theories in general, and neoclassical realism in particular. As we explain below, there is no deductive reason why neoclassical realism cannot incorporate unit-level variables, while at the same time maintaining the causal primacy of structural variables.

Neoclassical realist conceptions of the state

As we stated earlier, neoclassical realism builds upon the complex relationship between state and society found in classical realism without sacrificing the central insight about systemic constraints and opportunities found in neorealism. What exactly does this mean?

---

[59] See Stephen M. Walt, "The Enduring Relevance of the Realist Tradition," in Katznelson and Milner, *Political Science: The State of the Discipline*, p. 211; and Legro and Moravcsik, "Is Anybody Still a Realist?" pp. 27–34.

[60] See Patrick James, *International Relations and Scientific Progress: Structural Realism Reconsidered* (Columbus: Ohio State University Press, 2002).

[61] On the desirable attributes of social science theories, see Stephen Van Evera, *Guide to Methods for Students of Political Science* (Ithaca, NY: Cornell University Press, 1997), pp. 17–21.

[62] See Legro and Moravcsik, "Is Anyone Still a Realist?" pp. 21–5.

What is neoclassical realism's conception of the state and how, if at all, does that conception improve upon the treatments of the state found in neorealism and other schools of international relations theory? Neoclassical realism identifies states as the most important actors in international politics. Gilpin writes, "The essence of social reality is the group. The building blocks and ultimate units of social and political life are not the individuals of liberal thought nor the classes of Marxism [but instead] conflict groups."[63] Tribalism is an immutable aspect of the human condition and political life. Human beings cannot survive in an anarchic environment as individuals, but only as members of a larger group. While groups may come into existence for a variety of reasons, the one necessary condition is that they differ from some outside entity. Fear plays a crucial role in group formation, if only because physical security is a prerequisite for the pursuit of any other individual or collective goal. *Metus hostilis* or the fear of enemies – whether manifested in the form of xenophobia directed at internal minorities or a fear of external groups – is indispensable for the creation and maintenance of political groups, because it offers a way of overcoming collective action barriers. The concept of the *metus hostilis* appears, in one form or another, in the writings of Thucydides, Hobbes, Morgenthau, Waltz, and Mearsheimer.[64] Research in the fields of evolutionary biology and social psychology provides additional support for long-standing realist assumptions about the centrality of in-group/out-group discrimination, intergroup comparison, and competition in political life.[65]

We acknowledge there is no universally accepted definition of the "state," and the term itself has different connotations within the disciplines of anthropology, history, and sociology, and in the comparative politics and international relations subfields of political science. Nonetheless, Max Weber's classic definition is often a starting point: "A state is a human community that (successfully) claims the

---

[63] See Gilpin, "The Richness of the Tradition of Political Realism," p. 305.

[64] See Ioannis D. Evrigenis, " 'Carthage Must Be Saved': Fear of Enemies and Collective Action" (PhD dissertation, Harvard University, 2005), esp. chap. 3.

[65] Sterling-Folker, *Theories of International Cooperation*, pp. 70–6; Sterling-Folker, "Realism and the Constructivist Challenge"; Bradley A. Thayer, "Bringing in Darwin: Evolutionary Theory, Realism, and International Politics," *International Security* 25, no. 2 (fall 2000), pp. 124–51; and Jonathan Mercer, "Anarchy and Identity," *International Organization* 49, no. 2 (summer 1995), pp. 229–52.

monopoly of the legitimate use of physical force within a given territory. Note that 'territory' is one of the characteristics of the state."[66] While Weber's definition captures the essential coercive nature of political authority and the existence of an administrative apparatus, it fails to encompass cases where territorial control is incomplete (or non-existent) or where the monopoly on the legitimate use of force is contested. Most international relations theorists would conceive of the state as: (1) a set of institutions, (2) placed within a geographically bounded territory that (3) at least *claims* a monopoly on legitimate rule within that defined territory.[67]

Neoclassical realism presents a "top-down" conception of the state, which means systemic forces ultimately drive external behavior. To this end it views the states as epitomized by a national security executive, comprised of the head of government and the ministers and officials charged with making foreign security policy.[68] This executive, sitting at the juncture of the state and the international system, with access to privileged information from the state's politico-military apparatus, is best equipped to perceive systemic constraints and deduce the national interest. Nonetheless, while the executive is potentially autonomous from society, in many contexts political arrangements frequently compel it to bargain with domestic actors (such as the legislature, political parties, economic sectors, classes, or the public as a whole) in order to enact policy and extract resources to implement policy choices. Therefore, in contrast to liberalism and Marxism, neoclassical realism does not see states as simply aggregating the demands of different societal interest groups or economic classes.[69] Rather, leaders define the "national interests" and conduct

---

[66] Max Weber, *Economy and Society*, vol. II, ed. Guenther Roth and Claus Wittich (Berkeley: University of California Press, 1978), pp. 904–05.
[67] See Michael C. Desch, "War and Strong States, Peace and Weak States?" *International Organization* 50, no. 2 (spring 2006), pp. 237–68, at p. 240 (emphasis added).
[68] See Ripsman, *Peacemaking by Democracies*, pp. 43–4; Margaret G. Hermann, Charles F. Hermann, and Joe D. Hagan, "How Decision Units Shape Foreign Policy Behavior," in Charles F. Hermann, Charles W. Kegley, and James N. Rosenau, eds., *New Directions in the Study of Foreign Policy* (Boston: Allen and Unwin, 1987), pp. 309–36.
[69] For discussions of the state in liberal international relations theories, see Moravcsik, "Taking Preferences Seriously," esp. pp. 514–20; and Moravcsik, "Liberal International Relations Theory: A Scientific Assessment," in Elman and Elman, *Progress in International Relations Theory*, pp. 159–203.

foreign policy based upon their assessment of relative power and other states' intentions, but always subject to domestic constraints. This means that substate actors are far from irrelevant and that the definition and articulation of national interests is not without controversy. On the contrary, threat assessment, strategic adjustment, and policy implementation are inherently difficult and may entail considerable bargaining within the state's leadership and with other stakeholders within society.

In this volume we use the term "state" as a generic term for a variety of autonomous polities with different geographic scopes, internal attributes, and relative material capabilities that coexist and interact in an anarchic environment. We would not confine the term to the sovereign territorial states that first appeared in early modern Europe and later spread throughout the world. For our purposes, polities as varied as ancient Greek city-states (the *polis*), the Roman, Byzantine, and Chinese empires, the principalities and kingdoms of medieval Europe and pre-colonial India, and the city-state leagues of the Holy Roman Empire and Italy fall under the generic category of "states."

States are not necessarily synonymous with nations, as the many examples of stateless nations, multinational or multiethnic states, and contested national identities between and within different states, illustrate. While states may claim a monopoly on legitimate rule within a defined territory, we recognize the actual degree of territorial control by central political institutions varies. Finally, while we do not equate statehood with what Stephen Krasner calls "international legal sovereignty" or Westphalian sovereignty, we do exclude colonies, protectorates, tributaries, and other polities based on formal hierarchic relationships and de facto territorial control by another state.[70]

Neoclassical realism builds upon the explicit distinction between the state and society made by German classical realists like Weber, Otto Hintze, and Leopold von Ranke and carried over into the writings of their Anglo-American counterparts.[71] Classical realism

[70] Stephen D. Krasner, *Sovereignty: Organized Hypocrisy* (Princeton, NJ: Princeton University Press, 1999), chap. 1.

[71] See Otto Hintze, "Military Organization and the Organization of the State," in Felix Gilbert, ed., *Historical Essays of Otto Hintze* (New York: Oxford University Press, 1975), pp. 180–215; and Leopold Ranke, "A Dialogue on Politics," reprinted in Theodore H. Von Laue, *Leopold Ranke: The Formative Years* (Princeton, NJ: Princeton University Press, 1950), pp. 152–80.

and neoclassical realism do not see the state – that is, the central politico-military institutions and top officials of the polity – as completely autonomous from society. On the contrary, Morgenthau, Kissinger, and other classical realists lament the gradual erosion of state autonomy from society in the European great powers in the nineteenth century. Greater accountability to legislatures and greater vulnerability to the whims of nationalism and public opinion diminished statesmen's ability to pursue policies necessary to preserve the balance of power.[72] Nonetheless, the national security executive has interests which transcend any class or sector, namely the national interest. Moreover, since the executive receives privileged information from state agencies, it is frequently more aware of the national interest and the dictates of the international system than are other domestic actors. Limitations on executive autonomy in different national contexts, however, may undermine their ability to respond as necessary to shifts in the balance of power. Neoclassical realists consequently view policy responses as a product of state–society coordination and, at times, struggle. Less autonomous states must frequently build coalitions and make compromises to mobilize social and political actors in order to enact policy, as George H. W. Bush did in preparation for the 1991 Gulf War.[73] Most states must also frequently bargain with societal actors in order to secure the provision of key national security goods to implement policy. Thus, for example, as Michael Barnett has demonstrated, the Egyptian and Israeli states had to make considerable policy concessions and barter away degrees of executive autonomy in order to prosecute the 1967 and 1973 Arab–Israeli wars.[74]

As several contributors show, the degree of state autonomy vis-à-vis society varies over time and across different states. This variation, in turn, affects whether states respond to international pressures in a timely and efficient fashion.[75] Finally, neoclassical realism recognizes

---

[72] See Morgenthau, *Politics among Nations*, pp. 220–3 and pp. 248–59; and Henry A. Kissinger, *World Restored: Metternich, Castlereagh, and the Problems of Peace, 1812–1822* (Boston: Houghton Mifflin, 1957), pp. 324–30.

[73] For a discussion of executive autonomy in the conduct of foreign policy, see Ripsman, *Peacemaking by Democracies*, pp. 43–57.

[74] See Michael N. Barnett, *Confronting the Costs of War* (Princeton, NJ: Princeton University Press, 1992).

[75] See Ripsman, *Peacemaking by Democracies*, chap. 5; and Michael Mastanduno, David A. Lake, and G. John Ikenberry, "Toward a Realist

that many states or regimes do not necessarily function as "unitary" actors. Elite consensus or disagreement about the nature and extent of international threats, persistent internal divisions within the leadership, social cohesion, and the regime's vulnerability to violent overthrow all inhibit the state's ability to respond to systemic pressures.[76]

The neoclassical realist conception of the international system

Neoclassical realism identifies elite calculations and perceptions of relative power and domestic constraints as intervening variables between international pressures and states' foreign policies. Relative power sets parameters for how states (or rather, those who act on their behalf) define their interests and pursue particular ends. But what is the neoclassical realist conception of the international system? After all, as even Waltz admits, the international system does not dictate exactly *how* each state will respond within those parameters. David Dessler's office-building analogy is illustrative. The exterior walls and the configuration of the internal spaces generate broad behavioral patterns for the people working within them. Most office workers do not attempt to walk through walls, crawl through air conditioning ducts, or leave the building via windows on the twentieth floor.[77]

Pervasive uncertainty and potential threats are central to the conception of anarchy in neorealism and neoclassical realism. To return to the office-building analogy, the workers may be aware of hidden trapdoors and that the consequence of falling through them is severe injury or death, but they have no knowledge or control over the placement of these traps. It is not simply that anarchy leaves states unregulated and unsupervised so that war may break out at any time, Jennifer Sterling-Folker observes, "It is instead that the anarchic environment allows death to occur in the first place while providing no guidance for how to avoid it in the short-term and ultimately no means of doing so in the long-term."[78] This lack of guidance automatically renders anarchy a self-help environment. It also suggests that systemic incentives and

---

Theory of State Action," *International Studies Quarterly* 33, no. 4 (December 1988), pp. 457–74.
[76] Schweller, *Unanswered Threats*, pp. 46–68.
[77] David Dessler, "What's at Stake in the Agent-Structure Debate?" *International Organization* 43, no. 3 (summer 1989), pp. 441–73, at p. 466.
[78] Sterling-Folker, *Theories of International Cooperation*, p. 73.

threats, at least in the short run, are rarely unambiguous. This means there is often not a single, optimal response to such incentives and, due to the operation of the security dilemma, actions designed to counter threats may actually make states less secure.

State leaders, like the employees in Dessler's office analogy, try to anticipate other states' likely reactions and future power trends. However, feedback may be delayed and indirect. The difficulties leaders encounter in assessing relative power shifts and systemic feedback are persistent themes in the neoclassical realist literature. For example, Wohlforth details how, in the late 1970s and early 1980s, Soviet leaders faced the dual dilemma of assessing the extent of relative decline and discerning whether the Reagan administration's defense buildup was *sui generis* or feedback to the Brezhnev doctrine, the invasion of Afghanistan, and Kremlin support for revolutions in the Third World.[79] Similarly, Aaron L. Friedberg chronicles the difficulties competing Whitehall departments and ministers serving under prime ministers Lord Salisbury and Alfred James Balfour experienced in assessing and responding to the relative decline of Britain between 1895 and 1905. In both the Soviet and British examples, debates among top decision-makers and within state bureaucracies over the appropriate power measures made strategic adjustment even more difficult, because, as Wohlforth observes:

Power cannot be tested; different elements of power possess different utilities at different times; the relation of perceived power to material resources can be capricious; the mechanics of power are surrounded by uncertainty; states possess different conversion ratios and comparative advantages; the perceived prestige hierarchy and the military distribution may not coincide for prolonged periods; states adopt asymmetrical strategies to maximize their positions and undercut rivals; signals get confused among allies, rivals, and domestic audiences.[80]

In addition to long-term trends, feedback can also come in the form of exogenous shocks, such as the sudden defeat of a frontline ally or the unexpected escalation of a crisis. These shocks can suddenly make leaders aware of the cumulative effect of long-term power trends. For example, Christensen notes that the extent of Britain's collapse in

[79] Wohlforth, *Elusive Balance*, pp. 223–51; Schweller and Wohlforth, "Power Test," pp. 86–9.
[80] Wohlforth, *Elusive Balance*, pp. 306–7.

spring 1947 shocked the Truman administration into recognizing the true bipolar distribution of power and shifting toward active containment of the Soviet Union. Elsewhere, Christensen argues that ambiguity about the distribution of military power in Europe in the 1860s led the French emperor Napoleon III and his generals to overestimate Austria's ability to withstand a war with Prussia. Consequently, French leaders did not seek a prewar alliance with Austria. Zakaria notes the resounding US victory over Spain in the 1898 Spanish–American War solidified the perception of increasing US state power both at home and abroad. Conversely, the Japanese attack on Pearl Harbor on December 7, 1941 or the terrorist attacks on New York City and Washington on September 11, 2001 solidified perceptions of homeland vulnerability, while the Vietnam War solidified perceptions of the limits of US military power.[81] Feedback, whether positive (or self-amplifying) or negative (or dampening), is often subject to multiple interpretations by top decision-makers and national security bureaucracies. Furthermore, the interaction of different states' strategies may produce unforeseen or unintended systemic outcomes. While explaining the likelihood of such systemic outcomes lies outside the purview of neoclassical realism, several contributors to this volume do address the manner in which states interpret and react to such outcomes.[82]

Neoclassical realism accepts the importance of competitive pressures and socialization effects in shaping the internal composition of states. What motivates such adaptive behavior is not the normative appeal of others' practices or domestic institutions, but rather the desire to enhance competitive advantage and the probability of survival. "The nation-state is by no means the teleological end-point of group identification," observes Sterling-Folker, "but its development as the primary constitutive unit of the present global system is explicable as a result of anarchy's imitative dynamics."[83] Indeed, as much of the state-building literature argues, the territorial state simply proved more effective than other polities in early modern Europe in

---

[81] See Christensen, *Useful Adversaries*, p. 22; and Thomas J. Christensen, "Perceptions and Alliances in Europe, 1860–1940," *International Organization* 51, no. 1 (winter 1997), pp. 65–97.

[82] For a discussion of feedback and non-linearity in international politics see Jervis, *Systems Effects*, pp. 125–76.

[83] Sterling-Folker, *Theories of International Cooperation*, p. 73.

mobilizing internal resources and responding to external threats. This process of intergroup comparison, emulation, and innovation led to the spread of the territorial state as an institutional form, first throughout Europe and later around the world. It also led to the demise of competing institutional forms over time. Thus, the international system is of paramount importance to neoclassical realists, which distinguishes them from inside-out approaches.

Research questions and contents of the volume

We asked the contributors to reflect on several questions about neoclassical realism, the state, and foreign policy. The questions fall into three groups: (1) the politics of threat assessment; (2) the politics of strategic adjustment; and (3) the politics of resource extraction, domestic mobilization, and policy implementation.[84]

1. Threat assessment
   - How do states, or rather the decision-makers and key institutions that act on behalf of states, assess international threats and opportunities?
   - Who are the relevant actors within the state with respect to international threat assessment?
   - How are disagreements within the state over the nature of international threats and appropriate remedies ultimately resolved?
2. Strategic adjustment
   - Who decides how to respond to international threats?
   - To what extent can domestic actors bargain with the state and influence foreign and security policies in different state settings?
   - Do domestic actors determine the content of foreign and security policy or merely its style?
   - Which domestic actors have the greatest influence on security policy? Under what circumstances?
   - What bargains do leaders need to strike with domestic actors in order to respond to international threats and opportunities?

---

[84] One area of neoclassical realism that this volume does not examine is variation in the interests of states. Structural realism assumes that all states have comparable missions, namely to survive in an anarchic international system. Drawing upon classical realism, however, Schweller differentiates between states on the basis of differing motivations, be they status quo or revisionist. See Schweller, *Deadly Imbalances*, esp. pp. 19–36, and pp. 64–91.

3. Resource extraction, domestic mobilization, and policy implementation
   - How do states mobilize the resources necessary to pursue their chosen security policies?
   - How much power do domestic actors have to obstruct the state when it seeks to mobilize resources in different settings?
   - What determines who is more successful in bargaining games between the state and societal groups?

In subsequent chapters, our contributors provide a range of answers to these questions to provide a better understanding of neoclassical realism and the intersection of international and domestic forces in shaping foreign policy. Some, like Randall Schweller, view the role of society as episodic and rare, accounting only for surprising deviations from systemic requirements. Others, like Colin Dueck, contend that societal forces regularly affect foreign policy, but their effects are limited to the style and form of policy choices, rather than the substance of policy. Still others, like Steven Lobell, Mark Brawley, and Benjamin Fordham, view the role of domestic interests as more pervasive and powerful in shaping foreign policy choices. Finally, others, such as Norrin Ripsman, Jeffrey Taliaferro, and Jennifer Sterling-Folker, construct theories positing the conditions under which societal forces will affect foreign policy choices and implementation. The chapters thus posit a variety of neoclassical realist hypotheses that purport to explain variation in different aspects of states' grand strategies – diplomacy, military doctrine and force structure, and foreign economic policy. Some chapters are largely theoretical, while others test hypotheses against historical and contemporary cases.

The process of strategic adjustment must begin with elites' recognition of impending shifts in the distribution of power, changes in the intentions of other states and non-state actors, or feedback that suggests existing strategies are suboptimal or counterproductive. However, neoclassical realism suggests that elite perceptions and calculations of international pressures and a lack of consensus within the top leadership and national security bureaucracies often skew the process of net assessment. Furthermore, even if elites correctly perceive the nature and magnitude of international threats, domestic political dynamics can nonetheless force them into pursuing arguably counterproductive foreign and security policies.

In chapter 2, Steven E. Lobell lays out a complex threat identification model within neoclassical realism. Contrary to neorealist balance of power theory, he argues states not only respond to aggregate shifts in the international distribution of power, but also to shifts in power differentials and specific components of other states' material capabilities. Divisions among the top officials of the state charged with the formulation of grand strategy – what Lobell calls the foreign policy executive (FPE) – and key societal elites can adversely affect the threat assessment process and ultimately strategic adjustment. The result is often the pursuit of grand strategies that appear anomalous from the standpoint of neorealist balance of power and balance of threat theories.

Lobell's complex threat identification model begins with the observation that the FPE stands at the intersection of international and domestic politics. The FPE has responsibility for grand strategic planning, including the identification of changes in the global or regional balance of power. Yet, in order to implement foreign and security policies, the FPE must forge and maintain a coalition with various societal elites. These societal elites include the leaders of different economic sectors (such as finance, heavy industry, agriculture, and manufacturing), state actors (such as the military, the diplomatic service, and colonial bureaucrats), and domestic interest groups. These groups, in turn, have a material interest in the pursuit of different types of foreign economic policies and often focus on different components of rising or threatening states' material capabilities.

Lobell argues that where a shift in a component of power of a foreign state *enables* a foreign security policy coalition (that is, consensus among FPE and key societal supporters), the FPE will be unconstrained in assessing international threats. Consensus on threat assessment enables more timely and efficient balancing against rising or threatening adversaries abroad to occur. Conversely, where a shift in an element of power of a foreign country *disables* a foreign security policy coalition (that is, where there is no consensus among FPE and societal supporters), the FPE will be constrained since there is no agreement on threat assessment. As a result, the ability of the FPE to pursue balancing strategies against overly powerful or threatening states will be curtailed or delayed. To illustrate his argument, Lobell draws on the examples of the British threat assessment of Germany before the two world wars.

In chapter 3, Mark Brawley examines the dilemmas of threat assessment and strategic adjustment in permissive international environments – postwar periods marked by considerable ambiguity among the victorious great powers and their vanquished foes over long-term power trends, future intentions, and potential patterns of alignment and enmity. In such environments, systemic constraints on the victorious great powers are relatively weak or indeterminate, thus leading to considerable variation in how they define the core security interests, make tradeoffs between short-term military security and longer-term economic prosperity, and discount the future. However, the types of strategic tradeoffs great powers make can effect subsequent strategic adjustment, when systemic constraints are stronger and international threats are immediate. Brawley reexamines the dilemmas encountered by Britain, France, and the Soviet Union in responding to the latent (and later the proximate) threat of Germany in the 1920s and 1930s.

Initially, the trauma and costs of the First World War, along with the fact that the Weimar Republic was in no position to instigate another conflict in the near future, shaped British, French, and Soviet strategic thinking. Officials in London, Paris, and Moscow could consider various strategies for balancing or deterring Germany in the long term. Moreover, all leaders believed that in the case of another war, it would take considerable time and effort to get their economies back on a wartime footing. Expectations about the time frame for balancing German power, and assumptions about the difficulties in converting economic assets into military power, shaped decisions in the 1920s. Since the threat was not proximate, British, French, and Soviet leaders proposed different strategies for achieving the same end. In the permissive environment of the immediate postwar years, their preferences reflected factors typically ignored by neorealists, but at the heart of neoclassical realism. As Germany recovered in the 1930s, the leaders of these countries reassessed the time-horizon in which they needed to balance the German threat, leading them to prefer different strategies. Their decisions in the 1920s drove them to incompatible stances in the 1930s, however. Therefore, the failure of Britain, France, and the USSR to balance against Nazi Germany did not stem from disagreements or misperceptions about the nature and the location of the threat, but rather from the difficulties associated with changing long-standing strategies.

Why do states continue to perceive each other as security threats despite increased economic interdependence between them? How is it possible for military rivals to continue trading with each other despite the continuing risk that their rivalry might escalate to war? Why does the so-called peace dividend predicted by advocates of greater economic cooperation often fail to materialize? Liberal theories (particularly complex interdependence and neoliberal institutionalism) posit a causal connection between economic interdependence and a greater likelihood of peace. States learn that cooperation is the most functionally efficient means to maximize societal wealth. Likewise, consumers, firms, and other societal groups tend to become dependent on overseas markets and will withdraw support from leaders who pursue foreign policies that are commercially harmful.

In chapter 4, Jennifer Sterling-Folker presents a neoclassical realist framework that challenges this interdependence/peace dividend thesis. Liberal theories ignore nationalism and unilateralism entirely, or treat them as irrational "historical residues" to be overcome through ever greater institutionalized cooperation. Consequently, they cannot explain how states (and their leaders) can simultaneously view and treat one another both as valued trading partners and security threats. Neoclassical realism, according to Sterling-Folker, can resolve this seeming paradox, in part because it builds upon a core realist assumption about the immutability of tribalism and centrality of conflict groups. Group (or national) identity differentiation plays an enduring role in the domestic politics and foreign policies of nation-states. That is, just as states compete with one another over the allocation of scarce resources at the international level, within each state different groups compete with one another over the allocation of resources to group members and who has the ability and legitimacy to make these decisions for the state. Since international (or interstate) competition has ramifications for *intra*-national (or intra-state) competition, and vice versa, one cannot be isolated from the other.

To illustrate the utility of this framework, Sterling-Folker examines relations between the United States, China, and Taiwan. While trade and direct investment between China and Taiwan has dramatically increased since the late 1980s, security tensions between the two have remained high, peaking during the 1995 Taiwan Straits crisis and again during the 2000 and 2004 Taiwanese presidential elections. Similarly, although economic linkages between the United States and

China have increased, each continues to define the other as its principal adversary in the Asia-Pacific region. Sterling-Folker argues that an interactive combination of national subgroups in Taiwan, China, and the United States each drove their respective countries toward more confrontational foreign and security policies, despite increasing economic ties and clear power asymmetries. In the United States, competition between the free trade and national security wings of the Republican and Democratic parties led the Clinton and the George W. Bush administrations to increase military aid to Taiwan and to grant entry visas to Taiwanese president Lee Teng-hui and his successor Chen Shui-bian, despite Beijing's protests. In Taiwan, questions of national identity and the island's ultimate political status became intertwined in the electoral competition between the Kuomintang (KMT) and the Democratic People's Party (DPP). Consequently, Lee and later Chen pursued policies to assert Taiwanese nationalism and political equality on the mainland, even at the risk of military confrontation with China. Finally, although the mainland's economic boom is largely due to increased trade with Taiwan and the United States, the Chinese Communist Party has become increasingly dependent upon Chinese nationalism to justify its continued monopoly on political power. Consequently, any perceived move by Taiwan to assert its independence from the mainland prompts a forceful diplomatic (and sometimes military) response from the PRC, despite the risk of confrontation with the United States.

Successive presidents of the United States have engaged in major military interventions abroad, but existing theoretical explanations of such intervention often emphasize either third image (international) or second image (domestic) factors.[85] In chapter 5, Colin Dueck presents a neoclassical realist theory to show exactly how, why, and to what extent domestic politics matters in shaping such interventions. According to this theory, when facing the possibility of major military intervention, presidents usually begin by consulting what they perceive to be the national interests. Subsequently, however, they consider how best to pursue those conceptions of the national interest in the light of domestic political incentives and constraints. These

---

[85] The classic discussion of the three images of international politics is in Kenneth N. Waltz, *Man, the State, and War* (New York: Columbia University Press, 1959).

constraints frequently lead presidents to implement the precise conduct, framing, and timing of US intervention in a manner that may appear suboptimal or dysfunctional from a neorealist perspective. In this sense, domestic politics "matters," not as a primary cause of intervention, but rather as a powerful influence on its exact form. Dueck lays out the theoretical rationale for this approach, and illustrates its plausibility in case studies of the Truman administration's decision to intervene in the Korean War in June 1950 and the Johnson administration's decision to escalate US involvement in the Vietnam War in 1964 and 1965. He concludes with observations and implications regarding the current war in Iraq.

When are systemic forces more likely to override domestic politics in shaping states' external behavior? Alternatively, when are domestic political institutions and the preferences of societal actors more likely to inhibit leaders' responses to the external environment? In chapter 6, Norrin M. Ripsman seeks to delimit the scope of neoclassical realism and the relative causal importance of domestic-level and systemic variables within it. He hypothesizes that, in general, the more influential domestic actors will be those with sufficient power to remove national executives from office (whether through the ballot box, legislative no-confidence votes, or coups d'état), those that can act as "veto players" to obstruct the government's programmatic goals, or those that can shape the definition of the national interests. These actors are more likely to have a significant impact on foreign and national policies when the international threat level is low, when leaders have a weak hold on power, and when the national security executive lacks structural autonomy. In general, however, neoclassical realism suggests domestic actors are far more likely to influence the timing and style of a state's national security policies, rather than the basic definition of the national interest, which is usually determined from without, unless the state inhabits a security-abundant environment. Ripsman's chapter illustrates the plausibility of these hypotheses with examples drawn from Great Britain, France, the United States, the Soviet Union, Turkey, Israel, and Egypt over the past century.

Threat assessment and strategic adjustment are inherently difficult processes, even in those rare situations where international threats and opportunities are unambiguous and elite consensus exists on the appropriate foreign and military strategies to address them. Nonetheless, states still face the considerable task of extracting the material and human resources of their societies and directing them into measurable economic and military power in the pursuit of national security objectives. Neoclassical realism identifies states' extractive and mobilization capacity as a crucial intervening variable between systemic imperatives and the actual foreign and defense policies states pursue. However, extractive and mobilization capacity are not simply a function either of a state's bureaucracy or of the composition of a regime's power base. In addition to institutions, ideational factors such as ideology and nationalism can play an instrumental role in helping the leadership extract, mobilize, and direct societal resources and cultivate support among its power base. Chapters 7, 8, and 9 examine the ways in which institutions, nationalism, and political ideology interact to constrain or facilitate states' ability to exact and mobilize resources for national security, and consequently the types of national security policies states will likely pursue.

Under what circumstances will states emulate the successful military institutions, governing practices, and technologies of more powerful states? When confronted with similarly threatening international environments, why do some states emulate, while others fail to do so? Under what circumstances will states create entirely new military institutions, practices, and technologies in an effort to offset the perceived advantages of rival states? Neorealist balance of power theory holds that the international system compels states to adopt similar adaptive strategies – namely, balancing and emulation – or risk possible elimination as independent entities. Yet, in practice, states do not always emulate the successful practices of the system's leading states in a timely and uniform fashion. Moreover, states can also respond to external threats by persisting in existing security strategies or by developing entirely new military practices, doctrines, technologies, and institutions. In chapter 7, Jeffrey W. Taliaferro outlines a "resource extraction" model of the state in neoclassical realism. External vulnerability provides incentives for states to emulate others' practices or to counter such practices through innovation. However, neoclassical realism suggests that state power, defined as the relative ability of the state to extract and mobilize resources from domestic society, shapes the types of internal balancing strategies countries are likely to pursue. State power, in turn, is a function of the politico-military institutions of the state, as well as nationalism and ideology.

Taliaferro argues that states with higher extraction and mobilization capacity, but that also face high external vulnerability, are more likely to emulate the military, governing, and technological practices of the system's most successful states, at least in the short run. On the other hand, states with low extraction and mobilization capacity but confronting high external vulnerability will have greater difficulty in pursuing emulation, at least in the short run. States with higher extraction and mobilization capacity but low external vulnerability have the luxury of engaging in innovation to enhance their long-term security and power. Conversely, states lacking high mobilization and extraction capacity, but facing low external vulnerability, are less likely to pursue emulation or innovation. In the long term, states can try to increase their extractive and mobilization capabilities, and consequently their ability to pursue emulation or innovation, by purveying nationalism or statist ideologies. Lack of nationalist sentiment or an anti-statist ideology, however, can limit the state's ability to emulate or innovate. In these circumstances, vulnerable states will likely persist in existing strategies. To illustrate the plausibility of these hypotheses, Taliaferro uses historical examples from the experiences of seven rising or declining great powers over the past 300 years: China, France, Britain, Japan, Prussia (later Germany), Russia (Soviet Union), and the United States.

In chapter 8, Randall Schweller addresses the problem of resource mobilization and extraction from a somewhat different perspective. He asks: why have instances of territorial conquest and bids for regional hegemony by modern great powers been relatively rare? After all, offensive realism contends that the international system compels all great powers to maximize relative power as the best route to security. According to Mearsheimer, across history, great powers strive for regional hegemony and will look for opportunities to expand their territorial control and weaken potential rivals.[86] Yet, in the twentieth century, only Germany, Japan, and to a lesser extent Italy, embarked upon calculated drives for territorial aggrandizement.

Schweller presents a neoclassical realist theory to explain the phenomena of under-aggression and under-expansion in the age of mass politics – circumstances under which great powers forgo opportunities for regional expansion despite favorable power balances, and systemic

---

[86] Mearsheimer, *Tragedy of Great Power Politics*, chap. 5.

and battlefield opportunities. Contrary to offensive realism and balance of power and balance of threat theories, he contends the barriers to hegemony lie not in the deterrence effect of opposing great power coalitions, but rather the difficulties revisionist great powers (or their leaders) have in mobilizing the domestic resources necessary to make a credible hegemonic bid. Furthermore, leaders have never been able to use appeals to balance of power logic as a means to rally and maintain public support for expensive and risky foreign ventures. Instead, Schweller argues, the keys to extracting and mobilizing the resources necessary for a hegemonic bid lie in the ability of national leaders to mobilize support for expansionist foreign ventures in an age of mass politics. More than any other ideology, fascism provided the necessary political and ideological content missing from realism to implement the principle that states should expand when they can. Fascist ideology in its various manifestations gave the German, Italian, and Japanese states in the 1930s a vehicle through which to mobilize popular support and material resources for total war. Schweller certainly does not endorse fascism; he is quick to point out the social Darwinist and racist elements of Nazism, and Italian and Japanese fascism provided the ideological justification for genocide (in the case of Nazism), war crimes, and the pursuit of reckless grand strategies. Yet he also notes several surprising similarities between the conception of state and society found in realist thought and in fascism.

Benjamin O. Fordham addresses the limits of neoclassical realism in chapter 9. He argues that theories of foreign policy, such as neoclassical realism, err in treating international pressures and domestic political constraints additively – that is, by treating them as separate, but complimentary, influences on a state's policy choices. One cannot know the policy implications of systemic forces without knowing the preexisting interests and motives of domestic political actors, and one cannot know the policy preferences of domestic political actors without knowing about international conditions. Fordham proposes an additive model of foreign policy that arguably challenges neoclassical realism by positing a symbiotic relationship between domestic and international factors. He presents a case study of US defense spending during the Cold War to illustrate the plausibility of competing neoclassical realist and integrative hypotheses on foreign policy.

Fordham observes that Democratic and Republican parties essentially switched positions over the course of the Cold War, largely in response to the perceived successes and failures of military policies abroad. House and Senate Democrats moved from being strongly supportive of increased military spending in the 1940s and 1950s to being its major opponents in the 1960s and 1970s. Congressional Republicans followed the opposite course, moving from a relatively skeptical view of higher defense spending in the 1940s and 1950s to favoring large increases in the defense budget in the 1970s and 1980s. This shift also manifested itself in the defense priorities of successive Republican and Democratic administrations. The Truman and Kennedy administrations championed large increases in the defense budget, while the Eisenhower, Nixon, and Ford administrations favored reductions in defense spending. By the mid-1970s, the positions reversed, with the Carter administration only agreeing to defense increases after the 1979 Soviet invasion of Afghanistan, and the Reagan administration presiding over the largest increase in the defense budget (in relative and absolute terms) since the Korean War.

In chapter 10, Ripsman, Taliaferro, and Lobell undertake three tasks. First, they reflect upon the scope of neoclassical realism as set forth in the previous chapters. They conclude that neoclassical realism is a far more coherent and broadly applicable research program than previously realized. Contrary to the assertions of some critics and even some neoclassical realists (such as Schweller), the empirical scope of neoclassical realism is not restricted to cases of arguably dysfunctional or self-defeating foreign policy behavior. Instead, neoclassical realism is most useful in explaining foreign policy behavior where the international system provides unambiguous information about threats and opportunities, but no clear guidance about how states ought to respond. Second, Ripsman, Taliaferro, and Lobell compare the relative performance of neoclassical realism and other leading theories of international relations and foreign policy, including other variants of realism, systemic and domestic-level liberal (or pluralist) theories, other *Innenpolitik* approaches, and rationalist models of bargaining and foreign policy. Finally, they lay out some potential avenues for future research.

2 | Threat assessment, the state, and foreign policy: a neoclassical realist model*

STEVEN E. LOBELL

How do states perceive international threats? Which domestic actors are the most important in threat definition? What happens when domestic actors and interests disagree on the nature of threats? As we state in chapter 1, these are central questions to the neoclassical realist agenda and require a theory of the state to answer. In this chapter I will develop a neoclassical realist theory of threat assessment to fill this gap and illustrate it with reference to the British experience between the two world wars.

Neorealist theories are theories of international outcomes.[1] They highlight the role of polarity and international structure, black box the state, and focus on shifts in aggregate military power or threat. Debates include whether bipolar or multipolar distributions of power are more war-prone; whether anarchy encourages states to maximize relative power or security; whether equal or unequal distributions of power contribute to war; and the prevalence of buck-passing or balancing against threats.[2]

* I would like to thank Ben Fordham, Ben Frankel, Norrin Ripsman, Jeff Taliaferro, and the participants of the workshop on "Neoclassical Realism and the State" at Concordia University for their comments and suggestions.

[1] See Kenneth Waltz, *Theory of International Politics* (Reading, MA: Addison-Wesley, 1979); John Lewis Gaddis, "The Long Peace: Elements of Stability in the Postwar International System," *International Security* 10, no. 4 (spring 1986), pp. 99–142; Christopher Layne, "The Unipolar Illusion Revisited: The Coming End of the United States' Unipolar Moment," *International Security* 31, no. 2 (fall 2006), pp. 7–41; and Barry Posen, "European Union Security and Defense Policy: A Response to Unipolarity?" *Security Studies* 15, no. 2 (April–June 2006), pp. 149–86.

[2] On alternative forms of counterbalancing in the contemporary world, see the chapters in T.V. Paul, James J. Wirtz, and Michel Fortmann, eds., *Balance of*

Proponents of balance of power theory and balance of threat theory would argue that prior to World War I Britain balanced against the rising power (or threat) of Wilhelmine Germany in the form of the Anglo-French Entente Cordiale, the Triple Entente, and the naval arms buildup.[3] Granted, prior to 1914, balancing may not have happened in an optimal fashion. Balance of power theory and balance of threat theory, at least in their current forms, predict a general tendency toward balancing and do not expect an efficient or quick balancing process under all circumstances.

As discussed in chapter 1, neoclassical realist theories are theories of foreign policy.[4] First, as a theory of foreign policy, neoclassical realism explains the foreign and security policy of great powers, but can also account for the distinctive characteristics of regional and small powers, developing countries, or divided, warring, or failed states to mention a few other types of states.[5] Second, neoclassical realists include both external and internal variables in their models. While shifts in power at the international system dominate, threats can also emanate from the subsystemic or regional and domestic environments. As a number of authors in this volume note, the foreign policy executive (hereafter the FPE) is Janus-faced, existing at the intersection of the international and the domestic.[6] This perspective can either constrain or enable the FPE's behavior. For instance, leaders can act

Power: Theory and Practice in the 21st Century (Stanford, CA: Stanford University Press, 2004).

[3] On balance of threat theory, see Stephen M. Walt, *The Origins of Alliances* (Ithaca, NY: Cornell University Press, 1987).

[4] Jeffrey W. Taliaferro, "Neoclassical Realism: Psychology of Great Power Intervention," in Jennifer Sterling-Folker, ed., *Making Sense of International Relations Theory* (Boulder, CO: Lynne Rienner, 2006), pp. 38–53.

[5] Steven R. David, "Explaining Third World Alignment," *World Politics* 43, no. 2 (January 1991), pp. 233–56; Mohammad Ayoob, "Subaltern Realism: International Relations Theory Meets the Third World," in Stephanie G. Neuman, ed., *International Relations Theory and the Third World* (New York: St. Martin's Press, 1998), pp. 31–54.

[6] Thomas J. Christensen, *Useful Adversaries: Grand Strategy, Domestic Mobilization, and Sino-American Conflict, 1947–1958* (Princeton, NJ: Princeton University Press, 1996). On the foreign policy executive, see David A. Lake, *Power, Protection and Free Trade: International Sources of US Commercial Strategy, 1887–1939* (Ithaca, NY: Cornell University Press, 1988); Norrin Ripsman, *Peacemaking by Democracies: Domestic Structure, Executive Autonomy and Peacemaking after Two World Wars* (University Park, PA: Penn State University Press, 2002).

internationally for domestic reasons or domestically for international purposes.[7] Third, neoclassical realists place power at the center of political life. Yet, I argue in this chapter that states do not just respond to aggregate shifts in power alone, but also to shifts in power differentials and specific components of a foreign state's power.

Finally, for neoclassical realists, "there is no immediate or perfect transmission belt linking material capabilities to foreign policy behavior."[8] John Mearsheimer's book, *The Tragedy of Great Power Politics*, has numerous indicators of relative shares of national wealth, population, and the manpower of armies of regional and potential regional hegemons.[9] What these numbers cannot tell, and more broadly what neorealists ignore, is whether state leaders have the freedom to convert the nation's economic power into military power or translate the nation's economic and military power into foreign policy actions.[10] For neoclassical realists, the state is an intervening variable between the international system and foreign policy. Among other characteristics, the state can be strong or weak relative to society, its critical bureaucratic agencies can operate based on parochial rather than national interests, the "state" can be motivated by

---

[7] In addition to Mastanduno, Lake, and Ikenberry's discussion of international and domestic goals, I add subsystemic or regional politics. See Michael Mastanduno, David A. Lake, and G. John Ikenberry, "Toward a Realist Theory of State Action," *International Studies Quarterly* 33, no. 4 (December 1989), pp. 457–74.

[8] Gideon Rose, "Neoclassical Realism and Theories of Foreign Policy," *World Politics* 51, no. 1 (October 1998), pp. 144–72. Friedberg writes "there would seem to be strong logical and historical reasons for questioning the explanatory and predictive power of theories that move directly from international structures to state behavior." Aaron L. Friedberg, *The Weary Titan: Britain and the Experience of Relative Decline, 1895–1905* (Princeton, NY: Princeton University Press, 1988), p. 7.

[9] John J. Mearsheimer, *The Tragedy of Great Power Politics* (New York: Norton, 2001). Wealth (i.e. material power) is important because it can be converted into military power. Manpower in armies is important because for Mearsheimer's argument only land armies can win wars. Also see the tables in Paul Kennedy's *The Rise and Fall of the Great Powers: Economic Change and Military Conflict from 1500 to 2000* (New York: Random House, 1987), pp. 199–202.

[10] For Zakaria, state power is the "portion of national power the government can extract for its purposes and reflects the ease with which central decision-makers can achieve their ends." Fareed Zakaria, *From Wealth to Power: The Unusual Origins of America's World Role* (Princeton, NJ: Princeton University Press, 1998), p. 9.

regime survival instead of national survival, and small group dynamics such as "groupthink" and loss aversion can affect the decision-making process of the FPE.[11]

This chapter examines constraints on threat assessment. It addresses three questions raised in chapter 1: how do states assess threats, who are some of the relevant domestic actors, and what happens when state and societal leaders disagree about whether a foreign state is a threat? Broadly, realists argue that as a major state's regional or global power increases it will seek more influence abroad.[12] For the other powers, this shift in relative material capability establishes the broad parameters of their international behavior, but cannot account for a state's particular foreign policy or a specific historical event. Only a theory of foreign policy which includes intervening variables can account for which states will balance, when they will balance, or why they fail to counterbalance. In this chapter I argue that the degree of consensus among the FPE and key societal supporters about foreign threats will affect the efficiency and appropriateness of counterbalancing behavior.

The first section of this chapter discusses threat assessment. I make two contributions. First, I develop a *complex threat identification* model outlining the nested and multitiered nature of threat assessment, and second, I argue that when identifying a foreign threat, what matters are shifts in specific components of the rising state's power rather than shifts in aggregate power alone. The second section discusses the relevant state and societal actors: the FPE and societal elites. State leaders or the FPE occupy critical positions in the administration, and are responsible for long-term grand strategic planning, including the identification of changes in the global or regional balance of power. Societal elites, made up of outward-oriented internationalists or inward leaning nationalists, are primarily concerned about immediate shifts in the domestic balance of political power.

The third section examines constraints on the FPE's threat assessment. I hypothesize that where a shift in a component of power of

[11] On the effect of small group dynamics on foreign policy, see Jeffrey W. Taliaferro, *Balancing Risks: Great Power Intervention in the Periphery* (Ithaca, NY: Cornell University Press, 2004); Steven E. Lobell, "The International Realm, Framing Effects, and Security Strategies: Britain in Peace and War," *International Interactions* 32, no. 1 (2006), pp. 27–48.

[12] And as the erstwhile leader's power declines its actions will be scaled back.

another state *enables* a foreign security policy coalition (consensus among FPE and key societal supporters), the FPE is unconstrained, and efficient counterbalancing can occur.[13] Where a shift in an element of power of a foreign country *disables* a foreign security policy coalition (no consensus among FPE and societal supporters), the FPE is constrained since there is no agreement on threat assessment. The latter scenario can result in delayed, inefficient, and arguably inappropriate balancing. To illustrate my argument, I draw on examples from Britain in the era of World War I and World War II.

How do states identify and assess threats?

Complex threat identification

The state, and specifically the FPE, exists at the nexus of domestic and international politics. The FPE focuses outward on the systemic and subsystemic balance of power (where states compete), and inward on the domestic balance of power (where societal blocs compete). Great powers face threats that originate from shifts either in the international system or in the internal domestic arena, while regional powers can face an additional threat from shifts in the subsystem.[14]

It is important to understand the nested and multitiered nature of threat assessment. As George Tsebelis warns, "The observer focuses attention on only one game, but the actor is involved in a whole network of games ... What appears suboptimal from the perspective of only one game is in fact optimal when the whole network of games is considered."[15] The boundary lines dividing these systemic–subsystemic–domestic tiers are blurred and interrelated. Leaders often act on one level, but the target is to influence the outcome on

---

[13] It is important to note that I examine a subset of dyadic relations – those where the FPE has identified a foreign state as a threat. This discussion does not include instances in which the FPE and its key societal supporters do not identify a component of power of the ascending state as a threat, which could be the vast majority of instances.

[14] On internal and external threats to the state, see Scott Cooper, "State-Centric Balance-of-Threat Theory: Explaining the Misunderstood Gulf Cooperation Council," *Security Studies* 13, no. 2 (2003/4), pp. 306–49.

[15] George Tsebelis, *Nested Games: Rational Choice in Comparative Politics* (Los Angeles: University of California Press, 1990), p. 7.

another level.[16] By focusing on a single threat or the wrong threat, FPEs such as diplomats, intelligence officers, and policy-makers will find it difficult to understand the motives and intentions behind a foreign state's behavior. That is, what appears suboptimal in a 'secondary' arena might be an optimal alternative in the 'primary' or 'target' arena.

Systemic threats (interstate competition)

The international systemic level is characterized by interstate competition. Neorealist scholars disagree on whether anarchy pressures the FPE to maximize security or to maximize relative power. For defensive realists, states generally seek to maximize their security through preserving the existing balance of power. Defensive realists maintain that the international system pushes states to pursue moderate behavior to ensure their survival and safety. The rationale is that a move to maximize relative power by seeking hegemony or preponderance is unproductive because it will generally provoke counterbalancing behavior, and thereby thwart the state's effort to gain power. For defensive realists, states expand when they are forced to by their environment – when they are threatened owing to insecurity or shifts in relative capability, or by states with aggressive designs.[17]

Offensive realists charge that the anarchic nature of the international system pushes states to maximize their relative share of world power in order to make themselves more secure.[18] The reasoning is that the more power and the stronger the state, the less likely it will be a target, since weaker powers will be reluctant to fight. For offensive realists, the international system creates powerful incentives for states to look for opportunities to gain power at the expense of present and potential future rivals. These include expansionist and aggressive

---

[16] See Carl Brown's "Rules of the Eastern Question Game," in Carl L. Brown, *International Politics and the Middle East: Old Rules, Dangerous Game* (Princeton, NJ: Princeton University Press, 1984), pp. 16–18.

[17] See, for example, Robert Jervis, "Cooperation under the Security Dilemma," *World Politics* 30, no. 2 (January 1978), pp. 167–214; Waltz, *Theory of International Politics*; Stephen Van Evera, *Causes of War: Power and the Roots of Conflict* (Ithaca, NY: Cornell University Press, 1999).

[18] Eric J. Labs, "Beyond Victory: Offensive Realism and the Expansion of War Aims," *Security Studies* 6, no. 4 (summer 1997), pp. 1–49; Mearsheimer, *The Tragedy of Great Power Politics*.

foreign policies, taking advantage of opportunities to gain more power, and weakening potential challengers through preventive wars or 'delaying tactics' to slow their ascent. In fact, only a misguided state will pass up such opportunities. For offensive realists, threatening states are identified as those that can expand – states that possess a combination of latent and land power.

For regional powers, systemic threats come from the great powers and their impact on regional dynamics. During the Cold War, the American–Soviet rivalry penetrated regional politics to different degrees.[19] One view is that in highly 'penetrated' locales, the great powers kept a lid on regional rivalries and restrained their allies by exerting influence and thereby ensuring that regional conflicts did not escalate into global conflicts between the superpowers. A contrary view is that the bipolar superpower competition for global influence, bases, and facilities internationalized and stoked regional and local threats.[20]

In the current unipolar world of the new security environment, some scholars argue that American hegemony contributes to regional stability because Washington provides important public goods and services which moderate local and domestic rivalries, as well as regional services such as mediation, security guarantees, and other confidence-building and conflict-resolution mechanisms.[21] Others counter that American preponderance allows Washington to act in an unconstrained manner and without the fear of retaliation.[22]

---

[19] Benjamin Miller, *When Opponents Cooperate: Great Power Conflict and Collaboration in World Politics* (Ann Arbor: University of Michigan Press, 1995); Arthur A. Stein and Steven E. Lobell, "Geo-structuralism and International Politics: The End of the Cold War and the Regionalisation of International Security," in David Lake and Patrick M. Morgan, eds., *Regional Orders: Building Security in a New World* (University Park, PA: Penn State University Press, 1997), pp. 101–22. Scholars such as Walter LaFeber and Geir Lundestad differ on whether the American "empire" was imposed or invited.

[20] This is what Glenn H. Snyder referred to as the stability–instability paradox. For the original formulation see Snyder, "The Balance of Power and the Balance of Terror," in Paul Seabury, ed., *The Balance of Power* (San Francisco: Chandler, 1965), pp. 198–99.

[21] William Curti Wohlforth, "The Stability of a Unipolar World," *International Security* 24, no. 1 (1999), pp. 5–41; Benjamin Miller, *States, Nations, and the Great Powers: The Sources of Regional War and Peace* (Cambridge: Cambridge University Press, 2007).

[22] Stephen M. Walt, *Taming American Power: The Global Response to US Primacy* (New York: W. W. Norton, 2005).

Subsystemic threats (interstate competition)

While the unipolar system is the dominant one in the world today, subordinate or regional international systems are often ignored.[23] Regions have their own dynamic which is semi-autonomous but not independent of the global great power system and domestic politics. Competition occurs between the major regional players for leadership or hegemony over the locale.[24] A classic example of this subsystemic perspective is Malcolm Kerr's account of the 1960s "Arab Cold War" or competition between the moderate conservative states of Saudi Arabia and Jordan and the more radical revolutionary states led by Nasser's Egypt, but also including Syria, Algeria, Iraq, and the Republic of Yemen. In the preface to *The Arab Cold War*, Malcolm Kerr makes clear that "one of my main concerns in the book has been to dispel the notion of Arab politics as a projection of decisions made in Washington, London, Moscow, and Jerusalem."[25] Likewise, Paul Noble outlines the major "properties" of the Arab system.[26] Leonard Binder notes that "the existence of a bipolar system, or the counterbalancing of the United States and the Soviet Union, cannot explain all post-World War II developments in the Middle East."[27]

Great power induced shifts in the regional distribution of power can create new threats and opportunities for local states. The defeat of the French in the Seven Years War (French and Indian War) weakened a major continental threat and emboldened the American colonists against Britain. The destruction of Iraq's army during the current Gulf War and in its aftermath means that Iran is now the dominant power in the region, with Iraq unable to act as a counterbalance. This

[23] Leonard Binder, "The Middle East as a Subordinate International System," *World Politics* 10, no. 3 (April 1958), pp. 408–29.

[24] The most serious threats come from proximate neighbors, not the distant great powers or other extra-regional states. This characteristic results in foreign meddling, support for ethnic and religious kin in neighboring states, and subversion in domestic politics rather than conventional military intervention or invasion. See Walt, *The Origins of Alliances*.

[25] Malcolm Kerr, *The Arab Cold War: Gamal' Abd al-Nasir and his Rivals, 1958–1970* (New York: Oxford University Press, 1971), p. vi.

[26] Paul Noble, "The Arab System: Pressure, Constraints, and Opportunities," in Bahgat Korany and Ali E. Hillal Dessouki, eds., *The Foreign Policies of Arab States* (Boulder, CO: Westview Press, 1991), pp. 50–60.

[27] Binder, "The Middle East as a subordinate International System," p. 414.

regional imbalance has unleashed Tehran (and Iraq's other neighbor, Syria) to pursue a more activist and aggressive foreign policy.[28] The regional danger of weakening Iraq was made clear in an interview conducted with General H. Norman Schwarzkopf, commander of the US Central Command (CENTCOM), prior to the first Gulf War:

There are alternatives to destroying Saddam Hussein or to destroying his regimes. I like to think that the ultimate objective is to make sure that we have peace, stability, and a correct balance of power in the Middle East ... Obviously one way would be the total destruction of Iraq, but I am not sure that is in the interest of the long-term balance of power in this region.[29]

The rise of China as a major economic and military power is bound to upset the balance of power in Asia.[30] China's growing assertion of power in South Asia was a contributing factor in India's decision to renew its nuclear program.[31] Related to this is the fact that while Sino-American relations have dramatically improved following the collapse of the Soviet Union, and especially after Clinton's "engagement" of Beijing, this détente put India on edge. According to some, Sino-American courting accounts for the timing of New Delhi's nuclear tests in 1998.[32]

Domestic threats (intra-state competition)

Domestic politics is characterized by intra-state competition. Many states in nonwestern regions and great powers in previous eras were not classic nation-states, where the geographical territory overlaps with a group of people who have a common identity. Instead, there exist divided loyalties amongst the population, with subnational groups owing allegiance to leaders based on ethnic, religious, or

[28] Michael Slackman, "Wary of US, Syria and Iran Strengthen Ties," *New York Times*, June 25, 2006, p. A1.
[29] General H. Norman Schwarzkopf, "Excerpts from Interview with Commander of American Forces in Gulf," *New York Times*, November 2, 1990, p. A8.
[30] Aaron Friedberg, "Ripe for Rivalry: Prospects for Peace in a Multipolar Asia," *International Security* 18, no. 3 (winter 1993/4), pp. 5–33.
[31] P. M. Kamath, "US–China Relations under the Clinton Administration: Comprehensive Engagement or the Cold War Again?" *Strategic Analysis* 22, no. 4 (1988), pp. 699–704.
[32] Prem Shankar Jha, "Why India Went Nuclear," *World Affairs* 2, no. 3 (1998), pp. 80–96.

regional groupings other than the state government. In these instances, Steven David defines the state as merely the "representative of a group that holds power in the capital ... [and] do not want to relinquish their only opportunity to acquire and keep wealth and influence."[33] The primary threat to these narrowly based regimes' survival comes from internal competitors, with neighboring states posing as secondary threats.[34] With the high stakes of domestic politics, leaders are primarily concerned about the ruling regime's survival rather than the nation-state's survival.

More broadly, in all states, socioeconomic elites ask Harold Lasswell's classic question, "Who gets what, when, and how?"[35] Societal leaders are concerned about the uneven distributional (and redistributional) effects of foreign policy on the internal balance of political and economic power. The perennial fear is that in capturing the distributive gains, an empowered coalition will lobby the government for policies that will further strengthen their bloc, at the expense of the opposing faction's interests (and perhaps the nation's too). As Helen Milner notes, these "domestic consequences are the 'stuff' of politics."[36] The long-term consequence can be a change in the state's economic and political institutions.

Multitiered threats

What can this complex threat identification model tell us about threat assessment and foreign policy behavior? This model highlights that the FPE assesses threats at the systemic level, but also at the sub-systemic and domestic levels. Specifically, threats can emanate from other great powers and extra-regional actors, regional powers in the locale, or domestic opponents. The implication is that state leaders can act on one level, but the objective is to influence the outcome on another level(s). Both Jennifer Sterling-Folker and Benjamin

---

[33] David, "Explaining Third World Alignment," pp. 239–40.

[34] See Mohammed Ayoob, "The Third World in the System of States: Acute Schizophrenia or Growing Pains?" *International Studies Quarterly* 33, no. 1 (1989), pp. 67–79.

[35] Harold. D. Lasswell, *Politics: Who gets What, When, How* (New York: Meridian Books, 1958).

[36] Helen V. Milner, *Resisting Protectionism: Global Industries and the Politics of International Trade* (Princeton, NJ: Princeton University Press, 1988), p. 16.

Fordham's chapters in this volume highlight this interactive nature of domestic and international politics.

First, this model tells us that the FPE can act externally with the intention of manipulating the political and economic power within their society. A hard-line foreign policy and interstate conflict can divert attention and create internal solidarity due to the "rally-around-the-flag" effect, expand the power of the state over society, punish and thereby weaken internal opposition, or mobilize internal backing for costly grand strategies the population would otherwise not support.[37] For example, for King Philip IV (1605–65) of Spain, total warfare on several fronts had the domestic effect of weakening the Cortes of Castile, the primary internal constraint on the crown's extraction of public revenue.[38] In 1619, with the resurgence in their autonomy, the Cortes encroached further on the royal prerogative, requiring the crown to apply for the appropriation of funds and to consult with them about the expenditure of the funds. With the resumption of war in 1621, the Cortes' deputies opposed the crown's request for additional funding because it imposed burdens on the already overtaxed cities. By engaging in total warfare, the crown forced the Cortes to increase the sales tax on basic foodstuffs (*millones*), and thereby undermined its fiscal, administrative, and distributive powers. As royal absolutism triumphed in Castile and the Cortes was subdued, the king annexed the commission of *millones* to his Council of Finance, dissolving the Cortes in 1664.

Second, this model tells us that the FPE can implement a foreign policy with the intention of manipulating domestic actors and interest groups in other states.[39] Specifically, a state's choice of arms, allies, or

---

[37] For illegitimate leaders, since the primary threat to a regime's survival is often internal, they may fear the domestic political cost from international compliance more than the economic or physical cost from international punishment.

[38] Charles Jago, "Habsburg Absolutism and the Cortes of Castile," *American Historical Review* 86 (1981), pp. 307–26; John H. Elliott, *Spain and its World, 1500–1700: Selected Essays* (New Haven, CT: Yale University Press, 1989); John Lynch, *The Hispanic World in Crisis and Change, 1598–1700* (Cambridge, MA: Blackwell, 1992).

[39] Scott C. James and David A. Lake, "The Second Face of Hegemony: Britain's Repeal of the Corn Laws and the American Walker Tariff of 1846," *International Organization* 43, no. 1 (1989), pp. 1–29; Rawi Abdelal and Jonathan Kirshner, "Strategy, Economic Relations, and the Definition of National Interests," *Security Studies* 9, no. 1 (1999–2000), pp. 119–56; John

appeasement can strengthen the political power of some societal and economic actors in foreign states while others will be weakened politically and economically. The domestic winners will then apply pressure on the government to support their preferred grand strategy. The long-term consequence can be the alteration in the foreign state's political and economic arrangements.[40] One goal of Britain's appeasement policy toward Japan and Germany in the 1930s was to strengthen domestic moderates over the hard-liners.[41] The intention of "targeted" appeasement (e.g. credits, loans, trade concessions, market guarantees, and export earnings in sterling) of conservative business, government officials, and economic circles in banking, light industry and finished goods, and even heavy industry, was to transform Japan and Germany's internal political-economic climate from the outside. If strengthened, these industrial, commercial, and official classes would pull Tokyo and Berlin away from economic autarky and militarism, and push to return to the international fold of open and orthodox economic policy – albeit a revised one.[42]

Third, this complex threat identification model tells us that the FPE can act locally with the intention of pulling reluctant extra-regional great powers into the conflict until all are involved.[43] North Korea has

M. Owen, "Transnational Liberalism and US Primacy," *International Security* 26, no. 3 (winter 2001/2), pp. 117–52. On reverberations (when international pressure affects the "Level II win-set size" by tipping the domestic constituent balance), see Robert Putnam, "Diplomacy and Domestic Politics: The Logic of Two-level Games," *International Organization* 42, no. 3 (1988), pp. 454–56.

[40] See Andrew Cortell and Susan Peterson, "Altered States: Explaining Domestic Institutional Change," *British Journal of Political Science* 29, no. 2 (1999), pp. 177–203.

[41] C. A. MacDonald, "Economic Appeasement and the German 'Moderates' 1937–1939. An Introductory Essay," *Past and Present* 56 (1972), pp. 105–35; Scott Newton, *Profits of Peace: The Political Economy of Anglo-German Appeasement* (Oxford: Clarendon Press, 1996); Kibata Yoichi, "Anglo-Japanese Relations from the Manchurian Incident to Pearl Harbor: Missed Opportunities," in Ian Nish and Yoichi Kibata, eds., *The History of Anglo-Japanese Relations, 1600–2000* (London: Macmillan, 2000), pp. 1–25; Steven E. Lobell, "The Second Face of Security: Britain's 'Smart' Appeasement Policy towards Japan and Germany," *International Relations of the Asia-Pacific* 7, no. 1 (2007), pp. 73–98.

[42] Ronald M. Smelser, "Nazi Dynamics, German Foreign Policy and Appeasement," in Wolfgang Mommsen and Lothar Kettenacker, eds., *The Fascist Challenge and the Policy of Appeasement* (Boston: George Allen and Unwin, 1983).

[43] Brown, *International Politics and the Middle East.*

used its weapons of mass destruction (WMD) program to provoke a crisis with the intention of involving China, Japan, and Russia as a counterbalance to US dominance on the Korean peninsula. Prior to World War I, both Austria-Hungary and Serbia used the July crisis of 1914 to draw in the great powers.

Finally, this model tells us that the FPE can act at the global level, with the leaders of second-tier states defying the great powers in order to flex their muscles and thereby gain status amongst regional competitors. Saddam Hussein turned severe sanctions and an intrusive UN inspection regime into a "victory" by not cooperating and by claiming that Iraq was the only Arab state to stand up against the "Great Satan" for broader pan-Arab security interests. This dynamic seems to go furthest towards explaining "why Saddam would choose to put his country through the pain of sanctions without having anything significant to hide."[44]

Component power versus aggregate power

Like balance of power and balance of threat theory, neoclassical realism places power at the center of political life. However, in contrast to conventional balance of power and balance of threat theories, I propose an alternative way to conceptualize balancing – foreign policy decision-makers and societal leaders do not balance against aggregate or net shifts in power alone; instead they also define threats based on specific components of a foreign state's power. I contend that instead of focusing on the consequence of another power's grand strategy, leaders pursue policies that address separate or specific components of an ascending or threatening state's power.[45] First,

---

[44] Michael Friend, "After Non-Detection, What? What Iraq's Unfound WMD Mean for the Future of Non-Proliferation," in Graham F. Walker, ed., *The Search for WMD: Non-Proliferation, Intelligence, and Pre-emption in the New Security Environment* (Halifax, Nova Scotia: Centre for Foreign Policy Studies, 2006), p. 15.

[45] See Wohlforth's discussion of American and Soviet definitions of what constituted "power." Americans emphasized economic and organizational resources and nuclear weapons, followed by economic and technical resources. The Soviets highlighted military capabilities. William Curti Wohlforth, *The Elusive Balance: Power and Perceptions during the Cold War* (Ithaca, NY: Cornell University Press, 1993), pp. 106–11, 120–29.

foreign policy decision-makers and societal leaders respond to shifts in the relative distribution of particular capabilities that might pose threats to specific strategic interests. Second, increases in the different components of others' relative power do not threaten an opposing state's interests equally. In the case of the pre-World War I period, it was the growth of German economic and land-based military power, not the naval buildup, that posed the primary threat to British interests on the continent. The German naval buildup was more of a threat to Britain's imperial interests abroad, given the strength of the Royal Navy's home fleet.

Whether a foreign state is viewed as threatening is in part a function of which component of its power is rising. Specific components might include shifts in territory, population, ideology, industry, land-based military, or naval and air power.[46] The importance for my argument is that different components of power pose different threats to societal actors in other states. For instance, export-oriented firms, large banking and financial services will view a foreign state whose economic component of power is ascending as a natural ally. Such leaders will emphasize the complementarity between the states and especially the ascending state's need for finished goods, loans, services, investment, and finances. In the case of pre-World War I Britain, "the interest of the City of London played an important role in setting out an economic and political framework under which it [Japanese industrialization] took place."[47] The assumption was that "the more Japanese cotton industries developed and construction of railways progressed, the more British machinery and railway materials tended to be imported."[48] In contrast, inefficient industry and agriculture, import-substituting manufacturing, and labor-intensive industry will identify the same ascending component of power as a threat. They are concerned that foreign industrialization will flood the home and third-party markets with cheaper and more competitive imports, divert

---

[46] Steven Spiegel, *Dominance and Diversity: The International Hierarchy* (Boston: Little Brown, 1972), pp. 39–91; Mearsheimer, *The Tragedy of Great Power Politics*, pp. 55–82.

[47] Shigeru Akita, " 'Gentlemanly Capitalism,' Inter-Asian Trade and Japanese Industrialisation at the Turn of the Last Century," *Japan Forum* 8, no. 1 (1996), p. 52. Also see Sir Fred Warner, *The Anglo-Japanese Financial Relations* (London: Basil Blackwell, 1991), pp. 53–6.

[48] Akita, "Gentlemanly Capitalism," p. 53.

capital overseas, raise the price of borrowing capital at home, and strengthen foreign competition.

As discussed in the final section, state and societal leaders can pursue policies that address the "wrong" component of an opposing state's power. By wrong, I mean state and societal leaders will view a state as a threat in so far as its ascending components of power endangers their specific interests. Therefore, the foreign state is viewed as more or less threatening as dictated by shifts in other components of power or its aggregate capabilities. One question addressed in the next section is why elites accord importance to different elements of power of a foreign state.

Who are the relevant actors?

Neoclassical realists make a number of assumptions about the state. First, they assume the FPE is a unified central decision-maker. Neoclassical realism accepts that these leaders sit at the intersection of domestic and international political systems, and can act internationally for domestic reasons or domestically for international ends. They further assume the FPE is primarily committed to advancing the security or power of the entire nation. Yet factors such as political and social cohesion, public support for foreign policy objectives, and the quality of a government and administrative competence affect whether the state can harness the nation's power. For this reason, a number of neoclassical realists differentiate between state power and national power.[49] Additionally, foreign policy choices are made by state leaders and it is their assessment of threat that matters. State leaders occupy critical positions in an administration, are the "sole authoritative foreign policymaker," and are responsible for national security and the formation of long-term grand strategies.[50] The FPE also possess private information and a monopoly on intelligence about foreign countries.

Like other neoclassical realists, I open the black box of the state, treating the state as an intervening variable. A limitation in the neoclassical realists' "top-down" model, including Norrin Ripsman's and

---

[49] On the distinction between state power and national power, see Zakaria, *From Wealth to Power*, pp. 35–41; and Christensen, *Useful Adversaries*, pp. 20–5.

[50] Lake, *Power, Protection and Free Trade*, p. 37.

Colin Dueck's chapters in this volume, is that they discount the influence of societal leaders in branding a foreign state as a "national" threat.[51] State and societal elites have a different "evoked set" of concerns about an ascending foreign power. As Robert Jervis notes, "The way people perceive data is influenced not only by their cognitive structure and theories about other actors but also by what they are concerned with at the time they receive the information."[52]

As discussed in this section: *societal elites* (i.e. socioeconomic leaders) maximize their sector or factor's economic welfare, and the *foreign policy executive* devises grand strategy and maximizes national security.[53] When societal leaders assess a foreign state they ask whether the shift in its components of power (such as territory, population, ideology, industry, land-based military, and naval and air power) threatens their firms, sectors, or factors of production. That is, is the shift in the element of power complementary (foreign state is a natural partner) or competitive (foreign state is a rival and threat)? Thomas Christensen and other neoclassical realists might be correct to state that "the public simply does not have the time or expertise to understand the subtleties of balance-of-power politics."[54] Yet it is wrong to infer that societal leaders do not understand when a specific component of a foreign state threatens their parochial interests. Societal leaders too are experts and have their "ear to the rail" to listen for approaching specific dangers to their firms, sectors, or factors. For instance, fearing further job losses, US labor leaders have pushed George W. Bush's administration to pressure the Chinese government to increase wages and improve working conditions.[55]

---

[51] Even Morgenthau acknowledges that "Domestic and international politics are but two different manifestations of the same phenomenon: the struggle for power." Hans J. Morgenthau, *Politics among Nations: The Struggle for Power and Peace*, 3rd edn (New York: Alfred A. Knopf, 1964), p. 38.

[52] Robert Jervis, "Hypotheses on Misperception," *World Politics* 20, no. 3 (April 1968), p. 472.

[53] Lars S. Skålnes, *Politics, Markets, and Grand Strategy: Foreign Economic Policies as Strategic Instruments* (Ann Arbor: University of Michigan Press, 2000), p. 585.

[54] Christensen, *Useful Adversaries*, p. 17.

[55] Meanwhile, American traders have profited from the sale of US mortgage-backed securities to Chinese investors.

Societal leaders: domestic balance of political power

While individual parochial groups have narrow interests, I distinguish between two broad and logrolled societal coalitions: *internationalist* and *nationalist*.[56] These coalitions form around shared interests – or as Peter Gourevitch notes, "What people want depends on where they sit."[57] Their policy preference is shaped by their international or domestic orientation and hence they have conflicting interests.[58] The composition of these domestic coalitions span state and private actors, and national interest groups, and their allegiance will depend on whether their incentives are inward and nationally oriented or outward and internationally oriented.

The internationalist coalition is defined as the internationally competitive sectors plus outward-leaning allies. They have overseas investments or interests, and benefit from foreign economic exposure or have strong international links. Supporters include fiscal conservatives, export-oriented firms, large banking and financial services, and skilled labor. Supporters favor a forward grand strategy that entails heightened participation in the international system. They prosper from greater economic, political, and military engagement in the international system.[59] Supporters require coordination and collaboration with foreign governments and business cohorts on matters of international trade and monetary and security policy to achieve

---

[56] Jeffrey A. Frieden, "Sectoral Conflict and US Foreign Economic Policy, 1914–1940," *International Organization* 42, no. 1 (winter 1988), pp. 59–90; Benjamin O. Fordham, *Building the Cold War Consensus: The Political Economy of US National Security Policy, 1949–51* (Ann Arbor: University of Michigan Press, 1998); Robert O. Keohane and Helen V. Milner, eds., *Internationalization and Domestic Politics* (Cambridge: Cambridge University Press, 1996); Etel Solingen, *Regional Orders at Century's Dawn: Global and Domestic Influences on Grand Strategy* (Princeton, NJ: Princeton University Press, 1998); Steven E. Lobell, *The Challenge of Hegemony: Grand Strategy, Trade, and Domestic Politics* (Ann Arbor: University of Michigan Press, 2003); and Kevin Narizny, *The Political Economy of Grand Strategy* (Ithaca, NY: Cornell University Press, 2007). The literature on structural adjustment makes similar coalitional assumptions.

[57] Peter Gourevitch, *Politics in Hard Times: Comparative Responses to International Economic Crises* (Ithaca, NY: Cornell University Press, 1986), p. 56.

[58] Peter Trubowitz, *Defining the National Interest: Conflict and Change in American Foreign Policy* (Chicago: University of Chicago Press, 1998).

[59] See Solingen, *Regional Orders*, pp. 26–9; and Fordham, *Building the Cold War Consensus*, p. 3.

mutual economic gains. This means membership in multilateral international organizations, and participating in conventions, treaties, and collective security arrangements. Their natural state allies are finance-oriented government bureaucracies.

The nationalist coalition is defined as the non-internationally competitive sectors and domestically oriented groups. They have few foreign assets, sales, or ties and compete with foreign imports. Backers include inefficient industry and agriculture, import-substituting manufacturing, and labor-intensive industry. They will contest calls for greater international engagement because it undermines their constituents' domestic power and position. For the most part, they oppose both the costs and risks of internationalism, and thereby favor limiting international involvement by restricting military spending to defense of the homeland, restricting foreign aid, and eschewing international commitments and entanglements.[60] Under certain circumstances nationalists will favor imperial conquest over isolation.[61] Their natural state allies are public sector managers and workers, colonial/settler/empire-oriented state bureaucrats, and civil servants.

In both factions, the supporters converge on a common position, often for different reasons and sometimes without any formal organization.[62] Some actors and interest groups might move between factions. Changes in the domestic and international environment can push members to defect and join the ranks of the opposing bloc. For instance, during the 1930s, many internationalists were harmed by the global trend toward self-sufficiency and exclusive commercial spheres. In Britain, these supporters pushed for a retreat behind the sterling area, where they aspired to maintain a high degree of financial authority to retain the confidence of sterling holders.[63]

---

[60] Fordham, *Building the Cold War Consensus*, pp. 3–4.

[61] James H. Nolt, "Business Conflict and the Demise of Imperialism," in David Skidmore, ed., *Contested Social Orders and International Politics* (Nashville, TN: Vanderbilt University Press, 1997), p. 99.

[62] The timing of development can play a role in differential domestic arrangements. In early developers, the state is less interventionist, while in the late developers the state plays a leading role in development. See Alexander Gerschenkron, *Economic Backwardness in Historical Perspective* (Cambridge, MA: Harvard University Press, 1962).

[63] Peter J. Cain and Anthony G. Hopkins, *British Imperialism: Crisis and Deconstruction, 1914–1990* (London: Longman, 1993).

Domestic balance of political and economic power

Societal leaders know that a shift in an element of power of a foreign state will alter the domestic balance of political and economic power in their state too. Specifically, nationalist and internationalist elites recognize the internal ramification of exogenous shifts – the rise or decline of a component of power of another major state is not distributionally equal but can have a differential effect on domestic political struggles, and thereby enhance some societal sectors while concomitantly weakening others. As mentioned above, pre-World War I Japanese industrialization had the concomitant effect in Britain of strengthening the internationalist bloc while undermining the nationalist faction.

The domestic process entails three calculations: (1) nationalist and internationalist elites recognize that shifts in an element of power of a foreign state can enable some societal actors and disable others; (2) nationalist and internationalist elites understand the domestic stakes involved in threat identification; (3) nationalist and internationalist elites know that counterbalancing a foreign threat will also create internal winners and losers.

Both nationalist and internationalist societal leaders will engage in political calculations about how threat assessment and counterbalancing will affect their relative domestic power and position.[64] That is, societal leaders will not only assess whether their constituents will be better or worse off as a result of threat identification, but will also consider the effect on the opposing faction. Societal leaders will seek to identify and brand states that have a component of power that harms their parochial interests as a national threat. The more their welfare depends on foreign threat identification, the harder societal elites will lobby the FPE. By getting the FPE to balance against the foreign state, the cost of balancing will be borne across society as a whole while the benefits will be reaped by their narrow constituency.[65]

---

[64] Here I differ from Schweller who ignores domestic distributional competition among elites over the domestic consequence of foreign policy. Randall L. Schweller, *Unanswered Threats: Political Constraints on the Balance of Power* (Princeton, NJ: Princeton University Press, 2006).

[65] Mancur Olson, *The Rise and the Decline of Nations: Economic Growth, Stagflation, and Social Rigidities* (New Haven, CT: Yale University Press, 1982), chap. 3; Jack L. Snyder, *Myths of Empire: Domestic Politics and International Ambition* (Ithaca, NY: Cornell University Press, 1991), pp. 17–18.

Societal leaders will also view counterbalancing as helpful or harmful to their constituency. This distributional perspective will affect the mobilization process since elites will either encourage or discourage their followers to provide critical support and resources for costly balancing.[66]

The beneficiaries will use the accrued gains from threat identification and counterbalancing to accelerate and expand the internal redistribution of political power. The concern of both blocs is that the domestic winners will then apply pressure on the government to advance their preferred domestic and foreign policies, further capturing the distributive gains. One real danger is that societal elites may push the FPE beyond what is in the nation's grand strategic interest. Elites might also challenge a policy because it will undermine their coalitional interests, even if it is in the national interest.[67]

FPE: grand strategy and the balance of power

The FPE formulates grand strategy and maximizes the state's national security. As Thomas Christensen tells us, "State leaders are more likely than average citizens to be concerned with the long-term security of the nation."[68] Grand strategy incorporates several components.[69] First, grand strategy is not only military, but also fiscal and political in nature. Second, grand strategy does not cease at the end of a war or start at the beginning of a war but is about balancing ends and means in both peacetime and wartime. Finally, grand strategy involves long-term planning over decades and perhaps longer.

State leaders are concerned about shifts in components of power of foreign states that will alter the broader systemic and subsystemic

---

[66] See Taliaferro and Schweller's chapters in this volume.

[67] How these actors discount the future might alter their strategy.

[68] Christensen, *Useful Adversaries*, p. 18.

[69] On definitions of grand strategy, see Barry R. Posen, *The Sources of Military Doctrine: France, Britain, and Germany Between the Wars* (Ithaca, NY: Cornell University Press, 1984), p. 6; Stephen M. Walt, "Analyzing US Grand Strategy," *International Security* 14, no. 1 (1989), p. 6; Richard Rosecrance and Arthur A. Stein, eds., "Beyond Realism: The Study of Grand Strategy," in *The Domestic Bases of Grand Strategy* (Ithaca, NY: Cornell University Press, 1993), pp. 4–5.

balance of power.[70] They focus on which components of power are increasing relative to their own and especially the power differential of the components.[71] They ask whether the foreign state's rising component will peak above (or below) their own component power and the size of the power gap, and in what areas the rising state will be superior and inferior. In focusing on shifts in a component power rather than net power, state leaders respond to shifts in the relative distribution of particular capabilities that threaten specific strategic interests. Furthermore, increases in different components of relative power do not threaten an opposing state's interests equally.

State leaders are not always unified in their assessment of threat. The bureaucratic politics model highlights the parochial nature of bureau chiefs too. In some instances, outward- or inward-oriented state leaders will align with or have strong ties to internationalist or nationalist societal leaders. Also it is important to note that many FPEs are erstwhile societal elites and will likely return to their former or similar positions.

What are the constraints and inducements on the FPE?

Chapter 1 offers two ways to understand the relationship between international systemic and unit-level forces.[72] First, systemic and subsystemic structural forces shape the broad parameters of a state's behavior in the international arena.[73] These external constraints and

---

[70] In contrast, on the effect of ideology and not power on threat identification, see Mark L. Haas, *The Ideological Origins of Great Power Politics, 1789–1989* (Ithaca, NY: Cornell University Press, 2005).

[71] By focusing on components of power, my argument is more than about broad transitions in power, such as A.F.K. Organski's *World Politics*, 2nd edn (New York: Knopf, 1968), or Robert Gilpin's *War and Change in World Politics* (New York: Cambridge University Press, 1981). On differentials of relative power, see Dale Copeland, *The Origins of Major War* (Ithaca, NY: Cornell University Press, 2000). State leaders might also look at other elements of state power of foreign states. These include a nation's quest for prestige and status, and the willingness of leaders (and citizens) to make the sacrifices needed to build material and military power. Other possible factors are the personalities and beliefs of leading statesmen, political and social cohesion, public support for foreign policy objectives (and its willingness to bear the costs of foreign involvement), and the quality of a government and its administrative competence.

[72] I would like to thank Norrin Ripsman for clarifying this point.

[73] Jennifer Sterling-Folker, "Realist Environment, Liberal Process, and Domestic-Level Variables," *International Studies Quarterly* 41, no. 1 (1997), pp. 1–25.

opportunities for action will create incentives or disincentives, but they alone cannot account for a state's particular foreign policy or specific historical events. Balance of power theory and balance of threat theory make no claims to do so. Only a theory of foreign and security policy, which includes unit-level variables, can explain which countries will balance, when countries will balance, or why countries will fail to balance against an emerging power or threat.

Second, unit-level obstacles can impede states from behaving in the rational manner that balance of power theory and balance of threat theory suppose. Specifically, variables such as domestic politics, civil–military relations, elite belief systems, organizational politics, state–society autonomy, and misperceptions can prevent states from adapting to changes in the international environment. According to this account, adjustment failures explain suboptimal outcomes and inefficient responses to systemic encouragements.[74] Problems include whether decision-makers can assess the state's foreign policy and adjust to shifts in relative power by building arms and forming alliances.

My argument on the constraints on foreign policy adaptation does not focus on the problem that decision-makers have in detecting, assessing, estimating, or calculating structural subsystemic changes in the relative distribution of power.[75] Such arguments focus on official assessment failure of the actual or net material capabilities among rising and declining powers. This might result from the nature of the indicators of national power, mistakes in estimates of material capabilities, or misperceptions of the distribution of power. In these instances, state leaders miscalculate shifts in net power. In failing to adjust to these changes, the states do not conform to the predictions of balance of power theory. Other arguments contend that leaders often face ambiguous, incomplete, and contradictory information about changes in relative power, especially during crises and periods of rapid change.[76]

[74] Snyder, *Myths of Empire*; Charles Kupchan, *The Vulnerability of Empire* (Ithaca, NY: Cornell University Press, 1994); Zakaria, *From Wealth to Power*.
[75] Friedberg, *The Weary Titan*; Wohlforth, *The Elusive Balance*; Randall L. Schweller, *Deadly Imbalances: Tripolarity and Hitler's Strategy of World Conquest* (New York: Columbia University Press, 1998).
[76] See Ole R. Holsti, "Theories of Crisis Decision-making," in Paul Gordon Lauren, ed., *Diplomacy: New Approaches in History, Theory, and Policy* (New York: Free Press, 1979), pp. 99–136.

In assessing threats I argue that the FPE faces constraints and inducements that emanate from the systemic, subsystemic, and domestic levels. When forces on all three levels converge, the FPE is unconstrained in its threat identification and in implementing its counterbalancing foreign policy (see scenario "A" and scenario "B" below). When forces on the systemic, subsystemic, or domestic levels diverge, the FPE is constrained in its threat assessment (see scenario "C" below).

Unconstrained FPE: scenario "A" and scenario "B"

Both systemic and subsystemic structural and unit-level forces influence the behavior of state leaders. When a shift in a component of power of a foreign state enables a foreign policy coalition, the FPE is unconstrained in its threat identification, and efficient counterbalancing is likely to follow. Specifically, this exogenous shift in power will foster consensus among the FPE and its key societal supporters that the emerging state is a threat.

In scenario "A" the FPE is the least constrained in branding a foreign state as a threat (and counterbalancing against it). At each level there is consensus that the foreign power is a sufficient danger. At the systemic-subsystemic level, the FPE has identified a component of power of the foreign state as a threat to the national interest. At the domestic level, both nationalist and internationalist leaders have identified different elements of power of the same foreign state as a threat to their parochial interests (i.e. the components are competitive). Neither nationalist nor internationalist elites believe that branding the state as a threat or counterbalancing it will redistribute the domestic balance of power; any benefits are "washed" or "canceled" out by the gains of the other bloc. For instance, by 1937, there was agreement among British elites in identifying Tokyo as a threat due to declining support among internationalists for accommodating Japan. Japan's actions in China threatened Britain's position in Shanghai, its stake in the Maritime Customs, and its shipping and railway interests.[77]

---

[77] Shanghai represented three-quarters of Britain's holdings in China. The city was also important to shipping firms, handling much of the extensive inland trade on the Yangtze River. Ann Trotter, *Britain and East Asia: 1933–1937* (Cambridge: Cambridge University Press, 1975), p. 18.

Scenario "A" approximates the Waltzian unitary actor. The foreign policy consequence is a smooth adaptation to changes in relative power, and counterbalancing should reflect shifts in the distribution of power.

In scenario "B," the FPE is more constrained than in scenario "A" but still mostly free to identify foreign threats.[78] At the systemic-subsystemic level, differentials in growth rates lead the FPE to identify a component of power of the foreign state as a threat to the national interest. Meanwhile, at the domestic level, while the FPE's societal supporters identify a component of power of the aspiring state as a threat to their parochial interests (i.e. the components are competitive), the opposition does not view the same component of power or other components as a danger (i.e. the components are complementary). From the perspective of the opposing societal elites, given the complementary nature of the components of power of the states, the foreign country is a natural partner. The more extensive the economic ties between the states, the more these elites will reject branding the foreign power as a threat, since such behavior will undermine its constituency's relative power and position.[79] If the opposition has strong ties to state leaders or can argue that the component of power is not a general threat to the national interest, they might be able to moderate the FPE's threat assessment.

For the FPE, scenario "B" has positive systemic, subsystemic, and domestic externalities – that is, policies at one level will have positive consequences for the others. Specifically, identifying and balancing against the foreign state will concomitantly empower the FPE's domestic supporters. Meanwhile, the FPE's societal opponents will be weakened by these policies. In fact, when systemic, subsystemic, and domestic forces converge, the FPE can target societal blocs. For Christensen, the FPE adopts a more hostile or more ideological foreign policy in order to mobilize public support for costly and necessary security strategies.[80] However, he ignores that the FPE can act internationally in order to redistribute societal power-strengthening

---

[78] Domestic institutions, regime type, and politics can affect whether the FPE can insulate itself from interest group pressure.

[79] Paul A. Papayoanou, *Power Ties: Economic Interdependence, Balancing, and War* (Ann Arbor: University of Michigan Press, 1999); Skålnes, *Politics, Markets, and Grand Strategy.*

[80] Christensen, *Useful Adversaries*, pp. 25–9.

internal supporters and weakening societal opposition. Specifically, Christensen neglects the fact that foreign policy is not distributionally equal, but instead can create different domestic winners and losers. Thereby, the FPE can act as "kingmaker" and pursue foreign policies that strengthen some societal groups at the expense of others. This is what the American FPE did after World War II. According to Jeff Frieden, "The Depression and eventually World War II weakened the economic nationalists and allowed the state to reshape both policies and policy networks. By the late 1930s, economic nationalists were isolated or ignored, and most relevant decisions were placed within the purview of relatively internationalist bureaucracies."[81]

In scenario "B," although the FPE is fairly unfettered in its threat assessment, the subsequent counterbalancing policy can still be inappropriate (although it will not be delayed, slow, or inefficient). As noted in the final section, the FPE and its societal supporters might focus on the wrong component of power of a foreign state. That is, elites might ignore a threatening state that does not have certain components of power or they might identify a non-threatening state as a threat that has certain components of power.

Constrained FPE: scenario "C"

When a shift in a component of power of a foreign state disables a foreign policy coalition, the FPE is constrained in its threat identification and inefficient counterbalancing can occur. Specifically, this exogenous shift will foster disagreement among the FPE and its key societal supporters on whether the foreign state is a danger.

In scenario "C," threat assessment at the systemic-subsystemic and the domestic levels diverge and work at cross purposes.[82] (1) The FPE has identified a component of power of the foreign state as a threat and is inclined to be more confrontational toward the rising or threatening nation. (2) The FPE's societal supporters do not identify the element as a threat to their parochial interests (i.e. the components

---

[81] Jeff Frieden, "Sectoral Conflict and Foreign Economic Policy, 1914–1940," *International Organization* 42, no. 1 (winter 1988), p. 88.

[82] Outside the scope of the discussion in this chapter, it is possible that the FPE will not identify a component of power as a threat, but that societal leaders will view it as a danger. In this instance, societal elites will lobby the FPE to brand the state a national threat.

are complementary), and are reluctant to believe there is a danger given the positive and complementary relationship. The more the supporters' welfare depends on maintaining the overseas trade, commercial links, and investments, the more they will oppose identifying the foreign state as a threat, and want to treat it kindly. Hence, if societal elites have strong ties to the FPE, the result is delayed, slow, or inefficient threat assessment (and counterbalancing).

One import of this disagreement over threat assessment is that power will be redistributed in either the systemic-subsystemic or the domestic arena. Identifying the foreign state as a threat will have the consequence of redistributing the domestic balance of economic and political power. Specifically, this choice will undermine the FPE's key societal supporters while strengthening the opposing societal bloc – and thereby alter the internal balance of power. Alternatively, the FPE can downplay the foreign state as a threat, and thereby defend the domestic position of its key societal supporters. But this option will permit a shift in the international or regional balance of power.

London's threat assessment between 1933 and 1936 of Germany, Japan, and Italy was hamstrung by elite disagreement. British nationalists identified these states as significant threats and called for massive rearmament (two-power naval standard, continental army, and air force with reserves), peacetime state intervention in the economy (termed national efficiency), abandonment of the gold standard (the gold standard meant higher export prices), binding international trade agreements (covering production, prices, and the allocation of markets), and imperial preferences that would link the empire and the domestic economy.[83] The internal consequence of this foreign policy agenda would enhance supporters of the nationalist bloc including inefficient industry, settler groups, and empire-oriented bureaucrats.

British internationalists, including the City of London, the Treasury, and the Bank of England, lobbied the government to oppose this policy. Outward-oriented internationalists fretted that the nationalists' security program meant the "establishment of a 'new economic

---

[83] Robert Paul Shay, Jr., *British Rearmament in the Thirties: Politics and Profits* (Princeton, NJ: Princeton University Press, 1977); G.C. Peden, *British Rearmament and the Treasury: 1932–1939* (Edinburgh: Scottish Academic Press, 1979).

order' in which price-fixing and the control of production and competition would replace the market as the main regulatory mechanisms of economic life."[84] Even a massive rearmament program carried risks, since it would require state intervention in industry and would divert resources and factories from export to rearmament. As the Treasury warned, state intervention in managing the economy was turning Britain into "a different kind of nation."[85]

Constrained by their close ties to the entrenched internationalist bloc (for instance, Prime Minister Neville Chamberlain had been chancellor of the exchequer from 1931 to 1937), the British government elected to: (1) restrain Britain's military buildup by imposing fiscal orthodoxy and laissez-faire economics, and opposing a continental army because it was expensive and would divert manpower from production; (2) extend credits and loans to Germany, Japan, and Italy; grant economic and territorial concessions; and lobby for their return to the League of Nations, participation in collective security, and naval and air limitation agreements; and (3) press for free trade within the sterling area, which required fiscal discipline at home. The outcome was a delay in Britain's rearmament program.

Inappropriate balancing

Constraints or inducements on threat assessment can contribute to inappropriate balancing when: (1) leaders respond to the wrong elements or to shifts in particular capabilities that pose a threat to specific geopolitical, strategic, or domestic groups; (2) increases in a component of relative power do not threaten the opposing state's societal interests equally; (3) the FPE's response is shaped by the domestic distributional consequence of foreign policy.

First, the FPE will identify adversaries based on shifts in a component of power rather than shifts in aggregate power or threat. State leaders might perceive a foreign state's capabilities as posing a greater or lesser threat than aggregate economic and military capabilities dictate. By focusing on a component of power instead of aggregate

[84] Clemens A. Wurn, *Business, Politics, and International Relations: Steel, Cotton, and International Cartels in British Politics, 1924–1939*, trans. Patrick Salmon (Cambridge: Cambridge University Press, 1993), p. 49.

[85] G. C. Peden, "A Matter of Timing: The Economic Background to British Foreign Policy, 1937–1939," *History* 69, no. 225 (February 1984), p. 24.

Table 2.1. *Unconstrained and constrained FPE*

	Exogenous shift	Systemic/subsystemic and domestic ramifications	FPE	Threat assessment and counterbalancing
Scenario "A"	Shift in a component power of a foreign state →	FPE and societal leaders identify component as a threat (enables coalition)→	Unconstrained →	Highly efficient threat assessment and counterbalancing
Scenario "B"	Shift in a component power of a foreign state →	FPE and societal supporters identify component as a threat (enables coalition)→	Limited to moderate constraints →	Efficient to limited threat assessment and counterbalancing
Scenario "C"	Shift in a component power of a foreign state →	FPE identify component as a threat, but societal supporters do not identify component as a threat (disables coalition)→	Constrained →	(a) No threat assessment and no counterbalancing (b) Inefficient threat assessment and counterbalancing

power, the FPE will view the intentions of emerging states as more benign or hostile than reality might dictate. Such leaders might under- or overreact to external threats and hence fail to adopt prudent foreign policies. There is also the real danger of blowback, with the component threat becoming embedded and believed by elites and thus institutionalized.[86]

Second, societal leaders are less likely to view emerging states that do not possess specific threatening components as hostile. In these instances, societal leaders will not rally their constituents to support balancing efforts. In fact, leaders might view threat identification as counterproductive and harmful to their constituents' interests. For example, after 1919, British merchant and joint stock banks raised money for the reconstruction of German cities and financed German transactions. The Bank of England and its governor, Montagu Norman, encouraged British financial penetration of Germany.[87] Norman and other international capitalists countered that any attempt to block these short-term loans and credits would weaken German economic moderates and Britain's interests too.[88] Supporters of trade concessions to Germany argued that British protectionism, and more specifically the Ottawa Agreement (1931) and imperial preferences (1931–32), had pushed the German industrial and commercial classes into the militarist camp.[89] More broadly, early and firm balancing policies are conducive to peace. These policies might deter the challenger and thereby prevent a war or could make war less costly than it would otherwise have been by limiting the challenger's time to prepare and catch up.[90]

Societal leaders will also favor balancing strategies that benefit their constituents. There may be several substitutable policies. Politics may

[86] Snyder, *Myths of Empire*, pp. 41–2.
[87] Neil Forbes, "London Banks, the German Standstill Agreements and 'Economic Appeasement' in the 1930s," *Economic History Review* 40, no. 4 (1987), pp. 571–87; Scott Newton, "The 'Anglo-German Connection' and the Political Economy of Appeasement," *Diplomacy and Statecraft* 2 (1991), p. 196.
[88] Paul Kennedy, *Strategy and Diplomacy, 1870–1945* (London: Allen and Unwin, 1983), p. 103.
[89] More generally, supporters pointed to Britain's abandonment of the gold standard, adopting imperial preferences, tariffs, quotas against Japanese exports, loan and credit embargoes against Germany, and trade sanctions against Italy. Gustav Schmidt, *The Politics and Economics of Appeasement: British Foreign Policy in the 1930s* (New York: St. Martin's Press, 1986).
[90] Randall L. Schweller, "Unanswered Threats: A Neoclassical Realist Theory of Underbalancing," *International Security* 29, no. 2 (2004), pp. 159–201.

narrow the range such that the final choice serves both constituent and national interests. However, it is also possible that policies are not substitutable. In this instance, the choice will undermine the state's national security.

Third, given the multitiered nature of threat assessment, inappropriate balancing can occur when leaders act on one level, but the target is to influence the outcome of game(s) played on another level. In the decade before World War I, Britain's domestic politics led London to overbalance in naval construction, and underbalance in its land army and alliance commitments. Between 1905 and 1912 Germany and Britain engaged in a naval arms race.[91] In 1908, the British Admiralty projected that in the spring of 1912 Germany could have twenty-one Dreadnoughts and twenty-five by the autumn. To match German construction, it was estimated that Britain would need nine new Dreadnoughts by the spring of 1912 and four more by the autumn. However, Berlin never came close to the estimates for German naval construction.[92] By 1913, Britain had completed thirty Dreadnoughts to Germany's seventeen, exceeding the defunct two-power naval standard and above the 1912 official 60 percent naval standard.[93] The gap was even larger when measured in overall naval

[91] John C. Lambelet, "The Anglo-German Dreadnought Race, 1905–1914," *Papers of the Peace Science Society* 22 (1974), pp. 1–45; Rhodri Williams, *Defending the Empire: The Conservative Party and British Defence Policy 1899–1915* (New Haven, CT: Yale University Press, 1991). London's initial concern was that German naval construction would hold the maritime balance between the British and the opposing Franco-Russian fleets.

[92] As Michael Howard notes, "By 1912 the German navy had, not 21 dreadnoughts, not 17, not even 13, but only 9." See Howard, "The Edwardian Arms Race," in Donald Read, ed., *Edwardian England* (London: Croom Helm, 1982), pp. 156–7.

[93] A two-power standard, defined in 1889, meant a navy should "at least be equal to the naval strength of any two other countries." Arthur J. Marder, *The Anatomy of British Sea Power: A History of British Naval Policy in the Pre-Dreadnought Era, 1880–1905* (New York: Alfred A. Knopf, 1940), p. 106. The two-power standard was based on modern battleships, but extended to first-class cruisers too. Measured in tonnage, Germany had the next largest navy after Great Britain, followed by the United States. A one-power standard was calculated as being a force equal to that of Germany plus a margin of 60 percent. The two-power naval standard would have required 26 Dreadnoughts, built against the United States and Germany, while the 60 percent naval standard would have required 27 Dreadnoughts. Jon Tetsuro Sumida, *In Defence of Naval Supremacy: Finance, Technology, and British Naval Policy, 1889–1914* (Boston: Unwin Hyman, 1989), table 21.

tonnage – nearly equal to a three-power naval standard.[94] Though Germany's naval construction clearly pushed Britain to rearm, London overbalanced in its naval rearmament, approaching the combined fleet tonnage of the United States, France, and Germany.

The People's Budget of 1909 used naval rearmament to achieve the party goal of ratcheting up taxes to a new limit – higher than the Conservatives believed possible – without alienating a large portion of the electorate.[95] By generating new revenue for their social agenda and redistributing wealth, the beneficiaries were the Liberal Party's core base of middle-class supporters and working-class voters.[96] The net outcome was a substantial increase in government spending, with social welfare rising from £2.1 million in 1908–9 to £19.7 million in 1913–14 and navy expenditure increasing from £32.2 million to £48.7 million.[97] The working- and middle-class supporters gained significant tax reductions, with the burden of new taxes imposed in the 1909–10 budget (and 1914–15 budget) falling on the opposing aristocracy, by taxing unearned income.[98]

[94] Measured in terms of battleships, armored ships, armored cruisers, and protected cruisers. David D'Lugo and Ronald Rogowski, "The Anglo-American Naval Race and Comparative Constitutional 'Fitness,'" in Richard Rosecrance and Arthur A. Stein, eds., The Domestic Basis of Grand Strategy (Ithaca, NY: Cornell University Press, 1993), table 4.2.

[95] Hugh V. Emy, "The Impact of Financial Policy on English Party Politics before 1914," Historical Journal 15, no. 1 (1972), pp. 122–3; G.C. Peden, British Economic and Social Policy: Lloyd George to Margaret Thatcher (New York: Philip Allan, 1991). In framing his budget for 1909–10, David Lloyd George, Chancellor of the Exchequer of the Liberal government, had to include additional funding for the armed services and for old age pensions, which was scheduled to come into full effect. For Conservatives the answer to the revenue shortage was an end to free trade, which would help British industry and reduce the need for increases in direct taxation. For Liberals the solution was to raise new revenue to provide for the government's long-term social agenda.

[96] To meet the estimated deficit, the People's Budget raised direct taxes rather than indirect taxes through an income tax. The Liberals called for a graduation of income tax or a progressive tax, the differentiation between earned and unearned incomes, and the taxation of land values. In addition, they increased death duties, stamp duties on all sales, and duties on liquor, tobacco, and automobiles. Finally, the budget levied a new tax, called a super tax, to be paid in addition to income tax by all those with an income of over £5,000 a year. Peden, British Economic and Social Policy, pp. 23–32.

[97] Sumida, In Defence of Naval Supremacy, p. 189.

[98] Emy, "The Impact of Financial Policy," pp. 122–3; Bruce Murray, The People's Budget of 1909/10: Lloyd George and Liberal Politics (Oxford: Clarendon Press, 1980), pp. 9–10.

Unfortunately, while naval rearmament boosted the Liberal Party's base, London underbalanced in its alliance commitments with France and Russia, and the buildup of the British Expeditionary Force (BEF). Historian Niall Ferguson concurs. He writes that Britain's greatest foreign policy failure in the decade prior to the Great War was that while London "identified a serious German threat to the continental status quo," Britain "made no serious attempt to prepare to check that threat by the only viable means: the creation of a comparably large land army."[99] The import of excessive naval construction is that Britain diverted scarce resources that could have been allocated to the army, which was underfunded and only had five divisions of the BEF to send to the continent.[100]

Conclusion

This chapter has addressed how states assess foreign threats, identified who are the relevant domestic actors, and examined what happens when elites disagree about whether a foreign state is a danger. Neoclassical realist theories are theories of foreign policy, not international outcomes. For neoclassical realists, systemic and subsystemic pressures are translated through intervening variables at the unit level to explain a particular state's foreign policy or a specific historic event.

In this chapter I made several arguments. First, I developed a complex threat identification model and contended that threats can emanate from systemic (global), subsystemic (regional), and domestic sources. The import is that the FPE can act on one level with the intent of influencing the outcome on another level. Second, in contrast to many realist theories, I have argued that what matters are shifts in components of the rising or threatening state's power, rather than shifts in its aggregate power alone. Third, in disaggregating the concept of the state, I argued that the FPE occupy critical positions in the administration, and are responsible for long-term grand strategic planning, including the identification of changes in the global or regional balance of power. In contrast, societal elites, reflecting outward-oriented internationalists and inward-leaning nationalists,

[99] Niall Ferguson, *The Cash Nexus* (New York: Basic Books, 2001), p. 411.
[100] David French, *British Economic and Strategic Planning, 1905–1915* (Boston: George Allen and Unwin, 1982).

are primarily concerned about immediate shifts in the domestic balance of political power.

The significance of these arguments is that shifts in components of power of a major state can have an uneven or differential effect on domestic political struggles in other countries. Where this exogenous shift enables a foreign security policy coalition, the FPE is unconstrained in threat identification and efficient counterbalancing can occur. In this instance, there is consensus among the FPE and its societal supporters on threat assessment. Where this exogenous shift disables a foreign security policy coalition, the FPE is constrained in threat identification since there is no agreement on threat assessment. Specifically, there is no consensus among the FPE and societal supporters on whether the emerging state is a danger. The latter outcome can result in delayed, inefficient, and inappropriate balancing. Thus, as Kenneth Waltz acknowledges, to explain a specific state's policies or to account for a historical event requires unit-level variables.[101]

---

[101] Waltz, *Theory of International Politics*, pp. 121–3.

3 Neoclassical realism and strategic calculations: explaining divergent British, French, and Soviet strategies toward Germany between the world wars (1919–1939)

MARK R. BRAWLEY

This chapter addresses two questions raised in chapter 1 by Jeffrey Taliaferro, Steven Lobell, and Norrin Ripsman. These questions are how did decision-makers in France, Britain, and the Soviet Union assess foreign threats and opportunities, and how and under what circumstances did domestic factors impede these leaders from pursuing the strategies predicted by balance of power and balance of threat theories? These are some of the central questions raised by the neo-classical realist research agenda and they require a concept of the state to understand the differential and incompatible foreign policy responses to the Nazi German threat in the 1920s and 1930s.

Europe's fate, and perhaps the fate of the world, hung in the balance in 1941. Britain stood isolated, and Nazi Germany appeared not merely ascendant, but on the verge of amassing overwhelming power. In the summer of 1941, Hitler's decisions had sown the seeds of the Third Reich's destruction. With German troops heading into the Balkans and Mediterranean, and then the invasion of the Soviet Union, the odds of a German victory were significantly diminished. (The decision to declare war on the United States stacked the odds decisively against Germany.) I do not raise this turning point in history to question military strategies or to discuss the war itself, but to suggest why the interwar period continues to fascinate us. In 1941, an effective counter-alliance formed because of Hitler's recklessness. Still, the question remains: why did this coalition not form in the 1930s? Might not the war have been prevented if a balancing alliance had been constructed earlier?

There are many explanations for the European great powers' failure to form an effective balance against Hitler's Germany. These accounts emphasize a host of factors, with explanations varying from one country to another. One line of argument focuses on particular individuals; the responsibility, these authors argue, lies in the faults of particular leaders. Some, for example, scrutinize British Prime Minister Neville Chamberlain's decisions, arguing he preferred peace above all other goals. With Britain refusing to deter Hitler's Germany, other states were left to their own devices. French and Soviet leaders acquiesced to appeasement, failing to come up with alternative policies. Yet, increasingly, historians have given us a more realistic portrait of these leaders, illustrating they were neither naïve nor weak.[1]

A second line of arguments looks at domestic political constraints to suggest why an alliance failed to form. This approach is often applied to the French, who were wracked with domestic instabilities. The constant shifting of party alliances and cabinet shakeups made French foreign policy appear inconsistent. Internal strife in the Soviet Union, including the forced reorganization of the economy and then Stalin's purges, made Soviet policy appear erratic, and undercut that country's desirability as an ally. With the only available allies weak and unsteady states such as France or the Soviet Union, who else could Britain have turned to? If British leaders were unwilling to run risks, and refused to support larger military forces, why would the others turn to Britain?

Whereas historical accounts often focus on the foreign policies of a single country, seeking to drive the systemic outcome either from domestic instability or the idiosyncratic flaws of a particular leader, analyses by political scientists often focus on a particular policy. Appeasement has drawn the most attention, but others have looked at defense plans, reparations, disarmament, or collective security as policy instruments. Few have attempted to give the broader account of how these differing policies interacted, or the reasons why one policy

---

[1] See several recent works, including James P. Levy, *Appeasement and Rearmament, Britain 1926–1939* (New York: Rowman and Littlefield, 2006), and Keith Neilson, *Britain, Soviet Russia and the Collapse of the Versailles Order, 1919–1939* (New York: Cambridge University Press, 2006).

held appeal for one state's leaders but not those of another. In the sections below, I seek to give the broader systemic picture, but also discuss why these different policies should be thought of as different routes to balance against Germany. Anyone familiar with the details of interwar diplomacy must be struck by the way German power consistently remained the focus of concerns. The eventual resurgence of German power – and the consequent threats this posed to France, Britain, the Soviet Union, and other states – was unquestioned. These great powers were continually searching for an effective counter to this likely threat.

In the next section, I provide a simple description of balance of power theory, then turn it into a more practical tool for assessing past decisions by unpacking two of its implicit assumptions. I then endogenize these two assumptions – concerning the time frame for decisions and the ability to convert economic assets into realized military resources – to give a better appreciation of the sort of decisions political and military leaders must make when managing power and their international relations. This political economic interpretation of balancing yields a new framework for contrasting the policy instruments various countries employed in the interwar period. As outlined in chapter 1, a permissive systemic environment means that each state can pursue a different foreign policy.[2] Similarly, in chapter 10, Ripsman, Taliaferro, and Lobell discuss scenarios where the international system provides clear information about foreign threats but little guidance about the optimal response. I argue that in the 1920s state preferences varied because systemic imperatives were channeled through countries with different economic positions. In order to manage their power over time, state leaders developed balancing strategies that were consistent with their own idiosyncratic economic needs. As the systemic imperative increased in the 1930s, these past decisions constrained each country's options. Although leaders in Britain, France, and the Soviet Union may have agreed consistently throughout the interwar period that Germany posed the greatest potential threat to their security in the long run, this shared evaluation of the location of the threat did not drive them to form a balancing coalition.

---

[2] This scenario also reflects World 2 that Ripsman, Taliaferro, and Lobell outline in chapter 10 of this volume.

A political economic interpretation of balancing

A simple realist version of balance of power theory is straightforward.
In a system of two states, at a minimum each state seeks to maintain a
rough equilibrium of power with a potential rival, with some states
seeking greater power than the opposition.[3] We can state this with a
simple equation. If we use M to stand for each country's realized
military resources, then state A will seek to have:

$$M^A \geq M^B \tag{1}$$

Once we introduce additional states, then each will seek allies to tilt
the balance in their favor. The equation then becomes:

$$M^A + M^{A\text{'s allies}} \geq M^B + M^{B\text{'s allies}} \tag{2}$$

To execute this calculation, decision-makers must figure out which
state poses the greatest threat to their own security, and then fashion
alliances accordingly. Recent debates among realists, including
chapters in this volume, focus on how threat is assessed – is it purely
based on the distribution of power, what is the role of domestic distributional politics, and are intentions included in threat assessment?[4]

A structural realist version of balance of power theory fails to provide much insight to interwar diplomacy because it emphasizes a single
factor: the current distribution of power (under the constant situation
of anarchy). This factor identifies both the source of threat and also
what other states can do about it. In this case, the three countries
central to the story – Britain, France, and the Soviet Union – all agreed

---

[3] Some realists question whether states will be satisfied with a mere balance of
power. For overviews of the literature on balance of power theory, see Ernest
B. Haas, "The Balance of Power: Prescription, Concept, or Propaganda?"
World Politics 5, no. 4 (July 1953), pp. 442–77; Dina A. Zinnes, "An
Analytical Study of the Balance of Power Theories," *Journal of Peace
Research* 4, no. 3 (1967), pp. 270–88; Inis L. Claude, Jr., "The Balance of
Power Revisited," *Review of International Studies* 15, no. 2 (April 1989),
pp. 77–85; Michael Sheehan, *The Balance of Power: History and Theory*
(London: Routledge, 1996); and Jack S. Levy, "What Do Great Powers
Balance Against and When?" in T. V. Paul, James J. Wirtz, and Michel
Fortmann, eds., *Balance of Power: Theory and Practice in the 21st Century*
(Stanford, CA: Stanford University Press, 2006), pp. 29–51.

[4] This debate took off with the contribution of Stephen Walt, *The Origins of
Alliances* (Ithaca, NY: Cornell University Press, 1987).

on the current distribution of power and the likely source of any threat to their own security. (Both Britain and the Soviet Union were also concerned by Japan's ambitions, of course. But this was in addition to the threat posed by Germany, and Germany clearly threatened their homelands while Japan did not.) Having recognized and agreed on the threat, these three powers still failed to form an alliance.

Moreover, statesmen recognized the anarchic environment as an obstacle to achieving a balance versus Germany in the long run. They directed their efforts at cooperation and institution-building for that very reason. It is actually a mistake to say they failed to react to the potential German threat. If anything, they responded through too many policies. The structural realist account emphasizes alliances as the tool for balancing, and thus ignores how alternative policies might have worked; it also accentuates the tendency to ignore disarmament, collective security, or other policies as viable alternatives.

To place these other policies in comparable terms, I first explain why the structural realist version of balancing is underspecified. It implicitly assumes that a balance needs to be constructed immediately (and continuously reconstructed), and that economic assets can be converted into military power very rapidly.[5] These two assumptions of time-horizons and resource convertibility considerably simplify the choices decision-makers face, by eliminating considerations of how power and economic resources are managed. In the structural realist view, the best way to increase one's power is to find allies. Diplomacy collapses down to a single policy dimension.

---

[5] This approach is reminiscent of the remarks Stephen G. Brooks has made about realism, because he also focused attention on time as a variable. See Brooks, "Dueling Realisms," *International Organization* 51, no. 3 (summer 1997), pp. 445–77. Brooks argues, however that Waltz explicitly argues for a short time-horizon, while Gilpin explicitly argues for a long one. I argue time-horizons should be treated as variable. Secondly, Brooks argued that assumptions about time-horizons made for distinct versions of realism: one where conflict was probable, the other where conflict was treated as possible. My reading of Robert Gilpin was not that he argued that economic capacity was subservient to the management of power, but rather that states had other goals alongside security. See Gilpin, *War and Change in World Politics* (Cambridge: Cambridge University Press, 1981), esp. chaps. 3–4. In that sense, by making the time-horizon and the ability to convert economic wealth into power variables, I seek to reconcile different versions of realism, not pull them apart.

The world is obviously more complex. By taking these two implicit assumptions and treating them as variables, we get a better sense of the challenges statesmen faced when conducting foreign policy in the interwar period. Leaders had to manage their country's power relative to Germany's over time – aiming to achieve maximum strength when it would be needed, not every day. In the peace talks at Versailles, it would have been foolish to seek to counter German power in 1920. The goals the allied leaders had when constructing the peace, and when formulating policies in the later 1920s, would have been to ensure their countries' security by producing a favorable balance at some point in the future. The statesmen needed to think about their economic assets relative to Germany's, how this comparison would change over time, and the speed at which each country could convert economic assets into realized military forces.

Compared to the earlier equation, this political economic interpretation of balancing is taking a step behind the scenes. Realized military resources, M, now need to be considered across time (denoted by subscripts t and t+1). The amount of realized military resources is a function of three variables: economic resources (E), the amount currently spent on the military (S), and a rate of transformation (RT). The rate of transformation represents the speed at which economic assets can be converted into usable military force. (On this conversion, Jeffrey Taliaferro's chapter discusses when states will likely emulate military and technological practices of more powerful states or try to offset others' perceived advantages through innovation.) Policy-makers must still try to achieve a positive balance (equation 2), but in terms of equations 3 and 4, as well as seeking allies.

$$E_t^A \times S_t^A \times RT_t^A = M_t^A \tag{3}$$

$$E_{t+1}^A \times S_{t+1}^A \times RT_{t+1}^A = M_{t+1}^A \tag{4}$$

Current expenditures can be problematic, because they may reduce future economic resources (by diverting funds from productive investments). However, expenditures on military production facilities may change the future rate of transformation in advantageous ways, making it possible to convert economic resources into viable military force more rapidly. Moreover, given their ability to enforce conditions on Germany in the Paris peace talks, the leaders of France and Britain could target not only these variables in managing how they constructed their own military forces, but also intervene in Germany's choices as well.

The key to my argument about the interwar period lies in the lax nature of the structural imperatives in the early 1920s (versus the strong imperative in the late 1930s). British and French leaders (as well as their Soviet counterparts) knew German power would return, but they did not need to strike the balance in realized military resources in the short run. Instead, they each looked at possible ways to ensure the future balance of power would be in their favor. Instead of a single variable to concentrate on (alliance commitments), they had several to choose from. In that sense, reparations, the League of Nations, disarmament talks, and other policies need to be viewed as substitutes for achieving the same goal: balancing German power at some point in the future. Because of their different domestic situations, and their shared belief that it would take any state considerable time to convert peacetime economies to war production, they were free to select different policies in the permissive environment of the 1920s. Each state preferred a different policy. These earlier policy choices shaped their military postures, interactions with each other, and desirability of alliances. As the time-horizon for balancing shortened in the late 1930s, providing more concrete information on how to respond, the European great powers found themselves on incompatible paths that had originated a decade earlier.

Individual countries' strategic choices in the 1920s

France

From the end of World War I, the French consistently perceived Germany as the greatest threat to their security. While Germany lay defeated in 1919, the sacrifices France had made on the battlefields of the First World War seemed destined to place the country at a continued disadvantage versus Germany. The gap between the two in terms of economic resources or manpower could only be expected to grow over time. French leaders assumed the two would have conflicting interests in the future; therefore the French felt a compelling desire to ensure they would have a favorable balance of power.

The initial French preference was for firm alliance commitments from stronger states. As Premier Georges Clemenceau announced to the Chamber of Deputies in early 1919 (before the Paris peace talks began): "There is an old system of alliances called the Balance of Power – this system of alliances, which I do not renounce, will be my guiding thought at the Peace Conference."[6] Yet France could no longer turn to its most important prewar ally, Russia. Instead, French leaders sought, and believed they had attained, commitments from the United States and Britain.

The British and Americans placed emphasis on collective security, to be achieved in the League of Nations. Clemenceau, French President Raymond Poincaré, and other leaders were persuaded the League could substitute for bilateral alliance commitments, but they recognized the potential problems with the League. During the peace conference, the French therefore argued for a strong League, with a standing military planning staff and significant intelligence-gathering capabilities. Since Germany was outside the organization, if the League was militarily prepared it could serve as an instant alliance for balancing an aggressive Germany.[7] President Woodrow Wilson and others opposed the idea of the League as an armed camp, however. To get the French to commit to a more neutral League Wilson and British Prime Minister David Lloyd George offered to arrange security commitments for French borders alongside the League. Unfortunately, when the US Senate rejected the peace treaty, they not only canceled American participation in the League but also the American security commitment to France. When that happened, the British quietly gave up their commitment as well.

The French would continue to search for firm alliance arrangements in the later 1920s, but they already knew that other major powers were unlikely to commit to their assistance. They sought and received some guarantees at Locarno in October 1925, for instance. But since the commitments others made at Locarno were vague, this did little to assuage their fears.

Instead, French leaders immediately focused their attention on other ways to manage this future gap between their potential military

---

[6] As quoted in Margaret Macmillan, *Paris 1919: Six Months that Changed the World* (New York: Random House, 2002), p. 23.

[7] David Stevenson, "France at the Paris Peace Conference: Addressing the Dilemmas of Security," in Robert Boyce, ed., *French Foreign and Defence Policy, 1918–1940* (London: LSE/Routledge, 1998), pp. 10–29, esp. pp. 12–13.

strength and that of Germany. In terms of the equations above, French leaders aimed to manipulate all the variables they could, via the conditions imposed upon Germany in the Treaty of Versailles. The gap between their economic base and Germany's could be narrowed via economic policies. The French wanted to shape reparations in ways that would both limit the speed of Germany's economic recovery from the war (while hastening France's), but also hold down the rate at which Germany could transform economic power into military force. Similarly, the arms limitations imposed on Germany in the peace treaty, as well as negotiated in later disarmament talks, were aimed at not simply holding down current military forces but also stunting the growth of Germany's military-industrial capacity. This would keep Germany's ability to transform economic capacity into military forces at a low rate.

These goals were expressed by Clemenceau in the peace talks, and then echoed by later leaders. When the allies met to discuss the level of German reparations in early 1922 in the Cannes and Genoa Conferences, President Raymond Poincaré and other French leaders made it clear they desired high amounts because the transfers would both weaken Germany and strengthen France in the long run.[8] This was also why the French (and Belgians) were insistent on enforcing the collection of reparations. As will be discussed below, the British held a different perspective on this, because they calculated the relative position of their economy vis-à-vis Germany's differently, and also because they feared such transfers would simply stunt everyone's economic growth.

While reparations targeted the relative economic capacity of both Germany and France, with an indirect impact on Germany's ability to convert economic wealth into power, another strategy for keeping the balance of power in France's favor was to impose arms limitations on Germany. In 1926, the League began more serious pursuit of disarmament talks. The French used these forums to ensure their cadre of forces was larger than Germany's. The importance of such agreements had less to do with the short-run level of forces than with the longer-term ability to convert economic power into military forces rapidly. With little construction of forces in Germany, the military-industrial base would remain small. Yet again, the British would take a different stand on disarmament, as described below.

[8] Doerr, *British Foreign Policy 1919–1939*, esp. pp. 66–67.

Of course, none of these policies could resolve the essential problem for the French: the relative size of the French and German economies. The French were in a quandary. If they invested heavily in their military forces (or even their militarily oriented industries), that would likely worsen the gap between their economy and their rival's over the long run. If they did not invest in military forces, however, they risked leaving themselves vulnerable should the threat emerge sooner than expected. To reconcile these two goals, the French adopted a defensive military stance. Though French military leaders have been criticized for preparing to fight the last war rather than the next, their emphasis on fortifications was driven by the economic and political constraints France faced at the time. Construction of the Maginot Line began in 1929. These forts represented the investment they believed adequate to survive an initial German onslaught. Behind these defenses, they could then go about mobilizing their economy for a war effort.[9]

Deductively and inductively, we can observe the French ranking in the 1920s for preferred ways to balance Germany for the long run:

- firm alliance commitments
- a strong League of Nations
- reparations
- disarmament
- a weakened League.

Britain

British and French policy-makers held similar notions in the early 1920s on many issues, but not all. British decision-makers believed Germany would take a very long time to recover economically from the war. They also believed that each country would take some time to convert back to peacetime production, and that reversing that process to a war footing again would take considerable time. These assessments of the situation shaped their preferences and policies in the 1920s.

---

[9] See, for example, Robert A. Doughty, "The Illusion of Security: France, 1919–1940," in Williamson Murray, MacGregor Knox, and Alvin Bernstein, eds., *The Making of Strategy: Rulers, States, and War* (Cambridge: Cambridge University Press, 1994), pp. 466–97; and Barry R. Posen, *The Sources of Military Doctrine: France, Britain, and Germany between the World Wars* (Ithaca, NY: Cornell University Press, 1984), pp. 105–21.

This evaluation left British decision-makers confused about what to do, however. They considered the French to be overly paranoid about German power. Moreover, the very policies the French wound up emphasizing – limitations on Germany's economic recovery – threatened to disrupt efforts to regenerate international trade and investments, harming Britain's recovery. Before the war, Britain had benefited from its dominant position in trade and finance. This position was threatened in the 1920s, both by the rise of an important rival (the United States) and also by the damage and disruption caused by the war. Reparations threatened to worsen that situation.

The very thing the French desired – stunting German economic recovery – was against long-run British economic interests. Indeed, British economist John Maynard Keynes was critical of French pro- posals for high reparations, not because they were irrationally high, but precisely because they were based on a strategy of balancing German power. Here is Keynes' own description of French thinking:

It was the policy of France to set the clock back and to undo what, since 1870, the progress of Germany had accomplished. By loss of territory and other measures her population was to be curtailed; but chiefly the economic system, upon which she depended for her new strength, the vast fabric built upon iron, coal, and transport, must be destroyed. If France could seize, even in part, what Germany was compelled to drop, the inequality of strength between the two rivals for European hegemony might be remedied for many generations.[10]

Keynes argued these French goals were impractical; these efforts would not limit German power, he claimed, but definitely exacerbate conflicts between the two. As he put it, Clemenceau's determination to exact resources from Germany would "only have the effect of shortening the interval of Germany's recovery and hastening the day when she will once again hurl at France her greater numbers and her superior resources and technical skill."[11] He also argued these countries' economic fates were intertwined. By weakening Germany, he argued, France would weaken itself. This claim was surely less true for France than it was for Britain.

The French insistence on a security alliance was considered unnecessary. This has been primarily described by historians in terms

[10] J. M. Keynes, *The Economic Consequences of the Peace* (London: Macmillan, 1920), p. 32.
[11] Keynes, *The Economic Consequences of the Peace*, pp. 31–2.

of a British refusal to reenter the prewar days of "secret diplomacy" and hard alliance blocs. It is worth unpacking these concerns and thinking about them more abstractly. The British did not desire a renewed commitment to the continent because that would entail continued development and maintenance of expensive ground forces. These demands would depend not only on British diplomacy, but on French tact as well. Britain had been forced into the First World War because of great power quibbling over the Balkans, where Britain had little directly at stake. A formal commitment to France might produce the same result all over again.[12]

Although the British eventually signed up to a guarantee of French borders in the form of the Locarno Treaty, it never developed the military forces that would have been needed to uphold that guarantee.[13] The wording in Locarno was deliberately vague too, giving British diplomats wiggle room – perhaps even enough to wiggle all the way out of any action. Much the same thinking had shaped British attitudes towards the League. It promised possible benefits, but demands by other League members on Britain were likely to come sooner than any needs Britain might have.

Lloyd George and other British leaders were concerned with getting their economy back on its peacetime footing, which meant inspiring international trade and investment to return to something like its prewar patterns. These leaders also believed their long-run economic prosperity (and thus indirectly their power) would be accentuated by a return to low taxation and balanced budgets.[14] In the 1920s, this could be afforded by reducing current military expenditures due to the decreased threat from Germany. This was eventually expressed quite clearly in the famous "Ten-Year Rule" imposed on military expenditure.

The British were therefore attracted to several possible policies for dealing with threats that might arise in the future. Disarmament was

---

[12] Paul Doerr, *British Foreign Policy 1919–1939* (Manchester: Manchester University Press, 1998), esp. p. 61.

[13] Richard Grayson, *Austen Chamberlain and the Commitment to Europe: British Foreign Policy 1924–1929* (London: Frank Cass, 1997), esp. pp. 31–2.

[14] In this sense the argument put forward here overlaps with, or complements, the argument Randall Schweller makes in *Unanswered Threats* (Princeton, NJ: Princeton University Press, 2006), esp. p. 70. Schweller claims British leaders preferred domestic stability to balancing – my argument is that they believed they needed a balance later on, and domestic stability was the route to that later balance.

especially appealing since it would delay the point in time when balancing would be required. Britain was therefore a vigorous supporter of disarmament in the 1920s. Whereas the French committed themselves to a defensive military posture by the end of the 1920s, the British were still hoping to put off military expenditures. They still hoped to emphasize economic recovery, even as the economic climate was about to change drastically with the onset of the Great Depression.

Although the differences between French and British thinking in the 1920s were slight, these differences carried significant repercussions. The British refused to be tied to any immediate alliance commitments because they desired reductions on expenditures. Second, they believed reparations would not tilt the balance of economic resources in their favor in the way the French thought.

Therefore British preferences for balancing Germany in the 1920s were:

- disarmament
- the League of Nations
- firm alliance commitments
- reparations.

The Soviet Union

The Soviets feared German power even in the 1920s. Yet the Soviets too believed the danger Germany posed was in the future rather than the short term. There were several reasons the Soviet situation differed from the French position. The Soviets would be threatened by renewed German power, but more indirectly than the French. This would lead them to favor very different policies from either the British or French.

First, Germany and the Soviet Union were not contiguous – several countries served as a buffer against any German invasion of the Soviet Union. To get to the Soviets, the Germans would first have to conquer Poland, Czechoslovakia, or other states. In the 1920s, this buffer appeared to be meaningful, at least in the eyes of the Soviets. The Red Army fared poorly against the armies of Poland, Estonia, Latvia, and Lithuania in 1918–20. If the Germans were to get to the Soviets, they would have to fight their way through Poland and Czechoslovakia, thus giving the Soviets time to anticipate and react. (In addition, Soviet leaders rightly thought it was highly unlikely the Poles or Czechs would side with the Germans in a war against the Soviet Union.)

The Soviets presumed that Germany would have its sights zeroed in on the French first. This appeared to be one of the calculations in the 1920s – a point that made the Soviets willing to deal with the Germans, as they did at Rapallo. Their interaction was naturally helped along by the fact that both countries were diplomatic outcasts in those years. They also shared similar needs – improving their military training, their technologies for producing arms, and so forth. As long as any threat remained distant, the two were willing to help each other.

It is important to reiterate how the Soviet leaders – like their British and French counterparts – considered World War I's effects to be long-lasting. They knew the Germans' weaknesses, and felt they had time to develop their own power to counter Germany's resurgence. The Soviet Union was not represented at the Paris Peace Conference and did not sign the Versailles Treaty. Unlike Britain and France, it had no legal basis for (and little economic interest in) intervening in German domestic affairs. Instead, the key to their own fate lay in advancing their own economic interests and military-industrial capacity. It was this shared need which allowed them to work with the Germans covertly in the late 1920s. It made little sense to consider the policy options since the Soviets could not participate in reparations or the League. They were invited to enter agreements on stabilizing borders, and disarmament talks. Disarmament held appeal because it was consistent with lengthening the time frame for the country to gain a stronger economic footing, so they often endorsed disarmament as a principle, while offering little in the way of participation.

Conclusions on the 1920s

In the decade after World War I, Britain, France, and the Soviet Union each decided to deal with the German threat in different ways. It is impossible to say what would have happened had Britain and France decided to establish a firm alliance, or if they had supported reparations designed to enhance French power. Instead, each pushed in the direction it preferred, undercutting the other's options. Even with disarmament, which all three great powers might have preferred, each desired to emphasize limitation of arms in a different way. The French wanted unequal force levels for ground troops, while the British worried about the relative distribution of naval units. The Soviets viewed the German threat as even more distant, considering their own need for improving their military infrastructure too high, and therefore cooperated with Germany on military training and technological developments. While concerted efforts on any single one approach might have worked to offset or decelerate the resurgence of German power, the economic needs of each country led them to try and shape the future balance of power in different ways.

New strategic calculations as the German threat returns

The European great powers' calculations from the 1920s placed them in a poor position to react to the changed environment of the 1930s. Between 1929 and 1933, several shocks altered the variables decision-makers had to take into account. The onset of the Great Depression not only hampered short-term government budgets, but also altered the evaluation of each major power's economic capacity for the future. The depth of the depression appeared at first glance to make any future threat appear even more distant. Yet Hitler's rise to power, combined with the subsequent recovery of the German economy before those of Britain and France, forced the leaders of the other states to rethink their strategies. By the mid-1930s, British and French military intelligence believed Germany's economic policies were geared towards rearmament for a conflict in the near future.[15] They now had to balance Germany in the medium or even short run.

The great powers' options were now much more limited. The Great Depression led to the collapse of trade and international investments, seriously undermining Britain's economic position. The depression had nullified reparations. The League soon collapsed in the face of inaction over Ethiopia and Manchuria. The arms limitations previously negotiated were also irrelevant, since it became known that these had not always been honored; they were completely off the table once Hitler challenged the Treaty of Versailles. Compared to 1929,

---

[15] Peter Jackson, "Intelligence and the End of Appeasement," in Boyce, *French Foreign and Defence Policy*, pp. 234–60, esp. p. 242.

when France had begun construction of the Maginot Line and Britain was emphasizing the "Ten-Year Rule" and disarmament, the strategic environment had changed considerably.

France in the 1930s

France had invested more than just money in the Maginot Line. The string of fortresses was intended as a shield, as one part of a broader grand strategy. Using the shield to survive the onset of a war, France could then convert its peacetime economy to war production, relying on an attrition strategy to defeat Germany. The French were prepared to construct large, mobile military forces, but knew this was cost-prohibitive. The need to use few troops and stationary positions for initial defense was intensified because of the widening gap between the size of the French economy and Germany's. When France committed to the fortifications, they also altered the way they trained their troops for mobile warfare.[16]

The deeper problem was that the French lost their ability to restrain Germany's economy after 1933. Reparations were no longer possible, disarmament was given one more fling (with the Stresa Front), but the French now needed to balance German power in the near future. Quite soon it was evident this could not be done with the League, so France had to turn to either the Soviets or the British.

Britain was the obvious choice politically, yet British military forces did not complement France's; neither country's military forces were tailored to their diplomatic ends. While small, purely defensive forces appeared useful as complements to disarmament talks, membership in the League, or reparations, they were not the sort of assets diplomats needed in the 1930s. Once the potential enemy abandoned disarmament, defensive postures were only useful for deflecting an attack (buying time diplomatically or defensively).

In April 1935, at Stresa, the British, French, and Italian governments reaffirmed their commitments made at Locarno and for the League. Yet the League was already cracking under its failures, and even the disarmament deals attempted at Stresa quickly unraveled. The French then approached the Soviet Union, signing a mutual

[16] Jon Jacobson, *Locarno Diplomacy: Germany and the West 1925–1929* (Princeton, NJ: Princeton University Press, 1972), esp. pp. 105–7.

defense pact in May 1935. The Soviets appeared unreliable, however. More importantly, the lack of a contiguous border with Germany meant that the Soviets could not come to the aid of the French in any direct fashion. Direct Soviet pressure on Germany would require assistance from the Czechs or the Poles, who were unwilling to cede their sovereignty to allow the passage of the Red Army. The defensive posture of the French meant they were not likely to help any of their allies in the east, including even the Soviet Union.

Yet the French opposed appeasement and eventually stood up for Poland. By the mid-1930s, General Maurice Gauché, the chief of military intelligence, was arguing that Hitler would likely drive German forces east (or southeast) to control important natural resources. With those in hand, he could then lead Germany against France again, even hoping to win in a war of attrition. Ceding control of the Balkans or central Europe to Germany would leave France decisively weaker vis-à-vis Germany. Daladier echoed these sentiments in his comments to Neville Chamberlain before the latter met Hitler in Munich. Daladier told the British leader that if Germany dominated eastern Europe it would "be assured the resources necessary to turn against the west, which, out of weakness, will have provided her with the means to wage the long war which she is at present incapable of sustaining."[17] Still Chamberlain pursued appeasement.

After the Munich agreement, the French government accelerated its efforts to reach a firm commitment from Britain or the Soviet Union, and also began gearing up its rearmament programs. Only a firm alliance commitment could help France either deter or defeat Germany.

Britain in the 1930s

Faced with similar changing circumstances in the 1930s, why did Britain not respond in the same way? Why were British policy-makers reluctant to give France a firmer alliance commitment? Why did Chamberlain choose appeasement? Part of the answer lies in understanding the connection between appeasement and rearmament in the British plans. Even into the later 1930s, British leaders assumed that their country was not prepared for another war, and that the solution

[17] Jackson, "Intelligence and the End of Appeasement" p. 246.

lay in establishing and maintaining a stable economic recovery from the depression first.[18]

Britain abandoned the "Ten-Year Rule" in 1931, before Hitler ascended to power. This decision signaled the recognition of the need for rearmament, rather than an effort at rearmament per se. To rearm, British leaders had to think about the nature of the German threat. As in France, priority was given to surviving the initial German onslaught. The great lesson drawn from World War I in both Britain and France was that the war had been a near-run thing. By striking first, the Germans had used the initiative to their advantage. The allies had barely survived that initial onslaught, but had then been in a position to marshal their resources. With those in hand, they defeated Germany. Each country thus set about determining the proper strategy for repeating this success in the future. For Britain, a knock-out blow could only come by sea or air. Rearmament was programmed accordingly. Air defenses would have priority. In December 1937, Chamberlain specifically ordered anti-aircraft guns to be given the highest priority – in 1938 Britain produced more of these than either field pieces or anti-tank guns.[19]

Yet at first, in the early 1930s, Britain stuck with the policies it carried over from the 1920s. It continued to look to the League and disarmament as tools for extending the time frame for strengthening its economic position. Diplomacy was used to delay the date for needing a balance, thus putting off Britain's own rearmament as long as possible. Britain opposed French overtures to the Soviets in 1935 precisely because they feared this would hasten the date of any conflict, shortening the time-horizon for rearmament. Those talks between the Soviets and the French did allow Hitler to publicly announce Germany's rejection of the limitations imposed by Versailles.[20]

When Chamberlain ordered expenditures to focus on the Royal Air Force (RAF) rather than other branches, he specifically insisted that manufacturers be paid to construct additional assembly lines.[21] Orders were placed beyond capacity to produce. This helped Britain

[18] Lindsay W. Michie, *Portrait of an Appeaser* (Westport, CT: Praeger, 1996), esp. p. 128.
[19] Levy, *Appeasement and Rearmament*, esp. pp. 64–5.
[20] Neilson, *Britain, Soviet Russia, and the Collapse of the Versailles Order*, esp. pp. 120 and 132.
[21] Doerr, *British Foreign Policy 1919–1939*, esp. p. 193.

not only begin to build up realized military forces, but also altered the rate at which the country would be able to convert economic assets into military forces in the future. When Britain needed to ramp up aircraft production once the war started, it could. Admiral of the Fleet Lord Chatfield, the First Sea Lord, endorsed appeasement for the very same reasons: the Royal Navy too needed time to construct more modern production facilities, not simply increase its force levels.

Those countries that tried to build up realized military resources in the mid-1930s, including France, Italy, and the Soviet Union, may have increased their capacities, but also had equipment that was no longer cutting-edge when the real fighting began in 1940–41.[22] Some scholars have asked whether these earlier military expenditures really helped them or not. Nonetheless, the British would need assistance in any future conflict with Germany, so British leaders needed to consult with their French counterparts. The trouble was this: the British goal remained postponing the start of any fighting, whereas the French saw this as worsening their chance of winning. It was a poor basis for conducting joint diplomacy.

Compared to the French, the British were hesitant to approach the Soviet Union. This hesitancy came from several sources. Some policy-makers believed the Soviets would sit out any great war, hoping to foment widespread revolution in its wake. Others doubted the utility of any alliance with the Soviets, since the purges had stripped the Red Army of many of its best officers. British military chiefs thought the Soviets could defend their own territory, but the Red Army was now ineffective for major offensive actions of the sort that would be needed to relieve pressure on France or other countries to Germany's west.[23]

In the end, the British leaders favored appeasement because they believed it would buy the thing Britain needed most: time. This would allow them to adjust their own military forces, but also increase the country's ability to convert economic assets into military power at a more rapid rate. As Vansittart put it, writing on December 31, 1936: "Time is the very material commodity which the Foreign Office is expected to provide in the same way as other departments provide *other* war material ... To the Foreign Office falls therefore the task of

---

[22] Levy, *Appeasement and Rearmament*, esp. p. xiv.
[23] Doerr, *British Foreign Policy 1919–1939*, esp. pp. 250–4; Nelson, *Britain, Soviet Russia and the Collapse of the Versailles Order*, esp. p. 209.

holding the situation until at least 1939."[24] France and Britain therefore found themselves with different desires and needs, even as the German threat reemerged.

The Soviet Union in the 1930s

The Soviets, who had never had any support from the League anyway, looked for some kind of alliance support as Germany's strength was recovering in the 1930s. As mentioned above, the Soviets entered negotiations with France in 1935, which presaged the Soviets' entry into the League. This of course was just as the League was proving itself too weak to be of real use. Moreover, France was recognizing it needed to cooperate with the British, and thus was limited in what it could do in cooperation with the Soviet Union. In the face of these frustrations, the Soviets would turn to bandwagoning. Once again, however, this decision was based on the idea that other countries served as a buffer between themselves and the Germans. This buffer would buy them time to engage in further balancing.

The Soviets might have consistently backed away from their coopera-tion with Germany on military affairs in the 1930s, because they understood Hitler's aims better than the leaders of other countries. They had looked for assistance elsewhere, but found this wanting. ... Other countries were unlikely to come to their aid, even if the Kremlin wanted to assist them. Britain, for example, lacked the means and the will to come to the Soviet Union's aid in containing Germany. According to Sir William Strang (later Lord Strang), then Assistant Under-Secretary of State for Europe in the Foreign Office, in 1942 Winston Churchill had asked Stalin why the Soviets had joined Hitler in the partition of Poland in 1939. Stalin stated that he thought the British and French commitment to Poland was a bluff. The French military was unready for war, and Britain could mobilize a mere two divisions for immediate use. By bandwagoning with Germany, Stalin believed he could buy valuable time for the Soviets to continue their own preparations for war.[25]

[24] Quoted in Norton Medlicott, "Britain and Germany: The Search for Agreement, 1930–37," in David Dilks, ed., *Retreat from Power: Studies in Britain's Foreign Policy of the Twentieth Century*, vol. I: *1906–1939* (London: Macmillan, 1981), p. 100.

[25] Lord Strang, "The Moscow Negotiations, 1939," in Dilks, *Retreat from Power*, pp. 170–86, esp. p. 184.

Conclusions on the 1930s

All three European powers were committing themselves in different directions in the late 1920s. The French were emphasizing defensive land fortifications, the British were banking on disarmament and the League to put off the time when a balance would be needed, and the Soviets – believing the presence of a buffer would give them extra time – chose to cooperate with the Germans in order to enhance their own military infrastructure. In the 1930s, the French no longer saw a chance to catch up with Germany economically and thus sat behind the Maginot Line; the British continued to buy time, putting off the conflict with appeasement; and the Soviets were now ready to balance but saw no allies that might be able to come to their aid.

Lessons from the 1930s

Consequences of the failure to balance against Hitler

Despite their agreement on where a future threat was likely to come from, and even when this threat emerged, France and Britain could not reconcile their military postures in the 1930s to serve their united aims. Both thought any future conflict would be another war of attrition; economic resources would be pivotal for victory. In such a situation, building up their economic base was critical. They considered the ways to do this in very different terms – not simply in the means, but also in the time needed to do so. Both countries then constructed forces for defending their territory from direct German assault. Behind their defensive shields, each would then convert their peacetime economies to wartime production. Unfortunately, once fighting began, it was apparent the French had organized and trained their military for a war of attrition, rather than one of mobility.[26] The strategy had not changed since the end of World War I – "some diversionary thrusts across the German frontier, a blockade of Germany, and time, would assure ultimate victory."[27] Faced with the German army's ability to maneuver aggressively, the ill-prepared French forces crumbled.

[26] Levy, *Appeasement and Rearmament*, esp. pp. 44–8.
[27] Nathanael Greene, *From Versailles to Vichy: The Third French Republic, 1919–1940* (New York: Thomas Y. Crowell, 1970), esp. p. 115.

British forces did better but, as Stalin had foreseen, there were too few of them to bolster the French in the face of the German attack. The time purchased by appeasement had been used to build up British air and naval defenses, as well as to increase Britain's ability to produce war material. The improvements made in these areas paid off when Britain stood alone against Germany after France fell. Without the improvements appeasement afforded – the new fighter aircraft, the training facilities for pilots, the chain of radar stations, the destroyers, and patrol aircrafts – Britain might not have survived between mid-1940 and late 1941, when allies eventually entered the war.

The Soviets entered the conflict later, and Stalin had used some of that time to his country's advantage by developing its military capacity. The preparations did not spare the Soviet Union from terrible losses; it came close to suffering the catastrophic losses France had. Of course, the Soviets did not have many choices in the 1920s, and precious few in the 1930s. Each country's leaders managed their foreign policies as best they could in those decades, within the constraints imposed upon them by the needs they faced in managing their own internal economic needs. The lack of an imperative in balancing Germany in the 1920s allowed each to head off in directions that made it more difficult for them to coalesce around a single choice in the 1930s.

Implications for theory

One of the most striking things about the interwar diplomacy of Britain and France was how intensely divisive foreign affairs were internally, especially in the 1920s. Not only did policy decisions generate public outcry, they divided parties from parties, factions within individual parties, and even cabinets. Observing such outcomes, it is difficult to argue that domestic sources of foreign policy are easily discernible. If internal sources had been so clearly defined, then we would have seen parties distinguishing themselves along these lines, and using their stances to draw domestic support. While liberals might argue that domestic sources created a distribution of preferences that were incompatible, in fact it is apparent that Britain, France, and the Soviet Union all preferred the same end. The internal divisions, as well as the diplomatic wrangling, varied because they could not agree on the means to that end.

At the system level, it is hard to locate confusion about how the distribution of power was changing, or which state would be striving to alter the status quo. These assumptions were present from the end of the First World War on, and did not fluctuate. Decisions about the time-horizon for a future conflict were driven by the distribution of power much more than the changing leadership or regime in Germany. The real policy decisions in the 1920s (compared to the 1930s) appear to have been driven by the lack of any overriding structural imperatives – instead policy-makers considered numerous ways of achieving the same goal. Their preferences varied because they each believed their own economic needs required particular policies.

For these reasons, neoclassical realism offers the best insight into the outcomes. Neoclassical realists look to the state as the manager of the nation's resources for competition in the anarchic international environment. The state's position as mediator between the two realms of politics – domestic and international – gives it a unique role. It must coordinate diplomacy and domestic policies, harnessing economic capacity to generate military power in defense of interests. While France, Britain, and the Soviet Union might have been in similar positions in the system structurally, their ability to alter their positions over time differed because of internal characteristics. These differences, recognized by their own leaders, made them pursue different means towards the same end. That outcome cannot be easily explained by either structural realists, or by liberals.

Policy implications

While many may not appreciate the parallels, in fact the 1920s and the current period are quite alike in many ways. Many people predict the continued economic rise of China. While that country's industrialization is quite likely to continue, China's social and political trajectory is much harder to predict. The country is led by a non-democratic single party, which has successfully adopted a series of policies almost the antithesis of its ideological origins. That it has done so without major political upheaval may reflect the party leaders' remarkable skills; or we may merely be seeing the buildup of expectations and pressures. Should the economy falter, what sort of political changes might occur? How would a powerful China, governed by a single party steeped in capitalism and chauvinistic nationalism, behave?

Because we do not perceive China as an immediate threat to the
system, the western industrialized democracies find themselves in a
similarly permissive systemic setting. There are several possible ways
these countries could seek to maintain a more secure stance as power
in the system is redistributed. But who is to say arms limitation talks
are preferable to firm alliances, or that strengthening the UN would be
more successful in achieving a future balance against an aggressive
China than would continued American investment in military technology and infrastructure? Each of these policies offers genuine ways
to offset a future Chinese threat.

If we need to learn something from the 1930s, it should be about
the need to consider ways to continue to cooperate in the future.
Countries threatened by Germany in the 1930s were constricted by
their previous decisions, and thus could not coordinate their efforts
easily. Although the danger seems remote at the moment, the sorts of
decisions we make today shape our choices in the future. One must
remain cognizant of the need to keep multilateral channels open, and
to see ways to leave the option of building a broad coalition for times
when we might need it.

4 | Neoclassical realism and identity: peril despite profit across the Taiwan Strait*

JENNIFER STERLING-FOLKER

The introductory chapter of this volume by Jeffrey Taliaferro, Steven Lobell, and Norrin Ripsman suggests that neoclassical realism can add explanatory power to structural realism by considering the effect of the domestic political environment on policy. It also improves on liberal theories by asserting the primacy of international constraints. In this chapter, I examine whether a neoclassical realist approach can explain a liberal puzzle, namely the persistence of security competition between trade partners and the absence of peace dividends between economically interdependent states. In other words, why do states continue to perceive each other as security threats despite increased economic interdependence between them? How is it possible for states that are engaged in an active security conflict to continue trading with one another? Why does the purported peace dividend of economic interdependence so often fail to materialize?

That there should be a peace dividend is an assumption with deep philosophical roots. It is an assumption that has served as the analytical bedrock for a variety of liberal theoretical projects in the international relations discipline, and it continues to inform foreign

* Earlier drafts of this chapter have been presented at several forums, including the Fifth Pan-European Meeting of the European Consortium for Political Research, The Hague, the Netherlands, September 9–11, 2004; the Neoclassical Realism and the State Workshop, Concordia University, Montreal, Canada, May 25–26, 2006; and the Annual Meeting of the American Political Science Association, Philadelphia, August 31 – September 3, 2006. The author would like to thank the participants at these venues, and in particular Lene Hansen, Scott Kastner, and Ole Wæver, for their helpful comments and suggestions. Special thanks also go to Chua Boon Li at the National University of Singapore for providing information on relevant sources.

policy and decision-making throughout the globe. The result is, as Katherine Barbieri and Gerald Schneider note, that "most leaders still cling to the longstanding belief that expanding economic ties will cement the bonds of friendship between and within nations that make the resort to arms unfathomable," and "few scholars today question the belief that trade brings universal benefits and peace under all conceivable conditions."[1] Despite its continued popularity in academic and policy-making circles, however, it is also an assumption that has been subject to intense analytical scrutiny and criticism within the international relations discipline.

Much of this scrutiny has revolved around documenting a statistical correlation between trade, peace, and conflict.[2] Large datasets have

---

[1] Katherine Barbieri and Gerald Schneider, "Globalization and Peace: Assessing New Directions in the Study of Trade and Conflict," *Journal of Peace Research* 36, no. 4 (July 1999), pp. 387–404, at pp. 387 and 390.

[2] A sample of these studies includes Katherine Barbieri, *The Liberal Illusion: Does Trade Promote Peace?* (Ann Arbor: University of Michigan Press, 2002); Katherine Barbieri, "Economic Interdependence: A Path to Peace or a Source of Interstate Conflict?" *Journal of Peace Research* 33, no. 1 (February 1996), pp. 29–49; Katherine Barbieri and Jack S. Levy, "Sleeping with the Enemy: The Impact of War on Trade," *Journal of Peace Research* 36, no. 4 (July 1999), pp. 463–79; Mark J. Gasiorowski, "Economic Interdependence and International Conflict: Some Cross-national Evidence," *International Studies Quarterly* 30, no. 1 (March 1986), pp. 23–38; Hyung Min Kim and David L. Rousseau, "The Classical Liberals Were Half Right (or Half Wrong): New Tests of the 'Liberal Peace', 1960–88," *Journal of Peace Research* 42, no. 5 (September 2005), pp. 523–43; John R. Oneal and Bruce M. Russett, "The Classical Liberals Were Right: Democracy, Interdependence, and Conflict, 1950–1985," *International Studies Quarterly* 41, no. 2 (June 1997), pp. 267–94; John R. Oneal, Frances H. Oneal, Zeev Maoz, and Bruce Russett, "The Liberal Peace: Interdependence, Democracy, and International Conflict, 1950–85," *Journal of Peace Research* 33, no. 1 (February, 1996), pp. 11–28; and Solomon William Polachek, "Conflict and Trade," *Journal of Conflict Resolution* 24, no. 1 (March 1980), pp. 55–78. Work that reviews the interdependence-promotes-peace literature includes Katherine Barbieri and Gerald Schneider, "Globalization and Peace: Assessing New Directions in the Study of Trade and Conflict," *Journal of Peace Research* 36, no. 4 (July 1999), pp. 387–404; Michael W. Doyle, *Ways of War and Peace: Realism, Liberalism, and Socialism* (New York: Norton, 1997); Edward D. Mansfield and Brian M. Pollins, *Economic Interdependence and International Conflict: New Perspectives on an Enduring Debate* (Ann Arbor: University of Michigan Press, 2003); Edward D. Mansfield and Brian M. Pollins, "The Study of Interdependence and Conflict: Recent Advances, Open Questions, and Directions for Future Research," *Journal of Conflict Resolution* 45, no. 6 (December 2001), pp. 834–59; and Susan M. McMillan, "Interdependence and

been constructed or utilized for this purpose, and what have ensued are the usual arguments over scope conditions and how to define, observe, and code the phenomena in question. In this regard, much of the statistical "interdependence-promotes-peace" literature is very similar to, and hence subject to the same analytical problems as, the "democracies-love-peace" literature.[3] Alternatively many observers of and participants in these interdependence debates have expressed interest in examining the causal mechanisms that might link interdependence to outcomes such as peace or conflict. In their review of such mechanisms, Edward Mansfield and Brian Pollins argue that more attention needs to be focused on the boundary conditions and contingencies of interdependence, as well as "on exactly how interdependence interacts with domestic institutions, leaders' preferences, and the interests of societal actors to influence interstate violence."[4] Similarly, Scott Kastner discusses three broad causal mechanisms that are prevalent in the literature: economic ties constrain state behavior (due largely to pressure from powerful, affected domestic

Conflict," *Mershon International Studies Review* 41, no. 1 (May 1997), pp. 33–58. Additional works that are critical of the purported linkage include: Dale Copeland, "Economic Interdependence and War: A Theory of Trade Expectations," *International Security* 20, no. 4 (spring 1996), pp. 5–41; Norrin M. Ripsman and Jean-Marc F. Blanchard, "Commercial Liberalism Under Fire: Evidence from 1914 and 1936," *Security Studies* 6, no. 2 (winter 1996/97), pp. 4–50; Joanne Gowa, *Allies, Adversaries, and International Trade* (Princeton, NJ: Princeton University Press, 1994); Joanne Gowa and Edward D. Mansfield, "Power Politics and International Trade," *American Political Science Review* 87, no. 2 (June 1993), pp. 408–20; Joseph M. Grieco, *Cooperation Among Nations: Europe, America, and Non-Tariff Barriers to Trade* (Ithaca, NY: Cornell University Press, 1990); and John J. Mearsheimer, "The False Promise of International Institutions," *International Security* 19, no. 3 (winter 1994/5), pp. 5–49. See also additional citations in footnote 56.

[3] Compare, for example, the problems discussed by Mansfield and Pollins, "The Study of Interdependence and Conflict," pp. 846–54, to those discussed in Steve Chan, "In Search of Democratic Peace: Problems and Promise," *Mershon International Studies Review* 41, no. 1 (May 1997), pp. 59–91. See also Barbieri and Schneider, "Globalization and Peace"; Cullen F. Goenner, "Uncertainty of the Liberal Peace," *Journal of Peace Research* 41, no. 5 (September 2004), pp. 589–605; and, for a much earlier work that anticipated many of these measurement problems, R. J. B. Jones, "The Definitions and Identification of Interdependence," in R. J. B. Jones and P. Willetts, eds., *Interdependence on Trial: Studies in the Theory and Reality of Contemporary Interdependence* (New York: St. Martin's Press, 1984).

[4] Mansfield and Pollins, "The Study of Interdependence and Conflict," p. 843.

constituencies); economic ties change state goals over time (due to the growth of pro-interdependence domestic constituencies); and economic ties make it easier for states to signal their true level of resolve (due to the opportunity to exchange greater information).[5]

Regardless of causal focus, however, there is a common underlying analytical problem with much of the literature devoted to the interdependence-promotes-peace phenomenon. The bulk of this literature continues to assume that the politics of national identity difference plays little to no role in foreign economic policy-making. Although there are a few exceptions, proponents (and even many critics) tend to share a core assumption that outcomes are due to the *conscious* and *rational* recognition of and concern over disrupted profits that are then linked *consciously* and *rationally* to their corresponding foreign policy.[6] The link may be obtained through a variety of domestic political mechanisms, and what are frequently in dispute in this literature are the exact mechanisms for the translation, or the extent to which the anticipated outcome can be short-circuited. What is generally not in dispute in much of this literature is the extent to which *rational* self-interest in capitalist profit and the concomitant negation of *irrational* national collective identity politics are the unacknowledged foundation for the entire edifice.[7] Tug at this foundation too vigorously and the edifice crumbles of its own accord.

---

[5] Scott L. Kastner, "Does Economic Integration Across the Taiwan Strait Make Military Conflict Less Likely?" *Journal of East Asian Studies* 6, no. 3 (fall 2006), pp. 319–46, at pp. 322–3.

[6] See C. Jonsson, "Cognitive Factors in Explaining Regime Dynamics," in V. Rittberger, ed., *Regime Theory and International Relations* (Oxford: Oxford University Press, 1993), and Andrew A. G. Ross, "Coming in from the Cold: Constructivism and Emotions," *European Journal of International Relations* 12, no. 2 (June 2006), pp. 197–222, for analyses of these cognition assumptions in regime and constructivist theorizing respectively.

[7] Some exceptions include Rawi Abdela, *National Purpose in the World Economy: Post-Soviet States in Comparative Perspective* (Ithaca, NY: Cornell University Press, 2001); Eric Helleiner, "Denationalizing Money? Economic Liberalism and the 'National Question' in Currency Affairs," in E. Gilbert and Eric Helleiner, eds., *Nation-States and Money* (London: Routledge, 1999), pp. 139–58; Scott L. Kastner, "Commerce in the Shadow of Conflict: Domestic Politics and the Relationship Between International Conflict and Economic Interdependence" (Ph.D. dissertation, University of California, San Diego, 2003); and Harry G. Gelber, *Sovereignty Through Interdependence* (The Hague: Kluwer Law International, 1997). In his review of work on nationalism in IPE, Eric Helleiner, "Economic Nationalism as a Challenge to Economic

One of the purposes of this chapter is to engage in some rigorous analytical tugging within the context of neoclassical realism and with China–Taiwan–US relations as a prime example. I argue that neo-classical realism can explain this apparent paradox – namely, states that simultaneously view each other as military threats and valued economic partners – because it builds upon a core realist assumption about the immutability of tribalism and the centrality of conflict groups. Subsequent sections review the micro-foundations that already inform much of the interdependence literature and explain why such foundations make a neoclassical realist perspective neces-sary. The micro-foundations of neoclassical realism are discussed in turn, and the implications of its tribalism assumption are analyzed in particular. This assumption allows neoclassical realism to deductively incorporate and combine insights drawn from structural realism, about the influence of powerful external actors, and constructivism, about the dynamics of national collective identity formation. It combines these with a classical realist interest in the state, its rela-tionship to society, and its role in determining the "national interest." This combination indicates that external competitions with other states, internal competition for control of the state, and the process of national identity politics can be significantly entwined factors in for-eign policy choices and the assessment of external threat.

It is this entwining of internal competition with identity politics that allows trade and conflict to coexist, because internal competitions can encourage greater nationalism directed at a potential enemy while simultaneously encouraging greater economic exchange with it. The notion that such behavior should be impossible, or even just puzzling, is based on a set of faulty assumptions about the relationships between identity, nationalism, capitalist profit and exchange, cooperation, and

---

Liberalism? Lessons From the 19th Century," *International Studies Quarterly* 46, no. 3 (September 2002), pp. 307–29. Helleiner also cites work by George T. Crane, "Economic Nationalism: Bringing the Nation Back In," *Millennium* 27, no. 1 (1998), pp. 55–75; George T. Crane, "Imagining the Economic Nation: Globalisation in China," *New Political Economy* 4, no. 2 (July 1999), pp. 215–32; and Stephen Shulman, "Nationalist Sources of International Economic Integration," *International Studies Quarterly* 44, no. 3 (September 2000), pp. 365–90, along with several others. That Helleiner, "Economic Nationalism as a Challenge to Economic Liberalism?" repeatedly stresses just how controversial this body of work is in his review, underscores how antithetical nationalism is considered to be in the project of capitalist IPE.

the nature of nation-states in general.[8] It is perfectly possible for *irrational* national collective identity politics to coexist with *rational* self-interest in capitalist profits and cooperative policies to those ends. In fact, it may even be that the dynamics of internal competition and national identity politics are what inform the condition of inter-dependence, not vice versa. In other words, states can perceive each other as security threats despite increased economic interdependence between them, because nationalism and capitalism are not behavi-oral, analytical, or practical contradictions. Global capitalism has always functioned and will continue to function in a context of national collectives with internal competitive dynamics that make the "interdependent-peace-dividend" a phenomenon in name only.

The China–Taiwan–US relationship is certainly an appropriate case study to illustrate these claims. Trade and investment between China and Taiwan have increased even as security tensions between the two have remained high. Similarly, there have been growing economic linkages between China and the United States, and yet each continues to define the other as a potential security threat in the region. Numerous scholars have scrutinized both relationships in the context of interdependence arguments,[9] and the assumption that interde-pendence leads to peace has influenced not only scholarly assessments of these relationships but actual policy choices within all three states at various points in time. Thus the China–Taiwan–US relationship is a microcosm, both empirically and analytically, of the interrelated phenomena of economic interdependence, peace, and conflict.

Micro-foundations in the liberal interdependence literature

Although there may be increasing recognition that more attention needs to be paid to the micro-foundations of interdependence, it is legitimate to wonder why neoclassical realism is a necessary or even conducive platform from which to analytically proceed. Part of the answer lies in the traditional ways in which the "interdependence-promotes-peace"

---

[8] For an overview of the literature devoted to trading with the enemy, and an examination of its analytical propositions, see Barbieri and Levy, "Sleeping with the Enemy."

[9] See, for example, Kastner, "Does Economic Integration?" and Yun-han Chu, "Taiwan's National Identity Politics and the Prospect of Cross-Strait Relations," *Asian Survey* 44, no. 4 (July/August 2004), pp. 484–512.

thesis has been argued in the discipline. Despite calls for more work to be done on micro-causal mechanisms, there is already a considerable body of theoretical work, by liberal theorists such as Ernst Haas, Karl Deutsch, James Rosenau, Robert Keohane, and Joseph Nye to name a few, which delineates interdependent micro-foundations. This may seem surprising since some of the more influential versions of the "interdependence-promotes-peace" thesis were intentionally framed in systemic terms. In *After Hegemony*, for example, Keohane sought to "account for state behavior on the basis of attributes of the system as a whole," and in *Power and Interdependence*, Keohane and Nye argued that it was "essential to know how much one can explain purely on the basis of information about the international system."[10] These works set the stage for what has become a standard disciplinary assumption about the phenomenon of economic interdependence: when nation-states share a common goal in the maximization of capitalist profits, the functionally efficient means to this end are policies of transnational cooperation.[11]

---

[10] Robert O. Keohane, *After Hegemony: Cooperation and Discord in the World Political Economy* (Princeton, NJ: Princeton University Press, 1984), p. 25, and Keohane and Joseph S. Nye, *Power and Interdependence: World Politics in Transition* (Glenview, IL: Scott, Foresman and Company, [1977; reprint 1989]), p. vi. Obviously there have been many scholars and works on liberal interdependence that have been influential in the discipline, much of which is cited throughout this article. But if we define influence on the basis of citations, subsequently generated popular research agendas (in terms of numbers of devotees, their job placements, and placement of publications), and influence/appearance in international relations journals intended for policy-makers and lay audiences, then one would be hard pressed to find disciplinary work on interdependence that has been more influential than the work of Robert O. Keohane and Joseph S. Nye. See also Keohane and Nye, eds., *Transnational Relations and World Politics* (Cambridge, MA: Harvard University Press, 1971); Keohane and Nye, "Power and Interdependence in the Information Age," *Foreign Affairs* (September/October 1998), pp. 81–94; and Keohane, "Governance in a Partially Globalized World 'Presidential Address', 'American Political Science Association, 2000,'" *American Political Science Review* 95, no. 1 (March 2001), pp. 1–13.

[11] Some examples of IR theoretical scholarship that explicitly make or rely upon this argument include Emanuel Adler, Beverly Crawford, and Jack Donnelly, "Defining and Conceptualizing Progress in International Relations," in Emanuel Adler and Beverly Crawford, eds., *Progress in Postwar International Relations* (New York: Columbia University Press, 1991); James M. Goldgeier and Michael McFaul, "A Tale of Two Worlds: Core and Periphery in the Post-Cold War Era," *International Organization* 46, no. 2 (spring 1992), pp. 467–91; Robert Jervis, "The Future of World Politics: Will

Yet this assumption rests upon questionable, normative assumptions about individual cognition and domestic politics that have remained largely unexcavated.[12] Keohane and Nye, for example, acknowledged that the state and its leaders do not automatically recognize that cooperation is the functionally efficient policy. What stand in the way of this recognition are the state itself and the cognitive mind-set of autonomy and territoriality which it supposedly engenders among its publics and decision-makers. These are presumed to be historical residues, and ridding state leaders of this mind-set allows international marketplaces to produce greater profits and hence a stake in continued peaceful relations. Decision-makers are expected to cognitively and behaviorally adapt to new systemic conditions in trade and economics, then, and they do so when it becomes increasingly clear that profits and hence higher standards of living for their societies can only be realized through interstate cooperation. Analytically this means that domestic and individual variables are expected to change in response to newly evolved systemic constraints, which can only occur if causal priority has been assigned to capitalist profit over any other domestic or international goals state leaders and their societies might have.

Although other aspects of interdependence are argued to have a pacifying effect on conflict as well, the basic formula proposed in the early theoretical interdependence literature has retained a firm grip on the imagination of scholars. Mansfield and Pollins note, for example, that the most "widespread liberal argument is that open economic exchange leads private traders and consumers to become dependent on overseas markets," that "these actors have incentives to withdraw support for public officials who take actions ... that are commercially harmful," and that "realizing this, public officials who need such support have reason to resolve interstate disputes."[13] Analyses of interdependent micro-foundations inevitably begin with this basic formula and assume

it Resemble the Past?" *International Security* 16, no. 3 (1991/2), pp. 39–73; Richard Rosecrance, *The Rise of the Trading State: Commerce and Conquest in the Modern World* (New York: Basic Books, 1986); John Gerard Ruggie, *Constructing the World Polity: Essays on International Institutionalization* (New York: Routledge, 1998).

[12] The arguments that follow are more extensively developed in Jennifer Sterling-Folker, *Theories of International Cooperation and the Primacy of Anarchy: Explaining US International Monetary Policy-Making After Bretton Woods* (Albany: State University of New York Press, 2002).

[13] Mansfield and Pollins, "The Study of Interdependence and Conflict," p. 841.

that domestic politics and individual cognition are reshaped by the condition of interdependence to suit a primary interest in capitalist profit, whether it is on behalf of particular constituencies or societies at large. This is, for example, what Helen Milner argues in her domestic-level analysis of international cooperation, as do Paul Papayoanou, in his study of how domestic political institutions aggregate economic interests, and Jeffry Frieden, in his analysis of US monetary policy.[14] In so doing, these and other scholars replicate all the essential features of Keohane and Nye's original formula. That is, the assumption of rational, conscious, and collective self-interest in capitalist profit is combined with an economic pluralist perspective on state–society relations which assumes, as Garrett and Lange point out, that "changes in the constellation of preferences in the private sphere will be quickly reflected in commensurate changes in public policies and institutions."[15]

Yet parochial unilateralism and the obsession with territorial autonomy are not mere historical residues, as most liberal scholars assume; nor are such attributes disconnected from the interests of particular economic constituencies within nation-states. Nationalists do not stand on one side of the nation-state, while capitalists seeking profit or workers seeking employment and better wages stand on the other.

---

[14] Helen Milner, *Interests, Institutions, and Information: Domestic Politics and International Relations* (Princeton, NJ: Princeton University Press, 1997); Paul Papayoanou, *Power Ties: Economic Interdependence, Balancing, and War* (Ann Arbor: University of Michigan Press, 1999); Jeffry A. Frieden, "Economic Integration and the Politics of Monetary Policy in the United States," in Robert O. Keohane and Helen Milner, eds., *Internationalization and Domestic Politics* (Cambridge: Cambridge University Press, 1996).

[15] Geoffrey Garrett and Peter Lange, "Internationalization, Institutions, and Political Change," in Keohane and Milner, *Internationalization and Domestic Politics*, p. 74. Or what Mansfield and Pollins, "The Study of Interdependence and Conflict," p. 843, note is "a key weakness of most liberal explanations of international relations, namely, the tendency to rely on pluralist models of domestic politics, which lack a theory of the state specifying how social actors' interests are aggregated, how such actors translate their interests into foreign policy, and which societal actors are most influential." Similarly, David H. Bearce and Sawa Omori, "How Do Commercial Institutions Promote Peace?" *Journal of Peace Research* 42, no. 6 (November 2005), pp. 659–78, at pp. 662–3, observe that "the interdependence literature, especially the commercial liberal variant, has yet to convincingly explain how internationally oriented societal actors successfully impose their preferences for peace on the autonomous state, especially when there are other societal actors pressuring the state for conflict and when the state stands to benefit from possible military conquest."

National collective identity differentiation is an active, on-going process which undergirds the very activities of economic exchange. As Rawi Abdelal points out, "national identities frame societal debates about trade and monetary relations, especially fundamental choices about trade and monetary integration with other states."[16] Liberal interdependence arguments insist upon treating nationalism as an irrational, unconscious mind-set that can and should be dislodged by the recognition of the more rational, conscious self-interest in collective profit. But collective capitalist profits do not constitute a collective identity, and nationalism is not easily reshaped by rational, self-interested capitalist calculations, even when these are pursued in the name of a collective (a point already well recognized by scholars of various Marxist orientations). Instead, national identity and nationalism continue to play an enduring, foundational role in domestic political struggles and foreign policy, even in the context of increased interdependence.

This insight is essential for understanding the relationship between conflict and economic interdependence, because processes of national identity formation always involve the delineation of difference, and difference can be deadly. This is one of the reasons why economically interdependent nation-states can still be security threats to one another and hence why "trading with the enemy" is not as surprising as it might first appear. The continued relevance of national identity politics to economic ideas, decisions, and outcomes is also one of the reasons why collective profit is so frequently (and, one could argue, easily) sacrificed in the Westphalian system. Because liberalism contains no theory of collective identity that acknowledges difference as an essential, enduring component of identity, it is not surprising that liberal interdependence theories fail to recognize the role that collective identity difference plays in individual cognition and domestic politics. Political categories in liberalism are, as Michael Williams points out, "in significant ways constituted by unwillingness to ask the question of identity," and this "conscious *exclusion* of its significance from the political realm" is due to "the conflict it was seen to entail."[17] The

---

[16] Abdelal, *National Purpose in the World Economy*, p. 42.

[17] Michael C. Williams, "Identity and the Politics of Security," *European Journal of International Relations* 4, no. 2 (1998), pp. 204–25, at pp. 213–14 (emphasis in original). Alternatively he notes, at p. 217 (emphasis in original), that neorealism "emerged as a conscious response *to* such questions" and hence it "does not lack a grasp of identity practices, it *is* an identity practice."

problem with this exclusion, from an analytical perspective, is that national identity is not a mere irrational, unconscious barrier to universally better solutions; it is the stuff of politics itself. As Linda Bishai puts this, "politics, in other words, is about the never-ending negotiation of identity."[18]

There are scholars, such as Rawi Abdelal, Eric Helleiner, and Scott Kastner, among others, who recognize that nationalism plays a greater role in international political economy than is commonly assumed, and who are on the right track if we are to understand how economic foreign policies *actually* come about in a world order that continues to be dominated by *nation*-states.[19] Similarly, neoclassical realism is, as Anders Wivel observes, a variant of realism that has "attempted to combine structural factors with domestic politics in order to explain foreign policy."[20] Because neoclassical realism also questions the extent to which domestic politics and individual cognition actually work as liberal international relations theory assumes, it is a natural platform from which to engage with and challenge liberal interdependence-promotes-peace arguments. Yet this begs a second obvious question: why realism at all? Here the answer lies in realism's continued focus on the state and its assumption of tribalism, which serves as the analytical link between individual identity and collectives. Realism's focus on groups as its core unit of analysis also allows it to incorporate insights from constructivism regarding the process of collective identity formation. It is to this assumption that the analysis now turns.

Tribalism as an analytical foundation for neoclassical realism

The neoclassical realism of this chapter starts with the observation, confirmed in the work of realist scholars such as Robert Gilpin, Jonathan Mercer, Randall Schweller, and David Priess, as well as chapter 1 of this volume, that realism's core analytical unit is not the

---

[18] Linda Bishai, "Liberal Empire," *Journal of International Relations and Development* 7, no. 1 (April 2004), pp. 48–72, at p. 60.

[19] See footnote 6 for bibliographic information and additional sources.

[20] Anders Wivel, "Explaining Why State X Made a Certain Move Last Tuesday: The Promise and Limitations of Realist Foreign Policy Analysis," *Journal of International Relations and Development* 8, no. 4 (December 2005), pp. 355–80, at p. 360.

individual, nor the state, but human collectives as a broad category.[21] Realism assumes that human beings are social animals who naturally form groups, and, as constructivists have argued, groups shape and bind individuals together via distinct social practices, institutions, and common identities. Individual identity is only realized through a process of collective social construction, which involves making self–other distinctions. As Franke Wilmer notes, identity is a "paradoxical beginning," because it "is constituted by referring the bounded self to something else, something with which the self is either *identified* (as the same) or from which it is *different*."[22] Hence collective identity formation always entails the creation of in-group/out-group distinctions that have implications for external relations as well as for internal politics and competitions. The fact that human beings are naturally social, and hence predisposed to form groups, has implications for both politics within groups as well as how groups interact with one another.

The neoclassical realism to which I subscribe obviously starts from a bio-political foundation, because it explicitly adopts particular human nature assumptions which it argues are transhistorical. The particular assumptions that it adopts do not involve power lust or aggression, however; rather I concur with Yosef Lapid that there is a more foundational realist "tradition that subscribes to an ontology of conflictual group fragmentation," which leads to a central "problematique (survival/war)."[23] In a sense, then, neoclassical realism represents the return to a realist insight largely lost in the structural rush to neorealism: tribalism is a fact of human existence. But it

---

[21] Robert Gilpin, "No One Loves a Political Realist," in Benjamin Frankel, ed., *Realism: Restatements and Renewal* (London: Frank Cass, 1996); Robert Gilpin, "The Richness of the Tradition of Political Realism," in Robert O. Keohane, ed., *Neorealism and its Critics* (New York: Columbia University Press, 1986); Jonathan Mercer, "Anarchy and Identity," *International Organization* 49, no. 2 (spring 1995), pp. 229–52; Randall L. Schweller and David Priess, "A Tale of Two Realisms: Expanding the Institutions Debate," *Mershon International Studies Review* 41, no. 1 (May 1997), pp. 1–32.

[22] Franke Wilmer, *The Social Construction of Man, the State, and War: Identity, Conflict, and Violence in the Former Yugoslavia* (New York: Routledge, 2002), p. 69; see also Bishai, "Liberal Empire," pp. 60–3.

[23] Yosef Lapid, "Nationalism and Realist Discourses of International Relations," in Francis A. Beer and Robert Hariman, eds., *Post-Realism: The Rhetorical Turn in International Relations* (East Lansing: Michigan State University Press, 1996), pp. 239–40.

subsequently moves from there to a realist-constructivist position in which group identity, social practices, and intergroup interaction become paramount to explanation and understanding, within very broad boundaries set by the sociability of the species itself. These boundaries are the stuff of traditional realist analysis. Because human beings will always form groups, there will always be intergroup competition, a concern with relative power, and a tendency to imitate one another's social practices. Hence realist structural patterns are an essential starting point for analysis.

Yet realist structural expectations are so broad that most of the heavy explanatory lifting must be done by constructivism instead, which is why neoclassical realist scholarship typically produces historical narratives. To understand how history evolves and why politics and economics look the way they do, it is essential to examine how groups construct their identity via differentiation, how groups marry identity differentiation to institutions that determine who gets what within the group (whether it is the state or another process of collective decision-making), and how that marriage of individual identity and decision-making institutions is maintained. This process is "natural" and "realist" in the sense that human beings are predisposed to it; that is, to forming groups, differentiating them, and developing institutions that continually reify those differences. But it is a process that is simultaneously "fictional" and "constructed" since there are infinite ways in which human groupings can differentiate themselves, and the ultimate source for these differentiations is the social practices human beings create and control.

This still does not say very much, since there are a variety of types of groups and individuals who can be members of multiple groups simultaneously, a point highlighted by the work of Yale Ferguson and Richard Mansbach.[24] One can be a member of an ethnic group, a national group, a religious group, a professional association, an economic class, an interest group, a racial group, and so on. As Lowell Barrington argues, it is important to establish clear definitions when discussing different types of groups. A nation, for example, may be distinguished from an ethnic group in that a nation is a "collective of people" that is "not just unified by culture; they are unified by a sense

---

[24] Yale H. Ferguson and Richard W. Mansbach, *Polities: Authority, Identities, and Change* (Columbia: University of South Carolina Press, 1996).

of purpose: controlling the territory that the members of the group believe to be theirs."[25] Although multiple group membership is the norm, at any given historical moment particular collective identities are more pertinent than others to the allocation of intra-collective resources and the decision-making processes and institutions that attend it. Put another way, the control of resource allocation decision-making for its constituent members is the surest indication that a particular collective identity is first among equals.

In this regard, it is the nation that is most pertinent to contemporary life, but this was not always the case (although nations certainly existed prior to the Westphalian system), nor will it necessarily be so in the future (although nations certainly will continue to exist after Westphalia's demise). What makes contemporary nations unique is not simply the prominence they have assumed over other group identities, but their marriage to states as a particular type of social institution or process for determining intra-group resource decisions. It is, after all, the state that serves as "the preeminent structure carrying out or ... 'containing' the resources necessary to carry out two kinds of political activities: allocative and authoritative."[26] Too often, however, scholars conflate the nation with the state as if they were interchangeable, but as Barrington points out, the state "is the principle political unit in the inter*national* political system" which is distinct from "a collective of people" whose belief in the right to territorial self-determination is what unites them.[27] Because the state has become the primary allocative and authoritative unit of contemporary nations, subgroups within nations spend a great deal of time

[25] Lowell W. Barrington, " 'Nation' and 'Nationalism': The Misuse of Key Concepts in Political Science," *PS: Political Science and Politics* 30, no. 4 (December 1997), pp. 712–16, at p. 713. Similarly, Alexander B. Murphy, "The Sovereign State System as Political-Territorial Ideal: Historical and Contemporary Considerations," in Thomas J. Biersteker and Cynthia Weber, eds., *State Sovereignty as Social Construct* (Cambridge: Cambridge University Press, 1996), pp. 81–120, at p. 95, defines a nation as "a group of people who saw themselves as a cultural-historical unit," while nationalism was "fundamentally concerned with the rights of a nation ... to control its own territory." On the other hand, see Sheila L. Croucher, "Perpetual Imagining: Nationhood in a Global Era," *International Studies Review* 5, no. 1 (March 2003), pp. 1–24 for a review of the analytical difficulties with defining the term "nation."

[26] Wilmer, *The Social Construction*, p. 126.

[27] Barrington, " 'Nation' and 'Nationalism,' " p. 713 (my emphasis).

fighting over who will control it. This is not unique to nation-states, however. When resource allocation decisions are involved, all collectives are subject to a common logic of competition that affects intra- as well as intergroup relations.

Hence despite the human predisposition to form groups, group construction is a contentious internal process because group resource decisions matter a great deal to its individual members. Realist dynamics may be found at both levels as a result. That is, there is competition *between* groups over access and control of resources for group disposal, and there is competition *within* groups over how resources will be divided and distributed to group members and who has the ability and legitimacy to make these decisions for the group. Yet groups do form and are maintained, despite the ongoing threat of centrifugal collapse, in a process whereby members seek to both differentiate their group from other external groups and bound (or regulate) the amount of intra-group competition. This bounding involves the creation of a fictitious internal unity, out of what are often disparate subgroups and competing interests, and it creates this unity by juxtaposing it against an external, comparative difference that other groups represent. All societies at all times are in the process of constructing an identity of self that is in juxtaposition to external others, but this always has ramifications for resource allocations within and for internal subgroups who do not fit neatly into the juxtaposition (Muslim Americans after 9/11, for example, or Latino "illegal" immigrants in the 2006 American political debates). What is constructed is never complete or entirely coherent, and it involves the sort of "constructed power-disguising myths" that are the subject of Coxian critical theory, in which the arbitrary exercise of internal power – of who gets to decide what resources the rest of us get – is rationalized as normal.[28]

While such constructs may indeed be internally directed, they also involve juxtaposition to otherness. To understand such juxtapositions, one must go beyond the container of the nation-state. As Iver Neumann puts this, "the formation of the self is inextricably intertwined with the formation of its others and ... a failure to regard the

[28] Jeffrey Harrod, "Global Realism: Unmasking Power in the International Political Economy," in Richard Wyn Jones, ed., *Critical Theory and World Politics* (Boulder, CO: Lynne Reinner, 2001), pp. 120–1.

others in their own right must necessarily have repercussions for the formation of the self."[29] That there *are* other groups that are also engaging in the same process is important to remember, since group formation and identity construction does not generally occur in isolation.[30] But collectives also remain internally obsessed with themselves, and in particular with whom and how intra-group decisions will be made, because intra-group resource allocation decisions will affect internal subgroups and individuals differently. In other words, internal subgroups compete with one another over who will control the state, because control allows for the allocation of collective resources and the determination of choices toward other collectives. Subgroups maintain this obsession with internal affairs even as they develop and behave in juxtaposition to and in competition with other groups. Thus who controls resources, how they are allocated, and what role relative power plays in final resource decisions is as important *within* nation-states as it is *between* them.

In the Westphalian system, where collective identity construction is linked to national collective autonomy and territorial self-determination, subgroup competition for state control can manifest itself as electoral, bureaucratic, and/or leadership struggles, depending on whether or not a polity is a democracy. Obviously not all such competitions involve national identity formation and reproduction, but national identity symbols are typically implicated, evoked, or encouraged as a means of winning such competitions.[31] And state leaders always attempt to encourage, reiterate, or impose particular visions of national identity in order to obtain support for their policies and preferences. The result is, as Roxanne Doty points out, that "the state plays a particularly significant role in producing and reproducing

---

[29] Iver B. Neumann, *Uses of the Other: 'The East' in European Identity Formation* (Minneapolis: University of Minnesota Press, 1999), p. 35.

[30] That is, while the construction of content difference may be fictional, the existence of difference is not due simply to the ubiquitous predisposition to form groups. Group formation and identity construction typically involves a material and ideational interrelationship between groups. It is this claim that allows neoclassical realism to deductively link the internal to the external, and to incorporate insights from constructivism (regarding identity construction and social practices) and neorealism (regarding anarchy and polarity) under the same analytical umbrella.

[31] See in particular the essays in Michael E Geisler, *National Symbols, Fractured Identities* (Middlebury, VT: Middlebury College Press, 2005).

national identities."[32] It does so, she argues, by producing "sovereignty effects," which are the "practices that seek to reaffirm the foundational elements of belonging to one group as opposed to another and to exclude those represented as 'other.'"[33] Thus the processes of national group identity formation are intimately linked into internal subgroup competitions for state control, and this process can derail even the most rational and consciously desired peace dividends anticipated from economic interdependent conditions.

Neoclassical realism argues, then, that because *inter*-national competition has significant ramifications for *intra*-national competition and vice versa, these logics of competition should not be analytically isolated from one another. Group formation simultaneously links individual identity to internal political and economic decision-making practices *and* juxtaposes this identity to something normatively different, external, and, ultimately less desirable. These are constructed fictions, of course, since internal decision-making practices do not always work in the individual's favor, and external difference may actually be normatively more desirable, but they are fictions dependent on the competitive interaction with other collectives, who are themselves engaged in similar intra-group processes. Given that group identities are never settled and remain ongoing processes, it is impossible to understand those processes and their particular contents unless we consider how group formation is always, simultaneously, driven by internal and external competitions that are crosscutting and interrelated.

The interrelation between national internals and externals is one of the reasons why national group formation and transformation are not easily subject to conscious and rational manipulation. While leaders and particular subgroups certainly attempt such manipulations, crosscutting competitive developments, opportunities, and challenges will deflect and surprise both leaders and scholars alike. So too will the vehemence and power of national identities, which, once galvanized, can take off in unexpected, and at times deadly, directions that, in the dual context of intra- and inter-national competition, cannot be anticipated or controlled by leaders and subgroups. This should really come as no surprise,

---

[32] Roxanne Lynn Doty, "Sovereignty and the Nation: Constructing the Boundaries of National Identity," in Biersteker and Weber, *State Sovereignty as Social Construct*, pp. 121–47, at p. 128.

[33] Ibid., p. 142.

however, since the formation and maintenance of nations is ultimately an individual-level phenomenon, involving the construction and maintenance of individual identity which is bound to and developed within the context of group social practices and institutions. As Wilmer notes, "the ability to arouse powerful emotions by invoking solidarity on the basis of group identities derived from symbolic as much as (or more than) substantive differences remains as pervasive as ever in modern societies."[34] No wonder, then, that national identity is a force well beyond the control of rational actors and that while "politics must be understood through reason, yet it is not in reason that it finds its model," because "the social world is always complicated, incongruous, and concrete."[35]

It is only within this context that phenomena such as economic interdependence, "trading with the enemy," and threat assessment can be understood. Foreign policy choices result from a crosscutting interrelationship between national identity formation and reproduction, domestic political struggles for control of the state and external actors and conditions. This is not merely a two-level game conducted by state officials, as Robert Putnam has argued, but a complex process in which internal and external resource competitions implicate differing collective self-definitions.[36] Which self-definitions dominate state policy choices at any point in time can have as much to do with internal competitions as external events; more typically the external and internal events are linked and feed back on one another. In such a context, the phenomenon of "trading with the enemy" has as much to do with how, or even whether, a collective defines itself in juxtaposition to an enemy other as it has to do with economic exchange with that enemy other. Collectives can pose threats to one another and still have crosscutting linkages of an economic, political, or cultural nature. In fact, as Erik Gartzke and Kristian Gleditsch have argued, violence is actually more likely among states with similar cultural ties than with dissimilar ones, as the case of China and Taiwan amply demonstrates.[37]

---

[34] Wilmer, *The Social Construction*, p. 11.

[35] H. J. Morgenthau, *Scientific Man vs. Power Politics* (Chicago: University of Chicago Press, 1946), p. 10.

[36] Robert D. Putnam, "Diplomacy and Domestic Politics: The Logic of Two-Level Games," *International Organization* 42, no. 3 (summer 1988), pp. 427–60.

[37] Erik Gartzke and Kristian Skrede Gleditsch, "Identity and Conflict: Ties that Bind and Differences that Divide," *European Journal of International Relations* 12, no. 1 (March 2006), pp. 53–87.

Setting the stage: The history of China–Taiwan–US relations

How, then, does a neoclassical realist perspective challenge the assumption that growing interdependence between China and Taiwan is a potential path to peace between them? That there is growing interdependence and rising profit maximization on both sides of the Strait is undeniable. In the late 1980s, Taiwan's government, the Republic of China (ROC), lifted its ban on visits to the mainland and initiated trade investment talks with the People's Republic of China (PRC). By 1998, Taiwanese investment in China had reached $38 billion, and in 2003, China became Taiwan's largest export market before the United States or Japan.[38] Smith points out that "as much as $10 billion has poured into China from Taiwan in the last two years, compared with $40 billion in the previous decade," much of it in high-technology industries, and by 2004, 1.5 million Taiwanese lived on the mainland.[39] Yet this growing economic interdependence occurred at the same time as the potential for violence remained palpable. Much of this potential can be explained with a realist structural perspective, which, as noted above, serves as a first cut for neoclassical realist analysis.

Taiwan (or Formosa as it was called by the Portuguese) was a province of China that was occupied by the Japanese until the end of World War II. In 1949, the Nationalists (Kuomintang or KMT) fled to the island as the Communists claimed victory on the mainland. Both the Nationalists and the PRC maintained that they were the sole legitimate government of China and both made plans to reclaim the other's territory. One of the major reasons why neither launched such an invasion, however, was the US interest in balancing Chinese

[38] Richard L. Russell, "The 1996 Taiwan Strait Crisis: The United States and China at the Precipice of War?" Case Study 231, Institute for the Study of Diplomacy (School of Foreign Service, Georgetown University, Washington, DC, 2000), p. 4; Joseph Kahn, "Taiwan Voters Weighing how Far to Push China," *New York Times*, March 18, 2004, p. A8.

[39] Craig S. Smith, "Signs in China and Taiwan of Making Money, Not War," *New York Times*, May 15, 2001; Kahn, "Taiwan Voters Weighing," p. A8. For additional figures on Taiwanese-Chinese trade and economic investment, see Chu, "Taiwan's National Identity Politics," p. 493, and Scott L. Kastner, "Ambiguity, Economic Interdependence, and the US Strategic Dilemma in the Taiwan Strait," *Journal of Contemporary China* 15, no. 49 (November 2006), pp. 651–69, at p. 666.

aggression in light of the Korean War and increasing Cold War tensions in the region. In 1950, the United States declared Taiwan a neutral territory and, from 1950 until 1953, sent the Seventh Fleet into the Taiwan Strait, which is a major commercial shipping avenue between the island of Taiwan itself and the coast of China's Fukien province. The United States also began to supply the ROC with economic aid, and the two countries signed a mutual defense treaty in 1954 in response to the first in a series of Taiwan Strait crises that have continued to occur intermittently up to the present day.[40] During the second crisis, in 1958, the US sent military forces into the Strait, and it issued a joint communiqué confirming its commitment to Taiwan's security.

Throughout this same period, Taiwan occupied the Chinese seat in the UN Security Council and other intergovernmental organizations (IGOs), and it enjoyed full diplomatic relations with the majority of nation-states. All of this was with US blessings and encouragement, as it attempted to freeze the PRC out of world politics by refusing to legally acknowledge its existence. Taiwan became an important cornerstone in the US Cold War strategy to balance potential communist expansionism in Asia. It is probably no exaggeration to say that a ROC that is politically and territorially independent from the PRC would not exist today had it not been for this larger balance of power context to which neorealism draws our attention.

This Cold War context had changed by the early 1970s, however, as China had by then developed a mutual interest in balancing the Soviet Union, and the US and China began to explore the possibility of improved relations. In 1971, the US stood by as the UN General Assembly voted to expel Taiwan and give the China seat to the PRC instead, and the vast majority of other nation-states ended their formal diplomatic relationship with Taiwan at that time. Taiwan lost its seat in most IGOs, along with its diplomatic status in the UN, as the PRC insisted that other nation-states could not recognize the sovereignty of both states. In 1972, the US and China signed the Shanghai Communiqué, which stated that "there is but one China and that Taiwan is a part of China" and agreed that US forces and military

---

[40] These crises typically involve Chinese artillery attacks on the off-shore islands of Quemoy and Matsu, which are Nationalist-held territory but generally unpopulated.

installations should be withdrawn from Taiwan. In 1979, the US established full diplomatic relations with the PRC, terminated its 1954 mutual security pact with Taiwan, and reaffirmed the one-China principle. In the ensuing decades, the US has consistently acknowledged and acquiesced to Chinese claims that Taiwanese independence, a two-China system, or Taiwanese membership in IGOs are unacceptable.

It would be a mistake to assume, however, that the US had actually abandoned Taiwan to the PRC. While the US pursued improved diplomatic relations with China, it also adopted the Taiwan Relations Act in 1979, which declares that the US has a commitment to Taiwan's security and is obligated to sell sophisticated defensive arms to it. These arms sales have been extensive, involving fighter planes, spy planes, helicopters, torpedoes, anti-ship missiles, anti-missile defense systems, and submarines. By 1997, Taiwan was the world's number one purchaser of arms in dollar amounts, and most military strategists rank its military technology as far superior to that of the PRC.[41] The Taiwan Relations Act also reserved the American right to "resist any resort to force or other forms of coercion" that might jeopardize the security of Taiwan, and the US has been consistently willing to militarily signal this right to the PRC. When the Chinese conducted war games off Taiwan's coast in 1996, the US dispatched two aircraft carrier groups to the region in the largest show of naval force since the Vietnam War, and it explicitly stated that it would not allow the PRC to close the Strait. The US has also consistently monitored the Chinese military buildup and activities along the Strait. The 2001 diplomatic crisis over a US navy surveillance plane's collision with a Chinese fighter jet was a direct result of the continued US concern over Chinese aggression and its commitment to Taiwanese security. In addition, American economic linkages with Taiwan expanded so that by the early 2000s Taiwan was the US's seventh-largest trading partner.[42]

This contradictory behavior on the part of the US is consistent with its contradictory strategic interests in the region. It seeks to avoid direct confrontation with China and remains interested in accessing its

---

[41] John F. Copper, *Taiwan*, 3rd edn (Boulder, CO: Westview Press, 1999), p. 168. John F. Copper, *Taiwan: Nation-State or Province?* (Boulder, CO: Westview Press, 1999), p. 168.

[42] Russell, "The 1996 Taiwan Strait Crisis," p. 4.

growing markets; hence it has severed its formal diplomatic ties with Taiwan and does not challenge Chinese claims to the island directly. At the same time, the US is wary of future Chinese intentions and so it has attempted to pacify China with regards to Taiwan, while also protecting Taiwan from China, which is no small feat considering that the PRC and the ROC see the very existence of each other as a political anathema. Yet, during the late 1980s and early 1990s, it seemed more likely that the PRC and the ROC were going to reach an acceptable accord. The ROC gradually renounced its goal to militarily reclaim the mainland and in the late 1980s it lifted its ban on visits to the mainland and the publication of mainland books. Throughout the 1990s, economic ties between China and Taiwan increased dramatically, and the ROC espoused a pro-unification position, concurring with the PRC that the one-China policy was desirable, but only if it could occur on terms acceptable to both sides. In 1991, the ROC renounced any intention of using force to reclaim the mainland, and direct negotiations between PRC and ROC officials began in 1993. When Hong Kong and Macao were returned to the PRC in 1997 and 1999 respectively, China suggested that the "one country, two systems" principle it applied to them, in which they would be allowed to maintain their capitalist systems and a high degree of autonomy, would remain a viable formula for its relationship with Taiwan.

Yet, by the mid-1990s, relations between China and Taiwan had deteriorated again, and the two were increasingly at odds over the Taiwanese refusal to publicly renounce the goal of independence, as well as its pursuit of diplomatic ties and IGO membership throughout the world. The Chinese staged war games and conducted military tests in the Strait in 1995, 1996, and 2001, with the stated purpose of intimidating Taiwan into accepting the one-China principle, and not unsurprisingly reunification talks ended. Since the 1980s, China has consistently demonstrated its willingness to be patient (and not force political and economic unity), but only if Taiwan accepts this principle. Taiwan has just as consistently sought to maintain its independence, while attempting to avoid a direct military confrontation with China. Taiwan has also been careful not to alienate American support, and when China contemplates military action against Taiwan, China has to consider the possibility of a direct military confrontation with the US. The 2001 Chinese military exercises meant to simulate an assault on Taiwan were not merely for

Taiwanese consumption; they included a third-stage counterattack against "an enemy fleet attempting to intervene in the war."[43]

A tangled web: the link between internal and external competitions

What happened in the mid-1990s to resolidify antagonism between China and Taiwan at a time when economic trade and investment between them was growing dramatically? To understand this dynamic, it is necessary to examine the subgroups within each nation-state involved, their competition over control of their own state, and the impact that their interaction with other nation-states has on internal competitions and vice versa. Also important is how nationalism continues to play a role in delineating larger group boundaries, particularly in China and Taiwan, and how these elements have interacted with the kinds of strategic systemic elements highlighted in a typical structural realist analysis. What emerges is a story of competition and power that is not simply between nation-states but within them, so that systemic structural elements work through the subgroups and institutions within the nation-state to produce foreign policy choices and behaviors. How these choices and behaviors come about tells us a great deal about how states and societies assess external threat, how increased trade and hostility can occur simultaneously, and why the interdependence-promotes-peace argument should be treated with a great deal of skepticism.

Throughout the late 1990s and early 2000s, the interactive combination of particular subgroups and their ascendance within China, Taiwan, and the US drove each nation-state toward a greater tendency for crisis, in spite of the increased levels of economic exchange between all three of them. In the case of the US, for example, the commitment to protect Taiwan cuts across both political parties, which essentially support a policy of "strategic ambiguity" in which Taiwan is protected but not allowed to become independent.[44]

---

[43] "Chronology," *Frontline Special: Dangerous Straits, Exploring the Future of US–China Relations and the Long Simmering Issue of Taiwan.* First aired October 2001, available at: www.pbs.org/wgbh/pages/frontline/shows/china/etc/cron.html.

[44] See Kastner, "Ambiguity, Economic Interdependence," for a review of this policy, its controversies in the American context, and the literature (both scholarly and policy-focused) associated with it.

However there are important splits within the Republican Party over whether China can be pacified via trade (according to liberal inter-dependence claims) or whether, according to neorealist suspicions, trade is simply a means for China to improve its military and later become an even greater national security threat to US interests in the region. David Sanger refers to those Republicans who favor the trade perspective as "the Boeing camp," which consists primarily of business executives who seek stronger ties between the US and China and want US foreign policy to be "tough-minded militarily, but fundamentally open to the embrace of China into a capitalist system."[45] Alternatively the second camp within the Republican Party is "a containment camp," which believes that the Boeing camp is being "naïve about the growing military threat from China."[46] This latter camp, Kurt Campbell notes, believes that "China is the next great enemy of the United States," and, as a result, "there is a raging debate, sometimes in full view, sometimes behind the scenes, about how to conceptualize China."[47]

The Republican Boeing camp scored a major victory in 1999, when the Senate passed a bill granting China permanent normal trade relations and thus paved the way for Chinese membership in the World Trade Organization. That there are powerful economic interests in the Democratic Party that share the Boeing camp vision means that the economic conceptualization of China carries considerable weight in US foreign policy. But when China has behaved belligerently toward Taiwan, the containment camp has claimed confirmation for their concerns and insisted that the US adopt a series of tougher measures toward it and in defense of Taiwan. Such concerns prompted a series of decisions early in the first George W. Bush administration which upset and angered the Chinese, but were also meant to pacify the containment camp of the Republican Party. The administration authorized the first sale of US submarines to Taiwan since 1974, eventually sold Taiwan destroyers equipped with the

[45] David Sanger, "Interview," *Frontline Special: Dangerous Straits, Exploring the Future of US–China Relations and the Long Simmering Issue of Taiwan.* First aired October 2001, available at: www.pbs.org/wgbh/pages/frontline/shows/china/interviews/sanger.html

[46] Ibid.

[47] Kurt Campbell, "Interview," *Frontline Special,* available at: www.pbs.org/wgbh/pages/frontline/shows/china/interviews/campbell.html.

Aegis radar system, announced that the US would do "whatever it took" to help Taiwan defend itself, and in 2001 allowed Chen Shui-bian, the Taiwanese president, to visit New York and meet with legislators, while simultaneously entertaining Tibet's exiled spiritual leader, the Dalai Lama, at the White House.

These last two acts reverberated in Chinese domestic politics. Chinese officials continue to worry about secessionist movements within their borders, which are linked, of course, to the process of national identity construction, and they are particularly sensitive to the idea that contacts between the state and secessionists legitimize the latter. Chinese officials take this point so seriously that they initially insisted on party-to-party rather than state-to-state talks when dealing with Taiwan, because the latter would accord Taiwan the status of a sovereign nation-state which, China insists, Taiwan is not and never will be. Since Taiwan has become a democracy, however, this has proved to be an important impediment to improved relations, because it amounts to insisting that political parties which are not necessarily in control of the state should conduct foreign policy on its behalf.[48] Its equivalent, in the American context, would be to insist that Republicans allow Democrats to be the chief negotiators for US–Chinese relations, even when they do not hold the White House.

Because Taiwan's status is entwined with US–Chinese relations and vice versa, granting permission for a visit from the Taiwanese president has been the surest way for the US to provoke a Chinese military response directed at Taiwan.[49] The military exercises China conducted in the Taiwan Strait in 1995 were held in the months immediately following a Taiwanese presidential visit to the US, as was the simulated Chinese military assault on Taiwan in 2001. In the 1995 case, the Clinton administration had initially refused the Taiwanese

[48] Copper, *Taiwan*, p. 170. Since 1995, the Chinese have been more conciliatory on this point, suggesting that all Taiwanese political parties or officials can be included, although this still raises serious problems for foreign policy-making in a competitive democracy.

[49] Recognition of this pattern may be one reason why, in May 2006 (and given its already extensive military commitments in Afghanistan, Iraq, and its own border with Mexico), the second administration of George W. Bush would only permit Chen Shui-bian, en route from Latin American, to stop over in the US in Alaska, rather than his preferred stop in New York City (an offer that he refused).

president a visa, fearing the visit would unnecessarily anger the Chinese, but the Republican-dominated Congress passed a non-binding resolution demanding he receive one. Out of fear that Congress might pass legislation to amend the Taiwan Relations Act and force compliance, the Clinton administration granted the visa.[50] In this way, the internal political competition among subgroups and decision-making institutions forced an outcome with systemic ramifications which then reverberated in the internal competitions of others. American party politics and institutional competitions affected the decision to grant a visa. These subsequently influenced political competitions within Taiwan, reinforced Taiwanese preferences for national identity-building rather than bridge-building with China, made enmity between China and Taiwan more likely, and increased the chances that the US would have to intervene militarily on Taiwan's behalf, which it did in 1996.

The American decision also played into the internal competitions within China, by confirming a military hard-liner stance, in ascendance since the events in Tiananmen Square in 1989, that the only way to deal with Taiwan was through threats and force. Although there are moderates within China who, similar to the Boeing camp, focus on economic reform and wish to improve relations with Taiwan, intense bureaucratic competition has pitted them against hard-liners and the People's Liberation Army (PLA).[51] Moderates in the PRC have had some success in separating China's political and economic relationships with Taiwan, as has been done with Hong Kong and Macao, and all three are allowed to remain separate members of the WTO because they have their own rules governing imports. But Taiwan's status continues to evoke issues of historical memory and national identity that are linked to Chinese domestic political competitions. Frank Dikötter argues that Chinese nationalism is a form of "racial nationalism" in that the nation is "a

---

[50] Russell, "The 1996 Taiwan Strait Crisis," p. 1.
[51] See Joseph Wu, "Interview," *Frontline Special*, available at: www.pbs.org/wgbh/pages/frontline/shows/china/interviews/wu.html; and June Teufel Dreyer, "Regional Security Issues," *Journal of International Affairs* 49, no. 2 (winter 1996), pp. 391–411. For a valuable analysis of the influence of the Chinese "selectorate" on Chinese officials and their open economic policies in general, see Paul A. Papayoanou and Scott L. Kastner, "Sleeping with the (Potential) Enemy: Assessing the US Policy of Engagement with China," *Security Studies* 9, no. 1–2 (1999/2000), pp. 157–87.

pseudo-biological entity united by ties of blood" and portrays "outer China, from Taiwan to Tibet, as 'organic' parts of the sacred territory of the descendants of the Yellow Emperor that should be defended by military power if necessary."[52] Taiwanese talk of independence strikes at the heart of this entity, and hence it serves as a threat to the construction of Chinese national identity itself.

In addition, Dikötter notes that constitutive western outsiders have been essential in the formation and unity of China's national identity and the feeling of humiliation at their hands has been a catalyst for collective responsibility. Lowell Dittmer seconds this observation, noting that Taiwan is "the last remaining symbol of China's 'national humiliation'" and that "China has consistently viewed Taiwan as a missing piece to be appropriated in order that China's identity might be fully realized."[53] It is easy to see how American interference in the China–Taiwan relationship would constitute an ongoing humiliation for China and a catalyst in this regard. Small wonder, then, that even moderate subgroups within China had a difficult time challenging a hard-line stance toward Taiwan. As Joseph Wu puts it, "no political leader in China is able to appear to be soft on Taiwan, because that is dangerous to their own political career," and they are "likely to be portrayed by ... political opponents as too soft on Taiwan as a traitor in their nationalism."[54] The result has been regularly staged Chinese war games and missile tests in the Strait in order to warn Taiwan against overtly declaring its independence.

Not unexpectedly, this has the reverse effect of convincing the Taiwanese people that there are real differences between Taiwan and China, and that Taiwan should be considered a separate entity from (and not a province of) China. Since Taiwan began direct elections in the mid-1990s there has been a surge of support for the pro-independence candidates in both its presidential and parliamentary elections, and Chinese lobbying efforts to keep Taiwan out of the World Health Organization in 2003, just as it was battling the

---

[52] Frank Dikötter, "Culture, 'Race' and Nation: The Formation of National Identity in Twentieth Century China," *Journal of International Affairs* 49, no. 2 (winter 1996), pp. 590–605, at pp. 591 and 604.
[53] Lowell Dittmer, "Taiwan as a Factor in China's Quest for National Identity," *Journal of Contemporary China* 15, no. 49 (November 2006), pp. 671–86, at pp. 671 and 685.
[54] Wu, "Interview," pp. 2, 4.

SARS epidemic, further angered the Taiwanese population.[55] These heavy-handed Chinese policies, coupled with its military exercises in the Strait, were largely driven by a combination of China's own national identity politics and internal subgroup competitions over decisions and control of Chinese foreign policy-making. However what it then produced externally, in the politics of Taiwan and the US, was the very outcome it wished to avoid: a Taiwan bent on independence and a United States intent on protecting it.

These outcomes are not due to irrationality, stupidity, or lack of foresight, since the policy-makers involved are often acutely aware that the decisions made will have negative consequences elsewhere. Instead they are due to the primacy and immediacy of decision-making competitions within groups and are made expediently with the internal subgroup political struggles in mind. The fact that hard-line actions will have ramifications for the decision-making process in other groups, and hence produce consequences that could negatively affect one's own internal power struggles, is by political necessity an afterthought in a world of multiple national collectives.

The tail that wags the dog: Taiwanese identity politics

Although the link between US and Chinese internal and external competition helps us understand how foreign policy can be driven toward increased trade and conflict simultaneously, it is also necessary to look at internal developments within Taiwan since the late 1980s. Eric Eckholm notes that, "to some degree both the United States and China are a hostage to what the Taiwanese people decide," and Michael McDevitt characterizes Taiwan as "the tail that wags dogs."[56] These are unfair exaggerations to some extent, since it is China that refuses to yield on the issue of national sovereignty, and the US has its own geostrategic reasons for protecting Taiwan. Thus political and economic competition among subgroups within Taiwan has consistently and overtly been affected by the internal competitions of Chinese and American subgroups. But it is also true that national identity

---

[55] Kahn, "Taiwan Voters Weighing," p. A8.
[56] Erik Eckholm, "Interview," *Frontline Special*, available at: www.pbs.org/wgbh/pages/frontline/shows/china/interviews/eckholm.html, p. 2; and Michael McDevitt, "Taiwan: The Tail that Wags Dogs," *Asia Policy* 1, no. 1 (January 2006), pp. 69–93.

politics has become more overtly pertinent to internal political struggles for control of the Taiwanese state since it became a competitive democracy in the early 1990s. Democratization has been coupled with a process of national identity reconstruction that involves competing ethnic groups, nationalisms, political parties, and governing institutions, and these are as concerned with one another as they are with Chinese intentions or American commitments.

Whether democratization itself is entirely responsible for promoting this surge of Taiwanese nationalism and identity reconstruction is an open question, although certainly a legitimate one given the place democracies occupy in the "Kantian Tripod."[57] Wang and Liu observe it was after democratization that "local politicians started to advocate ethnic harmony" as a means "to maximize electoral votes," thus underscoring how greater self–other differentiation becomes part of internal electoral competitions.[58] On the other hand, issues of

---

[57] The phrase was coined by Oneal, Oneal, Maoz, and Russett, "The Liberal Peace," to indicate three phenomena (or legs of the tripod) that liberalism has traditionally assumed have pacifying effects: democracy, economic interdependence, and membership in international institutions. Much of the subsequent statistical work by these authors has found a correlation between all of these phenomena, for example, Oneal and Russett, "The Classical Liberals Were Right," and Bruce Russett and John Oneal, *Triangulating Peace: Democracy, Interdependence, and International Organizations* (New York: Norton, 2001), while other statistical work has found that the tripod correlation does not hold or must be analytically bounded, for example, Bearce and Omori, "How Do Commercial Institutions?"; Christopher Gelpi, and Joseph M. Grieco, "Economic Interdependence, the Democratic State, and the Liberal Peace," in Edward D. Mansfield and Brian M. Pollins, eds., *Economic Interdependence and International Conflict: New Perspectives on an Enduring Debate* (Ann Arbor: University of Michigan Press, 2003), pp. 44–59; Goenner, "Uncertainty of the Liberal Peace"; Omar M. G. Keshk, Brian M. Pollins, and Rafael Reuveny, "Trade Still Follows the Flag: The Primacy of Politics in a Simultaneous Model of Interdependence and Armed Conflict," *Journal of Politics* 66, no. 4 (November 2004), pp. 1155–79; Kim and Rousseau, "The Classical Liberals Were Half Right;" and Michael Mousseau, Håvard Hegre, and John R. Oneal, "How the Wealth of Nations Conditions the Liberal Peace," *European Journal of International Relations* 9, no. 2 (June 2003), pp. 277–314). The Taiwan case would seem to better support Mansfield and Snyder's claim that new democracies tend to be bellicose: Edward D. Mansfield and Jack Snyder, "Democratization and the Danger of War," *International Security* 20, no. 1 (summer 1995), pp. 5–38.

[58] T. Y. Wang and I-Chou Liu, "Contending Identities in Taiwan: Implications for Cross-Strait Relations," *Asian Survey* 44, no. 4 (July/August 2004), pp. 568–90, at p. 572. See also Chu, "Taiwan's National Identity Politics."

collective identity have always been an undercurrent in Taiwan's politics and its relationship to China. Taiwan is comprised of three ethnic groups – Taiwanese, Mainlander, and Aborigines – which are differentiated according to the date of their arrival in Taiwan.[59] The Aborigines are the original inhabitants of the island, from Malay–Polynesian descent, and constitute 1 percent of the population. The Taiwanese emigrated from mainland China before World War II and may be divided into two groups (Hoklos and Hakkas) based on linguistic differences. They constitute 85 percent of the population. Mainlanders are the Mandarin-speaking KMT, who retreated to Taiwan from 1945 to 1949, and constitute 14 percent of the population.

It was this latter group that came to politically and economically dominate the island, and did so through martial law and authoritarian rule from 1947 until the late 1980s. It banned the formation of political parties, jailed and executed political opponents, gave the military legal and censorship powers, and ruled Taiwan as a virtual police state. Although their economic policies also helped transform Taiwan into an advanced industrial economy, the KMT remained obsessed with reclaiming mainland China and this obsession determined some of the more important aspects of Taiwan's collective identity during that time. These included insisting that Mandarin be the ROC's official language while other local languages were banned, the adoption of Chinese-related textbooks and curriculums in schools, and restrictions on ethnic programming in TV and radio broadcasts.[60]

Alternatively, many "native" Taiwanese, who constituted the majority under KMT rule, did not share the goal of reunification with China and preferred Taiwanese independence instead. Early pro-independence movements were as much about secession from China as they were opposition to the KMT's authoritarian rule, and there was an ethnic link between China and the KMT that was in juxtaposition to the ethnic Taiwanese majority on the island. Joseph Kahn notes that for many Taiwanese, "they belong to a separate nation that has no more enduring connection to China than it does to Japan or

---

[59] Xiaokun Song, "Intellectual Discourses in the Taiwan Independence Movement," in Bruno Coppieters and Michel Huysseune, eds., *Secession, History and the Social Sciences* (Brussels: Brussels University Press, 2002) p. 228.

[60] Wang and Liu, "Contending Identities in Taiwan," p. 572.

even the Netherlands, its former colonial rulers."[61] Thus Taiwanese independence is not simply a political security issue; it is an ethnic issue and it involves whether Taiwanese identity is Mandarin Chinese, which is what the KMT insisted, or whether it is something different and indigenous. Taiwanese who favored independence developed underground or overseas movements, which later evolved into a rival political party to the KMT/Nationalists known as the Democratic Progressive Party (DPP).

This evolution would not have been possible if the KMT had not also allowed the ROC to evolve into the full-fledged democracy it is today, and it is that development which has provided pro-independence forces with legitimate access to and control over the state. Why the KMT did so has a great deal to do with the US decision in the 1970s to improve its relations with China at the expense of its formal relationship with Taiwan. This was a shock for ROC leaders, who were forced to consider alternative means to end Taiwan's sudden international isolation. Democratization was one means, because it could raise national consciousness and commitment, while simultaneously indicating to other nation-states that, since the ROC government had the legitimate support of its population, it had a legitimate claim to sovereignty (in opposition to China's claim that it was simply a province).[62] Economic reforms also encouraged democratic awareness, and pro-democracy activists joined forces with pro-independence movements so that a 1979 rally against authoritarian

---

[61] Kahn, "Taiwan Voters Weighing," p. A8.

[62] It is interesting to note that this last calculation is similar to the assumption that the Democratic League of Kosovo (LDK), and its leader Ibrahim Rugova, made in Kosovo in the early 1990s, but with entirely different results. The region was under Serbian control and the LDK held underground elections and developed what was essentially a parallel Albanian state functioning alongside or under the official Serb-dominated state, which had a democratically elected president and parliament, and its main responsibility was to develop and oversee parallel educational and health care systems for Albanian Kosovars. Rugova and other leaders of the LDK were convinced that if they could demonstrate to the west that they could handle their own affairs, they would be rewarded with their own independent nation-state when the war in Bosnia-Herzegovina ended. They were sorely disappointed, and that disappointment was one of the reasons for the development of the Kosovo Liberation Army (KLA) and the violence in Kosovo in 1998 and 1999. The comparison with Taiwan's situation is instructive on a number of levels, including comparative differences in great power strategic interests, claims of sovereignty, and use of force.

rule became violent and was crushed by force.[63] Rather than tighten its grip, however, the KMT began to publicly consider political reforms and it lifted martial law in 1987. The KMT also enacted major constitutional reforms, including the abolition of the National Assembly's role as an electoral college, and provisions for the direct, popular election for the president and the vice-president of the ROC beginning in 1996. The Nationalists won the first two presidential elections, while the DPP won the subsequent two.

The Chinese are intensely interested in these elections, and their rhetorical and physical hostility toward Taiwan increases just before Taiwanese presidential elections. The Chinese war games, missile tests, and live fire drills that were staged in 1996, and to which the US responded by sending two aircraft carrier groups to the Strait, were conducted in an attempt to scare Taiwanese voters away from the DPP candidates in the Taiwanese presidential election. Just prior to the 2000 elections, Chinese premier Zhu Rongji threatened Taiwan with "bloodshed" if the DPP were elected, and its military exercises staged a year after the elections were conducted both to express displeasure over the Taiwanese president's visit to New York and to send a warning not to continue pushing for independence. In fact, however, the DPP candidate, Chen Shui-bian, was elected in both 2000 and 2004, with a platform that sought to achieve independence by 2008 via constitutional referendums and amendments that involved restructuring the government, redefining Taiwan's territory, and changing the island's name from the Republic of China to the Republic of Taiwan.[64] To many observers at the time, this platform suggested that Chen "is determined to be the founding father of a new nation by 2008."[65]

Chen did not receive a parliamentary majority in December 2004, however, which he needed in order to pass pro-independence legislation, and his popularity among the Taiwanese electorate continued

[63] Xiaokun Song, "Intellectual Discourses in the Taiwan Independence Movement," in Bruno Coppieters and Michel Huysseune, eds., *Secession, History, and Social Sciences* (Brussels: VUB Brussels University Press, 2002), pp. 220–47, at pp. 234–5.
[64] Yao Chia-wen, interview by Ko Shu-Ling, "Forging a Democracy, One Step at a Time," *Taipei Times*, July 6, 2004.
[65] Yan Xuetong, a foreign policy expert at Beijing's Qinghua University, quoted in Joseph Kahn, "Election Fallout: Mounting Tension: Fears of Ethnic Conflict, and More Confrontation with Beijing," *New York Times*, March 22, 2004, p. A9.

to sink for a variety of reasons. But the project of reconstructing Taiwanese national identity as a means of confirming Taiwanese independence actually cuts across both political parties. The Nationalists did as much to initiate this reconstructed national identity project, in both encouraging democratization and winning the first two presidential elections, as the DPP has done to capitalize on it in subsequent presidential elections. Certainly it was the Nationalist Party that in the 1980s sought more cooperative ties with China, lifted travel bans there, held reconciliation talks with Chinese officials, and developed economic interdependent linkages with the mainland. In this latter goal the Nationalists could be characterized as the Taiwanese counterparts to the American Boeing camp and the Chinese economic moderates, both with regard to their electoral dependence on big business interests and in the belief that peaceful relations are required for efficient economic exchange. But it would be inaccurate to say that the Nationalists sought reconciliation with China at the expense of Taiwanese independence or that they actively promoted a common ethnic identity with China.

It was the Nationalists, after all, who sought to strengthen Taiwanese diplomatic relations and membership in IGOs, and it was the first democratically elected president, Lee Teng-hui, whose visit to the US caused such a furor in 1995. Lee was the first Taiwanese leader since the ROC's inception to have been born in Taiwan, rather than on the mainland, and he frequently referred to a "Taiwanese consciousness" or "sense of national identity," while publicly arguing that the ROC "has been sovereign and independent since its founding."[66] It was during Lee's second term in office that, as Britain was returning Hong Kong to China in 1997, Taiwan purposely conducted its own live military exercises in the Strait to demonstrate that it would not necessarily follow Hong Kong's example. It was also Lee's 1999 remarks that Taiwan and China enjoyed a "special state-to-state relationship," thus implying that Taiwan was sovereign, that angered China enough to end reconciliation talks for the second time. While the Nationalists may have talked of reunification, agreed publicly with the "one-China" principle, and encouraged greater economic exchange with China, their terms for reunification have always involved a

---

[66] Lee Teng-hui, "Understanding Taiwan: Bridging the Perception Gap," *Foreign Affairs* 78, no. 6 (November/December 1999), pp. 9–14, at p. 10.

Chinese conversion to democracy. Barring the immediate realization of this goal, the Nationalists pursued a dual-track foreign policy of economic cooperation with and continued political independence from China.

Analysts have also observed that it was the Nationalists who, as a means of consolidating electoral victories and Taiwanese political independence, engaged in a state-directed project to strengthen Taiwanese national identity. Chu notes that President Lee "turned out to be a diehard Taiwanese nationalist" who overhauled the state media, revamped school textbooks, and encouraged native literature and performing arts in an effort "to promote the burgeoning Taiwanese consciousness while deemphasizing Chinese culture and history."[67] The Taiwanese electorate was responsive to this identity project, and by the late 1990s the DDP could exploit this for its own political fortunes. The DPP's platform clearly aligned pro-independence with Taiwanese ethnicity. Under Chen's first term in office Taiwanese identity began "enjoying a tailwind of popular support," as the use of the Taiwanese dialect, Minnanese, increased dramatically, and numerous polls began to "show that a majority have begun identifying themselves as Taiwanese rather than Chinese."[68] The March 2004 presidential elections were cast "as a choice between subjugation to communist China and Taiwanese nationalism," thus evoking self–other differentiations that are typical of identity politics.[69] And Chen's dominant campaign theme was that the DPP were "the best promoters of Taiwan's national identity," while he "sometimes disparaged rivals as representing the interests of Beijing."[70] Chen also called for a "defensive referendum" on national security issues related to external threats to be held simultaneously with the Taiwanese election.

Thus one of the dominant themes of the 2004 campaign was Taiwanese nationalism and Taiwan's relationship to China. Chen's Nationalist opponent, Lien Chan, attempted to focus the election on Chen's handling of the economy by pointing out that economic exchanges with China could be harmed by insisting on independence. Chen's initiation of a defense referendum was also criticized for

[67] Chu, "Taiwan's National Identity Politics," p. 499. See also Lowell Dittmer, "Taiwan's Aim-Inhibited Quest for Identity and the China Factor," *Journal of Asian and African Studies* 40, no. 1/2 (April 2005), pp. 71–90.
[68] Kahn, "Taiwan Voters Weighing," p. A8.
[69] Ibid., p. A1 (continued on A8).   [70] Kahn, "Election Fallout," p. A9.

"purposefully baiting Beijing" and "putting domestic politics ahead of national security."[71] But during the campaign even Lien used Minnanese, thereby stressing his ethnic Taiwanese background, and rarely mentioned reunification. The margins of victory also indicated that Taiwanese nationalism played a role in the election. In the 2000 election, Chen won with 39 percent of the vote in a three-way race and with a moderate pro-independence platform. In 2004, Chen won with 50 percent of the vote and a moderate pro-independence platform explicitly linked to Taiwanese nationalism. As Liao Dai-chi, a political expert at National Sun Yat-sen University of Kaohsiung observed at the time, "any politician has to stand with 'Taiwan identity' to win election," and as another Taiwanese political expert put it, "this election was really the point of no return for Taiwanese identity," as "it gives Chen a mandate on that question."[72]

This increasing Taiwanese nationalism does not translate into a simplistic collective desire for Taiwan to declare itself a sovereign nation-state because, as Wang and Liu note, "it is the intertwining of the cultural and political components that constitutes the very essence of public discourse on national identity in Taiwan."[73] Public opinion polls conducted in 2002 by Wang and Liu demonstrated that while the majority in Taiwan self-identified as distinctly Taiwanese politically, a sizable portion of the population saw itself as ethnically Chinese. This distinction between politics and ethnicity is important, because these same polls indicated that while the public favored cultural and economic contacts with China, and wanted to avoid unnecessarily provoking it, the vast majority (almost 90 percent) preferred to remain an independent political entity if it meant integration on China's terms.[74]

[71] Ralph A. Cossa, "Taiwan Referendum: Waving a Red Flag," *Pacific Forum CSIS*, PacNet, No. 48 (December 3, 2003), Honolulu, Hawaii, available at: www.csis.org/media/csis/pubs/pac_0348.pdf.
[72] Quoted respectively in Kahn, "Taiwan Voters Weighing," p. A8, and Kahn, "Election Fallout," p. A9.
[73] Wang and Liu, "Contending Identities in Taiwan," p. 574.
[74] More specifically, Wang and Liu, p. 581, found that "less than 10% of respondents find the 'one country, two systems' formula appealing if it were to limit Taiwan's rights of judicial adjudication, conducting foreign affairs, or electing public officials." And 70 percent of respondents would oppose this formula if it meant limitations on Taiwan's ability to acquire arms from foreign countries. These findings are in direct contradiction to Chu's claims, "Taiwan's National Identity Politics," pp. 502–3 that public opinion polls

Thus the foreign policy that has consistently received the most public support, regardless of ethnicity, is not independence immediately but a continuation of the status quo (at 80 percent), and this is what both political parties have essentially pursued once in office and despite their campaign rhetoric.[75] In other words, both parties have used nationalism as a means to win elections, as well as maintain and even increase Taiwan's political distinction from China. In so doing, they are maintaining the Taiwanese state itself and their own base of power. At the same time, both the Nationalists and the DPP have sought greater economic and cultural contact with China, which serves the interests of particular domestic constituents who desire greater links for cultural and economic reasons.[76]

Increasing Taiwanese nationalism has not translated into a popular and rabid anti-Chinese movement seeking to sever all economic ties and declaring legal independence immediately and at all costs. It *has* served, however, as the context through which Taiwan's political and economic relations with China have been pursued and maintained by

demonstrate that Taiwanese national identification has plateaued, particularly among the younger generation.

[75] See not only Wang and Liu's findings, "Contending Identities in Taiwan," pp. 584–5, but also the public opinion data that is provided by the ROC government at their official website, and may be downloaded at www.mac.gov.tw. As Wu, "Interview," p. 1, notes, however, what exactly the Taiwanese people want "is complicated because status quo has been indicated or interpreted by different people in different ways," so that it has been defined alternatively as having already achieved independence, or as already having one China, two systems.

[76] The result is that even the DPP's pro-independence goals were moderated once in office. After Chen Shui-bian won the 2000 election, he stated that he would not declare independence unless Taiwan came under military attack, and (in a similar vein to Lee) claimed that there was no need to make such declarations since Taiwan was already sovereign. Taiwanese investment in mainland China also grew at a faster pace under Chen's first administration than it had under Lee's, prompting one optimistic economist to claim, "I'm convinced that the cross-strait issue will resolve in 10 years," in Smith, "Signs in China and Taiwan." Kastner, "Does Economic Integration?," pp. 331–3, provides an analysis of this growing Taiwanese business constituency with links to mainland China and its preferences with regard to Chinese relations. Kastner points out, p. 332, that it is unclear how much it influences Taiwan's foreign policy, and notes that Chen still won a second term, despite ongoing provocations, "because he was able to craft a winning coalition that included both those seeking to build a stronger Taiwanese identity and those who are threatened, economically, by growing commercial links with Mainland China."

both parties. Some (although not all) Taiwanese businesses clearly profit from access to China, and these interests have pressured the Taiwanese government to maintain good relations with the mainland. At the same time, officials in Taipei have pursued economic engagement with China within the domestic context of rising Taiwanese national identity. The parties have encouraged the reconstruction of a Taiwanese national identity as a means of winning elections against one another, as well as maintaining the Taiwanese state as a politically distinct entity from China. Paradoxically, the increased nationalism this has unleashed helps maintain and even strengthen a division that is, in itself, the source of the security threat Taiwan faces. This places collective difference on the first rung of the causal ladder, making the recognition of rational self-interests in capitalist profits secondary to the maintenance of these political divisions. As it turns out, national collective difference is the context for both the increased tensions *and* the increased economic exchange.

Far from being a phenomenon that is due to the state's rational calculation of capitalist profit on behalf of society, then, "trading with the enemy" in the China–Taiwan case has resulted from their continued political division and the desire on the part of the Taiwanese state leaders (and the majority of Taiwan's people) to maintain that division in practice. Taiwan has no desire to integrate on China's terms, nor does it wish to provoke China into an attack. To walk this fine line between independence and provocation, Taiwanese decision-makers have pursued policies of military balancing and economic linkage simultaneously. This is why the Taiwanese state engages in trade with China even as it prepares to fight it, although "trading with the enemy" also takes on a different nuance when a portion of your population ethnically identifies itself with that "enemy." The primary goal that Taiwan's presidential political parties appear to have shared is the maintenance of political division, while avoiding an outright attack by China. Yet the project of Taiwanese identity reconstruction has external repercussions, because it pulls Taiwanese political parties, elections, and society toward greater nationalism and independence, thereby simultaneously exacerbating tensions with the Chinese government. This has led to overt hostility and aggression toward Taiwan by Chinese officials, which has had the effect of driving Taiwanese national unity and the conviction that it should remain independent from China. Thus the "politics of national identity" has become "a major driving force boxing Beijing, Washington, and Taipei into an ever-tighter strategic corner over the past few years."[77]

In this evolving, intertwined, competitive context, Taiwan's relationship with China is, simultaneously, an ethnic identity issue, an electoral issue, an economic issue, and a security issue. The project of national identity reconstruction has reinforced Taiwan's material and ideational separation from China, by portraying China as the other against which a unified Taiwanese identity may be known and manifest, *even as* its policy-makers have encouraged greater economic linkages with China. The pursuit of profits via economic exchange – whether for the benefit of society or particular constituents – is secondary to the goal of maintaining this political separation from China. It is little wonder, then, that Dittmer observes economic integration has not "had any perceptible impact on 'creeping independence' on the island," and that "from the perspective of classic political economy, the implication is counter-intuitive: where one lives is more determinative of political preferences than the functional logic of one's economic interests."[78] From the perspective of economic nationalism, on the other hand, these outcomes are perfectly understandable. What is driving the increased economic exchanges is not the desire to maximize profits, nor the concomitant shift in the cognitive mind-set of decision-makers that is anticipated in the liberal interdependence literature. What is driving the economic interdependence is a combination of nationalism, electoral competitions, and the territorially autonomous structures of the state that liberal interdependence arguments assume must be displaced for higher levels of exchange to even occur.

Peril despite profit: whither the interdependent peace dividend?

The process that is occurring in Taiwan is one that underscores precisely why a neoclassical realist analysis of the interdependence-promotes-peace proposition is necessary. It is a process in which the Nationalist–DPP electoral competition over the levers of internal power (i.e. the state and decision-making institutions) has been intimately related to and just as important as Taiwan's external

---

[77] Chu "Taiwan's National Identity Politics," p. 486.
[78] Dittmer, "Taiwan's Aim-Inhibited Quest," p. 78.

competitions with other states. Those internal competitions have involved a process of national identity reconstruction which pushes the very envelope that China, due to its own identity politics, has consistently warned should not be opened. As Thomas Christensen notes, "What will determine whether China takes actions that will lead to Sino-American conflict will likely be politics, perceptions, and coercive diplomacy involving specific military capabilities in specific geographic and political contexts, not the overall balance of military power across the Pacific or across the Taiwan Strait."[79] The more Taiwan has pushed, the more it has promoted a hard-line, nationalist response in China that encourages increasing nationalism in Taiwan. Meanwhile, the more aggressively China acts toward Taiwan, the more likely it has been that the US will intercede on Taiwan's behalf, since both American political parties are committed to doing so and Chinese aggression strengthens the hand of the containment crowd in the ongoing conceptual debates within US policy-making communities.

The phenomenon of economic interdependence is caught up in this matrix of internal competition and identity politics, and it should only be understood within this context. The Boeing camp in each country has acted rationally to protect its own economic interests within the interdependent relationship, and on this score it is functionally effi-cient for particular types of corporations, industrial sectors, and their elected or bureaucratic representatives to argue for moderation. But the liberal interdependence literature has taken this argument and turned it into an explanation for the international phenomenon of interdependence itself, as well as a normative justification that it can deliver more peaceful international relations. The US–China–Taiwan case underscores why the phenomenon should not be treated with such sanguinity. Interdependence among nation-states does not arise from a commonly shared recognition of joint profit and a cognitive shift among state decision-makers that cooperation and peace are the best means to obtain these profits for themselves or particular interest groups or corporations or society as a whole.

Instead, economic interdependence occurs within the context of political competition between nation-states as well as inside them.

---

[79] Thomas J. Christensen, "Posing Problems Without Catching Up: China's Rise and Challenges for US Security Policy," *International Security* 25, no. 4 (spring 2001), pp. 5–40, at p. 13.

Such internal competitions involve the fundamental issue of who controls the decision-making structures that allocate resources within the nation-state. Those structures are the subject of intense competition, and controlling them involves more than demonstrating that profit can be maximized, whether it is for everyone or just for particular con- stituents. It involves identity politics – that is, the ongoing process of national identity reconstruction both internally and in juxtaposition to other national groupings – and this process of identity politics works to reinforce nationalism, not displace it. It is this linkage between intra- group competition and national identity politics that drives interde- pendence. The ongoing relevance of nationalism and collective identity difference to world affairs means that the purported interdependence peace dividend will not be cashed in any time soon.

5 Neoclassical realism and the national interest: presidents, domestic politics, and major military interventions

COLIN DUECK

Presidents of the United States have frequently decided to engage in military interventions abroad, but existing explanations of such intervention tend to emphasize *either* third-image (international) *or* second-image (domestic) factors. Third-image theories of intervention point to factors such as the international distribution of power and external threats. Second-image theories of intervention point to factors such as electoral incentives, together with the governing coalition's economic or political interests in war. However, as Jeffrey Taliaferro, Steven Lobell, and Norrin Ripsman argue in chapter 1, neoclassical realist theories generate more explanatory leverage over the national security behavior of states by incorporating both the domestic and international milieus. In this chapter I put forward a neoclassical realist model and show exactly how, why, and to what extent domestic politics matters in shaping US military interventions abroad. According to this model, when facing the possibility of major military intervention, presidents usually begin by consulting what they perceive to be the national security interests of the United States. Subsequently however, they consider how best to pursue those conceptions of the national interest in the light of domestic political incentives and constraints. These constraints frequently lead presidents to implement the precise conduct, framing, and timing of US intervention in a manner that may appear puzzling or anomalous from a neorealist perspective. In this sense, domestic politics "matters," not as a primary cause of intervention, but rather as a powerful influence on its exact form. I lay out the theoretical rationale for this approach, and test it empirically in two historical cases – Korea and Vietnam – using archival evidence along with secondary sources. I then conclude with observations and implications regarding the current war in Iraq.

Third image, second image, and military intervention

The issue of why states engage in military intervention is really a subset of the broader question of the causes of war. In his classic study, *Man, the State, and War*, Kenneth Waltz discerned three "images," or three kinds of theories, that are typically used to explain the outbreak of war: the first image, at the level of individual decision-makers; the second image, at the level of domestic politics or socioeconomic systems; and the third image, at the level of the international system.[1] Leaving aside for a moment Waltz's "first image," the dichotomy between domestic and international causes of war can certainly be used as a starting point for explaining military intervention.

Realists have long maintained that military intervention and war have their source in the anarchic nature of the international system. The realist or third-image premise is that because the international system is anarchic, states are forced to rely upon their own devices in order to survive. One of these devices is military intervention. International pressures are therefore the ultimate cause of military intervention on the part of individual states. Realists, however, differ on the extent and manner in which international conditions can be said to cause particular military interventions. In *Theory of International Politics* and elsewhere, Kenneth Waltz denies that his neorealist balance of power theory can be used to explain the foreign policies of individual states; consequently he would deny that it can be used to explain particular military interventions. Other realists try to account for patterns of military intervention by pointing to factors such as the international distribution of power, or state-centered perceptions of external threat to vital national interests. Joanne Gowa, for example, suggests that a rise in relative power makes the use of force by American presidents more likely. Stephen Krasner, on the other hand, accounts for US Cold War interventions in Latin America by pointing to autonomous conceptions of the national interest on the part of leading state officials. Realists therefore disagree on the precise mechanism by which third-image or international factors cause military intervention, but they share in

[1] Kenneth N. Waltz, *Man, the State, and War* (New York: Columbia University Press, 1959).

common the belief that such factors are the best starting points for explanation.[2]

Neoclassical realists bridge the gap between the second and the third images, arguing that, while the international system imposes certain generalizable pressures on all countries, foreign policy behavior can only be explained by layering in unit-specific variables.[3] They suggest that international systemic pressures are the most important cause behind the foreign policy behavior of particular states, but only through the mediating effect of unit-level variables such as elite perceptions and domestic political conditions. As Taliaferro, Lobell, and Ripsman suggest in the introduction, even if leading state officials seek to advance the national interest, the internal characteristics of states may constrain their ability to do so. A distinct contribution of neoclassical realism therefore lies in the exploration of mechanisms by which domestic political dynamics force leaders into seemingly counterproductive foreign policies. In the final analysis, however, neoclassical realists share with other realists a "top-down" conception of the state, in which systemic factors powerfully pressure and constrain foreign policy behavior. This is the approach taken by other authors in this volume, including Ripsman and Taliaferro. The implication is that the ultimate cause of particular military interventions lies with the third image, and that even the primary and immediate cause is likely to be some perception of national interest on the part of state officials rather than narrow domestic concerns per se.

The contrary argument – that is, that political leaders are more likely to use force abroad for domestic reasons – has an ancient lineage in the study of international relations, drawing upon liberal as well as Marxist traditions. Liberals have frequently suggested that democracies would be less likely than autocracies to engage in war for purely domestic reasons; Marxists have argued that socialist regimes

---

[2] Waltz, *Man, the State, and War*, chaps. 6–8; Kenneth Waltz, *Theory of International Politics* (Reading, MA: Addison-Wesley, 1979), pp. 116–28; Joanne Gowa, "Politics at the Water's Edge: Parties, Voters, and the Use of Force Abroad," *International Organization* 52, no. 2 (spring 1998), pp. 307–24; Stephen Krasner, *Defending the National Interest* (Princeton, NJ: Princeton University Press, 1978); and Robert Gilpin, "The Richness of the tradition of Political Realism," *International Organization* 38, no. 2 (spring 1984), pp. 287–304.

[3] Gideon Rose, "Neoclassical Realism and Theories of Foreign Policy," *World Politics* 51, no. 1 (October 1998), pp. 144–72.

would be less likely than capitalist ones to resort to such behavior. The relevant literature in this regard is known as diversionary war theory. According to this school of thought, leaders use international disputes to externalize and sublimate domestic conflict. External conflict, so the argument goes, distracts and refocuses attention from domestic disagreements toward international ones. Lewis Coser was an early proponent of this approach, suggesting that "in-group" cohesion is strengthened by conflict with "out-groups."[4] A wide body of contemporary work in international relations also explains foreign policy choices of all types by referring to domestic coalitional profiles. Authors such as Peter Trubowitz, Helen Milner, Jack Snyder, and Michael Hiscox conceive of trade policy or national security policy as essentially the result of specific sectoral and/or sectional interests, pulling and hauling for special advantage.[5] For these authors, foreign policy does not reflect the national interest per se. Instead, specific diplomatic, military, and foreign economic strategies reflect the ability of narrow, subnational coalitions to capture the levers of state power and direct policy toward their particular interests. The chapters in this volume by Fordham, and to a lesser extent Lobell, are influenced by this tradition. Especially in areas such as trade policy, this approach is, if anything, the preponderant one in political science, and the relevance to presidential uses of force is not hard to find. If major foreign policy decisions are in essence the reflection of narrow special interests, then domestically motivated military interventions would appear to be a predictable pattern of behavior for presidents.

The idea that American presidents specifically engage in military intervention for domestic political reasons has been investigated by political scientists, and has a theoretical basis in the literature on presidential uses of force. Authors within this tradition seek to

---

[4] Waltz, *Man, the State, and War*, chap. 4; Lewis Coser, *The Functions of Social Conflict* (New York: Free Press, 1956). See also Jack Levy, "The Diversionary Theory of War: A Critique," in Manus Midlarsky, ed., *Handbook of War Studies* (Boston: Unwin Hyman, 1989), pp. 259–88.

[5] Peter Trubowitz, *Defining the National Interest: Conflict and Change in American Foreign Policy* (Chicago: University of Chicago Press, 1998); Helen Milner, *Resisting Protectionism* (Princeton, NJ: Princeton University Press, 1988); Jack Snyder, *Myths of Empire: Domestic Politics and International Ambition* (Ithaca, NY: Cornell University Press, 1993); Michael Hiscox, *International Trade and Political Conflict* (Princeton, NJ: Princeton University Press, 2002).

determine what kinds of conditions make presidents more likely to engage in the use of force overseas. In an influential and trend-setting 1986 article, Charles Ostrom and Brian Job argued that presidents are more likely to use force when politically unsuccessful at home, or when economic conditions are bad. Other articles since then have built upon or modified these basic insights. Clifton Morgan and Ken Bickers, for example, suggested in a 1992 piece that presidents are more likely to use force when faced with a loss of support from core partisan supporters. Benjamin Fordham argued in 1998 that high unemployment makes the use of force more likely. What these authors have in common is the thesis that presidents engage in the use of force primarily on the basis of domestic rather than international conditions.[6] To understand why this is unlikely in the case of major military interventions undertaken by a US president requires a little elaboration.

Why presidents are reluctant to intervene for domestic political reasons

There are good reasons to believe that presidents are unlikely to engage in major military interventions for second-image reasons. For one thing, the domestic political incentives for such behavior are simply not that strong, and if anything run in the opposite direction – that is, away from military conflict. The prospect of war is rarely popular with the American public. Certainly, a segment of the public will often rally to the president's side in the immediate aftermath of a decision for intervention, but this "rally-around-the-flag" effect is usually superficial and short-lived. It is also highly contextual, and impossible to reliably or wholly manufacture apart from the inherent circumstances of the case. Mass public opinion in the United States, that is to say, is not infinitely malleable; the public is to some extent able to make broad distinctions between potential cases of military intervention based upon the plausibility of both the stated interest and

---

[6] Charles W. Ostrom and Brian L. Job, "The President and the Political Use of Force," *American Political Science Review* 80, no. 2 (June 1986), pp. 541–66; T. Clifton Morgan and Kenneth N. Bickers, "Domestic Discontent and the External Use of Force," *Journal of Conflict Resolution* 36, no. 1 (March 1992), pp. 25–52; Benjamin Fordham, "The Politics of Threat Perception and the Use of Force: A Political Economy Model of US Uses of Force, 1949–1994," *International Studies Quarterly* 42, no. 3 (September 1998), pp. 567–90.

the stated threat. If military conflict turns out to be costly and prolonged, support for war within the United States inexorably declines. And given the inevitable uncertainties of military intervention, it is usually hard to guarantee that a given intervention will not turn sour, undermining rather than bolstering the president's popularity. Military intervention overseas is therefore potentially a very risky and costly means by which to boost one's domestic political standing. Moreover, presidents *know* all of this to be true, or they would be unlikely to become president in the first place. They know that war is not particularly popular with the American public; they know that rally effects are temporary and unreliable; they know that the public will eventually turn against costly military ventures; and they know that such ventures are often uncertain. For all of these reasons, they are unlikely to engage in military intervention simply as a way of overcoming domestic political problems. On the contrary, they are only likely to do so if they (rightly or wrongly) perceive some compelling external threat.

Similarly, during an election campaign, if military conflict seems probable overseas, presidents are unlikely to campaign on a straightforwardly pro-war platform. Instead, they are more likely to stress the ways in which they seek to avoid war, precisely because they understand the electoral advantages of such a public stance. Indeed, it is worth noting that no American president over the past century has ever campaigned for election or reelection in peacetime on a pro-war platform. The pattern seems to be that the immediate prospect of elections pushes US presidents *away* from decisions for war, while the successful conclusion of such elections frees up their hands to pursue interventions that they may very well have viewed as necessary in the first place.[7]

Not only do domestic incentives within the United States tend to work against major military intervention, but the very assumption that presidents focus *solely* upon narrow domestic political concerns when making such decisions is itself strangely unrealistic. There are a whole host of considerations that presidents take into account when

---

[7] Richard Brody, *Assessing the President: The Media, Elite Opinion, and Public Support* (Stanford, CA: Stanford University Press, 1991), pp. 57–67, 77–8; Kurt Taylor Gaubatz, *Elections and War* (Stanford, CA: Stanford University Press, 1999), pp. 49–50, 78–9, 126–27, 142–5; John Mueller, *War, Presidents and Public Opinion* (New York: John Wiley, 1973), pp. 60, 65; Bruce Russett, *Controlling the Sword: The Democratic Governance of National Security* (Cambridge, MA: Harvard University Press, 1990), pp. 35, 38–49.

deciding for or against the use of force overseas, and what many of these other considerations amount to is the president's perception of the national interest. Presidents, that is to say, often have distinctive, internalized ideas and convictions on matters of national security, and these convictions in turn shape decisions for war. The fact that outside analysts may not agree with such convictions does not automatically invalidate their reality or sincerity. Indeed, most past US presidents of any party would have viewed it as outrageous to engage in a major foreign war primarily for narrow political gain. It is therefore remarkable with what ease and lack of empirical support such accusations are commonly made. But even assuming that presidents conduct life and death decisions regarding major military interventions primarily with an eye toward reelection, there is little reason to believe that electoral incentives usually favor intervention. Presidents are ultimately punished or rewarded by the voters for their ability to provide crucial public goods such as national security. If the public comes to believe that a president is pursuing narrow self-interest or private goods, in the form of a domestically driven military adventure, rather than responding to some genuine or at least plausible external threat, then that president will suffer politically. International threats have varying degrees of severity, and the American public knows as much. It is precisely because such threats are variable, externally presented, and not entirely subjective that presidents must respond to them – if only for domestic political reasons – with some discrimination.[8] In sum, within the American context, domestic politics is unlikely to be the immediate cause behind the resort to war. Yet there is no doubt that domestic political or second-image considerations "matter" in shaping presidential uses of force. The question then becomes not *whether*, but exactly *how* and to what *extent* do domestic political pressures determine patterns of US military intervention?

A neoclassical realist model of military intervention

A compelling alternative to second-image explanations of US military intervention lies in neoclassical realism. A neoclassical realist

---

[8] Gowa, "Politics at the Water's Edge"; James Meernik, "Presidential Decision Making and the Political Use of Military Force," *International Studies Quarterly* 38, no. 1 (March 1994), pp. 121–38.

model begins by positing that state officials inevitably have some conception of the national interest in the face of potential external threats. These conceptions may be misguided but they are nevertheless genuine. The anarchic condition of the international arena forces states to pay close attention to their security, and military intervention is one tool by which policy-makers attempt to pursue this goal. Neoclassical realist authors would add, however, that domestic political or second image causes can have a powerful impact on patterns of military intervention, shaping or skewing foreign policy choices in ways that are surprising from a neorealist perspective.[9]

The process of identifying national interests and then mobilizing resources to pursue those interests is not a given, and cannot even be usefully taken as such. As the contributions to this volume by Schweller and Taliaferro demonstrate, a wide variety of domestic political factors may influence this process. Military intervention can be very costly in societal terms; state officials face varying domestic political hurdles in building support for such interventions. Insofar as domestic political conditions are loose and permissive, both the fact and the form of military intervention will tend to follow state officials' perceptions of the national interest. Insofar as domestic conditions are restrictive and constraining, these officials face a difficult choice. They can give up pursuing what they believe to be a necessary policy course, or they can redouble their efforts to mobilize and build support for intervention. In the latter case, this may involve pursuing or packaging the decision in such a way as to create new sources of domestic support. Yet these very efforts to increase support at home may cause a particular military intervention to be implemented in a manner that is puzzling from a neorealist perspective. Under such circumstances, domestic political conditions certainly have a significant influence on

---

[9] Rose, "Neoclassical Realism and Theories of Foreign Policy"; Randall Schweller, "The Progressiveness of Neoclassical Realism," in Colin Elman and Miriam Fendius Elman, eds., *Progress in International Relations Theory* (Cambridge, MA: MIT Press, 2003), pp. 311–47; Jeffrey Taliaferro, "Security Seeking under Anarchy: Defensive Realism Revisited," *International Security* 25, no. 3 (winter 2000/1), pp. 128–61, at pp. 132–5, 142–3; Fareed Zakaria, *From Wealth to Power* (Princeton, NJ: Princeton University Press, 1998), chap. 2; Colin Dueck, "Realism, Culture and Grand Strategy: Explaining America's Peculiar Path to World Power," *Security Studies* 14, no. 2 (winter 2004/5), pp. 195–231.

the precise manner of intervention, but they cannot be said to be its ultimate cause.[10]

In the United States, domestic political constraints on military intervention are especially noticeable, for both institutional and cultural reasons. As in any democracy, leading state officials contend with an array of interest groups, public opinion, normative considerations, electoral pressures, and legislative prerogatives when making foreign policy decisions. These domestic constraints are multiplied in America by the effects of a deliberate division of power between Congress and the president, a classically liberal political culture, and an exceptionally robust civil society. Nevertheless, even in the case of the United States, state officials have considerable autonomy with which to formulate and pursue foreign policy goals. Presidents typically have more leeway over national security policy than over domestic issue areas. Congress and public opinion set ultimate limits to executive control over foreign policy, but these limitations are usually rather broad and elastic. If a president decides to engage in a given military intervention, he automatically holds major advantages over any potential domestic opponents in terms of prestige, position, and information. Domestic political constraints certainly influence the president, but with decisions for intervention the president also has some ability to bend and shape domestic political constraints. Indeed, presidents invest considerable effort in building domestic support – often successfully – for major military ventures. If the president decides to take the nation into war, a significant portion of American opinion will frequently follow the president's lead and hope for the best, especially during the early phases of intervention.[11] On matters

---

[10] Thomas Christensen, *Useful Adversaries: Grand Strategy, Domestic Mobilization, and Sino-American Conflict, 1947–1958* (Princeton, NJ: Princeton University Press, 1986), pp. 3–7, 13, 28; Charles Kupchan, *The Vulnerability of Empire* (Ithaca, NY: Cornell University Press, 1996), pp. 22–3; Michael Mastanduno, David A. Lake, and G. John Ikenberry, "Toward a Realist Theory of State Action," *International Studies Quarterly* 33, no. 4 (December 1989), pp. 457–74; Randall L. Schweller, "Unanswered Threats: A Neoclassical Realist Theory of Underbalancing," *International Security* 29, no. 2 (fall 2004), pp. 159–201, at pp. 161, 169.

[11] Benjamin Page and Robert Shapiro, *The Rational Public* (Chicago: University of Chicago Press, 1992), pp. 348–50; Jon Western, *Selling Intervention and War: The Presidency, the Media, and the American Public* (Baltimore, MD: Johns Hopkins University Press, 2005), pp. 4–5, 16–17.

of military intervention, therefore, the president is neither entirely free, nor entirely constrained, but rather "semi-constrained," with a certain range of choice and maneuver in the face of domestic political factors. This semi-constrained condition creates both an opportunity and an incentive. The opportunity is for the president to pursue perceived national security interests in something like the manner he sees fit; the incentive is to do so in such a way as to also create, build, and maximize domestic political support.

A neoclassical realist model of American military intervention, therefore, has the following features. First, executive officials necessarily hold some conception of the national interest, and of potential threats to that interest emanating from developments abroad. Second, when perceived external threats to vital interests seem to necessitate military intervention, executive officials consider how best to pursue such intervention in the light of domestic political conditions. The desire to build domestic support for intervention may, for example, encourage the president to oversimplify circumstances in his public rhetoric. The same desire may also lead him to add or subtract elements of intervention that might have been desirable from a purely international, realist perspective. None of this is to excuse any president's manner of portraying or implementing a given intervention in ethical or legal terms. Indeed, if presidents have some freedom of decision over such matters, as I have argued, then strictly speaking they cannot be said to have been "forced" into any particular foreign policy decision. Rather, this is only to identify and explain a striking pattern in the manner in which the United States tends to go to war. That pattern, simply put, is that presidents do not undertake major military interventions primarily out of domestic political concerns. Yet the specific forms of intervention, including their timing, implementation, and public representation, are frequently powerfully influenced by domestic political constraints and incentives.

The question of whether presidents engage in major military interventions for domestic political reasons, or whether they instead go to war in the manner I suggest, is ultimately an empirical one. Fortunately the number of such cases is rather limited. If, for the sake of argument, I define "major military interventions" as involving at least one hundred thousand American troops sent into a combat situation, then there are only four such cases since World War II: Korea 1950, Vietnam 1965, Iraq 1991, and Iraq 2003. Archival evidence for the latter two cases has yet to be released. I propose in the next few pages to undertake a limited, comparative case study, using both the Korea and Vietnam cases, and supplement them with a brief additional discussion of the current war in Iraq. The analysis of each case will be based upon primary as well as secondary sources. The method will be that of structured, focused comparison. The goal will be to confirm or disconfirm, insofar as we can, a neoclassical realist model of military intervention, as opposed to a primarily domestic political model of the same.[12]

Before going into the details of each case, the issue of the distinctively structural causes of these three interventions must be addressed. In all three cases, international structural factors acted as a crucial permissive cause of intervention. That is to say, the United States was powerful enough in 1950, 1965, 1991, and 2003 to intervene in Korea, Vietnam, and Iraq, respectively, without encountering overwhelming opposition from other major powers. America's very considerable relative capabilities gave it the opportunity to act militarily in each case, if it chose to do so. This same relative power gave the United States the luxury of being able to define its national security interests in an exceptionally broad manner in all three cases.[13] In this sense, America's relative power was a permissive cause of military intervention, and an absolutely necessary one at that. Beyond this, however, the precise impact of structural factors becomes hazier. As Taliaferro, Lobell, and Ripsman indicate, neoclassical realists understand that structural or systemic imperatives are often ambiguous. One can argue that the US was forced to intervene in each of these cases due to some intolerable external threat, but in fact the crucial

---

[12] The question of whether presidents employ *minor* uses of force for domestic political reasons is a separate one, which has received much attention in large-N studies already, and is beyond the scope of this chapter. There is no reason to assume that the causal mechanism will necessarily be identical in such cases to the one laid out here. But by process-tracing the impact of domestic politics upon major interventions, we can at least suggest potential hypotheses and avenues of research for the study of minor uses of force as well.

[13] Waltz, *Theory of International Politics*, pp. 188–90, 194–5, 205–6; Melvyn Leffler, *A Preponderance of Power: National Security, the Truman Administration, and the Cold War* (Stanford, CA: Stanford University Press, 1992); Gareth Porter, *Perils of Dominance: Imbalance of Power and the Road to War in Vietnam* (Berkeley: University of California Press, 2006); Colin Dueck, "Ideas and Alternatives in American Grand Strategy, 2000–2004," *Review of International Studies* 30, no. 4 (October 2004), pp. 511–35.

immediate variable was the perception of it on the part of senior officials, and not the international system as such. Here we have already left the pristine realm of international structure and descended into the murky reality of policy ideas and belief systems. We can certainly say that particular international factors and events made the perception of threat more *likely* in each case, especially in combination with reigning policy paradigms. The invasion of South Korea by the North in 1950 made American intervention very probable, given the paradigmatic framework of anti-communist containment. Given that same framework, the impending collapse of South Vietnam in 1964–5 appeared to make US intervention quite pressing. And the terrorist attacks of 2001 made it more likely that American officials would be newly inclined to militarily overthrow hostile, "rogue state" dictators such as Saddam Hussein, particularly under a paradigm of American primacy. International conditions and events therefore permitted certain courses of military action, and also made them more probable. But the immediate cause of intervention, in all three cases, was the perception of vital national interests on the part of leading state officials. This is still distinct from and in opposition to a primarily second image or "bottom-up" explanation, in that leaders are not presumed to have been motivated primarily by domestic political concerns. The question then becomes: even if leaders sought to pursue their understanding of the national interest in response to international pressures, how exactly *did* domestic politics influence the resort to war in each case?

Korea, 1950

On June 25, 1950, North Korean forces attacked the Republic of South Korea. From their first meeting at Blair House that very same day, President Truman and his advisors took it for granted that this attack represented a dramatic and intolerable threat to US interests. For one thing, a unified communist Korea would constitute a direct danger to one of America's key allies, Japan. But the real threat was indirect. Under the strategy of containment, conceived and implemented after World War II, the United States was presumed to have a vital interest in checking communist expansion worldwide. The entire global network of US-led, anti-communist alliances and commitments was viewed as being highly interdependent. The Korean invasion was assumed to be part of a global strategy under the guidance and direction of the Soviet Union.[14] This attack therefore seemed to represent an unusually frontal challenge to containment and to the United States on the part of the Soviet Union. The blatant and stunning nature of the North's attack helped clarify matters. Memories of appeasement and the 1930s were fresh in everyone's mind. Truman, in particular, was convinced that Korea represented the first real test of the United Nations and of the principle of collective security since 1945. A failure to respond would no doubt send a message of weakness around the world. The USSR and its clients would be emboldened; US allies and neutrals would be tempted to doubt the credibility of American commitments. A vigorous American response, conversely, would demonstrate to Moscow the costs of aggression. For all of these reasons, Truman heartily agreed with General Omar Bradley, chairman of the Joint Chiefs of Staff, that "the Korean situation offered as good an occasion for action in drawing the line as anywhere." Within six days of the North's attack, consequently, American officials entered into their first major military intervention since the Second World War by deploying US air, sea, and ground forces to Korea, while securing United Nations approval for their actions.[15]

The public reasons given for American intervention in Korea were in many cases simpler, but not unrepresentative of those given in private among elite officials. In a major July 19, 1950 radio and television address to the American public, for example, Truman hit on several regular themes: that the North Korean attack had been "an act of raw aggression, without a shadow of justification"; that it demonstrated a new willingness of "the international Communist

---

[14] Since the end of the Cold War, archival evidence has suggested that the USSR did in fact play a critical supporting role in the North Korean attack – albeit under considerable prodding from Pyongyang. See Sergei Goncharov, John Lewis, and Xue Litai, *Uncertain Partners: Stalin, Mao, and the Korean War* (Stanford, CA: Stanford University Press, 1993), pp. 130–54; Kathryn Weathersby, "The Soviet Role in the Early Phase of the Korean War: New Documentary Evidence," *Journal of American–East Asian Relations* 2, no. 4 (winter 1993), pp. 425–58.

[15] See "Intelligence Estimate Prepared by the Estimates Group, Office of Intelligence Research, Department of State," and "Memorandum of Conversation, by the Ambassador at Large (Jessup)," both dated June 25, 1950, in *Foreign Relations of the United States* [hereafter, *FRUS*] *1950*, vol. VII: *Korea* (Washington, DC: United States Government Printing Office, 1976), pp. 148–54, 157–61, at p. 158.

movement ... to use armed invasion to conquer independent
nations"; that it represented "an outright breach of the peace and a
violation of the Charter of the United Nations"; and that "free nations
have learned the fateful lesson of the 1930s ... that ... aggression
must be met firmly." In such addresses, Truman did not go into great
detail regarding the geopolitical subtleties of his administration's
thinking. But he did give encapsulated versions of a number of his
genuine core concerns; he made many of the same points in private.
Indeed, one of the most striking things about Truman's public
rhetoric was how constrained, sparse, and careful it was during the
early days of the Korean War. In hoping to keep the Korean intervention limited in its effects – from both an international, and a
domestic perspective – Truman went so far as to deny that the United
States was at war at all.[16]

Domestic incentives certainly existed for Truman to intervene
militarily in Korea. For several months prior to June 1950, his
administration had weathered fierce and continuing attacks from
Republican critics such as Senator Joseph McCarthy (R-WI) on the
issues of China policy, communism, and domestic subversion.
Decisive action by the president would presumably have the effect of
quietening such criticism, at least temporarily. As the liberal journal
The Nation put it in July 1950, "McCarthyism will have a hollow
sound when applied to the government that stood up to the
Russians."[17] Truman's series of decisions between June 25 and June 30
to provide major military support to South Korea in fact received
virtually unanimous support from American political elites. During

[16] "Radio and Television Address to the American People on the Situation in
Korea," July 19, 1950, in *Public Papers of the Presidents of the United States:
Harry S. Truman, 1950* (Washington, DC: United States Government Printing
Office, 1965), pp. 537–42.
[17] Alonzo Hamby, *Beyond the New Deal: Harry S. Truman and American
Liberalism* (New York: Columbia University Press, 1973), pp. 408–9. On the
domestic political context of the Korea decision, see Rosemary Foot, *The
Wrong War: American Policy and the Dimensions of the Korean Conflict,
1950–1953* (Ithaca, NY: Cornell University Press, 1985), pp. 62–3; David
Kepley, *The Collapse of the Middle Way: Senate Republicans and the
Bipartisan Foreign Policy, 1948–1952* (New York: Greenwood Press, 1988),
pp. 69–85; and Stephen Pelz, "US Decisions on Korean Policy, 1943–1950:
Some Hypotheses," in Bruce Cumings, ed., *Child of Conflict: The Korean–
American Relationship, 1943–1953* (Seattle: University of Washington Press,
1983), pp. 119–31.

this very early period of the war, even Truman's bitterest political opponents supported his decision to intervene in Korea. On the left, liberal and New Deal Democrats, lobbies, and interest groups rallied to the president; even former anti-Cold War critics such as Henry Wallace praised Truman's actions on behalf of the United Nations. On the right, almost every Republican senator and representative – including Joseph McCarthy – heartily approved of US intervention in Korea. The mainstream press was universally supportive. And in public opinion polls from the summer of 1950, over 75 percent of the American populace indicated its support for the president on this issue.[18]

It is not clear, however, that a less decisive response on Truman's part would have met with similarly universal criticism. Nor is there much evidence to suggest that the president was primarily motivated by domestic political factors in making his Korea decision. Rather, it would be more accurate to say that Truman himself not only shared but played a leading role in creating the hawkish, Cold War foreign policy consensus that had come to dominate American politics by 1950. The former haberdasher hardly needed to be told to take a hard line against communism internationally. Beneath an overarching Cold War consensus, public opinion and other domestic political constraints were somewhat fluid in the final days of June 1950. It was the administration that led public opinion, not the other way around. In making its central decision whether to intervene in Korea, most historians today agree that international geopolitical factors were the administration's primary concern.[19] Domestic political factors were ultimately secondary; they reinforced but did not create the decision to act. In the words of Barton Bernstein, a leading

[18] Ronald Caridi, *The Korean War and American Politics* (Philadelphia: University of Pennsylvania Press, 1968), pp. 33–8; Robert Donovan, *Tumultuous Years: The Presidency of Harry S. Truman, 1949–1953* (New York: W. W. Norton, 1982), p. 209; Hamby, *Beyond the New Deal*, pp. 403–5; Mueller, *War, Presidents and Public Opinion*, pp. 45–8.

[19] Charles Dobbs, *The Unwanted Symbol: American Foreign Policy, the Cold War and Korea, 1945–1950* (Kent, OH: Kent State University Press, 1981), pp. 160–92; Leffler, *A Preponderance of Power*, p. 368; James Matray, *The Reluctant Crusade: American Foreign Policy in Korea, 1941–1950* (Honolulu: University of Hawaii Press, 1985), pp. 251–8; William Stueck, *Road to Confrontation: American Policy toward China and Korea, 1947–1950* (Chapel Hill: University of North Carolina Press, 1981), p. 186.

revisionist Cold War historian who is otherwise quite critical of Truman's foreign policy:

The administration plunged the nation into war to establish credibility to block likely Soviet moves elsewhere; and to make clear that the United States would not accede to Soviet attacks or aggression by proxy in the Middle East, Asia (especially Japan), and Europe ... Their toughness in Korea might defuse potential attacks and reestablish the fierce anti-communist credentials of the administration. But domestic politics did not compel the administration to send troops into the war.[20]

During the initial period of combat, Truman and his advisors worked within a relatively permissive domestic political environment to mobilize resources for war. Beyond that, the administration took the opportunity to implement new US military efforts around the world. Congress and public opinion proved receptive. Within weeks, Congress approved an effective doubling of US military spending in supplemental and emergency measures. The country and the economy were placed on something like a wartime footing. With the Defense Production Act of September 1950, the president was authorized to allocate strategic raw materials toward defense, and if necessary to impose wage and price controls. Taxes were raised, draft calls accelerated, and foreign aid increased. Indeed, the entire framework of the administration's fiscal priorities shifted toward defense, and away from either balanced budgets or domestic social spending.[21] All of these changes are well understood in the literature on American Cold War national security policy, a literature that tends to emphasize the extent to which the Korean War lifted domestic political constraints on military spending.[22] Yet the Truman administration faced a

---

[20] Barton Bernstein, "The Truman Administration and the Korean War," in Michael Lacey, ed., *The Truman Presidency* (Cambridge: Cambridge University Press, 1989), p. 426.

[21] George Gallup, *The Gallup Poll: Public Opinion, 1935–1971* (New York: Random House, 1972), vol. II, pp. 962–4, 998–9; Warner Schilling, Paul Hammond, and Glenn Snyder, *Strategy, Politics, and Defense Budgets* (New York: Columbia University Press, 1962), pp. 351–9; Donald McCoy, *The Presidency of Harry S. Truman* (Lawrence: University Press of Kansas, 1984), p. 230.

[22] John Gaddis, *Strategies of Containment: A Critical Appraisal of Postwar American National Security Policy* (Oxford: Oxford University Press, 1982), p. 109; Michael Hogan, *A Cross of Iron: Harry S. Truman and the Origins of the National Security State, 1945–1954* (Cambridge: Cambridge University Press, 1998), pp. 266, 313; Leffler, *A Preponderance of Power*, pp. 371–3.

difficult balancing act, in that it sought to fight a strictly limited war – limited in its international scope, and also limited in its domestic effects. Truman feared that it might be possible to "over-mobilize" the American public, as well as the American economy, in a military effort that in the final analysis was necessarily restricted in scope. The shadow of a potential third world war involving the USSR loomed large over all the administration's wartime decisions. It was partly for this reason that Truman never went to Congress to ask for any sort of formal approval regarding the use of force in Korea – to avoid alarming the Soviet Union. Domestic mobilization for war was therefore extensive, but in the end also deliberately limited.[23]

For the most part, with regard to Korea, Truman acted primarily in response to his perception of the national interest. In some specific and important instances, however, the president authorized very aggressive and even counterproductive actions on particular military and foreign policy issues, in order to build domestic political support for his broader approach. The first example of such an instance was Truman's June 26 decision to deploy the Seventh Fleet to the Taiwan Strait, in effect indicating that the United States would defend and support the nascent government of Taiwan ("Formosa") against the People's Republic of China. Given the possibility at that time of an expanding military conflict in east Asia, there were certainly plausible arguments in favor of such a move; Truman had been reconsidering America's China policy in any case. But a leading and equally important reason for this decision appears to have been the desire to secure the White House from domestic criticism on the issue of Taiwan, as the United States moved toward war in Korea.[24] The issue of supporting Chinese nationalists was a longtime favorite of conservative Republicans; the administration had just been subjected to months of withering criticism on this very matter. The prospect of silencing or at least appeasing his critics on the issue of Taiwan must have been attractive to Truman, under the circumstances. As one of the leading chroniclers of the period, Robert Donovan, put it, "It would have been next to impossible for them [i.e. Truman and his

---

[23] Donovan, *Tumultuous Years*, pp. 217–24; Hamby, *Beyond the New Deal*, p. 415.

[24] Christensen, *Useful Adversaries*, pp. 134–7; Foot, *The Wrong War*, pp. 66–7; Stueck, *Road to Confrontation*, pp. 196–8; Nancy Tucker, *Patterns in the Dust: Chinese-American Relations and the Recognition Controversy, 1949–1950* (New York: Columbia University Press, 1983), p. 197.

advisors] to justify to Republican critics the commitment of American air and naval power to South Korea while leaving Formosa undefended. Defending Formosa would help win support for Korean policy in Congress."[25] In this sense, the administration took a very assertive and potentially flawed military and political action in relation to Taiwan, in order to build domestic support for what was deemed to be the larger effort in Korea. A similar, second example of this sort of action was in the administration's September 1950 decision to cross the thirty-eighth parallel with US armed forces, and reunify Korea under non-communist control. Again, plausible military and geopolitical arguments existed for such action, but an equally compelling reason was undoubtedly the realization that to halt at the thirty-eighth parallel would have been entirely unacceptable to a critical mass of politically significant opinion within the United States.[26]

In the end, of course, the decision to send American forces well north of the thirty-eighth parallel triggered a major intervention by Chinese forces into Korea during the fall of 1950. This is turn led to the most politically difficult period of the war for the Truman administration, characterized by continuing US casualties, bitter partisan criticism, and eventual military stalemate. Popular support within the United States for the administration's wartime efforts, which had previously been over-whelming, dropped to about 50 percent and stayed there for the next two years. The stalemated conflict in Korea ruined Truman's second term, politically speaking, and helped ensure that a revived Republican Party would be able to capture the White House in 1952. Truman did not intervene in Korea in order to boost his chances of reelection, but if he had done so, it would have been a disastrously misguided strategy, since in the end the war had precisely the opposite effect.[27]

Vietnam, 1964–1965

It is often suggested that Lyndon Johnson took America to war in Vietnam in order to stave off domestic criticism that he had "lost"

[25] Donovan, *Tumultuous Years*, p. 206.
[26] Foot, *The Wrong War*, pp. 69–70; Burton Kaufman, *The Korean War: Challenges in Crisis, Credibility and Command* (Philadelphia, PA: Temple University Press, 1986), pp. 84–6; Leffler, *A Preponderance of Power*, pp. 374–80.
[27] Kepley, *The Collapse of the Middle Way*, pp. 97–150; Mueller, *War, Presidents and Public Opinion*, pp. 50–2.

that country to communism. Johnson himself said that the loss of Vietnam would produce "a mean and destructive debate ... that would shatter my Presidency, kill my administration, and damage our democracy."[28] Undoubtedly this concern influenced and reinforced Johnson's decision to escalate military involvement in Vietnam, but domestic politics was not the primary cause of US intervention. Rather, the decision for war was ultimately rooted in an overarching perception of American strategic interests shared by Johnson, his advisors, and the overwhelming majority of political opinion leaders within the United States at that time.

Previous administrations laid the groundwork. Under Presidents Eisenhower and Kennedy, the survival of a non-communist government in South Vietnam was defined as a vital US national security interest. Kennedy, in particular – whatever his misgivings about escalation – increased the number of US military "advisors" in Vietnam to over 16,000, because he saw it as a crucial test case of America's ability to successfully conduct low-intensity wars. When Johnson became president in November 1963, he inherited what he took to be Kennedy's firm commitment to the independent existence of South Vietnam. He also inherited Kennedy's military and foreign policy team, the leading members of which – Secretary of State Dean Rusk, National Security Advisor McGeorge Bundy, Secretary of Defense Robert McNamara, and the Joint Chiefs of Staff – encouraged Johnson to escalate American military engagement in Vietnam. Johnson was inclined to do so in any case. Like most politically influential Americans of the early Cold War era, Johnson believed that the United States had to demonstrate strength, avoid appeasement, and contain communism wherever practically possible. As vice-president in 1961–3, he had been one of the Kennedy administration's more hawkish spokesmen and advisors on the issue of Indochina. Within days of taking over the presidency, Johnson urged his national security team to stop "bickering" and "win the war" in Vietnam, while denouncing compromise neutralization schemes as "another name for a Communist take-over."[29] Indeed,

---

[28] Doris Kearns, *Lyndon Johnson and the American Dream* (New York: Harper and Row, 1976), pp. 252–3, at p. 252. For a leading example of the domestic political argument in relation to Johnson, see Larry Berman, *Planning a Tragedy: The Americanization of the War in Vietnam* (New York: W. W. Norton, 1982).

[29] *FRUS, 1961–1963*, vol. IV, pp. 636–8, 745–7.

throughout the complicated deliberations of 1964–5, the Johnson administration pursued one goal quite consistently, namely, the continued survival and defense of a non-communist government in Saigon. This is not to deny that Johnson and his advisors agonized over these decisions, revealing considerable frustration, pessimism, and doubt along the way. But in the end, the prevention of a communist victory in South Vietnam was a fixed point in his administration's thinking and dictated escalation as circumstances worsened on the ground.[30]

Both Congress and public opinion were willing to offer considerable deference to the president on matters of national security, especially in the Cold War era of the early 1960s. Conservative Republicans and foreign policy hawks certainly held the president's feet to the fire on the issue of Vietnam in 1964–5, but on balance the domestic political constraints on Johnson's actions were ambiguous and fluid. Mass public opinion was initially not so much hawkish on Vietnam so much as it was uninterested. As Johnson put it to Senator Richard Russell in May 1964, "I don't think the people of this country know much about Vietnam and I think they care a hell of a lot less."[31] Even after the issue rose to the public's attention in 1964–5, opinion over specific policy options was strikingly divided and uncertain. In an April 1965 Gallup poll, respondents were divided over whether to "go all out" in Vietnam (19 percent), disengage and "get out" (17 percent), hold the line while negotiating (14 percent), or "stop fighting" and try diplomacy (12 percent).[32] The notion of a diplomatic option or solution remained very popular throughout 1964–5. Ultimately, a clear majority of the American public was willing to follow Johnson's lead during this period, and to support military escalation in Vietnam, not

---

[30] Vaughn D. Bornet, *The Presidency of Lyndon B. Johnson* (Lawrence: University Press of Kansas, 1983), pp. 64–75; George Herring, *America's Longest War: The United States and Vietnam, 1950–1975*, 4th edn (Boston: McGraw-Hill, 2002), p. 136; Michael Hunt, *Lyndon Johnson's War: America's Cold War Crusade in Vietnam, 1945–1968* (New York: Hill and Wang, 1996), pp. 75–106; Robert Schulzinger, *A Time for War: The United States and Vietnam, 1941–1975* (New York: Oxford University Press, 1997), p. 132.

[31] Michael Beschloss, *Taking Charge: The Johnson White House Tapes, 1963–1964* (New York: Simon and Schuster, 1997), p. 365.

[32] Other responses were as follows: step up military activity (12 percent); other (5 percent); no opinion (28 percent). (The total adds to more than 100 percent since some persons gave more than one response.) George Gallup, *The Gallup Poll*, vol. III, p. 1934.

so much because of strong inherent preferences on the issue itself, but because Johnson was the "commander-in-chief." Yet because much of that following was based upon uncertainty and deference to the president, rather than intense feelings about Vietnam per se, popular support for Johnson and for escalation was broad but at the same time shallow. A similar dynamic was at work in Congress. Within the context of the early Cold War, and especially in an apparent crisis, the vast majority of senators and representatives were inclined to support the president if he chose to take a hard-line stand on the containment of communism. Yet many members of both the Senate and the House were unenthusiastic about escalating American military involvement in Vietnam, some openly and strongly so. It is not quite accurate, therefore, to suggest that Johnson was "forced" into Vietnam by domestic political pressures. Rather, on this issue – as Johnson well knew – the White House led, while majorities in both Congress and public opinion followed behind.[33]

If the administration's decision for war in Vietnam was determined primarily by official perceptions of external threats, the precise manner in which that war was launched was profoundly shaped by domestic political considerations. From a strictly military perspective, *given* that the United States was going to embark on a major military intervention against an extremely determined and capable adversary, an alternative approach would have been to take the administration's case forthrightly to Congress, mobilize a serious national effort, call up the reserves, initiate a rapid and dramatic buildup of US forces in Vietnam, attack North Vietnamese military and economic capabilities through a massive bombing campaign, and make it clear to the American people that the United States was in fact at war. Indeed, Johnson was encouraged at various moments to do each one of these things, not only by members of the Joint Chiefs of Staff, but by numerous civilian advisors. He rejected such recommendations, partially for fear of provoking China, but also very much for domestic political reasons. Johnson's great domestic political concern was that

---

[33] Robert Dallek, *Lyndon B. Johnson: Portrait of a President* (New York: Oxford University Press, 2004), pp. 224–5; Fredrik Logevall, *Choosing War: The Lost Chance for Peace and the Escalation of the War in Vietnam* (Berkeley: University of California Press, 1999), pp. 275–9; William L. Lunch and Peter W. Sperlich, "American Public Opinion and the War in Vietnam," *Western Political Quarterly* 32, no. 1 (March 1979), pp. 21–44.

rapid or massive escalation in Vietnam might undermine, first, his reelection campaign, and second, his ambitious domestic policy agenda. As he put it, he did not want "that bitch of a war" to destroy "the woman I really loved – the Great Society."[34] He therefore chose a painfully incremental backdoor approach to military intervention and mobilization in 1964–5, in the hopes of preventing a great national focus or debate around the issue of Vietnam. Escalation was halting and gradual; the bombing of the North was tightly constrained and ineffectual; the ground buildup was piecemeal and stopgap; and neither Congress nor the American public were directly asked to join with the administration in a serious national wartime effort.[35]

The Johnson administration's misleading public statements on Vietnam are of course legendary, but it is worth specifying in what ways the administration knowingly misled the public and in what ways it did not. During the Gulf of Tonkin crisis of August 1964 – in which mistaken reports of successive North Vietnamese attacks on American destroyers led to congressional authorization for the use of force – Johnson and his advisors certainly misrepresented the full context and significance of the episode to Congress, but they do not appear to have "planned" the incident, or to have deliberately fabricated evidence of a second attack.[36] Johnson did not hide the fact that the preservation of a non-communist government in South Vietnam was a firm commitment in his mind; on the contrary, he reaffirmed it early and often, for example in March 1964 when he said on national television that "we must be responsible, we must stay there and help them, and that is what we are going to do."[37] When Johnson gave a major speech in April 1965, outlining the rationale for American military engagement in Vietnam, he listed considerations that also weighed heavily with him in private: notably, that "to leave Viet-Nam to its fate would shake the confidence of all these people [i.e. other

[34] Kearns, *Lyndon Johnson and the American Dream*, p. 251.
[35] Berman, *Planning a Tragedy*, pp. 123–8, 149–50; Jeffrey Helsing, *Johnson's War/Johnson's Great Society: The Guns and Butter Trap* (Westport: Praeger, 2000), pp. 255–6; H. R. McMaster, *Dereliction of Duty* (New York: Harper Perennial, 1997), pp. 324–33.
[36] Edwin Moise, *Tonkin Gulf and the Escalation of the Vietnam War* (Chapel Hill: University of North Carolina Press, 1996), pp. xi–xv.
[37] *Public Papers of the Presidents: Lyndon B. Johnson, 1963–64* (Washington DC: Government Printing Office, 1965), vol. I, p. 370.

US allies] in the value of an American commitment."[38] Such statements were not a misrepresentation of the administration's central concerns. Rather, they were extremely general – hardly surprising under the circumstances. The real credibility gap, as it came to be described, was therefore not between Johnson's public and private representation of the stakes in Vietnam – stakes that he genuinely considered to be high, for reasons of national security. Rather, the truly important gap was between the scope of Johnson's actual decisions on Vietnam by July 1965, which amounted to taking the country into a major war, and the public representation of those decisions, in which their full significance was deliberately obscured.

Johnson played down the prospect of a major military conflict in 1964–5 because he believed that domestic political incentives pulled in the direction of constraint. His public stance on Vietnam was frequently misleading, but not because he sought to gain electoral benefit from going to war. In the Gulf of Tonkin incident, to be sure, he seized the opportunity to strike at North Vietnam while securing the congressional stamp of approval. The American public rallied to his side in that crisis, which had the effect of neutralizing hawkish criticism from Republican presidential candidate Barry Goldwater heading into the November elections. Consider, however, that Johnson ran as *less* of a hawk than Goldwater, and reaped considerable electoral success in doing so. Johnson rejected early recommendations in 1964 for significant military escalation in Vietnam. He told American voters in October 1964 that "we are not about to send American boys 9 or 10,000 miles away from home to do what Asian boys ought to be doing for themselves."[39] He even downplayed or ignored several attacks on American troops in Vietnam, including one that occurred only days before the November election. Finally, he waited until *after* that election to begin planning in earnest for military escalation. He did all of these things because he knew that on balance the American people, like him, were unenthusiastic about going to war. The resulting impression that Johnson gave the public – of caution, reluctance, and restraint – helped secure broad bipartisan approval at home for his decision to escalate militarily.[40] Yet

---

[38] Ibid., vol. I, pp. 394–9, at p. 395.
[39] "Remarks in Memorial Hall, Akron University," October 21, 1964, ibid., vol. II, pp. 1387–93, at p. 1391.
[40] Herring, *America's Longest War*, p. 147; Schulzinger, *A Time for War*, pp. 155, 165.

this stealthy, skillful political maneuvering came at a heavy price. The halting, indirect manner in which the United States embarked upon war in 1964–5 was hardly the one most likely to achieve military or political success within Vietnam, if such success were even possible. Nor did Johnson escape fierce domestic political criticism on this issue – on the contrary, he simply delayed it. By 1966, popular support for the military effort in Vietnam began its inexorable decline, consuming the president's agenda and support.[41] By 1968, the war had divided the Democratic Party and destroyed Johnson's presidency.

Iraq, 2001–2006

The question naturally arises: is it probable that the George W. Bush administration invaded Iraq for second-image reasons? That is, did President Bush enter into a major military intervention primarily in order to boost his domestic political standing? The overarching caveat for anyone presuming to speak on this subject is that as yet we obviously have very little in the way of primary sources. In the cases of Korea and Vietnam, we have voluminous archival materials from which to work; in the case of Iraq, which is still ongoing, we have some good journalistic accounts, public statements, and early memoirs. Still, it is possible to piece together from those sources an initial, plausible picture of why and how the United States went to war in 2003. The evidence is as follows.[42]

Bush's popularity was in steady decline over the course of 2002, and inevitably so, since it had reached stratospheric levels in the aftermath of 9/11. Even then, his approval ratings were typically still in the

[41] Mueller, *War, Presidents and Public Opinion*, pp. 53–7.
[42] In addition to the sources listed in subsequent notes, see the following accounts of events leading up to the war in Iraq: Ivo Daalder and James Lindsay, *America Unbound: The Bush Revolution in Foreign Policy* (Washington, DC: Brookings Institution Press, 2003); Stefan Halper and Jonathan Clarke, *America Alone: The Neo-Conservatives and the Global Order* (New York: Cambridge University Press, 2004); Chaim Kaufmann, "Threat Inflation and the Failure of the Marketplace of Ideas: The Selling of the Iraq War," *International Security* 29, no. 1 (summer 2004), pp. 5–48; James Mann, *Rise of the Vulcans: The History of Bush's War Cabinet* (New York: Viking, 2004); George Packer, *The Assassins' Gate: America in Iraq* (New York: Farrar, Straus and Giroux, 2005); and Jon Western, *Selling Intervention and War: The Presidency, the Media, and the American Public* (Baltimore, MD: Johns Hopkins University Press, 2005), chap. 6.

sixties during the second half of 2002 – a high level by historical standards. The debate over Iraq – which really only began in earnest toward the end of summer 2002 – had little impact on Bush's approval ratings, which continued to slide as the year ended. Only with the actual invasion of Iraq in March 2003 did Bush's ratings go back up, and they did so in a rally that had faded by August 2003. Indeed by September 2003, with complications in Iraq becoming more obvious, Bush's ratings had dropped into the fifties; he was never to recover his earlier level of popularity.[43]

The issue of Iraq may very well have helped Republicans in the mid-term elections of 2002, not in the sense that most voters were enthusiastic for war, but in the sense that they trusted Bush's leadership on issues of national security and offered him and his party a vote of confidence for that reason. Certainly, with the congressional votes of October 2002, the administration was able to pin down Democratic senators, obliging them to go on record either for or against the potential use of force in Iraq. This could not have been an unappealing prospect for the White House, politically speaking, only weeks before mid-term elections.[44] In a more subtle sense, the idea of taking the "war on terror" into Iraq offered something to Bush's conservative supporters, kept Democrats divided, and maintained the focus of debate on issues of national security where Republicans were strong. Yet one hardly gets the impression that the American public – or even the grassroots base of the Republican Party, outside of Washington DC – was clamoring for war against Iraq in the winter of 2002–3. There was in fact widespread unease over the prospect of such a war, even among many traditional conservative hawks. Public support for war, in the abstract, rested between the low fifties and the mid-sixties from June 2002 right up until days before the invasion – never higher.[45] Nor was popular support for invading Iraq particularly deep or intense. There was, for example, little evidence of that widespread anger and overwhelming unity that existed as the United States went

---

[43] George Edwards III, "Riding High in the Polls: George W. Bush and Public Opinion," in Colin Campbell and Bert Rockman, eds., *The George W. Bush Presidency: Appraisals and Prospects* (Washington, DC: Congressional Quarterly Press, 2004), p. 23.

[44] Bob Woodward, *Plan of Attack* (New York: Simon and Schuster, 2004), p. 168.

[45] Edwards, "Riding High in the Polls," p. 38.

to war with the Taliban in fall 2001. In fact, the weeks immediately prior to the invasion of Iraq saw the mobilization of fierce and widespread anti-war sentiment within the United States. Political incentives for war were therefore mixed, at best.

By spring 2004, as the Bush administration prepared for its reelection campaign, it was already abundantly clear that Iraq could turn into a political liability rather than a political asset.[46] As the Iraqi insurgency persisted and American casualties mounted, popular support for war within the United States gradually but steadily declined. In the presidential election of 2004, Bush continued to get credit from many voters for strong leadership, particularly on the issue of terrorism. But the specific issue of Iraq was already having domestic political effects that were as much negative as positive for the administration. In fact, the war was becoming increasingly unpopular, and among those who felt most strongly about Iraq, the vast majority voted for Bush's opponent John Kerry.[47] By fall 2005, even the majority of congressional Republicans felt compelled to vote in favor of gradual (albeit unspecified) disengagement from Iraq. And as the mid-term elections of 2006 approached, Democrats were increasingly confident that Iraq had become a losing issue for the Republican Party. With no visible end in sight, the war dragged on uncomfortably, crowding out the Bush administration's political agenda, harming the president's popularity, and playing into an increasingly common image of incompetence. Exit polls confirmed that the issue of Iraq was one of the key factors in the Republicans' loss of Congress in November 2006.[48]

Certainly by the beginning of 2007 it was obvious that the domestic political effects of Iraq were, on balance, negative for the president. But Bush must have known this was a possibility when he made the decision initially; he did not become president by being politically obtuse. He obviously knew, from his own father's example, that even a victorious war would not necessarily redound much to his benefit

---

[46] Woodward, *Plan of Attack*, p. 430.

[47] Pew Research Center for the People and the Press, "Voters Liked Campaign 2004, But Too Much 'Mud-Slinging'," November 11, 2004, available at: people-press.org/reports/print.php3?PageID=909.

[48] Andrew Kohut, "The Real Message of the Midterms," Pew Research Center for the People and the Press, November 14, 2006, available at: pewresearch.org/pubs/91/the-real-message-of-the-midterms; David D. Kirkpatrick and Adam Nagourney, "In an Election Year, a Shift in Public Opinion on the War," *New York Times*, March 27, 2006, p. A12.

politically. He knew that previous presidents had been destroyed by less successful wars. It is therefore improbable that he made the decision on war with Iraq primarily for domestic political reasons; it would have simply been naïve to do so. At the very least, domestic political incentives for or against war ran in multiple directions in 2002–3. The determining factor in Bush's initial decision, consequently, was most likely the administration's own perception of American national security interests in relation to Iraq. On this great issue, for better or worse, the president and his leading foreign policy advisors appear to have believed in what they were doing.[49]

The events of 9/11 shocked Bush into a new willingness to put national security policy first on his list of priorities; to be more aggressive against potential external threats; to put democracy promotion in the Middle East at the top of his agenda; and to make regime change in Iraq a reality. Yet the administration's public statements regarding the rationale for war were often more simplistic than its private reasoning. In speaking to American audiences, the administration stressed the danger that Saddam Hussein might build weapons of mass destruction and then hand them over to terrorists. In speaking to international audiences, the administration stressed Saddam's continuing refusal to abide by United Nations resolutions and disarm completely. The first rationale, at least, seems to have been a genuine concern on the part of leading administration officials, especially in the wake of 9/11. But there were also other crucial perceptions that were less emphasized by the administration in public forums, yet which apparently carried considerable weight in the end: namely, that an invasion of Iraq would be an inviting instrument by which to shake up the corrupt, sclerotic power structures of the Middle East, demonstrate American capabilities, and thereby undermine support for international terrorism. These sorts of reasons for war were more subtle and indirect than images of a mushroom cloud, but by all accounts they had a powerful impact on the administration's thinking.

---

[49] On this and the following paragraph, see Philip H. Gordon, "Bush's Middle East Vision," *Survival* 45, no. 1 (spring 2003), pp. 155–65; Michael Hirsh, "Bush and the World," *Foreign Affairs* 81, no. 5 (September/October 2002), pp. 18–43, at pp. 18–19; John Judis, "Why Iraq?" *The American Prospect* (March 2003), pp. 12–13; Nicholas Lemann, "How It Came to War," *The New Yorker*, March 31, 2003, pp. 36–40, at pp. 37–8; Woodward, *Plan of Attack*, pp. 1–8, 29–136, 443.

Overall, there is simply very little evidence that domestic political concerns were a primary reason for war with Iraq. There were no overpowering domestic political constraints on Bush's ability to invade Iraq. At the same time, there were hardly any overpowering domestic political incentives to do so. It would therefore be more accurate to say that Bush went to war in spite of domestic political concerns, rather than because of them. Still, the precise implementation of that war may very well have been shaped by such domestic concerns. Specifically, the war was conducted with an appalling lack of preparation for postwar stability operations, and while this lack of preparation no doubt had much to do with the administration's sincere bias against "nation-building," it probably also had something to do with anticipation of the domestic criticisms that would have mounted had Bush's advisors been more forthcoming early on about the potential long-term costs of invasion. Domestic political concerns, that is, may have discouraged discussion of or preparation for the postwar period in Iraq. In this sense, intervention was carried out in a suboptimal or dysfunctional manner, possibly for domestic political reasons, as well as cognitive or ideological ones.

Conclusions

In light of these case studies, we now return to our initial question, namely: how does domestic politics shape and influence the resort to war? What common patterns can we discern on that subject from these three cases of major military intervention by an American president? First, the desire to mobilize domestic support frequently creates a certain gap between a president's private rationale for war and his public representations. In itself this is hardly surprising. A more interesting finding is that this gap often lies in the direction not of overstating but rather understating the scale and significance of a given intervention. This would seem to indicate that presidents do perceive and respond to the American public's general reluctance to engage in costly or sustained military engagements, even if they sometimes do so in unfortunate ways. But it should also be added that in each of these three cases the publicly declared reasons for war appear to have overlapped considerably with private rationales, however misguided in retrospect. Public rhetoric, that is to say, was more simplistic but fundamentally similar to the reasons given for war in private. A second common feature of all these cases was that domestic political constraints on war were rather loose, ambiguous, and multidirectional. This means that in the end presidents were able to act with remarkable freedom and autonomy, given that they were working within a democratic polity. For the most part, in every case, the president led while the public followed.

A third common pattern was that in each case the president went to war because of his administration's perception of American national security interests, and not for domestic political reasons. This is what realists would expect to find. A fourth, related common feature, however, was also quite consistent with neoclassical realism, namely that domestic political incentives encouraged particular forms of intervention that were suboptimal from an international perspective. Truman authorized "rollback" against North Korea; Johnson chose stopgap escalation in Vietnam; and Bush failed to plan satisfactorily for postwar Iraq. Every one of these decisions was flawed from a structural realist point of view, but they can each be explained to some extent (albeit not excused) by the president's desire to maintain domestic support for the overall war effort. Finally, popular support for war in each case followed a very similar trend. Initially, the public rallied behind the president in overwhelming majorities as American troops entered combat. Then, as the war appeared stalemated, public support went into a slow but steady decline.[50] The electoral consequences of this last trend were also intriguing. In 1950, 1952, 1966, and 1968, incumbent presidents and their parties were politically damaged by the perception of stalemated wars. In 1964, an incumbent president reaped political benefits by campaigning as *less* hawkish than his opponent. In 2002 and 2004, on the other hand, the electoral consequences of military intervention – or prospective military intervention – were more ambiguous. Certainly Bush and his party benefited from the public's impression of their strength against terrorism, but the extent to which the issue of Iraq, specifically, helped the Republicans was less obvious. As a general observation, in none of these three cases did any party reap clear-cut

[50] John Mueller, "The Iraq Syndrome," *Foreign Affairs* 84, no. 6 (November/December 2005), pp. 44–54.

electoral benefits after taking the country into a major military intervention.

In terms of further research, it would be most interesting to know through a similar comparative case study analysis whether these same general patterns and processes hold true for minor as well as major US military interventions. Advocates of diversionary war theory have argued for the primacy of domestic politics in presidential uses of force, typically using large-N methods, but these authors tend to abstain from demonstrating causality and either proving or falsifying their hypotheses through in-depth case studies. It would also be useful to know whether the same processes of decision-making hold true in other advanced industrial democracies, or whether patterns of major military intervention are dramatically different from one country to the next. As we expand the scope of investigation into authoritarian and semi-democratic regimes, we may well find many more cases of major military intervention initiated for primarily domestic political reasons.

In the bare-knuckle sport that is American party politics, critics often grab whatever ammunition is at hand in order to discredit their opponents. An intellectually honest accounting should be more discriminating. It is entirely possible to argue, for example, that the 2003 invasion of Iraq was ill-advised, that postwar planning was poorly conceived, and that WMD intelligence was mishandled, while at the same time maintaining that Bush's motives were essentially sincere and that the invasion was not undertaken primarily for domestic political reasons. Domestic political concerns shaped the promotion and possibly even the implementation of the invasion, but at bottom there is little reason to doubt that Bush went to war because of an altered perception of US national security interests post-9/11. In fact the most striking feature of the war in Iraq is how little domestic politics seems to have mattered in shaping the decision for intervention. The real lesson of this war is not that presidents go to war in order to get reelected, but rather than presidents are remarkably free to go to war regardless of domestic factors if they are sufficiently determined. No doubt presidents have frequently used that freedom in ways that were ill-advised, but they have rarely used it with outright cynicism or simply in order to boost their political standings. Indeed, as I have shown, such behavior would be as politically foolish and unrealistic as it would be reprehensible. Certainly, domestic political concerns inform every stage of presidential decision-making on major military interventions: whether to initiate hostilities; how to implement the decision; and how to build and promote popular support for war. In the final analysis, however, presidents typically go to war first and foremost because they believe it to be necessary for international reasons. These are some of the insights that neoclassical realism can bring to the study of domestic politics and military intervention.

6 | Neoclassical realism and domestic interest groups *

NORRIN M. RIPSMAN

Neorealists, with their focus on the international structure and the relative capabilities of the great powers, have tended to neglect the impact of domestic political forces – such as public opinion, the legislature, and privileged interest groups – on foreign security policy. Recently, however, a new generation of realists has begun to draw upon the comparative political economy literature to account for the impact of domestic political considerations and to introduce the problematique of state autonomy to security studies. As chapter 1 indicates, though, this neoclassical realist literature is still underdeveloped. In particular, it needs to address five critical questions about the role of domestic actors in determining policy: (1) Which domestic actors matter most in the construction of foreign security policy? (2) Under what international circumstances will they have the greatest influence? (3) Under what domestic circumstances will domestic actors have the greatest influence? (4) In what types of states will they matter most? (5) How is their influence likely to manifest itself? In this chapter, I provide preliminary answers to these questions with the goal of building a theory of domestic actors and the national security state, although I do not build such a theory here. Specifically, I explain when domestic political factors affect foreign security policy and which domestic groups and actors matter most.

A few assumptions guide my approach. First, although public opinion, the legislature, the media, and organized interest groups are usually treated separately, they share common aspects that make it appropriate to treat them together in a comprehensive theory of

* I am grateful to Ben Fordham, Ben Frankel, Steven Lobell, Brian Rathbun, Jeff Taliaferro, Marie-Jöelle Zahar, and the workshop participants for their comments and suggestions. I also thank Martin Bergeron, Sébastien Mainville, and Jean Proulx for their research assistance.

170

domestic political actors. For example, public opinion usually influences policy, when it does, indirectly through its representatives in the legislature, rather than directly through the foreign security policy executive. The media, which seek primarily to mold public opinion, ultimately travel the same causal path. Similarly, while organized interest groups can make representations directly to the political leadership,[1] they frequently have easier access through the legislature. Thus a theory that specifies the extent and nature of the legislature's influence on policy will be relevant to all of these domestic political actors.

Second, although democratic and non-democratic governments will differ in the manner in which they interact with domestic actors, even non-democratic states must take into account the demands of powerful political actors, such as the military, economic elites, and even, occasionally, the public as a whole, if they wish to remain in power. Thus it is useful to build a theory that accounts not only for the differences between domestic pressures in these two types of regimes, but also the common domestic political incentives and costs they face. Below, I argue that relative state autonomy matters more than regime type.

Third, I make the assumption, as I do elsewhere, that policy is conducted by a foreign security policy executive, comprised of the head of government and the ministers and officials charged with making foreign security policy, and that all other domestic actors – including members of the legislature, political allies, and even members of the cabinet that are not in national security-related ministries – may try to influence the decisions of that executive.[2] This assumption allows us to separate the

---

[1] See, for example, Jack Snyder, *Myths of Empire* (Ithaca, NY: Cornell University Press, 1991), pp. 32–9.

[2] Norrin M. Ripsman, *Peacemaking by Democracies: The Effect of Structural Autonomy on the Post-World-War Settlements* (University Park, PA: Penn State University Press, 2002), pp. 43–4. This definition is similar to the "ultimate decision unit" of Margaret G. Hermann et al. which they describe as "a set of authorities with the ability to commit the resources of the society and, with respect to a particular problem, with the authority to make a decision that cannot be readily reversed." See Margaret G. Hermann, Charles F. Hermann, and Joe D. Hagan "How Decision Units Shape Foreign Policy Behavior," in Charles F. Hermann, Charles W. Kegley, and James N. Rosenau, eds., *New Directions in the Study of Foreign Policy* (Boston: Allen and Unwin, 1987), pp. 309–36, at p. 309.

dominant neorealist influences on policy from the domestic influences. The executive, aware as it is of all the relevant information available on international strategic affairs, determines its preferences largely in accordance with international constraints and incentives. When domestic actors, who are frequently unaware of the intricacies of the policy environment, attempt to intervene in security policy, they are primarily motivated by personal, parochial, or domestic political motivations.

This is, of course, a simplified assumption, as members of the executive also bring personal motives to the table, and domestic actors can be motivated by concern over the state's security too. Indeed, these additional motives are reflected in my discussion below. Moreover, as Benjamin Fordham's chapter argues, it is possible that the interpretation of international threats may have a lot to do with the composition of the governing coalition – e.g. if the Communist Party had been in power in France or Italy during the early Cold War, they would not have perceived the Soviet Union as threatening – and not simply objective international circumstances. Therefore, some would object to my decision to treat the states as distinct from society, with distinct preferences.[3] Indeed, Benjamin Fordham's chapter in this volume contends that the economic and political interests of the governing coalition exert considerable causal weight over the threats the state responds to and the policies it chooses to counter them. Nonetheless, it stands to reason that if, as realists contend, international imperatives are the primary inputs into national security policy, then these imperatives should be best reflected within the executive. Furthermore, anecdotal evidence does suggest that the world looks different to those in power. In part because of access to privileged private information, in part because of the heavy responsibilities of office, leaders share a "view from above" that is qualitatively different from the viewpoints of private citizens and political interest groups, which often leads people who achieve power to adopt policies that diverge sharply from their previously expressed preferences.[4] Thus, for example,

---

[3] Colin Dueck's chapter, like mine, adopts a top-down model of the state.

[4] For this reason, I would argue that Benjamin Fordham's focus in his chapter on political parties in Congress is misplaced. We should expect the foreign policy preferences of domestic actors to be influenced by domestic political and economic interests. What matters, however, is how the executive determines its policy preferences.

Conservative Foreign Secretary Anthony Eden judged that Labour Foreign Secretary Ernest Bevin – a former union leader who was the ideological opposite of the aristocratic Eden – pursued a policy that was completely in line with his own views of the realities of Cold War Europe.[5] Similarly, when Bill Clinton was running for office, he opposed the George H. W. Bush administration's policy of constructive engagement with China, preferring a more aggressive strategy of promoting human rights. After winning the 1992 election and meeting with the outgoing administration, however, he comprehended the wisdom of constructive engagement.[6] Consequently, there is evidence that what Fordham calls an additive model can be more appropriate than an interactive model, which may overstate the degree to which parochial domestic considerations affect the way governments evaluate geostrategic developments once in power. Finally, if, as domestic political analysts contend, domestic actors can influence policy-making, that should be best measured by looking at the impact of actors outside the national security executive. Thus the simplified separation of the national security executive from other domestic actors is warranted on analytical grounds, and it can allow us to examine the conditions under which domestic actors can influence the policies selected by the executive.

Finally, although I assume that the executive is more attuned to international imperatives than other actors, I also acknowledge that it has an important domestic political motivation that could have an impact on its policy decisions as well, namely its interest in preserving its own power position. When national leaders feel their hold on power is slipping, they may be more responsive to domestic preferences and may choose riskier security policies in order to secure themselves domestically.[7] Some might object that bringing such considerations into a theory of foreign security policy is distinctly unrealist, as realist theories should privilege the international system over

---

[5] See Anthony Eden, *Full Circle: The Memoirs of Sir Anthony Eden* (London: Cassell, 1960), p. 5.

[6] See Ramon H. Myers, Michel C. Oksenberg, and David Shambaugh, eds., *Making China Policy: Lessons from the Bush and Clinton Administrations* (Lanham, MD: Rowman and Littlefield, 2001).

[7] Indeed, this is the logic behind the diversionary theory of war, which assumes states may engage in risky war to shore up domestic political support. See Jack S. Levy, "The Diversionary Theory of War," in Manus I. Midlarsky, ed., *The Handbook of War Studies* (Boston: Unwin Hyman, 1989), pp. 259–88.

domestic political considerations.[8] As I elaborate below, however, it is perfectly consistent with neoclassical realism, which assumes that the international system plays the dominant role in shaping national security decisions, but international imperatives are filtered through the domestic political environment, which can lead to variations in the way states respond to common international pressures.[9]

In the next section, I will briefly overview existing realist approaches to the state and the recent efforts to incorporate domestic politics into the security studies literature. I then proceed to assess the types of actors that matter, as well as the international and domestic political circumstances under which they can have the greatest impact on national security policy.

Neorealism, neoclassical realism, and the state

Neorealist theory typically views the state as a strong entity that is largely unaffected by domestic pressures when conducting foreign security policy. For neorealists, the international system conditions state behavior, and states respond as they must in an anarchic international system or they may perish. Therefore, all states are socialized to behave in a similar manner, regardless of their political regime type and domestic politics.[10] While defensive structural realists attribute some causal weight to domestic political factors, they agree that most states and most regimes conduct foreign security policy without much attention to domestic political forces. In their judgment, all states behave rationally internationally and avoid excessively aggressive policies, except for those with regimes founded on dysfunctional ideologies, such as imperialistic cartel regimes and those led by militaristic general staffs.[11] These are largely ideological issues, however,

---

[8] I thank Brian Rathbun for this line of criticism.
[9] Gideon Rose, "Neoclassical Realism and Theories of Foreign Policy," *World Politics* 51, no. 1 (October 1998), pp. 144–72.
[10] Kenneth N. Waltz, *Theory of International Politics* (New York: McGraw-Hill, 1979), pp. 118–28. For Waltz's conclusion that democratic states perform no differently from other regimes, see Waltz, *Foreign Policy and Democratic Politics: The American and British Experience* (Boston: Little, Brown, 1967), pp. 306–11.
[11] See, for example, Snyder, *Myths of Empire*; Fareed Zakaria, "Realism and Domestic Politics: A Review Essay," *International Security* 17, no. 1 (summer 1992), pp. 177–98; Jeffrey W. Taliaferro, "Security Seeking under Anarchy:

rather than domestic political factors, that affect policy choices.[12] Neorealism, thus, has typically excluded domestic actors, such as legislators, public opinion, interest groups, and the media, from the discussion of national security policy.[13]

Anecdotal evidence, however, suggests that domestic political considerations can indeed affect national security policy. The public reaction to the March 2004 terrorist attack in Spain and the consequent election of the Socialist Party led that country to withdraw its troops from the American- and British-led coalition in Iraq. The food riots in Egypt in the late-1970s played a significant role in President Anwar el-Sadat's decision to visit Jerusalem and seek a peace treaty with Israel.[14] While British, American, and French leaders in 1950 all feared a Soviet challenge in central Europe, and all agreed that German rearmament was desirable, British and American leaders were able to push the plan forward, while French leaders were stymied by public and legislative opposition which caused them to delay the plan for five years.[15] It is significant that even Kenneth Waltz recognized the importance of domestic politics. While he stressed that the third image was the only coherent basis for a systematic and internally consistent theory of international politics, to explain why a given state took a given foreign policy decision at a given time, the analyst would also need to consider first- and second-image factors.[16]

For these reasons, realist-oriented scholars have begun to broaden their understanding of national security policy-making to acknowledge the impact of domestic politics. While some, such as Jeffrey Legro and Andrew Moravcsik, might question whether these are

Defensive Realism Revisited," *International Security* 25, no. 3 (winter 2000), pp. 128–61.

[12] Randall Schweller's chapter in this volume contends that ideology actually is a domestic factor that can affect the ability of states to implement, rather than make, policy.

[13] In contrast, traditional realists did assume that domestic politics could cause leaders – especially leaders of democratic states – to pursue suboptimal policy choices. See Ripsman, *Peacemaking by Democracies*, pp. 30–4.

[14] Melvin A. Friedlander, *Sadat and Begin: The Domestic Politics of Peacemaking* (Boulder, CO: Westview, 1983), pp. 2–9.

[15] Norrin M. Ripsman, "The Curious Case of German Rearmament: Democracy and Foreign Security Policy," *Security Studies* 10, no. 2 (winter 2001), pp. 1–47.

[16] Kenneth N. Waltz, *Man, the State and War* (New York: Columbia University Press, 1959), p. 232.

truly realist approaches, I contend that they remain realist in their acceptance of core realist assumptions about international politics.[17] These neoclassical realists believe that anarchy and the distribution of power condition the pursuit of security, that security is the most important value in an anarchic international system, and that states are the most important actors in the international arena. Nonetheless, they accept that, since leaders are interested not only in securing the state from without but also holding power at home, domestic political conditions can also affect security policy. More precisely, they assume that domestic political arrangements act as intervening variables through which systemic imperatives are translated into foreign policy responses.[18] Thus, according to Jack Levy, "greater recognition of the role of domestic factors by political scientists would increase the explanatory power of their theories and provide more useful conceptual frameworks for the historical analysis of individual wars."[19] Let us briefly explore a few of these domestic political avenues of inquiry.

One observation is that national security policy may be targeted at a domestic audience, rather than an international one. The diversionary war theory thus contends that leaders do not only wage war for international strategic reasons. Occasionally, domestically beleaguered leaders who fear defeat or overthrow at home may initiate a war in order to alter the domestic political landscape and preserve their hold on power. Their premise is that war inspires a "rally-around-the-flag" effect, which silences opposition on nationalistic grounds and even co-opts opponents to support the regime in the national interest.[20] If this is correct, then to predict wars we would have to supplement a

[17] Jeffrey W. Legro and Andrew Moravcsik, "Is Anyone Still a Realist?" *International Security* 24, no. 2 (fall 1999), pp. 5–55. Like Jeffrey W. Taliaferro, I view the inclusion of domestic political variables as an enhancement of realism, rather than a rejection of it. See Peter D. Feaver et al., "Brother, Can You Spare a Paradigm? (Or Was Anybody Ever a Realist?)" *International Security* 25, no. 1 (summer 2000), p. 181.

[18] See, for example, Rose, "Neoclassical Realism and Theories of Foreign Policy"; Randall L. Schweller, "The Progressiveness of Neoclassical Realism," in Colin Elman and Miriam Fendius Elman, eds., *Progress in International Relations Theory: Appraising the Field* (Cambridge, MA: MIT Press, 2003), pp. 311–47.

[19] Jack S. Levy, "Domestic Politics and War," *Journal of Interdisciplinary History* 18, no. 4 (spring 1988), pp. 653–73, at p. 653.

[20] See Levy, "The Diversionary Theory of War"; Alastair Smith, "Diversionary Foreign Policy in Democratic Systems," *International Studies Quarterly* 40, no. 1 (1996), pp. 133–53.

third-image theory of international politics with second-image variables capturing the stability of the government.

Another strand of the new realist writings focuses on the impact of domestic political institutions and practices on the national security policy choices states make. Inspired by democratic peace theory, Susan Peterson posits that crisis bargaining outcomes depend not only on relative power considerations, but also on the nature of the governments involved. She argues that the institutional structures of a state and the strategic beliefs of key actors in the domestic theater play the principal role in determining whether crises end in war or not.[21] Building on Peterson's work, Miriam Fendius Elman operationalizes institutional structure by subdividing the category of democracy into majoritarian parliamentary democracies, coalitional parliamentary democracies, and presidential democracies, and represents strategic beliefs with an assessment of the relative hawkishness or dovishness of the executive and the legislature. She argues that in majoritarian parliamentary democracies executive preferences trump legislative preferences; thus a hawkish executive will pursue belligerent policies and a dovish cabinet will behave peacefully. In coalitional parliamentary democracies and presidential democracies, however, the executive is non-autonomous and public preferences trump executive preferences.[22] And my own research concludes that executive autonomy derives not merely from the form of democracy (i.e. its institutional structure), but also from the decision-making procedures and procedural norms that govern the conduct of foreign security policy. States with structurally autonomous executives behave as structural realists expect in response to international threats; those whose domestic decision-making environments deny autonomy to national security executives are often paralyzed in the face of domestic opposition and are unable to respond effectively to systemic imperatives.[23] Thus, to understand national security decisions fully, we must

---

[21] Susan Peterson, "How Democracies Differ: Public Opinion, State Structure, and the Lessons of the Fashoda Crisis," *Security Studies* 5, no. 1 (autumn 1995), pp. 3–37; Susan Peterson, *Crisis Bargaining and the State* (Ann Arbor: University of Michigan Press, 1996).

[22] Miriam Fendius Elman, "Presidentialism, Parliamentarism, and Theories of Democratic Peace," *Security Studies* 9, no. 4 (summer 20001), pp. 91–126.

[23] Ripsman, "The Curious Case of German Rearmament"; Ripsman, *Peacemaking by Democracies*.

complement third-image theory with a theory of the domestic decision-making environment.

Yet another avenue of inquiry that has opened recently is how broad domestic social coalitions affect the pursuit of security. Some, such as Benjamin O. Fordham, Peter Trubowitz, and Etel Solingen, argue that the grand strategies that states pursue may be shaped by the international system, but are heavily influenced by the constellation of domestic political and economic interests that comprise the governing coalition. In their view, then, the dictates of the international system are not as clear as neorealists would seem to imply; the governing coalition must interpret the national interest and decide upon the means with which it is pursued.[24] Building on this approach, Steven Lobell constructs a model of the grand strategy choices made by declining hegemons that includes the distribution of capabilities, the behavior of rising challengers, and the domestic coalition politics of the hegemon. While his "second image reversed plus second image" theory privileges international factors, it asserts the importance of the domestic political processes through which they are translated.[25] This branch of theory suggests that an understanding of the underlying domestic interest group and coalition structure will be essential if we wish to explain and predict how states respond to international threats and opportunities.

Drawing on the latter two traditions, scholars have constructed neoclassical realist theories to explain surprising deviations from the expectations of standard neorealist theories. Randall Schweller, for example, has advanced a theory of underbalancing that hinges on the level of elite and societal divisions in the state facing a rising challenger.[26] Jack Snyder uses regime type to explain why some states,

---

[24] Benjamin O. Fordham, *Building the Cold War Consensus: The Political Economy of US National Security Policy* (Ann Arbor: University of Michigan Press, 1998); Peter Trubowitz, *Defining the National Interest: Conflict and Change in American Foreign Policy* (Chicago: University of Chicago Press, 1998); Etel Solingen, *Regional Orders at Century's Dawn: Global and Domestic Influences on Grand Strategy* (Princeton, NJ: Princeton University Press, 1998).

[25] Steven E. Lobell, *The Challenge of Hegemony: Grand Strategy, Trade, and Domestic Politics* (Ann Arbor: University of Michigan Press, 2003).

[26] Randall L. Schweller, "Unanswered Threats: A Neoclassical Realist Theory of Underbalancing," *International Security* 29, no. 2 (fall 2004), pp. 159–201; Randall L. Schweller, *Unanswered Threats: Political Constraints on the Balance of Power* (Princeton, NJ: Princeton University Press, 2006).

principally those run by imperialistic cartels and militaristic general staffs, engage in campaigns of dangerous overexpansion.[27] And William Wohlforth explains the superpower clash during the Cold War as a product of their differing elite perceptions of the international balance of power.[28]

I argue that these new twists on realism represent an advance, rather than a step backward, because the domestic political variables they employ expand the explanatory power and precision of realist theory. They also represent an important advance on *Innenpolitik* approaches that view foreign policy largely as the product of domestic political competition. Thus, for example, pluralist models and Marxist approaches, which treat foreign policy as the product of the dominance of particular classes or interest coalitions in particular states, obscure considerable areas of commonality, resulting from similar international pressures, that unite states with different regimes and governing coalitions.[29] As Mark Brawley's chapter indicates, for example, the Soviet Union, Great Britain, and France all acknowledged the threat posed by Germany's power potential in the 1920s and 1930s and constructed policy accordingly. Domestic political differences led them to select different responses, but it is clear that international dynamics drove threat perception and set the parameters of policy-making. Thus, neoclassical realism adds both depth to structural realist theories and an appropriate frame for *Innenpolitik* approaches. Nonetheless, we lack a systematic theory to explain when domestic political factors affect national security policy and which domestic groups and actors matter most. In the next sections, I address each of these issues preliminarily.

Which interest groups and domestic actors matter most?

A large number of domestic actors have at least some interest in foreign security policy. At a minimum, the public is interested in any

---

[27] Snyder, *Myths of Empire*.

[28] William Curti Wohlforth, *The Elusive Balance: Power and Perceptions During the Cold War* (Ithaca, NY: Cornell University Press, 1993).

[29] See, for example, the approaches in Martin J. Smith, *Pressure, Power, and Policy: State Autonomy and Policy Networks in Britain and the United States* (Pittsburgh, PA: University of Pittsburgh Press, 1993); and Gabriel Kolko, *The Roots of American Foreign Policy* (Boston: Beacon Press, 1969).

policies that could affect the likelihood of war and privation, tax rates, or the potential for a military draft. Members of the legislature, of course, are interested in all aspects of the state's business, and national security is no exception. Many businesses, industrial sectors, labor unions, and other organized economic interests have vested interests in decisions that affect the levels of defense spending, the procurement of specific weapons systems, or access to foreign markets. Key domestic political institutions, such as the military and the aristocracy, have an interest in national security decisions that might affect their societal power and privilege. Ethnic groups that have sustained ties to a mother country may have an interest in decisions affecting that country. And the media justify their existence by probing all aspects of national policy. Which of these groups are likely to have any actual influence over national security policy?

In general, domestic actors should have less influence over national security policy than over any other issue area. This is the case for two key reasons. First, because of the importance of national security policy and the high costs that could accrue to the state were it to be mishandled – potentially defeat in war and perhaps even the loss of sovereignty – the public, the legislature, and societal interests should be willing to give the government more leeway in its conduct. This is especially the case since the government is acknowledged to have access to more (often secret) information on national security than other domestic actors, making it a better judge of the nation's long-term interests.[30] Indeed, it may even be considered unseemly to interfere with compelling national interests for private gain.[31]

Second, both the costs and the benefits of most aspects of national security policy tend to be rather widely distributed across society as a whole. Most sectors of society share, although perhaps unequally, in the tax burden and the recruitment burden to meet a foreign

---

[30] Steven Lobell's chapter concurs on this point. See also Thomas Christensen, *Useful Adversaries: Grand Strategy, Domestic Mobilization, and Sino-American Conflict, 1947–1958* (Princeton, NJ: Princeton University Press, 1996), p. 17.

[31] Such, for example, was the case in Israel prior to the 1982 Lebanon War. Because of the intensity of the security dilemma the country faced, it was viewed as improper to challenge the government on matters of national security. See Tamar Hermann, "Grassroots Activism as a Factor in Foreign Policy-Making," in David Skidmore and Valerie M. Hudson, eds., *The Limits of State Autonomy* (Boulder, CO: Westview, 1993), pp. 127–47.

challenge. Although the costs and opportunities of alliance decisions could conceivably impact some business sectors and firms more than others, very few of the organized societal interests that typically exert influence in domestic political coalitions have significant direct interests at stake in alliance politics. And all elements of society benefit from the enhanced security provided by prudent national security policy decisions. As James Q. Wilson contends, when the costs and benefits of policy are diffuse, strong interest groups tend not to form and interest groups consequently have little motivation to interfere with policy choices.[32] This suggests that, except for issues of defense spending and procurement, which we shall touch upon below, the direct interests of domestic actors in, and their willingness to interfere with, foreign security policy-making, should be low.[33]

Nonetheless, there are still opportunities for certain types of societal actors to influence policy. Let us now consider which types of groups are most likely to exert influence. In order to influence policy, domestic actors need to be able to provide a sufficient payoff to policy-makers if they construct policies in the desired direction, or to impose sufficient penalties if they do not. Since the policy executive is dominated, above all, by individuals who wish to retain their hold on power, and secondarily to pass their preferred policy agendas, they should be most receptive to influence from domestic actors who can provide or deny electoral support or, in non-democratic states, preserve the leader's position or topple him/her. Therefore, in democratic states, interest groups should be most successful if they have large membership rolls. Size, however, should not always translate into greater influence. A large interest group that does not have a significant degree of control over its members' voting behavior is not as

---

[32] James Q. Wilson, "The Politics of Regulation," in James Q. Wilson, ed., *The Politics of Regulation* (New York: Basic Books, 1980), pp. 357–94, at pp. 367–8. Theodore J. Lowi similarly links the range of societal actors that a particular policy affects and the magnitude of the personal stake to the manner in which they are resolved. "American Business, Public Policy, Case Studies, and Political Theory," *World Politics* 16, no. 4 (July 1964), pp. 676–716; and Theodore J. Lowi, "Four Systems of Policy, Politics, and Choice," *Public Administration Review* 32, no. 4 (July/August 1972), pp. 298–310.

[33] It is, perhaps, for this reason that in his classic treatment of the societal influence on policy, Lowi deliberately excludes foreign policy, which he describes as "in many ways not part of the same universe" as domestic policy. "American Business, Public Policy, Case Studies, and Political Theory," p. 689.

likely to wield as much influence as one that can rely on its members to vote as a bloc. In this regard, single-issue groups whose members are passionately committed to that issue above all others – as, say pro-choice and anti-abortion supporters tend to be – should have greater credibility than those whose members are likely to consider a wider range of domestic political issues when voting.[34] Thus, in the foreign policy issue area, we might expect ethnic diaspora communities to have greater member voting consistency than, say, groups who favor greater military preparedness but whose members might be divided over a host of other cross-cutting economic and political issues. Moreover, groups that have a significant voter base in strategic regions (e.g. in political districts or states that are competitive and pivotal) should have greater potential influence than those who are scattered or concentrated in less important locales. For example, the influence of Cuban émigrés in the United States over American Cuban policy can be attributed to their concentration in Florida, a populous swing state that has been pivotal in at least one US federal election. Finally, in rare cases when it is sufficiently intense and united on a particular issue, public opinion as a whole may persuade the national security executive to alter its national security policies. Thus, for example, strong public opposition, particularly in Quebec, to participation in George W. Bush's "coalition of the willing" against Iraq led Canadian Prime Minister Jean Chrétien to remain on the sidelines, despite initial indications that he would send a token Canadian force.

In non-democratic states or quasi-democratic regimes that lack institutionalized democratic stability, the leadership's desire to retain power should make it more receptive to influencing attempts from two types of actors. First, they should pay more attention to kingmakers, or those with decisive power to select, back, or eject leaders. Indeed, during the 1996 tensions with Taiwan, there is evidence to suggest that Chinese leader Deng Xiaoping was compelled to adopt a softer stance by powerful provincial leaders and Shanghai business-minded elites, who were growing increasingly influential in the party.[35] Second, they should be especially attentive to groups, such as the military,

---

[34] Eugene R. Wittkopf, Charles W. Kegley and James M. Scott, *American Foreign Policy: Pattern and Process*, 6th en, (Belmont, CA: Wadsworth/Thomson Learning, 2003), p. 298.

[35] I thank Jean-Marc F. Blanchard for bringing this episode to my attention.

that have the capability to lead a coup or organized revolt against the regime. Thus, for example, the new Islamist government of Turkey – a state which has seen numerous coups by a military seeking to guarantee a secular constitution and a stable policy – has shied away from moves such as outright termination of Turkey's cooperative relationship with Israel. And in very rare cases when public sentiment is so completely charged and leaders fear a revolution or widespread unrest, leaders may change or tailor their policies to public preferences. Indeed, such would appear to be Egyptian President Mubarak's policy toward Israel after Sadat's assassination. He retained the peace treaty with Israel, but kept it a cold peace, rather than a constructive one, to minimize domestic hostility.

Aside from a direct electoral payoff, political leaders are also interested in those domestic actors who can provide resources that can be used either to retain power or, in cases of corrupt regimes, to line their pockets. In this regard, we might expect that wealthier groups would have more influence than those with only limited resources. Nonetheless, money and resources should be of only limited utility, since – unlike direct, coherent electoral clout – they tend to be spread across interest groups. Thus, while one group may offer a large material payoff for pursuing its preferred policy option, it is conceivable that one or more actors that oppose the policy will be able to provide a countervailing payoff that, even if smaller, would allow the executive to select its preferred policy without forgoing the bulk of the payoff.

For this reason, I do not expect so-called "military-industrial-complex" (MIC) or "iron triangle" interest groups to have any significant influence over foreign security policy.[36] These groups, particularly firms that produce armaments or otherwise supply the military, and those engaged in defense-related research and development, are supposed to exert – together with the military and their allies in the government – a decisive influence over issues ranging from defense spending and weapons procurement to decisions of war and peace. Yet it is not clear why they must do so. To begin with, on individual procurement decisions, firms compete against each other and can raise countervailing rewards for the executive; therefore, the

---

[36] See C. Wright Mills, *The Power Elite* (New York: Oxford University Press, 2000).

government should be able to choose its own preferred option independently of MIC interest groups at little cost. Furthermore, on those issues where the MIC interest groups are united (say in favoring higher overall defense spending or encouraging the use of force), firms and interest groups in other sectors of the economy that would lose out as a result can coalesce to offer a countervailing reward. So it seems unreasonable to privilege this one cluster of economic interests over other well-endowed interests.[37]

Beyond the ability to keep the government in power or defeat it, domestic actors with the ability to obstruct the government's agenda should also be able to bargain with the executive over the content of security policy. In a democratic state, this means that the legislature, either as a whole or through its key legislative committees on foreign affairs or defense policy, can impact upon policy choices, since it can act as a veto player over policy if no concessions are made to its preferences.[38] This is particularly the case, as it is in the United States, when the legislature controls the implementation of policy through its control over budgetary allocations. Thus, prior to the Persian Gulf wars of 1991 and 2003, the administration spent much time and effort garnering congressional declarations authorizing the use of force and was willing to bargain with Congress to receive them. In addition, in a democratic state with powerful and independent courts that can issue binding advisory opinions, the executive may also take judicial preferences into account when making policy, although this phenomenon is rare.[39] Finally, in non-democratic states, where courts and legislatures have little role, other potential veto players, such as

---

[37] For related critiques, see Jerome Slater and Terry Nardin, "The Concept of the Military-Industrial Complex," in Steven Rosen, ed., *Testing the Theory of the Military-Industrial Complex* (Lexington, MA: Lexington Books, 1973), pp. 27–50; Steven Rosen, "Testing the Theory of the Military-Industrial Complex," ibid., pp. 1–25.

[38] On veto players, see George Tsebelis, *Veto Players: How Political Institutions Work* (Princeton, NJ: Princeton University Press, 2002).

[39] The Canadian Supreme Court, for example, issued an opinion in 1985 on whether testing American cruise missiles in Canada was constitutional. In this case, the court's ruling did not constrain the government's subsequent behavior, but it could have done. Moreover, the decision explicitly asserted the court's right to review matters of foreign and defense policy, giving it an important veto in the foreign policy process. *Operation Dismantle* v. *The Queen* [1985] 1 SCR 441. I thank James Kelly for bringing this case to my attention.

powerful bureaucratic actors, religious leaders, professional guilds, or the military, can also manipulate their power to obstruct to extract policy concessions. Indeed, in Iran – where the power of the Shiite clerics extends into all facets of daily life – the mullahs effectively blocked former President Mohammed Khatami's efforts to moderate Iranian foreign and domestic policies.

Finally, domestic actors may influence policy choices not by exchanging something of value for a policy payoff, but by shaping the interpretation of international circumstances and helping define the national interest. In this sense, they can act as epistemic communities, shaping the mind-set of the national security executive.[40] In this regard, the US media, and think tanks such as the Council on Foreign Relations or the Brookings Institution, may be able to influence American security policy by framing the elite debate.

Therefore, in democratic states, we should expect the greatest influence from well-organized, coherent, vote-rich, single-issue interest groups that can provide an electoral payoff, the legislature that can act as a veto for the government's policy agenda, groups that can frame executive thinking on foreign affairs, and, occasionally, the public as a whole. A lesser and less frequent influence may be expected from wealthy or resource-rich groups, simply because of the countervailing resources of opposing groups. In non-democratic states, kingmaker societal groups, and those such as the military that can lead a revolt against the leader, should have the greatest influence on national security policy, followed by bureaucratic or economic actors that have the potential to obstruct policy implementation, and in unusual circumstances, public opinion as a whole.

One final issue pertains to the scope of the domestic actor's demands.[41] If the group demands minor modifications or tailoring of policy, it will be more likely to influence outcomes, for the costs to national security of these minor changes will likely be low. In

---

[40] On epistemic communities in the international arena, see Ernst Haas, *When Knowledge is Power* (Berkeley: University of California Press, 1990); Peter M. Haas, "Introduction: Epistemic Communities and International Policy Coordination," *International Organization* 46, no. 1 (winter 1992), pp. 1–36.

[41] See Robert H. Trice, "Interest Groups and the Foreign Policy Process: US Policy in the Middle East," *Sage Professional Paper in International Studies* 4, no. 02–047 (1976), p. 8.

contrast, an actor that demands programmatic change to national security policy should have great difficulty achieving its goals if the international incentives point to a different strategy. Similarly, those actors that mobilize for basic continuity of policy should be more successful than those who agitate for policy change, although it would be difficult to attribute policy continuity to the influence of domestic actors, rather than other factors such as continuity in the external environment, constant executive preferences, bureaucratic inertia, etc.[42]

Having determined which domestic groups have the greatest potential to impact upon national security decisions, I will now consider the circumstances under which they should have the greatest influence.

Under what international circumstances will domestic actors have the greatest influence?

We should expect domestic actors and interest groups to have the greatest influence over foreign security policy during stable periods when the state faces a low-threat international environment. In high-threat environments, the risks to the state and its survival are paramount, since war is always likely and potentially imminent. Under these circumstances, when the margin for error is minimal, the national security executive will have powerful incentives to ignore domestic political interests and formulate security policy with the overriding goal of securing the state. Conversely, in a low-threat environment, the costs of allowing domestic actors to contribute to the making of national security policy are low. Consequently, the national security executive will be more attuned to its domestic political environment and, in particular, more willing to make concessions to powerful actors and interests that could potentially either assist it in maintaining its hold on power or contribute to its overthrow.[43]

---

[42] Wittkopf et al., *American Foreign Policy*, p. 298.

[43] Bernard C. Cohen puts this another way. "Private interest thus seems generally to yield to public – or national – interest when the latter is clearly formulated. The political question then turns more on the formulation of 'national interest' in threatening circumstances than it does on the accommodation of private interests in non-threatening circumstances." "The Influence of Special-Interest Groups and Mass Media on Security Policy in the United States," in Charles

In the American context, there is some evidence that interest groups have more influence during periods of relative security. During the Cold War, when global security competition with a nuclear-armed Soviet Union raised the stakes of foreign policy, Lester W. Milbrath concluded "that interest group influence on foreign policy is slight."[44] Another study of US foreign policy similarly concluded that:

> While interest groups seek to persuade, their mere presence, indeed, ubiquity, does not guarantee their penetration of the foreign policy-making process ... Interest groups may be effective on certain special issues. More often, foreign policy making is relatively immune to interest group influence.[45]

Nonetheless, as James McCormick's more recent study indicates, interest groups have gained some traction in the post-Cold War era.[46] As McCormick suggests, this phenomenon can be linked to, amongst other factors, the increasing prominence of trade issues and the declining focus on traditional national security matters, and a shift from crisis management to a long-term approach to foreign policy. In other words, when security is not immediately at stake, interest groups have a greater say in foreign policy-making. To be sure, McCormick also points to institutional changes in Congress that give more lobby groups greater access. These reforms themselves, however, may be at least partially attributable to the stability of the early post-Cold War world which made a more transparent, less autonomous foreign policy process safer.[47] It remains to be seen what effect the new post-9/11 security environment will have on the influence of interest groups and other domestic actors.

W. Kegley, Jr. and Eugene R. Wittkopf, eds., *Perspectives on American Foreign Policy: Selected Readings* (New York: St. Martin's Press, 1983), pp. 222–41, at pp. 224–5. Mark Brawley's chapter in this volume similarly concludes that the time frame within which a threat is likely affects the intensity of balancing strategies and, consequently, the degree to which domestic difficulties are accommodated.

[44] Lester W. Milbrath, "Interest Groups and Foreign Policy," in James N. Rosenau, ed., *Domestic Sources of Foreign Policy* (New York: Free Press, 1967), pp. 231–51, at p. 251.

[45] Wittkopf et al., *American Foreign Policy*, p. 299.

[46] James McCormick, "Interest Groups and the Media in Post-Cold War US Foreign Policy," in James M. Scott, ed., *After the End: Making US Foreign Policy in the Post-Cold War World* (Durham, NC: Duke University Press, 1998), pp. 170–98.

[47] See, for example, Ripsman, *Peacemaking by Democracies*, pp. 237–8.

Under what domestic circumstances will domestic groups have the greatest influence?

In principle, domestic political actors should gain the most policy traction when the government is vulnerable. If the government expects that an electoral defeat, a military coup, or some other form of de-selection is potentially imminent, it will be far more likely to shore up its position by buying off a powerful interest group or the public at large. Thus a democratic national security policy executive might be most willing to bargain with domestic interests over national security policy as an election approaches and public opinion polls show that reelection will be difficult. This might explain, for example, why George W. Bush accelerated the pace of the handover of power to an interim Iraqi regime in June 2004, prior to the November election campaign. A non-democratic regime should be more willing to make national security policy with an eye toward domestic actors when a crisis looms that could topple the government. The Argentine junta's decision to invade the Falkland Islands in 1981 could thus be seen as an attempt to buy off domestic opposition dissatisfied with the regime's economic performance.[48]

Aside from governmental vulnerability, the degrees of both executive certainty and national consensus about policy should also affect the importance of domestic actors. When the executive is decided about the course of national security policy, there is little room for domestic actors with other agendas to influence policy choices. Similarly, when there is a national consensus, such as there was in favor of containment during much of the Cold War, groups with divergent views have little room to maneuver.[49] Only when ambiguity or confusion reigns in the policy environment can a domestic actor most effectively emerge as a policy entrepreneur and shape policy.

---

[48] See the discussion in Richard Ned Lebow, "Miscalculation in the South Atlantic: The Origins of the Falklands War," in Robert Jervis, Richard Ned Lebow, and Janice Gross Stein, eds., *Psychology and Deterrence* (Baltimore, MD: Johns Hopkins University Press, 1985), pp. 89–124.

[49] Cohen, "The Influence of Special-Interest Groups and Mass Media on Security Policy in the United States," p. 224. Daniel L. Byman and Kenneth M. Pollack similarly argue that the ability of individual leaders to shape policy also increases with ambiguity or confusion in the policy environment. "Let Us Now Praise Great Men: Bringing the Statesman Back In," *International Security* 25, no. 4 (spring 2001), pp. 141–2.

Even though he makes different assumptions about the nature of state–societal relations, Steven Lobell comes to similar conclusions in his chapter.

In what types of states will domestic actors matter most?

Simply put, domestic actors should have the greatest influence in states whose national security policy executives possess low levels of structural autonomy. As I argue elsewhere, a state's domestic decision-making environment – comprised of its institutional structures, decision-making procedures, and prevailing procedural norms – determines the degree to which its national security policy executive is insulated from its domestic opposition.[50] All things being equal, the more structurally autonomous an executive is, the lesser the ability of domestic actors to interfere with the government's foreign policy agenda. Autonomy varies not only across states, but also within the same state over time. For example, American governments varied in their independence from legislative opposition in forging postwar peace settlements in 1919 and after 1945. In 1919, Woodrow Wilson was constrained by opponents in the Senate because of an unresolved constitutional division of foreign policy powers and procedural norms that favored the full use of senatorial power. In contrast, Harry Truman's and Dwight Eisenhower's governments after World War II were able to act with substantial independence from domestic opposition because of judicial interpretations of the division of powers that privileged the president, the procedure of non-partisanship, and the emerging norm that, because of the Soviet threat, foreign policy was far too important to allow congressional interference.[51]

Since autonomy is the key variable affecting the influence of domestic actors on national security policy it should not matter that much whether they inhabit a democratic state or a non-democratic one. After all, both democracies and non-democratic states vary in the level of autonomy they possess in the national security area. It would

---

[50] Ripsman, *Peacemaking by Democracies*. As I indicate there, structural autonomy is calculated a priori based on a uniformly applied set of questions about state structure. Therefore, autonomy can be separated as a distinct independent variable from actual observed policy independence (the dependent variable) to avoid tautology.

[51] Ibid., chaps. 2–4.

be difficult to argue, for example, that after the Cuban Missile Crisis Soviet leader Nikita Khrushchev had anywhere near the national security policy autonomy from the Supreme Soviet that Iraqi dictator Saddam Hussein had from Iraqi society and institutions. Similarly, the executives of Fourth Republic France or contemporary Israel, both of which are/were comprised of fragile coalitions of poorly disciplined parties, have/had less foreign policy autonomy than postwar Great Britain, with its strong one-party majorities.[52] Thus we might expect that a structurally constrained non-democratic leader, such as Khrushchev, might possess even less autonomy to conduct policy than a highly autonomous democratic foreign security policy executive, such as the American national security state during the early Cold War. Relative autonomy, therefore, matters more than regime type.

It is easy to see how structural autonomy affects the influence of domestic groups. When a democratic executive is independent of the legislature, it minimizes the interference of individual parliamentarians, legislative committees, and the legislature as a whole. Furthermore, it reduces the impact of public opinion, which usually filters through to the executive indirectly through the legislature. Since interest groups typically have greater access to – and greater influence over – the legislature than the executive,[53] an autonomous executive is insulated from them to a greater extent as well. And the media's influence, flowing mostly through the public to the legislature, is similarly curtailed. In a non-democratic state, autonomy is even more profound, as insulation from societal elites and institutions directly shields the leader from their policy demands. In contrast, a non-autonomous national security executive is constantly bombarded by the demands of a vast array of domestic actors, each of which has the potential, subject to the conditions discussed above, to influence policy choices.

Another related aspect of the state that can affect the impact of domestic actors, particularly specific sectors or classes, is what Peter Evans calls the embeddedness of the state.[54] To the extent that the state has close ties to certain classes or sectors of society – to the point that state leaders and managers are typically drawn from those circles

---

[52] Ibid., chap. 2.   [53] Wittkopf et al., *American Foreign Policy*, p. 298.
[54] Peter Evans, *Embedded Autonomy: States and Industrial Transformations* (Princeton, NJ: Princeton University Press, 1995).

and socialized by them – those sectors will be able to shape the state's attitude to national security, and thereby influence the policy choices made by state leaders.[55] Nonetheless, the effect of embeddedness should not be overstated. Since the state is potentially autonomous and since, as I argued earlier, the view from above is different from the view out of office, we can expect leader preferences to deviate considerably from their societal cohorts, particularly when national security is at stake. Thus the degree of state autonomy is a more important factor than state embeddedness in determining the influence of domestic actors.

What are domestic actors most likely to affect when they have some influence?

When domestic actors are able to influence policy choices, what exactly do they help determine? Do they affect the way states define their national interests, the means that are used to implement those interests, or merely the timing and style of the response?

In general, the likelihood of influencing each of these aspects of foreign security policy declines considerably with the magnitude of influence. Thus it is only under a very restricted set of circumstances that domestic interests can determine the definition of the national interests that states pursue. Only when the security environment is very stable and the costs of faulty decisions are likely to be low can the state afford to allow the direction of national security strategy to be determined for domestic political reasons. In contrast, when weighty matters of war and peace threaten the state, domestic groups are likely to have a more restricted influence, affecting only the means employed to achieve a clearly defined end or the manner in which the response is crafted. Thus, as Colin Dueck's contribution to this volume indicates, domestic interests are unlikely to drive decisions of war and peace, but may affect the timing of war and the manner in which it is conducted.

Conclusion: domestic actors and foreign policy

Neorealists are correct to emphasize that the international system conditions national foreign policy choices and is their primary

---

[55] I thank Marie-Jöelle Zahar for bringing this line of argument to my attention.

determinant. But that does not mean that domestic political factors are unimportant. As neoclassical realists contend, at times domestic actors can exert a decisive influence on how the state interprets international threats and opportunities, and how it responds to them. In this chapter, I considered which domestic actors are likely to have the most influence on foreign security policy and the domestic and international conditions under which they are most likely to exert influence. In general, the domestic actors that can be most influential are those that have sufficient power to remove the leader or executive from office, those that can use their veto to obstruct the government's programmatic goals, or those that can shape the definition of national interests. These actors are more likely to have a significant impact on policy choices, principally when the international threat situation is low, when the leader's hold on power is weak, and when the national security executive lacks structural autonomy. On the whole, though, domestic actors are far more likely to influence the timing and style of a state's national security policies than the definition of the national interest, which is usually determined from without, unless the state inhabits a stable environment.

The implications of my chapter, then, are consistent with the overall thrust of this volume. To begin with, neoclassical realism presents a more nuanced and appropriate guide to the security choices that states make than either the externally driven neorealist model or the internally driven societal *Innenpolitik* models. While the international system sets the stage for policy choice and shapes the policy environment, as neorealists contend, its causal influence on national policy responses is tempered, and sometimes thwarted, by domestic political competition and institutions. Similarly, internal politics does not play as decisive a role in directing foreign policy as *Innenpolitik* theories assume, since domestic groups are forced to contend with the constraints of the international system, which when severe limit choices and compel certain policy alternatives. By asserting the primacy of the international system, moderated by domestic political competition within a potentially autonomous state, neoclassical realism provides a richer portrait of the dynamism and complexity of foreign policy-making.

In addition, this chapter underscores the utility of neoclassical realism as an approach to foreign policy, rather than merely as an explanation of suboptimal policy choices. Certainly, in a turbulent international system, when security is scarce, domestic actors have limited ability to influence foreign policy and interfere with the executive policy, potentially at the expense of the national interest.[56] When the security environment is more stable, however, states have a greater degree of freedom in choosing policies, and domestic actors have a greater role in directing the national foreign policy choices without serious consequences. In these circumstances, neoclassical realism can shed light on the ordinary foreign policy choices states make, rather than simply the dysfunctional errors they occasionally make.

[56] See, for example, Hans J. Morgenthau, *Dilemmas of Politics* (Chicago: University of Chicago, 1958), p. 326.

7 | Neoclassical realism and resource extraction: State building for future war*

JEFFREY W. TALIAFERRO

In the mid-nineteenth century, China and Japan faced the rising threat of western imperialism. Yet, despite the two countries' cultural ties and geographic proximity, their responses to that threat were quite different. When confronted with growing anti-Manchu rebellions at home and British demands for trade concessions in the 1830s, the Qing dynasty proved unable to mobilize the resources necessary to defend the empire. The first and second Opium Wars revealed disparities in military technology between China and the European great powers. Faced with internal unrest and the prospect of China's dismemberment, Chinese provincial leaders made an attempt at internal reform, the so-called Tongzi Restoration (1862–74), aimed at reforming the military, creating an arms industry, and strengthening traditional Confucian government. Although these and later reforms prolonged the Qing dynasty until 1911, they were insufficient to halt China's relative decline.

News of China's defeat in the Opium Wars, carried by Dutch and Chinese ships to Nagasaki and then relayed to the shogun at Edo (Tokyo), shocked Japan's feudal elite. The arrival of Commodore Matthew Perry and his "black ships" in Edo Bay in July 1853 ended Japan's two centuries of self-imposed isolation. The Tokugawa

* I thank Dale Copeland, Dan Drezner, Benjamin Fordham, Benjamin Frankel, Steven Lobell, Alex McLeod, João Resende-Santos, Julian Schofield, and Norrin Ripsman, the participants in the Program on International Politics, Economy, and Security (PIPES) seminar at the University of Chicago and the workshop on "Neoclassical Realism and the State" at Concordia University for comments and suggestions. Material from this chapter has appeared in "State Building for Future War: Neoclassical Realism and the Resource Extractive State," *Security Studies*, vol. 15, no. 3 (July–September 2006), pp. 464–95. Reprinted by permission of the publisher (Taylor & Francis Ltd, www.tandf.co.uk/journals).

shogunate's inability to defend the country led to its overthrow in 1867–8 by a group of samurai from Satsuma and Choshu, who acted to "restore" the sixteen-year-old Emperor Meiji. The new leadership spent the next twenty years methodically emulating the military, political, and technological practices of the European great powers. In particular, they built a mass army, a general staff system, a state bureaucracy modeled on those of Germany, and a navy modeled on the British Royal Navy. Between 1894 and 1905, Japan waged two wars: the first to supplant Chinese hegemony in East Asia and the second to prevent Russia from filling that power vacuum.[1]

Even when confronted with the same threat, states vary in their ability to mobilize domestic resources for defense. The creation of the mass army enabled Revolutionary and later Napoleonic France to enjoy ten years of battlefield victories. However, Austria, Great Britain, and Russia did not rush to emulate the French military model. Only Prussia, the weakest great power, was willing to risk upheaval to undertake a fundamental transformation of its military. Even then, Prussian reform efforts came relatively late. In 1794, King Friedrich Wilhelm II rejected proposals to institute *levée en masse*, fearing such a move would be "infinitely dangerous" to the social and political order. It took the catastrophic defeat of the Prussian army at Jena and Auerstädt in 1806 and the humiliating Treaty of Tilsit imposed by Napoleon to convince the king and his advisors of the need for sweeping military and political reforms.[2]

---

[1] For an overview of the impact of military modernization in Meiji Japan and Qing China, see David B. Ralston, *Importing the European Army: The Introduction of European Military Techniques and Institutions into the Extra-European World, 1600–1914* (Chicago: University of Chicago Press, 1990), pp. 107–41; Shin'ichi Kitaoka, "The Army as Bureaucracy: Japanese Militarism Revisited," *Journal of Military History* 57, no. 5 (October 1993), pp. 67–86; Ernst Presseisen, *Before Aggression: Europeans Prepare the Japanese Army* (Tucson: University of Arizona Press, 1965); and S. C. M. Paine, *The Sino-Japanese War of 1894–1895* (Cambridge: Cambridge University Press, 2003).

[2] See William H. McNeill, *The Pursuit of Power: Technology, Armed Force, and Society since A.D. 1000* (Chicago: University of Chicago Press, 1982), pp. 185–215; Peter Paret, "Napoleon and the Revolution in War," in Williamson Murray, MacGregor Knox, and Alvin Bernstein, eds., *Makers of Modern Strategy: From Machiavelli to the Nuclear Age* (Princeton, NJ: Princeton University Press, 1986), pp. 123–42; Barry R. Posen, "Nationalism, the Mass Army, and Military Power," *International Security* 18, no. 2 (fall 1993), pp. 80–124; and Geoffrey L. Herrera and Thomas G. Mahnken, "Military Diffusion in Nineteenth-Century Europe: The Napoleonic and

Neorealism, specifically Kenneth Waltz's balance of power theory, holds that the international system provides incentives for states, especially the great powers, to adopt similar adaptive strategies or risk elimination as independent entities. States generally balance against powerful states by forging alliances with weaker states or by arms racing. Furthermore, states tend to emulate the military, technological, and governing practices of the most successful states in the system.[3]

The problem, as both proponents and critics of neorealism point out, is that Waltz's theory does not explain why and how states choose between different types of "internal" balancing strategies, such as emulation, innovation, or the continuation of existing strategies.[4] Explaining this requires a theory that integrates systemic-level and unit-level variables.

Chapter 1 set forth three broad questions about the politics of resource extraction, domestic mobilization, and policy implementation in grand strategy: How do states mobilize the resources necessary to pursue their chosen security policies? How much power do domestic actors have to obstruct the state when it seeks to mobilize resources in different settings? What determines who is more successful in bargaining games between the state and societal groups?

The present chapter narrows this line of inquiry by focusing on one aspect of grand strategic change and implementation: namely, the diffusion of military institutions, technologies, and governing practices across states. Accordingly, the specific questions I address are the

Prussian Military Systems," in Emily O. Goldman and Leslie C. Eliason, eds., *The Diffusion of Military Technology and Ideas* (Stanford, CA: Stanford University Press, 2003), pp. 205–42.

[3] See Kenneth N. Waltz, *Theory of International Politics* (New York: Random House, 1979). Throughout this chapter, I use the terms "balance of power theory" and "neorealism" interchangeably to denote the theory Waltz developed in *Theory of International Politics*. The term "neorealism," however, also applies to several systemic realist theories that often make predictions that diverge sharply from Waltz's theory. See Jeffrey W. Taliaferro, "Security Seeking under Anarchy: Defensive Realism Reconsidered," *International Security* 25, no. 3 (winter 2000–1), pp. 128–61; and Colin Elman, "Horses for Courses: Why Not Neorealist Theories of Foreign Policy?" *Security Studies* 6, no. 2 (autumn 1996), pp. 7–53.

[4] The distinction between internal and external balancing originates in Waltz, *Theory of International Politics*, p. 168; and Barry R. Posen, *Sources of Military Doctrine: France, Britain, and Germany between the World Wars* (Ithaca, NY: Cornell University Press, 1984), pp. 17–18.

following: Under what circumstances will states emulate the successful military institutions, governing practices, and technologies of more powerful states? When confronted with similarly threatening international environments, why do some states emulate, while others fail to do so? Under what circumstances will states create entirely new military institutions, practices, and technologies in an effort to offset the perceived advantages of rival states? Finally, why are some threatened states willing and able to create efficient means to extract and mobilize greater resources from their societies, while other states will not or cannot?

In the pages that follow, I outline a resource-extraction model of the state in neoclassical realism. I argue that the competitive nature of the international system provides incentives for states to emulate the successful political, military, and technological practices of the system's leading states or to counter such practices through innovation. Domestic variables, however, limit the efficiency of states' responses to these systemic imperatives. Neoclassical realism suggests that state power – the relative ability of the state to extract or mobilize societal resources as determined by the institutions of the state, as well as by nationalism and ideology – shapes the types of internal balancing strategies a state is likely to pursue.

States that initially enjoy higher extraction and mobilization capacity, but also face high external vulnerability, are more likely to emulate the military, governing, and technological practices of the system's most successful states, at least in the short run. In contrast, states with low extraction and mobilization capacity, but confronting high external vulnerability, will have greater difficulty in pursuing emulation, at least in the short run. States with higher extraction and mobilization capacity but low external vulnerability have the luxury of engaging in innovation to enhance their long-term security and power. Conversely, states with constrained mobilization and extraction capacity, but facing low external vulnerability, are less likely to pursue emulation or innovation. In the long term, states can try to increase their extractive and mobilization capabilities, and consequently their ability to pursue emulation or innovation, by propagating nationalist or statist ideologies. Lack of nationalist sentiment or an anti-statist ideology, however, can limit the state's ability to emulate or innovate. In these circumstances, vulnerable states will likely persist in existing strategies.

As the introductory chapter explains, neoclassical realism stresses the causal primacy of structural variables, chiefly the relative distribution of material power and anticipated power trends, in shaping states' foreign policies. Systemic forces create incentives for all states to strive for greater efficiency in causing security for themselves. Yet, as Jennifer Sterling-Folker noted, "anarchy does not dictate how states should arrange their domestic processes to achieve that end. States are free to experiment, to emulate one another's practices, or to do nothing. Nonetheless, domestic processes act as the final arbiter for state survival within the anarchic environment."[5]

Constructivists charge that realism in general, and neorealist theory in particular, lacks a theory of the state.[6] Following others, I submit Waltz does present a theory of the state, albeit a restrictive and underdeveloped one.[7] Neoclassical realism provides a fuller conception of the state by specifying how systemic imperatives will likely translate, through the medium of state power, into actual foreign and security policies. Therefore, it might account for the different responses of late Qing China and Meiji Japan to the common threat of western imperialism or the variation in the European great powers' ability and willingness to emulate the mass army during the French Revolutionary and Napoleonic Wars.

It is important to note the limits of the model outlined on the following pages. I do not purport to offer a complete theory of state

[5] Jennifer Sterling-Folker, "Realist Environment, Liberal Process, and Domestic-Level Variables," *International Studies Quarterly* 41, no. 1 (March 1997), pp. 1–25, at p. 19.
[6] See Richard W. Cox, "Social Forces, States, and World Order: Beyond International Relations Theory"; and John Gerard Ruggie, "Continuity and Transformation in the World Polity," both in Robert O. Keohane, ed., *Neorealism and its Critics* (New York: Columbia University Press, 1986), pp. 204–54, esp. pp. 227–32, and 131–57; Alexander Wendt, "Anarchy Is What States Make of It," *International Organization* 42, no. 2 (spring 1992), pp. 391–426; and Hendrik Spruyt, *The Sovereign State and its Competitors* (Princeton, NJ: Princeton University Press, 1994), pp. 11–21.
[7] See Barry Buzan, Charles Jones, and Richard Little, *The Logic of Anarchy: Neorealism to Structural Realism* (New York: Columbia University Press, 1993), pp. 116–21; Sterling-Folker, "Realist Environment, Liberal Process and Domestic-Level Variables," *International Studies Quarterly* 41, no. 1 (March 1997), pp. 1–25. esp. pp. 16–22; Stephen Hobden, *International Relations and Historical Sociology* (London: Routledge, 1998), pp. 66–9; and John M. Hobson, *The State and International Relations* (Cambridge: Cambridge University Press, 2000), pp. 24–30.

formation and persistence. I agree with Stephen Walt that, "a realist approach to state formation would emphasize the imposition of sovereign authority to mobilize power and create security for ruler and ruled alike, as opposed to approaches that regard the state as a voluntary contract between sovereign and subject or between free and equal citizens."[8] Undertaking such a task is beyond the scope of this chapter. Likewise, the resource-extraction model treats states' external alignments as exogenous. Thus it does not address debates about the prevalence of balancing, buck-passing, chain ganging, appeasement, and hiding.[9] Finally, the objective of this chapter is merely to outline a neoclassical realist extraction model and not to empirically test hypotheses derived from that model. Consequently, the historical cases all involve instances in which the state in question faced high levels of external vulnerability. As discussed below, the variation in the level of external vulnerability is the independent variable, while variation in the level of state power is the intervening variable. By holding the value of the independent variable constant, I seek to establish the plausibility of state power as an intervening variable between systemic imperatives and the internal balancing strategy that a state will likely pursue.

This chapter consists of three sections: the first section establishes the theoretical context by examining the treatment of the state and the balance of power in classical realism and neorealism. The second outlines the resource-extraction model. I posit hypotheses about the circumstances under which state power will be likely to facilitate or inhibit a state's ability to adapt to changes in its strategic environment.

---

[8] Stephen M. Walt, "The Enduring Relevance of the Realist Tradition," in Ira Katznelson and Helen V. Milner, eds., *Political Science: State of the Discipline* (New York: W.W. Norton, 2002), p. 227. See also Ashley J. Tellis, "Reconstructing Political Realism: The Long March to Scientific Theory," in Benjamin Frankel, ed., *Roots of Realism* (London: Frank Cass, 1996), pp. 91–4; and Ioannis D. Evrigenis, "Carthage Must Be Saved: Fear of Enemies and Collective Action," (Ph.D. dissertation, Harvard University, 2005), esp. chaps. 1 and 2.

[9] For a discussion of what constitutes balancing, see Colin Elman, "Introduction: Appraising Balance-of-Power Theory"; Jack S. Levy, "Balances and Balancing: Concepts, Propositions, and Research Design"; and Richard Rosecrance, "Is There a Balance of Power?" all in John A. Vasquez and Colin Elman, eds., *Realism and the Balancing of Power: A New Debate* (Upper Saddle River, NJ: Prentice Hall, 2003), pp. 1–22, 128–53, and 154–65.

Historical examples from the experiences of seven rising or declining great powers over the past 300 years (Great Britain, France, Japan, China, Prussia/Germany, Russia/Soviet Union, and the United States) illustrate the plausibility of these hypotheses. The conclusion discusses directions for future research.

The state and the balance of power in classical realism and neorealism

The resource-extraction model in neoclassical realism integrates systemic and unit-level variables to explain variation in the types of internal balancing strategies states will likely pursue. Accordingly, this section delineates the range of likely internal balancing strategies and distinguishes the conception of the state and the balance of power in neoclassical realism from those of its theoretical forebear: classical realism and neorealism. Neoclassical realism incorporates classical realism's implicit complex model of state–society relations, while building upon neorealism's insights about the constraints of anarchy and the relative distribution of material power.

Delineating possible internal balancing strategies

When faced with external threats, states have a choice between three broad categories of internal balancing strategies: (1) to continue with existing politico-military strategies and technological practices; (2) to engage in emulation; or (3) to engage in innovation. The first strategy is self-explanatory. Senior officials recognize or anticipate an increasingly threatening strategic environment but conclude that a continuation or perhaps an escalation of current diplomatic and military policies or technological practices will likely ameliorate that threat. The other two strategies, however, entail the abandonment of existing institutions, technologies, or governing practices in favor of new ones.

Emulation is the "conscious, purposeful imitation, in full or in part, by one state of any institution, technology, or governing practice of another state."[10] It is distinct from the imposition of such practices by

---

[10] João Resende-Santos, "Anarchy and the Emulation of Military Systems: Military Organization and Technology in South America, 1870–1930," in

one state on another state or the imposition of such practices by one state on its colonies, protectorates, and other dependencies. Instead, emulation is a strategy voluntarily undertaken by a state in response to its strategic environment.[11] By definition, it is a large-scale and sustained process affecting the organization of a state's politico-military institutions, rather than the mere adoption of new weapons systems, minor adjustments to existing practices, discrete reforms guided by foreign models, or shifts in military doctrine. Innovation, in contrast, is a conscious, purposeful effort by one state to offset the perceived relative power advantage of another state by the creation of entirely new institutions, technologies, or governing practices. Both adaptive strategies – emulation and innovation – entail the reallocation of resources or increased extraction from society. They further entail the creation of new institutions or social structures and often the destruction of older ones.[12] Of the two, innovation is far more costly and time-consuming. Finally, both are future-oriented strategies undertaken to redress current vulnerabilities and to anticipate future competitive advantage. States emulate one another's military practices based on the perceived "lessons of the last war," but their objective in doing so is always to improve their competitive advantage in the event of a future war.

Benjamin Frankel, ed., *Realism: Restatements and Renewal* (London: Frank Cass, 1996), pp. 193–260, at p. 199.

[11] For example, Napoleon's imposition of the French military system on his protectorates – the kingdoms of Holland, Westphalia, Italy, and Naples, and the Grand Duchy of Warsaw – does not constitute emulation. See Herrera and Mahnken, "Military Diffusion in Nineteenth-Century Europe," pp. 210–12. The selective adoption of Soviet military doctrine, weapons, and organization by Egypt, Syria, and Iraq after the 1967 Middle East war, however, do constitute emulation. See Michael J. Eisenstadt and Kenneth M. Pollack, "Armies of Snow and Sand: The Impact of Soviet Military Doctrine on Arab Militaries," in Goldman and Eliason, *Diffusion of Military Technology and Ideas*, pp. 63–92.

[12] Matthew Evangelista defines innovation in terms of "new weapons that portend major organizational changes, reallocation of resources, [or] the possibility of diminished organizational autonomy ... The weapons innovations investigated ... entailed major restructuring of military organizations, significant changes in strategy, or both." Matthew Evangelista, *Innovation and the Arms Race: How the United States and the Soviet Union Develop New Military Technologies* (Ithaca, NY: Cornell University Press, 1988), p. 12.

Classical realism on the state and the balance of power

Twentieth-century classical realism implicitly assumes that the state is both distinct from and the agent of the nation or society.[13] Hans Morgenthau wrote, "A nation pursues foreign policies as a legal organization called a state, whose agents act as the representatives of the nation in international affairs. They speak for it, negotiate treaties in its name, define its objectives, choose the means for achieving them, and try to maintain, increase, and demonstrate its power."[14] Similarly, Henry Kissinger distinguished between state and society in his study of the Concert of Europe: "The statesman is inevitably confronted by the inertia of his material ... The acid test of a policy ... is its ability to obtain domestic support."[15] Arnold Wolfers argued:

There can be no "state behavior" except as the term is used to describe the combined behavior of individual human beings organized into a state ... Therefore, only when attention is focused on states, rather than on individuals, can light be thrown on the goals pursued and means employed in the name of nations and on the relationships of conflict or co-operation, of power competition or alignment that characterize inter-national politics.[16]

There are four noteworthy aspects of the classical realist view of the state and the balance of power. First, although classical realists rarely distinguish between levels of analysis, they clearly present a "top-down" conception of the state. Governments do not simply aggregate or respond to the demands of different segments of society. Rather, leaders define the "national interests" and conduct foreign policy based on their assessment of the relative distribution of power and

---

[13] Michael Mastanduno, David A. Lake, and G. John Ikenberry, "Toward a Realist Theory of State Action," *International Studies Quarterly* 33, no. 4 (December 1989), pp. 457–74, at p. 460.

[14] Hans J. Morgenthau, *Politics among Nations: The Struggle for Power and Peace*, 3rd edn (New York: Knopf, 1966), p. 102.

[15] Henry A. Kissinger, *A World Restored: Metternich, Castlereagh, and the Problems of Peace, 1812–1822* (Boston: Houghton Mifflin, 1957), pp. 326–8, at p. 326.

[16] Arnold Wolfers, "The Actors in International Politics," in Wolfers, *Discord and Collaboration: Essays on International Politics* (Baltimore, MD: Johns Hopkins University Press, 1962), pp. 8–9.

other states' intentions. Net assessment, however, is often difficult and prone to error. Edward Gulick wrote that "statesmen, whether accurate in their estimates or not, must measure power, regardless of the primitive nature of the scales at their disposal."[17] According to Morgenthau, "the task of assessing the relative power of nations for the present and for the future resolves itself into a series of hunches, of which some will certainly turn out to be wrong, while others may be proved by subsequent events to have been correct."[18] In a similar vein, Wolfers noted that, for great powers, particularly in the nuclear age, "neither the difficulties nor the importance of accuracy in the estimates of power can be exaggerated."[19]

Second, in conducting foreign policy, leaders must draw on domestic society for material resources and popular support. Morgenthau listed geography, natural resources, industrial capacity, military preparedness, population, national character, and national morale as components of national power. He also wrote, "The quality of government is patently a source of strength or weakness with respect to most of the factors upon which national power depends, especially in view of the influence the government exerts upon natural resources, industrial capacity, and military preparedness."[20] E. H. Carr argued, "Power over opinion is therefore not less essential for political purposes than military and economic power, and has always been closely associated with them. The art of persuasion has always been a necessary part of the equipment of a political leader."[21] Nevertheless, as in the case of net assessments, most classical realists devoted scant attention to the problems leaders encounter in extracting and mobilizing resources from domestic society.

Third, the capacity to extract and mobilize societal resources varies across different countries and historical periods. Classical realists do not assume states have similar extractive capacities, such that aggregate economic and potential capabilities are synonymous with a

[17] Edward Vose Gulick, *Europe's Classical Balance of Power* (New York: W. W. Norton, 1967), p. 14.
[18] Morgenthau, *Politics among Nations*, 154.
[19] Wolfers, *Discord and Collaboration*, p. 112.
[20] Morgenthau, *Politics among Nations*, p. 138.
[21] Edward Hallett Carr, *The Twenty Years' Crisis, 1919–1939: An Introduction to the Study of International Relations*, 2nd edn (1945; New York: Harper and Row, 1964), p. 132.

state's actual power and influence in the international arena. Instead, they assume states have varying levels of what neoclassical realists now call "state power," defined as the relative ability to extract and mobilize resources from domestic society.[22]

Classical realists draw a sharp distinction between the European balance of power in the age of "monarchical sovereignty" in the seventeenth to the nineteenth centuries and the age of "nationalist universalism" in the twentieth century. The operation of the balance of power succeeded in preventing any state from gaining universal dominion for 400 years. Yet, from 1815 to 1914, there were no major (or hegemonic) wars in Europe. In the twentieth century, by contrast, the great powers fought two devastating world wars in the span of 20 years. What might explain this?[23]

Morgenthau, Kissinger, Gulick, and Carr attribute the "long peace" of the nineteenth century to the "high" state power of the major states.[24] Monarchical sovereignty insulated governments from the masses, enabling states to conduct foreign policy free from the vicissitudes of public opinion and legislative interference, and thus to keep the international struggle for power within relatively peaceful bounds and avoid major war. The maintenance of the balance of power often required wholesale transfers of territory or even the elimination of weaker states, as in the three partitions of Poland in the eighteenth century or Prussia's annexation of 40 percent of Saxony after the Napoleonic Wars. Such moves maintained the equilibrium among the European great powers, but with little regard for the nationalist and political aspirations of subject peoples.[25]

The nationalist and democratic revolutions of the nineteenth and twentieth centuries eroded states' autonomy vis-à-vis their societies, which in turn led to a decline in their ability to sustain an international balance of power. The masses acquired a direct role in shaping foreign policy. A crusading "universalistic nationalism," in which states sought

[22] Hobson, *State and International Relations*, pp. 5–6 and 24–6.
[23] For a definition of major war, see Dale Copeland, *Origins of Major War* (Ithaca, NY: Cornell University Press, 2000), pp. 3–4.
[24] Hobson, *State and International Relations*, p. 51.
[25] See Morgenthau, *Politics among Nations*, pp. 205–6 and 218–19; and Kissinger, *World Restored*, pp. 156–7.

to impose their own ethics on all others, replaced the restraint that had embodied the age of monarchical sovereignty. The rise of nationalism allowed states to extract more resources from society and thus generate greater military power, but at the price of lost autonomy in the conduct of foreign policy and a heightened probability of all-out war.[26] Morgenthau lamented, "Nations no longer oppose each other, as they did from the Treaty of Westphalia to the Napoleonic Wars, and then again from the end of the latter to the First World War, within a framework of shared beliefs and common values, which imposes effective limitations upon the ends and means of their struggle for power."[27]

Fourth, classical realists see the balance of power as a system or pattern of relations created consciously and maintained by the great powers. Morgenthau contended, "The aspiration for power on the part of several nations, each trying either to maintain or overthrow the status quo, leads of necessity to a configuration ... called the balance of power and to policies that aim at preserving it."[28] A balance of power system functions only if the great powers (or at least most of them) adhere to the rules of that system. Chief among those rules are the following: the fluidity of alliances, respect for other great powers' vital areas of interest, postwar settlements that do not eliminate the defeated great power, and territorial compensation.[29] Nicholas Spykman commented, "Political equilibrium is neither a gift of the gods nor an inherent stable condition. It results from the active intervention of man, from the operation of political forces. States cannot afford to wait passively for the happy time when a miraculously achieved balance of power will bring peace and security."[30]

---

[26] For similar arguments see Alan C. Lamborn, "Power and the Politics of Extraction," *International Studies Quarterly* 27, no. 2 (June 1983), pp. 125–46; and Paul A. Papayoanou, "Interdependence, Institutions, and the Balance-of-Power: Britain, Germany, and World War I," *International Security* 20, no. 4 (spring 1996), pp. 42–76.

[27] Morgenthau, *Politics among Nations*, p. 256.   [28] Ibid., p. 167.

[29] For a recent discussion of the classical realist conception of the European balance of power as a type of "republic" or "society," see Marc Trachtenberg, "The Question of Realism: A Historian's View," *Security Studies* 13, no. 1 (autumn 2003), pp. 26–7.

[30] Nicholas John Spykman, *America's Strategy in World Politics: The United States and the Balance-of-Power* (New York: Harcourt, Brace, 1942), p. 25.

Neorealist balance of power theory and the "passive military adaptive" state

Waltz's balance of power theory is concerned primarily with explaining the high degree of continuity in international politics. As a systemic theory, it expects that outcomes produced by interacting states will fall within specified ranges. Since Waltz is not interested in explaining the foreign policies of individual states, but rather systemic outcomes over time, he begins with assumptions about the charac- teristics of the international system itself. Chief among the system's characteristics are its ordering principle (the "first tier" or "deep structure"), the differentiation of the units within the system (the "second tier"), and the distribution of capabilities among the units (the "third tier" or "surface structure").[31] The theory posits a single independent variable: the systemic distribution of power as measured by the number of great powers (or polarity). It makes two probabili- stic predictions: (1) that across different international systems, bal- ances of power tend to form, and (2) that states tend to emulate the successful practices of others.[32]

In an anarchic realm, states tend to keep up with one another's efforts and gains that might enhance their relative capabilities and competitiveness. States face pervasive uncertainty about one another's present and future intentions. A state must not overlook the possibility that potential adversaries will use their capabilities against it, and it therefore must focus on other states' capabilities, not their intentions. Unlike units in a hierarchic order, states in an anarchic realm cannot specialize but must instead perform roughly the same functions. Furthermore, if states are to survive, they must often eschew cooperation in favor of self-help.[33]

Due to the competition and socialization effects of anarchy, states tend to emulate the practices and institutions of the leading states in the system. A failure to emulate, and thus to conform to the logic of

---

[31] See Ruggie, "Continuity and Transformation in the World Polity," pp. 135–6.

[32] Waltz, *Theory of International Politics*, p. 124.

[33] For critiques of neorealism's "competition bias," see Charles L. Glaser, "Realists as Optimists: Cooperation as Self-Help," in Frankel, *Realism: Restatement and Renewal*, pp. 122–63, esp. pp. 128–9; and Stephen G. Brooks, "Dueling Realisms," *International Organization* 51, no. 3 (summer 1997), pp. 445–77, esp. pp. 447–50.

anarchy, would risk succumbing to relative power gaps, heightened vulnerability, or even extinction. Before interacting with one another, states may have vastly different internal attributes. Once states begin to interact, however, their military, institutional, and technological practices tend to converge.[34] Waltz does not expect that "emulation will proceed to the point where competitors become identical." Nevertheless, states that fail to conform to successful practices find themselves at a disadvantage. He writes, "Chilialistic rulers occasionally come to power. In power, most of them quickly change their ways [for fear of military defeat or political extinction]."[35]

Figure 7.1 illustrates what John M. Hobson calls the neorealist "passive military adaptive state." Several aspects of balance of power theory support this characterization.[36]

Unlike classical realists, who write about the state but say little about the constraints of the international system, Waltz does the opposite: his theory focuses on constraints imposed by the international system, but treats the state as a "black box." The second tier of the system, the characteristics of the units, effectively drops out. He writes, "A balance of power theory, properly stated, begins with assumptions about states: They are unitary actors who, at a minimum, seek their own preservation and, at a maximum, drive for universal domination."[37] States differ greatly in terms of relative capabilities, but over time, they become functionally alike due to the socializing effect of anarchy.[38]

Waltz assumes that even great powers must conform to systemic survival requirements through balancing and emulation or risk military defeat and extinction. He is careful to point out, however, that "structures shape and shove. They do not *determine* behaviors and outcomes, not only because unit-level and structural causes interact, but also because the shaping and shoving of structures may be successfully resisted."[39] Thus neorealist theory claims to delimit the

---

[34] Buzan, Jones, and Little, *Logic of Anarchy*, pp. 117–19.

[35] Waltz, *Theory of International Politics*, p. 128. Despite Waltz's warnings, the death rate of great powers is quite low. See Robert Jervis, *System Effects: Complexity in Political and Social Life* (Princeton, NJ: Princeton University Press, 1996), pp. 133–4.

[36] For a detailed discussion of the military-passive adaptive state, see Hobson, *State and International Relations*, pp. 24–30.

[37] Waltz, *Theory of International Politics*, p. 118.   [38] Ibid., p. 95.

[39] Waltz, "A Response to My Critics," in Keohane, *Neorealism and its Critics*, p. 343 (emphasis added). See also Waltz, *Theory of International Politics*, p. 69.

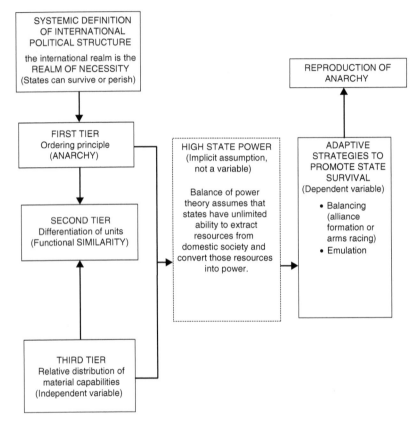

Figure 7.1 Waltz's basic neorealist model
Source: Adapted from John M. Hobson, *The State and International Relations* (Cambridge: Cambridge University Press, 2000), p. 25, fig. 2.2.

expected range of unit-level responses to structural constraints; it generates probabilistic expectations about international outcomes, not determinate ones. Yet the theory cannot explain exactly what the characteristic behavior of any state will likely be in the face of some structural constraint.[40]

[40] See Tellis, "Reconstructing Political Realism," pp. 80–4; Jervis, *System Effects*, pp. 107–10; Buzan, Jones, and Little, *Logic of Anarchy*, esp. pp. 29–80; Copeland, *Origins of Major War*, pp. 12–13; and Glenn H. Snyder, "Process Variables in Neorealist Theory" in Frankel, *Realism: Restatement and Renewal*, pp. 167–92.

Building on a microeconomic analogy, Waltz argued that anarchy pressures states to make continuous improvements in their internal organization. His restrictive definition of competition, however, results in a narrow view of competition's effects.[41] Just as free market competition need not lead all firms to produce identical projects, competition under anarchy need not lead to emulation. Waltz acknowledged, "Contending states imitate the military innovations contrived by the country of greatest capability and ingenuity."[42] Nevertheless, as João Resende-Santos observed, "competition in the system means constant striving, since the absence of a central agent forces states to seek the marginal advantages that innovation brings. Without *dynamic innovation*, selection will only lead to the dominance of those institutions or states that started the contest."[43] Waltz's theory does not explain why powerful states innovate in the first place, why they might do so in the absence of external threats, or why variation occurs in the relative innovativeness of states.

Finally, Waltz's theory assumes that units have an unlimited capacity to extract and mobilize resources from domestic society. What matters is a state's aggregate power, the sum of its economic and military capabilities (both actual and potential). One cannot separately weigh these capabilities. Therefore, great power status depends on states' relative scores on each of the following: population size, territory, resource endowment, economic capability, military strength, political stability, and competence. All else being equal, the great powers are better equipped, and therefore more likely, to engage in adaptive strategies such as balancing, emulation, or innovation, than are weaker states.[44]

Waltz's conception of the state represents the internal dimension of balance of power theory. Through balancing and emulation, states strive to maintain their competitive advantage and enhance their likelihood of survival. The recurrence of balancing and emulation, while intended mainly to ensure the survival of individual states, has

---

[41] Tellis, "Reconstructing Political Realism," pp. 75–82.
[42] Waltz, *Theory of International Politics*, p. 127.
[43] Resende-Santos, "Anarchy and the Emulation of Military Systems," pp. 207–8 (emphasis added). See also Buzan, Jones, and Little, *Logic of Anarchy*, pp. 40–41.
[44] See Waltz, *Theory of International Politics*, pp. 124–7 and 129–31.

the unintended consequence of sustaining an anarchic system.[45] Waltz, however, leaves the notion of emulation underdeveloped. In its spare form, therefore, his theory cannot account for variation in rate, scope, or extent of military diffusion or the likelihood that any particular state will pursue large-scale emulation, innovation, or any other internal balancing strategy. Resende-Santos, Emily Goldman and Richard Andres, and Colin Elman have sought to test neorealist hypotheses on the emulation and diffusion of military practices.[46] To explain variation in the rate and scope of emulation, they each add structural variables – chiefly the offense–defense balance, demonstration contexts, geography, and factor endowments. While each of these authors further specifies the external context in which emulation and innovation are more likely to occur, none of them systematically examines the domestic constraints that states face in responding to systemic imperatives.

Neoclassical realism and the resource-extractive state

As noted in this volume's introduction and in the subsequent chapters, neoclassical realism builds on the complex relationship between state and society found in classical realism without sacrificing the central insight of neorealist balance of power theory. Like classical realism, neoclassical realism holds that state power varies across states and across different historical periods. Yet, like neorealism, neoclassical realism holds that the international environment in which states interact is the primary determinant of their interests and behavior. Both neorealism and neoclassical realism, therefore, proceed from an environment-based ontology.[47]

As in the neoclassical realist theories that Norrin Ripsman and Colin Dueck developed earlier in this volume, the resource-extraction hypotheses build upon a top-down conception of the state. Systemic

---

[45] See Buzan, Jones, and Little, *Logic of Anarchy*, p. 44.
[46] See Resende-Santos, "Anarchy and the Emulation of Military Systems"; Colin Elman, "The Logic of Emulation: The Diffusion of Military Practices in the International System" (Ph.D. dissertation, Columbia University, 1999); and Emily O. Goldman and Richard B. Andres, "Systemic Effects of Military Innovation and Diffusion," *Security Studies* 8, no. 4 (summer 1999), pp. 79–125.
[47] Sterling-Folker, "Realist Environment," pp. 4–8.

forces shape domestic processes within states, which in turn constrain states' ability to respond to systemic imperatives. Put differently, unit-level variables are themselves dependent variables of prior structural conditions.[48] The cases of Great Britain and Brandenburg-Prussia in the sixteenth, seventeenth, and eighteenth centuries illustrate this dynamic. Since the English Channel lessened the chances of invasion, Britain never developed a large standing army and the extractive mechanisms necessary to sustain it. Instead, the navy was the first line of defense. Since navies are less useful for domestic repression than standing armies, the Tudor and Stuart monarchs were never able to create the absolutist state institutions that appeared on the continent. Britain's relatively benign security environment contributed to the gradual emergence of a liberal domestic political order. Conversely, Prussia's geopolitical location was very vulnerable. The Hohenzollern dynasty's original territories were not contiguous and lacked defensible borders. Prussia owed its existence to warfare, which in turn shaped the kingdom's internal organization. In the 1650s, the Great Elector Friedrich Wilhelm persuaded the Prussian Estates to raise a standing army under the direct control of the crown, without any legislative supervision. The result was the rise of a garrison state. A high degree of external vulnerability gave the Prussian army, and successive Hohenzollern kings, far greater autonomy and extractive capacity than might have been the case had security mattered less.[49]

Anarchy's competition and socialization effects provide no single guide or set of "best practices" for how states ought to arrange their domestic processes to maximize their probability of survival. To return to the case of Japan, from the late 1850s onward, there was consensus among Tokugawa and late Meiji elites about the country's vulnerability. There was no immediate consensus, however, about

---

[48] Again, I thank one of the anonymous reviewers at *Security Studies* for suggesting this point.

[49] See Peter Gouveritch, "The Second Image Reversed: The International Sources of Domestic Politics," *International Organization* 32, no. 4 (autumn 1978), pp. 881–912, at p. 896; Michael C. Desch, "War and Strong States, Peace and Weak States?" *International Organization* 50, no. 2 (spring 1996), pp. 237–68 at pp. 244–5; and Bruce D. Porter, *War and the Rise of the State: The Military Foundations of Modern Politics* (New York: Free Press, 1994), pp. 113–21.

which great power provided the most appropriate overall "model" for the new Japan, let alone over the specific technologies and institutions to emulate. Multipolarity and uncertainty about the actual distribution of land-based military power in Europe during the late 1850s and early 1860s led the Meiji oligarchs to consider emulating different types of constitutions, political and military institutions, and technologies.[50] The unexpected victory of Prussia and the North German Confederation in the Franco-Prussian War of 1870–1 convinced one of the Meiji oligarchs, Yamagata Aritomo, that the new Japanese army should emulate the Prussian army model. Likewise, after various trips to Europe and North America, Yamagata's fellow oligarch, Itō Hirobumi, concluded that Germany offered the best constitutional model for Japan to emulate.[51]

Neoclassical realism does not expect all vulnerable states to adopt authoritarian and centralized domestic institutions, nor does it expect more secure states to adopt uniformly liberal and decentralized institutions. Janice Thomson noted historical reasons for the state/society distinction: society was an adversary in the process of state-building because "it resisted state rulers' efforts to extract resources and monopolize political and judicial authority."[52] The arrangement of domestic institutions often reflects particular bargains reached between rulers and societal actors. This tension between the state and societal actors is one of the reasons why different polities always have different domestic institutions.[53]

---

[50] For a discussion see Thomas J. Christensen, "Perceptions and Alliances in Europe, 1860–1940," *International Organization* 51, no. 1 (winter 1997), pp. 65–97.

[51] See Richard J. Samuels, *Machiavelli's Children: Leaders and their Legacies in Italy and Japan* (Ithaca, NY: Cornell University Press, 2003), pp. 53–62; and W. G. Beasley, *The Rise of Modern Japan* (New York: St. Martin's, 1995), pp. 152–3.

[52] Janice E. Thomson, "State Sovereignty in International Relations: Bridging the Gap between Theory and Empirical Research," *International Studies Quarterly* 39, no. 2 (June 1995), pp. 213–33, at p. 216.

[53] Jennifer Sterling-Folker, *Theories of International Cooperation and the Primacy of Anarchy: Explaining US International Monetary Policy-Making after Bretton Woods* (New York: State University of New York Press, 2002), p. 85. See also Michael Barnett, *Confronting the Costs of War: Military Power, State, and Society in Egypt and Israel* (Princeton, NJ: Princeton University Press, 1992).

That said, there is no perfect "transmission belt" linking the relative distribution of power and states' foreign policies.[54] Officials make policy choices based on their perceptions and calculations of relative power and other states' intentions. This means that, over the short and medium terms, different states' foreign policies may not be objectively "efficient" or predictable based on an objective assessment of relative power.[55] Furthermore, states have varying amounts of state power. Even if leaders make "accurate" estimates of relative power and power trends, they do not always have complete access to the material resources of their own societies. Unit-level variables intervene between systemic incentives and policy responses. Domestic variables do not operate independently of structural variables in shaping states' foreign policies, though.

Figure 7.2 depicts the resource-extraction model. The level of external threat or vulnerability is the independent variable. This is a function of the relative distribution of power (both in the international system and in the particular region), the offense–defense balance in military technology, and geographic proximity.[56] The intervening variable is state power, defined as the relative ability of the state to extract or mobilize resources as determined by the institutions of the state, nationalism, and ideology. The dependent variable is the variation in the types and intensity of the adaptive strategies the state will pursue: emulation, innovation, or persistence in existing strategies.

The resource-extraction model assumes that states are reasonably cohesive and that leaders attempt to pursue foreign and security

---

[54] See Gideon Rose, "Neoclassical Realism and Theories of Foreign Policy," *World Politics* 51, no. 1 (October 1998), pp. 144–72, at p. 147.

[55] Elite calculations and perceptions of relative power are central themes in several neoclassical realist works. See Aaron L. Friedberg, *The Weary Titan: Britain and the Experience of Relative Decline, 1895–1905* (Princeton, NJ: Princeton University Press, 1988); William Curti Wohlforth, *The Elusive Balance: Power and Perception during the Cold War* (Ithaca, NY: Cornell University Press 1993); David M. Edelstein, "Managing Uncertainty: Beliefs about Intentions and Rise of Great Powers," *Security Studies* 12, no. 1 (autumn 2002), pp. 1–40; and Jeffrey W. Taliaferro, *Balancing Risks: Great Power Intervention in the Periphery* (Ithaca, NY: Cornell University Press, 2004).

[56] On threat, see Stephen M. Walt, *Origins of Alliances* (Ithaca, NY: Cornell University Press, 1987), pp. 22–6; and Walt, *Revolution and War* (Ithaca, NY: Cornell University Press, 1996), pp. 18–45.

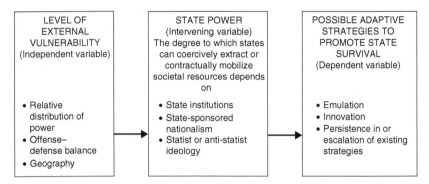

Figure 7.2 The neoclassical realist model of the resource-extractive state
Source: The resource-extraction model treats states' alignment behavior as exogenous.

policies based on their assessments and calculations of relative power and other states' intentions. It assumes that states do not suffer from various types of internal fragmentation, such as elite dissensus and fragmentation, a lack of social or ethno-nationalist cohesion, or regime vulnerability. In reality, the majority of states, particularly those in the developing world, have exhibited various kinds of fragmentation for some portion of their histories. Here, however, for the sake of developing the resource-extraction model, I assume states are reasonably coherent.[57]

States respond to shifts in their level of external vulnerability. In order to explain variation in the types and intensity of the adaptive strategies the state will likely pursue, however, we need to account for how systemic variables filter through a unit-level intervening variable: state power. The remainder of this section discusses how the institutions of the state, nationalism, and ideology might influence the level of state power, and then derives several hypotheses on how state power might constrain or facilitate a state's reaction to shifts in the external environment.

---

[57] For a neoclassical realist theory of how government or regime vulnerability and social cohesion inhibit timely balancing behavior, see Randall L. Schweller, *Unanswered Threats: Political Constraints on the Balance of Power* (Princeton, NJ: Princeton University Press, 2006).

State institutions

The politico-military institutions of the state are the first component of state power. Institutional arrangements affect the ability of central decision-makers to extract or mobilize resources from domestic society. Michael Mastanduno, David Lake, and John Ikenberry drew a distinction between mobilization and extraction. Mobilization generally takes two forms. A state can directly control economic activity and reallocate resources through centralized planning, the nationalization of key industries or particular firms, and other means. Alternatively, it can indirectly intervene in the economy to facilitate the accumulation of societal wealth and thereby the tax revenues available to the state. Neither strategy is cost-free. The state must make certain political and economic investments in these mobilizations, whether in the form of expenditures on a large administrative apparatus (direct mobilization) or in the form of subsidies and concessions to non-state actors as an inducement to expand production (indirect mobilization). In resource extraction, the state directly converts societal wealth into military power through taxation, requisition, and expropriation.[58]

Mastanduno, Lake, and Ikenberry noted a tradeoff between extraction and the two strategies of mobilization. They write, "As extraction increases, the state is likely to redouble its efforts at mobilization, but the effectiveness of the latter may decline because 1) the sum of investable wealth is now lower and 2) incentives for future wealth creation are undermined by discouraging investment and introducing inefficiencies into the economy."[59] Centralized and insulated states can extract societal wealth better than decentralized and constrained states can, but the authors' point is that even capitalist democratic states vary greatly in their ability to convert potential capabilities into actual economic and military power. The downside to this form of domestic-international strategy is that it may generate discontent among affected social groups.

Fareed Zakaria and Aaron Friedberg have examined how variation in extractive and mobilization capability affects grand strategic

---

[58] Mastanduno, Lake, and Ikenberry, "Toward a Realist Theory of State Action," p. 467.
[59] Ibid., p. 463.

adjustment. Zakaria developed the concept of state power, which he defined as the government's ability to extract resources for its own end, to explain why the United States did not expand abroad more rapidly between 1865 and 1899, but then expanded rapidly between 1899 and 1908. Despite a dramatic increase in its economy, population, and access to natural resources during the first period, the United States acquired no overseas territories, maintained a small military compared to the European great powers, and generally avoided entanglements in great power politics. Yet, in the second period, America not only fought a lopsided war against Spain, but acquired colonies in the Philippines, Guam, and Puerto Rico and a naval base in Cuba as a result, built the world's second-largest navy, and began to assert itself in great power diplomacy.

Zakaria attributed this shift in US grand strategy to an increase in the size and extractive capacity of the federal government in the late 1880s and 1890s. He measured the relative strength of a state along several dimensions: the degree of cohesion in central institutions (particularly the civil bureaucracy and the military); the degree of autonomy from society; the ability to generate revenue; and the scope of governmental responsibilities. Strong states have higher scores on each of these dimensions. Weaker states, by contrast, suffer from fragmentation, penetration by interest groups, lack of revenue, and minimal responsibilities.[60] All else being equal, stronger states have greater access to economic resources and are therefore more likely to adopt ambitious foreign policies.

Friedberg argued that, while anticipated power trends and uncertainty pushed the Soviet Union and the United States toward some form of confrontation after World War II, variation in state power ultimately shaped the types of grand strategies the superpowers pursued during the Cold War. A combination of weak institutions, the material interests of various societal actors, and a deeply embedded anti-statist ideology eventually led the United States to adopt an outward-directed force posture and military strategy. In support of this military strategy, the Truman, Eisenhower, and Kennedy administrations created a set of inward-directed power-creation mechanisms, including a de facto industrial policy whereby the federal government served as a procurement agent but eschewed any central planning role, and a reliance

[60] See Zakaria, *From Wealth to Power*, pp. 33–9.

on private industry to produce weapons systems and supporting technologies.[61] Taken together, these mechanisms allowed the United States to compete with the Soviet Union on a global scale for decades, without becoming a "garrison state" in the process.

Conversely, the Soviet Union lacked countervailing domestic constraints on extraction and mobilization; there were no powerful and independent societal actors. Friedberg noted, "To the contrary, the few influential groupings in the Soviet system were, in essence, state actors; all benefited from its growth. Communist ideology and the structure of Soviet political institutions combined to elevate the state and to permit, indeed to encourage, a strategically stimulated metastasis in its internal powers."[62] The highly centralized nature of the Soviet system allowed the second-ranked great power to acquire nuclear weapons quickly, control Eastern Europe, and compete with the US on a global scale for forty years. The downsides of the Soviet system were numerous: sluggish economic performance, strong disincentives for innovation, overinvestment in the military sector to the detriment of the consumer sector, lack of access to information technologies, and "imperial overstretch."[63]

The ability of states to extract resources from society is not simply a function of the strength of institutions: it also depends on leaders' ability to raise and maintain support for national security strategies. Thomas Christensen developed the concept of national political power, which he defined as "the ability of state leaders to mobilize their nation's human and material resources behind security policy initiatives."[64] The degree to which state–society relations distort policies that leaders prefer to use in dealing with extant threats depends on the heights of the domestic mobilization hurdles they face. The height of a mobilization hurdle depends upon the following: (1) the ability of the state to raise or maintain levels of taxation

---

[61] See Aaron L. Friedberg, *In the Shadow of the Garrison State: America's Anti-Statism and its Cold War Grand Strategy* (Princeton, NJ: Princeton University Press, 2000), chap. 4.

[62] Ibid., p. 75.

[63] See Stephen G. Brooks and William C. Wohlforth, "Power, Globalization, and the End of the Cold War: Revisiting the Landmark Case for Ideas," *International Security* 25, no. 3 (winter 2000–1), pp. 5–53.

[64] Thomas J. Christensen, *Useful Adversaries: Grand Strategy, Domestic Mobilization, and Sino-American Conflict, 1947–1958* (Princeton, NJ: Princeton University Press, 1996), p. 11.

before the mobilization drive; (2) the nature and immediacy of the international challenge and the expense of the leaders' preferred policies in comparison with past responses to similar challenges; and (3) the novelty and salient history of policy details within the preferred grand strategy.

Leaders often encounter difficulties convincing the public to make significant sacrifices for national security, even if such efforts are in the public's own long-term interests. This is especially true in liberal democracies, where the average citizen lacks the time and expertise to understand the balance of power. The average citizen tends to discount geographically distant and indirect external threats more than do foreign policy elites. Furthermore, citizens have an added incentive to free-ride on the efforts of others when called upon to make sacrifices for national security. In authoritarian or totalitarian regimes, Christensen observes, "the only significant hurdle to immediate, all-out mobilization ... [is] the morale and spirit of sacrifice in the population at large."[65]

Mobilization hurdles are likely to be particularly high where states currently face low levels of external vulnerability, but leaders nonetheless fear the emergence of new long-term threats. In order to mobilize and maintain broad support for strategies considered essential to national security, leaders might rationally adopt policies in secondary areas that objectively appear overly aggressive and ideological, that expend vast resources, or that foreclose alliance opportunities. Emulation and innovation both entail costs for societal actors in the form of higher taxation, the reallocation of resources, and conscription. Innovation is potentially more costly and disruptive.

The work of Friedberg, Zakaria, and Christensen suggests the following: states that initially enjoy high extraction and mobilization capacity, but that also face high external vulnerability, are more likely to emulate the military, governing, and technological practices of the system's most successful states, at least in the short run. On the other hand, states that must augment those capacities, but that also face high external vulnerability, will have greater difficulty in pursuing emulation, at least in the short run. States that initially enjoy high extraction and mobilization capacity, but that also face relatively low external vulnerability, have the luxury of engaging in innovation,

[65] Ibid., p. 245.

continuing existing strategies, or simply doing nothing to enhance their long-term security and power. Conversely, states that do not enjoy high mobilization and extraction capacity, but that also face low external vulnerability, are less likely to pursue emulation or innovation. Under these circumstances, states are more likely to continue or escalate existing strategies.

Ideology and nationalism

Ideology and state-sponsored nationalism are two other determinants of state power. In general, state-sponsored nationalism tends to increase social cohesion and the propensity of individuals to identify with the state, which in turn facilitates leaders' efforts to extract and mobilize resources from society for national security goals. Ideology, in contrast, can facilitate or inhibit leaders' efforts to extract and mobilize resources, depending on the content of that ideology and the extent to which elites and the public hold common ideas about the proper role of the state vis-à-vis society and the economy.

For the purposes of this chapter, I define nationalism as a political movement wherein individuals begin to identify their personal interests with a group that is too large to meet together; wherein they identify those interests based on a common "culture," "ethnicity," "civic" or "national identity" that the members of the group share to the exclusion of other groups; and wherein individuals come to believe that the members of the group share a common history; and to believe that the group requires its own state if it is to survive.[66]

Three points about this treatment of nationalism deserve emphasis. First, it assumes that leaders deliberately inculcate nationalism primarily as a means to achieve societal cohesion against external adversaries. This conception of state-sponsored nationalism deliberately excludes ethnic, secessionist, and vernacular nationalisms that might hinder and threaten the state from within.[67] Second, this

---

[66] See Posen, "Nationalism, the Mass Army, and Military Power," pp. 82–3; and Stephen Van Evera, "Hypotheses on Nationalism and War," *International Security* 18, no. 4 (spring 1994), pp. 6–7.

[67] For an overview, see Michael E. Brown, "The Causes of Internal Conflict: An Overview," in Michael E. Brown, Owen R. Coté, Jr., Sean M. Lynn-Jones, and Steven E. Miller, eds., *Nationalism and Ethnic Conflict* (Cambridge, MA: MIT Press, 2001).

definition of nationalism presumes that individuals' loyalty to the state supersedes their loyalty to more exclusive groups, such as those based on common kinship and location, and that such identification increases the cohesion of the group. Third, social cohesion is not the same as political unanimity or the absence of deep-seated political disagreements within society. All societies, including highly nationalistic ones, exhibit various conflicts and cleavages arising from divergent class interests, resource allocations, competing political goals, regional differences, and ethnic rivalries. Yet nationalism can enhance social cohesion and the willingness of individuals to make sacrifices to the extent that most individuals and societal groups view the state's institutions as legitimate. Particularly during periods of high external vulnerability, leaders have an incentive to inculcate nationalism as a means to extract greater societal resources for the production of military power.[68]

Consider the following: during the 1793–7 War of the First Coalition, France deliberately inculcated nationalism through the medium of compulsory primary education, propaganda campaigns, and the political indoctrination of military recruits, to generate public support for the *levée en masse* and the social and economic disruptions necessary to create a mass-conscription army. External vulnerability provided an impetus for the Committee of Public Safety and later the Directory to pursue military innovation. Nationalism, however, played a key role in increasing the state power of the French state and thus its ability to engage in large-scale military innovation in wartime.[69] In Japan, the Meiji oligarchs used the same methods to build a "'national essence' (*kokusui*) – the symbolic order that would unite the archipelago and enable Japan to achieve parity with the West."[70] State-sponsored nationalism was a precondition for the Meiji oligarchs' subsequent campaign to emulate the British and German military, economic, and governing practices in the 1870s and 1880s. In nineteenth-century China, however, the Qing dynasty was unable to respond to the rising threat of western imperialism by inculcating nationalism. On the contrary, the majority of ethnic

---

[68] On the other hand, in instances where states lack domestic legitimacy, or are vulnerable to overthrow, leaders will be wary of fomenting hyper-nationalism and mobilizing a mass army. See Schweller, *Unanswered Threats*, pp. 49–50.

[69] Posen, "Nationalism, the Mass Army, and Military Power," esp. pp. 92–5.

[70] See Samuels, *Machiavelli's Children*, pp. 33–4, at p. 34.

Chinese perceived their Manchu leaders as barbarians, largely because the Manchus "succeeded in their efforts to maintain an ethnically and, to a degree, culturally separate identity while ruling the country according to the Chinese mode and partaking of the benefits of Chinese civilization."[71]

Ideology is closely related, but not identical, to nationalism. Whereas state-sponsored nationalism focuses on the individual's identification with the nation or the state, the term "ideology" denotes a series of widely held beliefs, causal relationships, and assertions about the proper relationship of the state to domestic society and the role of the state in the international system across a range of issues – political, economic, social, and military. Ideology can facilitate or inhibit leaders' ability to extract and mobilize resources from society depending on its content and the extent to which the population and elites share it. For example, although the Bolsheviks had no coherent theory of international politics when they seized power in 1917, they developed one as they went along. As William Wohlforth has noted, the so-called correlation of forces or "détente through strength" thesis articulated by Joseph Stalin and his lieutenants in the 1930s held that the more powerful the Soviet Union became, the better its relations with the irrevocably hostile capitalist states would be. This thesis, along with Marxist-Leninist ideology, not only reflected the true beliefs of the Soviet leaders, but also gave the Kremlin an additional tool with which to extract greater resources for the crash industrialization program of the 1930s and the military buildup of the post-World War II period.[72] In the next chapter, Randall Schweller argues that fascism – in particular the embrace of social Darwinism, emphasis on territorial expansion, corporatism, and glorification of an all-powerful leader and the state – provided an excellent tool for the leaders of Nazi Germany and Fascist Italy to extract maximum resources from society and to mobilize broad support for aggressive grand strategies.[73]

---

[71] Ralston, *Importing the European Army*, p. 109.
[72] Wohlforth, *Elusive Balance*, pp. 51–3.
[73] That said, I have reservations about two other parts of Schweller's argument in chapter 8: (1) that the fascist state (specifically, its mobilization capacity and its grand strategic behavior) is the epitome of the "offensive realist state" and (2) that fascists and realists share many core assumptions about the nature of international politics, the role of the modern state, and the maximization of relative power through territorial expansion. In my view, Schweller downplays offensive realism's emphasis on calculated, limited

In other instances, ideology moderates leaders' efforts to extract or to mobilize resources. Friedberg has argued that an American anti-statist ideology, consisting of a deep-seated fear of concentrating power in the hands of the federal government and a commitment to economic liberalism, filtered the range of policy options under consideration in response to the perceived threat of the Soviet Union. This filtering process worked in two ways. First, since would-be state-builders had to assemble winning coalitions in Congress, they were unlikely to knowingly advocate policies that were impassable and not in keeping with what they perceived to be the country's basic ideological principles. "Whatever their initial preferences, more prudent, pragmatic leaders are likely to conclude that what the political traffic will bear and what is best for the country are, almost by definition, the same."[74] Second, while calculations of political advantage were never absent, senior officials in the Truman, Eisenhower, and Kennedy administrations subscribed to the dominant anti-statist ideology, which in turn drew them toward certain courses of action and away from others. "Ideology thus shapes the contours of the terrain, even if it does not determine the road that will finally be taken; it lays out signposts and warning signals that lead policy makers down certain paths and cause them to avoid or to overlook others."[75]

Conclusion

This chapter began by posing several questions: Under what circumstances are states more likely to emulate the successful military institutions, governing practices, and technologies of another? When

---

expansion as the best route for great powers to achieve security. See John J. Mearsheimer, *Tragedy of Great Powers* (New York: W.W. Norton, 2001), esp. chap. 3 ; and Eric J. Labs, "Beyond Victory: Offensive Realism and the Expansion of War Aims," *Security Studies* 6, no. 4 (summer 1997), pp. 1–49, esp. pp. 11–21. The second aspect of Schweller's argument obscures some important differences between realism and fascism, not the least of which is that the former purports to be both a political philosophy and a family of related empirical theories. Clearly, Morgenthau drew heavily on the work of Carl Schmitt. See Evrigenis, "Carthage Must Be Saved," chap. 4. However, fascism (at least in its German and Italian manifestations) rests upon a teleological conception of history and politics that realism clearly rejects.

[74] Friedberg, *In the Shadow of the Garrison State*, p. 22.   [75] Ibid.

confronted with similar international threats, why do some states respond by emulating the practices of the system's leading powers, while others respond through innovation or the continuation of existing strategies? Neorealist balance of power theory holds that the competitive nature and socialization effects of the international system provide incentives for states to emulate the practices of the system's leading states. In its spare form, however, the theory merely delimits a range of probable international outcomes; it does not explain why and how states choose between different types of "internal" balancing strategies. Explaining such variation in a state's foreign policy requires a theory that integrates systemic and unit-level variables.

Neoclassical realism can explain variation in states' abilities to adapt to changes in the international environment through internal balancing better than Waltz's balance of power theory can. Like classical realism, neoclassical realism expects variation in state power (the relative ability of the state to extract or mobilize resources from domestic society). Yet, like neorealist balance of power theory, neoclassical realism stresses the importance of the international system in shaping the parameters of states' external behavior. The arguments presented above are not a challenge to neorealist balance of power theory. Rather, they supplement balance of power theory by specifying how systemic variables interact with intervening variables at the unit level to explain variation in individual states' foreign and defense policies. Thus, neoclassical realism in general, and the resource-extraction model of the state developed here, seeks to explain phenomena that Waltz's theory does not.

Before concluding, let me address the critique of so-called additive models of foreign policy that Benjamin Fordham raises in chapter 9. Fordham criticizes neoclassical realism because it assumes that domestic and international variables are easily identifiable and that they have separable influences on states' grand strategies. In his view, the interests of the domestic coalition that governs the state determine whether or not particular international developments are seen as threats. Likewise, international circumstances affect domestic political and economic interests. As a solution, Fordham proposes an interactive model of foreign policy that both allows for and purports to explain variation in the preferences of both state leaders and domestic political and economic interest groups.

224 J. W. Taliaferro

I beg to differ with Fordham on various points. First, in order to create a foreign policy theory, one must begin with a set of assumptions about the broad preferences of those charged with making grand strategic decisions on behalf of states. Researchers do not test the validity of a theory (or, more properly, hypotheses derived from it) by assessing the validity of its underlying assumptions. Naturally the assumptions underlying any social science theory are simplifications of reality. That said, assumptions that never hold or that proceed from empirically false micro-foundations generate theories of limited explanatory power or policy relevance (at least in the study of international politics and foreign policy).[76]

Second, both neorealist balance of power theory (and other variants of neorealism) and most variants of neoclassical realism (including the resource-extraction model) proceed from a set of minimal assumptions about the core interests of states and the leaders who act on their behalf. At a minimum, states are assumed to strive to preserve their political autonomy and territorial integrity. That certainly does not preclude the pursuit of other goals, including territorial aggrandizement or universal domination. As to whether this assumption corresponds with reality, I would note that very few modern states have voluntarily surrendered their political autonomy or ceded their territory to other states.[77]

Third, the notion that central decision-makers discern and try to act upon the "national interests" based upon their assessments of the international environment is perfectly defensible. In any regime, the officials charged with the formulation and implementation of foreign

---

[76] See Alexander L. George and Andrew Bennett, *Case Studies and Theory Development in the Social Sciences* (Cambridge, MA: MIT Press, 2005), pp. 139–40; and Stephen Van Evera, *Guide to Methods for Students of Political Science* (Ithaca, NY: Cornell University Press, 1997), pp. 39–40. For a different view on the desirability of having realistic assumptions to underpin theories, see Milton Friedman, *Essays in Positive Economics* (Chicago: University of Chicago Press, 1953), pp. 14–23. "In general, the more significant the theory, the more unrealistic the assumptions," Friedman contends (p. 14).

[77] I can only think of two cases in the past century where states voluntarily surrendered their sovereignty to another state. The first was Syria's accession to the United Arab Republic with Egypt in 1958. The second was East Germany's decision to reconstitute the abolished eastern *Länder* (or states) and formally seek admission to the Federal Republic of Germany in 1990.

and national security policies will generally have more access to more information about international threats and opportunities than the average citizen, or even the leaders of domestic political or economic sectors with a direct stake in foreign policy decisions.[78] As Christensen notes, "Because of this information gap and competing claims for the public's attention, citizens are more likely than state elites to adopt stylized and ideological views of international conditions and proper responses to them."[79] In sum, researchers ought to evaluate the merits of what Fordham terms additive and integrative models of foreign policy based on their relative explanatory and predictive power across a range of cases (including an examination of causal mechanisms).

The resource-extraction model outlined in this chapter purports to explain variation in the likelihood that threatened states will pursue particular internal balancing strategies. External vulnerability provides incentives for states to emulate the practices of the system's leading states or to counter such practices through innovation. Unit-level variables affect the choices states make between innovation, emulation, or the continuation of existing military strategies and practices. The hypotheses derived in this chapter address the circumstances under which state power would likely affect a state's choice between these internal balancing strategies. Historical examples from the experiences of seven rising or declining great powers illustrate the plausibility of these hypotheses.

This chapter sought merely to outline a resource-extraction model of the state. It did not purport to test the hypotheses derived from that model against rival hypotheses from other theories, such as cultural theories of strategic adjustment.[80] The next stage of this research

---

[78] This does not imply that central decision-makers make objective assessments of the international environment and are therefore more likely to be correct. Certainly, they have more information than the average citizen or domestic interest group. However, despite information asymmetries, top leaders may still misperceive systemic imperatives. Moreover, even where elites do correctly perceive systemic imperatives, there is rarely a single optimum strategy for them to pursue. Thus my resource-extraction model straddles what Ripsman, Lobell, and I term World 1 and World 2 in the volume's concluding chapter.

[79] Christensen, *Useful Adversaries*, p. 17.

[80] On cultural theories of strategic adjustment, see Thomas Berger, *Cultures of Antimilitarism: National Security in Germany and Japan* (Baltimore, MD: Johns Hopkins University Press, 1998); Elizabeth Kier, *Imagining War: French and British Military Doctrines between the Wars* (Princeton, NJ: Princeton

entails creating measures of the different components of state power: the relative strength of existing state institutions, levels of nationalism, and the existence of state-sponsored or anti-statist ideology. This will not be an easy task. That said, every concept or variable of any interest to students of international relations is ambiguous, hard to operationalize and measure, and open to multiple interpretations. In the interests of outlining the resource-extraction model, the historical examples here all involved states arguably facing high levels of external vulnerability. Future research would involve identifying a universe of cases involving states facing different levels of external threat or a single state that experiences varying levels of external threat over time. Likewise, there should be variation in the level of state power across particular states or within the state over time. Other avenues for research might involve testing neoclassical realist hypotheses using cases involving second-tier and third-tier states in past international systems, as well as cases involving developing states today.

University Press, 1997); and Alastair Iain Johnston, *Cultural Realism: Strategic Culture and Grand Strategy in Chinese History* (Princeton, NJ: Princeton University Press, 1995).

8 | Neoclassical realism and state mobilization: expansionist ideology in the age of mass politics

RANDALL L. SCHWELLER

In chapter 1, Jeffrey Taliaferro, Steven Lobell, and Norrin Ripsman posed three questions about the politics of resource extraction and domestic mobilization in grand strategy: How do states mobilize the resources necessary to pursue their chosen security policies? How much power do domestic actors have to obstruct the state when it seeks to mobilize resources in different settings? Finally, what determines who is more successful in bargaining games between the state and societal groups? In this chapter, I address those questions as they pertain to variations in the ability of great powers to mobilize the resources required to pursue expansionist grand strategies, specifically bids for regional hegemony. I present a neoclassical realist theory to explain the puzzle of under-expansion and under-aggression: the suboptimal reluctance to use force or to build up military power in pursuit of profit or security or both. Neoclassical realism can explain why only certain great powers could make bids for regional hegemony in the late nineteenth and early twentieth centuries. In brief, I make the controversial argument that a particular type of ideology – fascism – enabled the leaders of Nazi Germany (and to a lesser extent Italy and Japan) to extract the resources and mobilize the domestic support necessary to undertake a sustained hegemonic bid.

This chapter consists of four sections: the first discusses how and why the puzzle of under-expansion and under-aggression arises. Offensive realism holds that the international system creates incentives for great powers to maximize relative power and seek regional hegemony as the best route to security. However, it cannot explain why there were so few bids for regional hegemony in the early twentieth century. Neoclassical realism, on the other hand, can explain this puzzle because it expects variation in the mobilization and extractive capacity of great powers vis-à-vis their domestic societies.

The second section makes the case that, in the age of mass politics, ideology plays an instrumental and necessary role in helping leaders extract resources and mobilize domestic support for novel and expensive grand strategies. This is particularly true in the case of revisionist great powers. Fascism, which extols the state, social Darwinism, militarism, and power, proved to be the perfect ideology for leaders to mobilize support for sustained expansion and serial aggression.

The third and arguably most provocative section highlights some surprising similarities between the conceptions of the state, international politics, and power found in both realist theory and fascist ideology, particularly in the writings of the interwar German political theorist Carl Schmitt. I certainly do not claim that realist scholars and practitioners do (or should) subscribe to fascist ideologies. As I acknowledge below, Adolf Hitler's overweening ambition ultimately brought ruin to Germany and Europe and caused the deaths of millions. However, I do make the case that fascist ideology allowed the Nazi and Italian fascist regimes to extract and mobilize the types of resources necessary to pursue an arguably offensive realist grand strategy. The fourth and final section addresses the implications of my argument for realism and for the operation of the balance of power in the modern age.

The puzzle of under-expansion and under-aggression in the twentieth century

In the world as portrayed by some major theories of international politics there should have been many more expansionist attempts than have actually occurred in recent history. Offensive realism tells us that states live in constant fear for their survival. To achieve security, therefore, states seek relative gains in national power over their potential rivals. One time-honored way to achieve these gains in military power is through conquest and expansion, which not only enhances the state's power in the immediate term but in the longer run as well: the added strength of successful conquest can be used to attack others in the future to make even greater gains. Across different historical periods, offensive realist theories expect pervasive uncertainty, constant positional competition, frequent bids for regional hegemony, and the ever-present possibility of war among the great powers to be the defining characteristics of international politics.

Offensive realism appears to explain the dynamics of European great power politics quite well from the sixteenth to the nineteenth centuries. For 300 years, the continent experienced intermittent great power wars. Dynastic states such as Prussia, Austria, Sweden, and Russia did not hesitate to forge alliances of convenience and to expand at the expense of weaker rivals. Habsburg Spain, France under Louis XIV and later Napoleon, and Wilhelmine Germany made concerted bids for regional hegemony. In the mid-twentieth century, however, only one pole – Nazi Germany – and two lesser great powers – Imperial Japan and Fascist Italy – embarked on all-out campaigns of territorial expansion at the expense of both weaker states and rival great powers lasting several years.[1] By contrast, the United States became a regional hegemon by default; there simply were no rival great powers in the western hemisphere. Although the Soviet Union had revisionist aspirations and did make a bid for regional hegemony, its territorial acquisitions were geographically limited. More often than not, Soviet leader Joseph Stalin and his successors exploited perceived power vacuums and avoided direct confrontations with other great powers whenever possible. Simply put, in the mid-twentieth century (before the advent of nuclear weapons), why were powerful states so timid?

The sources of this timidity may not lie in the polarity of the international system and the relative distribution of power alone, as offensive realists would suggest. Instead, the relative paucity of hegemonic bids in the early to mid-twentieth century may have its origins in the difficulties that even revisionist great powers face in extracting and mobilizing resources for national security. Neoclassical realism identifies extractive and mobilization capacity as a crucial intervening variable between systemic imperatives and the actual foreign and defense policies states undertake. As Taliaferro, Lobell, and Ripsman observed, ideational factors such as ideology and nationalism can play an instrumental role in helping a state's leadership extract, mobilize,

---

[1] On the distinction between poles and lesser great powers, see Randall L. Schweller, *Deadly Imbalances: Tripolarity and Hitler's Strategy of World Conquest* (New York: Columbia University Press, 1998), pp. 16–19 and 203–8.

and direct societal resources and cultivate support among its power base. Neoclassical realism suggests that in the age of mass politics and the nation-state political ideology became a necessary, but not sufficient, condition for great powers to pursue expansionist policies.

The problem, I argue, is that realpolitik arguments cannot generate the political heat necessary to launch costly mobilization campaigns for offensive purposes; its structural balance of power logic is too arcane to be of much use to elites as a mobilizing ideology in an age of mass politics. Most realists, even those who claim that states should seek to maximize their relative power for reasons of security and profit, such as E. H. Carr and John Mearsheimer, openly acknowledge realism's political and normative deficiencies. Still, offensive realists have not moved to fill this large normative-prescriptive hole in the theoretical perspective. The question is: how can modern elites sell to their publics the expansionist schemes that many offensive realists approve for structural-systemic reasons? What is needed is an ideational component to realist theory that explains why some states take advantage of systemic opportunities, while others do not. Contrary to standard social constructivist theory, however, I assert that interests and domestic politics typically drive identities, not the other way around. That said, identities do indeed matter a great deal: they determine to a large extent whether the state is willing and able to mobilize for expansion.

In a controversial twist, I maintain that the ideal "offensive realist" state is, in practice, best captured by a fascist state. Fascism provided the ideational rationale and "mobilizing passions" required for bold state action, while it eradicated the kind of internal dissent that I argue inhibits expansionist behaviors. Rooted in social Darwinism and geopolitics, fascism may be described as "ideologized" power politics for mass consumption. Inasmuch as this is true, little wonder that realists, who surprisingly share many of the geostrategic assumptions and views of the state that motivated the rise of modern fascism, have not addressed the question of what kind of political content (ideology) is best suited to motivate the masses for the expansionist behavior that their theories advocate.

To be sure, fascism's diabolical solution to the problem wound up throwing the realist baby out with the bathwater. Whereas fascism offered the necessary political content and internal unity for expansionist behavior, it failed miserably as a guidepost for prudent or moral state action. Rather than seizing sensible opportunities for expansion, fascist leaders, who did not believe in the balance of power, pursued excessive and greedy expansion that resulted in total disaster for themselves and the rest of the world.

The limits of offensive realism: the need for a mobilizing ideology

Opportunistic expansion has always been a core principle of the realist state – one that especially animates offensive realism and sets it apart from other strands of realism. The leading proponent of offensive realism, John Mearsheimer, claims that all great powers that have not achieved regional hegemony are revisionists with aggressive intentions. He further argues that states with the potential to dominate their regions will vigorously strive to achieve this form of hegemony. In his words, "anarchy and uncertainty about other states' intentions create an irreducible level of fear among states that leads to power-maximizing behavior ... the structure of the international system, not the particular characteristics of individual great powers, causes them to think and act offensively and to seek hegemony."[2] If this brand of offensive realism is correct, we should see many cases of bold state expansion throughout time and space. Yet there have been relatively few bids for hegemony in recent history.

This is especially true in the Third World, which consists of regions where significant power inequalities exist among neighboring states that should, according to offensive realism, engender opportunistic expansion. Since the end of the Cold War, however, very few developing countries have fought interstate wars, and the vast majority of them have not even confronted significant external threats. As Jeffrey Herbst observes,

Even in Africa, the continent seemingly destined for war given the colonially-imposed boundaries and weak political authorities, there has not been one involuntary boundary change since the dawn of the independence era in the late 1950s, and very few countries face even the prospect of a conflict with

---

[2] John J. Mearsheimer, *The Tragedy of Great Power Politics* (New York: W. W. Norton, 2001), pp. 43, 53. According to Mearsheimer there has only been one regional hegemon, the United States. Thus he writes: "Even when a great power achieves a distinct military advantage over its rivals, it continues looking for chances to gain more power. The pursuit of power stops only when hegemony is achieved." Ibid., p. 34.

their neighbors. Most of the conflicts in Africa that have occurred were not, as in Europe, wars of conquest that threatened the existence of other states, but conflicts over lesser issues that were resolved without threatening the existence of another state.[3]

Likewise, K. J. Holsti comments: "The search for continental hegemony is rare in the Third World, but was a common feature of European diplomacy under the Habsburgs, Louis XIV, Napoleon, Wilhelmine Germany, Hitler, the Soviet Union and, arguably, the United States."[4]

Potentially powerful states such as India, South Africa, China, Nigeria, Indonesia, and Brazil have chosen to remain potential regional hegemons rather than actual ones. None has even contemplated much less actively pursued a grand strategy to achieve this exalted status. And so what Gerald Segal claims about contemporary China can be said for all these countries: "China remains a classic case of hope over experience, reminiscent of de Gaulle's famous comment about Brazil: It has great potential, and always will."[5] Why have we seen so few wars of aggression in modern times? Why do we see so few regions with hegemons or even aspiring ones? What explains this contemporary timidity to maximize and exert power, and to dominate one's neighbors when it is possible to do so?

One might inquire whether we can resolve this puzzle with arguments that nationalism, the diffusion of defensive weapons, and the growth of the global marketplace have combined to increase the costs of conquering territory, making conquest comparatively inefficient.[6] As Peter Liberman demonstrates, however, sufficiently ruthless occupiers can extract gain from territory (especially industrialized countries) even in the modern era.[7] Thus, it would appear that the

---

[3] Jeffrey Herbst, "War and the State in Africa," *International Security* 14, no. 4 (spring 1990), pp. 117–39, at p. 123.

[4] K. J. Holsti, "International Relations Theory and Domestic War in the Third World: The Limits of Relevance," in Stephanie G. Neuman, ed., *International Relations Theory and the Third World* (New York: St. Martin's Press, 1998), p. 106.

[5] Gerald Segal, "Does China Matter?" *Foreign Affairs* 78, no. 5 (September/ October 1999), p. 28.

[6] See, for example, Stephen Van Evera, "Primed for Peace: Europe after the Cold War," *International Security* 15, no. 3 (winter 1990–1), pp. 7–57. I thank an anonymous reviewer for suggesting this argument.

[7] Peter Liberman *Does Conquest Pay? The Exploitation of Occupied Industrial Societies* (Princeton, NJ: Princeton University Press, 1996).

dearth of conquest has more to do with the nature of states than with the efficiency of conquest.

Although the British Empire, according to J. R. Seeley and Winston Churchill, was acquired in a fit of absentmindedness, territorial expansion usually advances through a deliberate and collective will to imperial power, through single-mindedness for expansion shared by both rulers and ruled.[8] This kind of single-mindedness on a national scale, however, is quite rare. Moreover, history shows that those restless leaders who have not only succumbed to imperial temptations but most zealously pursued their expansionist aims have generally led strong and unified polities, not weak and fragmented ones. This is not to say that domestic unity is a sufficient condition for ambitious territorial aims and the initiation of wars of aggression. It is, however, a permissive cause for such behavior and a prerequisite for sustaining the state's efforts once it has decided to embark on an offensive course of action. Because, as Geoffrey Blainey puts it, "international war is armed violence on a large scale rather than an episode of pick pocketing," national will and unity, in addition to motives, adequate financing, and organization, are essential for offensive wars of aggression.[9]

What Blainey terms the "pick pocketing" of national will and unity was not critical for the dynastic states of early modern and Enlightenment Europe to embark upon expansionist ventures. In the previous chapter, Taliaferro discusses the distinction that classical realists like Carr and Hans Morgenthau drew between the operation of the balance of power in the "age of monarchical sovereignty" and in the age of universal nationalism that began in the nineteenth century and reached its zenith in the twentieth century. Absolute monarchs such as Philip II of Spain, Louis XIV of France, and Frederick the Great of Prussia had considerable autonomy vis-à-vis other domestic actors in the conduct of grand strategy. Consequently, they could (and generally did) pursue strategies perfectly consistent with the relative power-maximizing logic of offensive realism. However, the emergence of

---

[8] See Niall Ferguson, *Colossus: The Price of America's Empire* (New York: Penguin Press, 2004), p. 294.

[9] Geoffrey Blainey, *The Causes of War* (New York: The Free Press, 1973), p. 88. Blainey makes a different point: motives alone are insufficient causes of war. States with motives for war also need arms, adequate finance, and government organization if they are to prosecute it with any chance of success.

nationalism and the military revolution associated with the French Revolutionary Wars and later the Napoleonic Wars heralded a gradual erosion of statesmen's ability to conduct grand strategy free of domestic constraints. Paradoxically, even as the destructive capacity of warfare increased throughout the nineteenth century, so did the need for elites to mobilize and sustain popular support and national unity in support of expansionist policies. For leaders to achieve this domestic unity and national will in the pursuit of power, they had to latch on to powerful expansionist ideas – ones capable of, at a maximum, whipping the masses into a mood of hysteria and, at a minimum, rallying the nation to arms when it is not under attack.

In practice, fascism was just such an ideology. In the modern age of mass politics, fascism provided the necessary political and ideological content missing from realism to implement the principle that states should expand when they can. Surprisingly, fascism shared many of realism's core assumptions about world politics and views about the nature and role of the state. There was one very significant difference, however: fascism activated realist principles with a racist ideology that, unfortunately for humankind, succeeded in mobilizing the passions of the multitudes. Through unparalleled ruthlessness and brutality, fascism managed to forge a unified national community with a will to power for power's sake. The fact remains, however, that fascism worked extremely well as a tool to mobilize national resources for state expansion.

By itself, mobilization capacity is only one important aspect of a realist foreign policy; it alone tells us nothing about how a state chooses to use its enhanced capabilities. In an anarchic realm, power is an essential means to any ends. To define state interests in terms of power, however, is to confuse means with ends. The particular shape that power takes – and its consequences for those that possess it – depends on the ideas that motivate how and when it is exercised. On this score, fascism proved an abysmal failure. The aggressive aims of fascist regimes far exceeded what realists would call prudent and necessary expansion. In the end, the hubris of fascist leaders set in motion recklessness in foreign policy that resulted in total disaster for themselves, their nations, and the rest of the world. That said, there is no reason why fascist states must be led by dictators with an insatiable and utterly reckless lust for territorial expansion. Indeed, had Munich succeeded or if Germany had not attacked the Soviet Union in 1941,

Hitler and Mussolini would have accomplished the bold but prudent expansion of their states – expansion that is consistent with an offensive realist view of appropriate state interests and behavior.

Shared foundations of the fascist and realist state

Fascism arose in the aftermath of the First World War as a new political philosophy that would solve the problem of eroding state power and the decline of Europe in the modern age of mass politics. It was a response to five interwar crises of liberal democracy: (1) the military crisis of the Great War and its destructive and demoralizing consequences; (2) the economic crisis of the Great Depression; (3) the political crisis created by the rapid and disruptive transition of many countries towards democratization; (4) the ideological crisis presented by the Russian Revolution and the communist threat; and (5) the cultural crisis of the perceived decline and decay of European civilization.[10] The basic assumption of fascism, advanced on a grand scale by the Great Depression, was that democratic capitalism had failed miserably as a form of political, social, and economic organization. Fascists detested liberal democracy because of its inherent weaknesses and distortion of the organic nation's collective will. Unlike fascist regimes, parliamentary systems do not recognize absolute truths or monopolies on virtue, but instead tolerate conflicts of interest and search for unprincipled compromises. For fascists, the endless wheeling and dealing by so-called representative elites, who prefer operating in smoke-filled back rooms, constituted nothing less than a "constant conspiracy against the public weal." Thus, fascists proclaimed that "democracy is not really a form of government but a kind of anarchy. The rule of the sum of individual spontaneity means the paralysis of the spontaneity of the common weal and its voice."[11]

A precise definition of fascism, one that all would agree on, is no easy matter. Unlike socialism, it did not offer a systematic theory.[12]

---

[10] See Michael Mann, *Fascists* (Cambridge: Cambridge University Press, 2004), pp. 23–4.

[11] Ernst Nolte, *Three Faces of Fascism*, trans. Leila Vennewitz (New York: Holt, Rinehart, and Winston, 1965), p. 107.

[12] H. R. Trevor-Roper, "The Phenomenon of Fascism," in S. J. Woolf, ed., *Fascism in Europe* (London: Methuen, 1981), pp. 20–1.

Instead, fascism comprised a list of essential and common elements: anti-liberalism, anti-Marxism, anti-conservatism, anti-Semitism, anti-parliamentarism, hyper-nationalism, authoritarian statism, corporatism and syndicalism, imperialism, idealism, voluntarism, romanticism, mysticism, militarism, and violence.[13] At its core, fascism combined aggressive hyper-nationalism with statism to form a highly militaristic and extreme version of nation-statism. Broadly speaking, the motivation behind this modern blueprint of the nation-state was to "forge a new, wholly disciplined state which would revive real or mythical glories of a past age or achieve a new pre-eminence for their race."[14] In the domestic sphere, fascists sought to transcend social conflict and build the "new man" by "cleansing" the nation of minorities and political opponents and by co-opting classes and other interests groups within state corporatist institutions. Along these lines, Michael Mann provides the most succinct and coherent definition: "Fascism is the pursuit of a transcendent and cleansing nation-statism through paramilitarism."[15]

As a solution to the fraud of liberal capitalism and the menace of communism, fascists attempted to provide a third way between capital and labor, right and left, that would rally elements of capitalist society among all classes that perceived themselves as most directly vulnerable and immediately imperiled by the Bolshevik threat. The passion which Mussolini and Hitler sought to inspire in their followers was whipped up as an antidote to Marxist-Leninist fervor; and, for this purpose, fascists borrowed many of their enemy's authoritarian methods.

Placing wars of conquest at the center of their aims, fascist regimes may be described as expansionist military dictatorships with a high degree of state-sponsored mobilization. The fascist mission was national aggrandizement and purification, not a socioeconomic revolution; "they never dreamed of abolishing property or social hierarchy." Instead, they wanted "a revolution in the world power position of their people. They meant to unify and invigorate and empower their decadent nation."[16]

---

[13] See Stanley Payne, *Fascism: Comparison and Definition* (Madison: University of Wisconsin, 1980); Payne, *A History of Fascism: 1914–1945* (Madison: University of Wisconsin, 1995); Nolte, *Three Faces of Fascism.*

[14] S. J. Woolf, "Introduction," in *Fascism in Europe*, p. 2.

[15] Mann, *Fascists*, p. 13.

[16] Robert O. Paxton, *The Anatomy of Fascism* (New York: Alfred A. Knopf, 2004), p. 142.

Through the use of modern techniques of mass mobilization that played on the fears, emotions, and passions of the citizens, fascists produced the ultimate mobilizing state motivated by the single-minded purpose (obsession) of expansion.

Fascists and realists shared many core principles about the nature of world politics, the role of the modern state, and the maximization of national power through territorial expansion. The practical problem with realist theory that fascists attempted to solve (whether deliberately or unwittingly) was the absence of an accompanying political doctrine or ideology – one that could be used by elites to energize their citizenry, and thereby facilitate the mass mobilization of national resources needed to fulfill realist prescriptions for state action. Seeking to animate politically lifeless realist principles in an age of mass politics, fascists championed a hideously racist ideology, which nevertheless proved wildly successful in generating a passionate nationalism, in subordinating the individual to the community, and in uniting the nation behind the state.[17] What, then, are the shared assumptions of realism and fascism that lead me to this conclusion?

First, realists and fascists view the group (or conflict group) rather than the individual or class as the primary unit of political order.[18] This is the most basic realist assumption: human beings do not face one another primarily as individuals but as members of groups that command their loyalty.[19] In the contemporary world, the primary

---

[17] In Robert Paxton's words: "At bottom is a passionate nationalism. Allied to it is a conspiratorial and Manichean view of history as a battle between the good and evil camps, between the pure and the corrupt, in which one's own community or nation has been the victim." Ibid., p. 1.

[18] Paxton writes: "Fascisms seek out in each national culture those themes that are best capable of mobilizing a mass movement of regeneration, unification, and purity, directed against liberal individualism and constitutionalism and against Leftist class struggle ... [A Fascist foundation is] the primacy of the group, toward which one has duties superior to every right, whether individual or universal, and the subordination of the individual to it." Ibid., pp. 40–1.

[19] See Robert Gilpin, "The Richness of the Tradition of Political Realism," in Robert O. Keohane, ed., *Neorealism and its Critics* (New York: Columbia University Press, 1986), pp. 304–5; Gilpin, "No One Loves a Political Realist," *Security Studies* 5, no. 3 (spring 1996), pp. 3–26, at p. 7 and pp. 18–26; and Randall L. Schweller and David Priess, "A Tale of Two Realisms: Expanding the Institutions Debate," *Mershon International Studies Review* 41, Supplement 1 (May 1997), pp. 1–32, at p. 6. For the argument that this assumption of group conflict most centrally distinguishes realism from liberalism, see Andrew Moravcsik, "Taking Preferences Seriously: A Liberal

conflict group is the nation-state, which, according to realists, is not only the major actor in world politics but an autonomous one; that is, the state's objectives cannot be reduced to the summation of powerful private and societal actors.[20] For fascists, the primary conflict group is the racially pure nation-state, people's community, or *Volk*.[21] In practice, this means that fascists, like realists, are state-centric in their approach to politics.

Second, both creeds view the world in terms of a constant struggle between groups for power and security. Humankind's "tribal nature" ineluctably leads to group conflict and competition; and so humankind cannot transcend conflict through the progressive power of reason to discover a science of peace.[22] Third, both realists and fascists place the concept of state power at the core of international politics and see the drive for power (whether for reasons of greed, prestige, or security) as the primary goal of state behaviors and grand strategies. Fourth, and related to the previous point, realists and fascists proclaim that states, because they operate within a fiercely competitive and dangerous realm, possess a natural will to power and right to control others. Thus fascism posits "the right of the chosen people to dominate others without restraint from any kind of human or divine law, right being decided by the sole criterion of the group's

Theory of International Politics," *International Organization* 51, no. 4 (autumn 1997), pp. 513–53, esp. pp. 516–20; and Jeffrey W. Legro and Andrew Moravcsik, "Is Anybody Still a Realist?" *International Security* 24, no. 2 (fall 1999), pp. 5–55.

20 See, for example, Stephen D. Krasner, *Defending the National Interest: Raw Materials Investments and US Foreign Policy* (Princeton, NJ: Princeton University Press, 1976).

21 To German romanticists, the term *Volk* connoted far more than just "people." Embodying the life spirit of the cosmos, the *Volk* conveyed the connection of the human soul with its native landscape – a virtuous "rural rootedness" that stood in contrast with urban dislocation. More specifically, *Volk* signified "the union of a group of people with a transcendental 'essence.' This 'essence' might be called 'nature' or 'cosmos' or 'mythos,' but in each instance it was fused to man's innermost nature, and represented the source of his creativity, his depth of feeling, his individuality, and his unity with other members of the Volk." George L. Mosse, *The Crisis of German Ideology: Intellectual Origins of the Third Reich* (New York: Howard Fertig, [1964] 1998), p. 4, and chap. 1.

22 Randall L. Schweller, "Realism and the Present Great Power System: Growth and Positional Conflict over Scarce Resources," in Michael Mastanduno and and Ethan B. Kapstein, eds., *Unipolar Politics: Realism and State Strategies after the Cold War* (New York: Columbia University Press, 1999), p. 30.

prowess within a Darwinian struggle."[23] This echoes the familiar realist theme drawn from Thucydides' Melian Dialogue "that right, as the world goes, is only in question between equals in power, while the strong do what they can and the weak suffer what they must."[24]

Fifth, both realists and fascists reject the notion that economic forces are the prime movers of history; instead, major events such as global war and change are driven by politics and the search for power.[25] Sixth, both realists and fascists embrace economic nationalism and champion autarky or economic self-sufficiency as an instrument of political power and a necessity for war preparedness.

Regarding the realm of international political economy, fascism attacked free trade and laissez-faire market mechanisms, striking at the heart of economic liberalism. Even in Britain, where Manchester liberalism had been a basic consensus value of Victorian politics, fascists advocated the twin policies of protection for British industry and the establishment of imperial preference as antecedent foundations for the establishment of an autarkic British Empire. According to British fascists, economic liberalism was the root cause of Britain's decline in power and rampant unemployment. In their eyes, only an economic program of protection, imperial preference, and a planned economy under firm governmental direction within a "corporate state" system could check the sharp decline in British power in the late Victorian and Edwardian eras.[26]

The central feature of the British fascist program to revive the national economy was the corporate state, which:

was to be the machinery of central direction. It would set the limits within which individuals and interests would function ... The economic system was to be divided into twenty corporations, ranging from agriculture, iron and steel, textiles and public utilities to professional, domestic and pensioners' sectors. All twenty corporations would be represented in a National

---

[23] Paxton, *The Anatomy of Fascism*, p. 41.

[24] Thucydides, *The Peloponnesian War*, trans. Richard Crawley (New York: The Modern Library, 1934), book V.

[25] For this core fascist tenet, see Paxton, *The Anatomy of Fascism*, p. 10. For the realist view on this issue, see Edward Hallett Carr, *The Twenty Years' Crisis, 1919–1939: An Introduction to the Study of International Relations* (New York: Harper and Row, [1939] 1964), pp. 114–20.

[26] Richard Thurlow, *Fascism in Britain: From Oswald Mosley's Blackshirts to the National Front* (New York: I. B. Tauris, 1998), pp. 6–7, 122–3.

Corporation ... The corporations were to be entrusted with the functions of planning, control, and social welfare. Strikes and lock-outs would be forbidden. Instead, each corporation would regulate wages, hours, and conditions of work.[27]

A similar "corporatist" or "statist" approach – one rooted in neo-mercantilist ideas – underpins most realist thought on national and international political economy.[28] Thus E. H. Carr proclaims: "Internationally, the consequences of absolute *laissez-faire* are as fantastic and as unacceptable as are the consequences of *laissez-faire* within the state. In modern conditions the artificial promotion of some degree of autarky is a necessary condition of orderly social existence."[29] In a different sense, realism's state-as-actor assumption rests on, among other things, the view that "individuals' shared knowledge reproduces an Idea of the state as a corporate 'person' or 'group self.'"[30]

Seventh, economic power is an instrument of national policy to be used as a weapon to acquire power and influence abroad, primarily through the use of the export of capital and the control of foreign markets.[31] For realists, economic statecraft is simply politics and the pursuit of power by national economic means. Realism promotes mercantilist notions of the subservience of the national economy to the state and its interests, which range from social welfare to international security to territorial aggrandizement.[32] Were not these precisely the national economic ideas espoused by Mussolini, Hitler, and the leaders of Imperial Japan? Were not these the rationales for – and operational doctrines that enabled – their expansionist foreign policies?

[27] Robert Benewick, *The Fascist Movement in Britain* (London: Allen Lane, Penguin, 1972), pp. 143–4; also see A. Raven Thomson, *The Coming Corporate State* (London: Greater Britain Publications, 1937).

[28] See, for example, Krasner, *Defending the National Interest*.

[29] Carr, *Twenty Years' Crisis*, p. 121. See also, Jonathan Kirshner, "The Political Economy of Realism," in Mastanduno and Kapstein, *Unipolar Politics*, pp. 69–102.

[30] Alexander Wendt, *Social Theory of International Politics* (Cambridge: Cambridge University Press, 1999), pp. 289–316, at p. 218.

[31] Carr, *The Twenty Years' Crisis*, pp. 124–5. For Nazi Germany's use of these kinds of policies, see Albert O. Hirschman, *National Power and the Structure of Foreign Trade* (Berkeley: University of California Press, [1945], 1980).

[32] See, for example, Robert Gilpin, *US Power and the Multinational Corporation: The Political Economy of Direct Foreign Investment* (New York: Basic Books, 1975); and Robert Gilpin, *The Political Economy of International Relations* (Princeton, NJ: Princeton University Press, 1987), esp. pp. 31–4.

Finally and most important to the present concerns, both creeds treat the state as a unitary actor with properties we associate with human beings. Thus standard realist theory attributes purposiveness to the state; it assumes that states act "as if" they were intentional actors or "persons." Pushing this realist assumption to the limit, Alexander Wendt asserts that "states are people too."[33] State persons are real not only in the important sense of being "'intentional' or purposive actors" but also in the more radical senses of being "*organisms*, understood as forms of life" that possess "*consciousness*, understood as subjective experience."[34] Likewise, a central foundation of fascism is "the need for authority by natural leaders (always male), culminating in a national chief who alone is capable of incarnating the group's destiny."[35] For fascists, the state really is a person; it is embodied in an all-seeing, all-knowing leader. To be sure, this popular "monolithic power" image of fascist dictatorships grossly simplifies the true nature of fascist rule and exercise of state power. The "all-powerful dictator" is a convenient myth: "the last triumph of fascist propagandists" that "personalizes fascism" and "offers an alibi to nations that approved or tolerated fascist leaders, and diverts attention from the persons, groups, and institutions who helped him."[36] Of course, dictators are not all-powerful; they cannot rule a country by themselves. Rather, fascist regimes rested on a complex arrangement between the fascist party and powerful conservative forces, on cartels of party, industry, army, and bureaucracy, all held together by "profits, power, prestige, and above all, fear."[37]

That noted, we should not let the overwhelming complexities of "reality" obscure us to a central fact: fascist regimes were dictatorships built on the principle of "the superiority of the leader's instincts over abstract and universal reason"; they were political regimes based on "mobilizing passions" shaped by powerful leaders, who, free from virtually all societal, legal, and governmental constraints, could act with extraordinary autonomy, speed, and decisiveness.[38] Dynamism,

---

[33] Wendt, *Social Theory of International Politics*, p. 215.
[34] Alexander Wendt, "The State as Person in International Theory," *Review of International Studies* 30, no. 2 (April 2004), pp. 289–316, at 291.
[35] Paxton, *Anatomy of Fascism*, p. 41.   [36] Ibid., p. 9.
[37] Franz Neumann, *Behemoth: The Structure and Practice of National Socialism, 1933–1944*, 2nd edn (New York: Oxford University Press, 1944), pp. 396–7.
[38] Paxton, *Anatomy of Fascism*, p. 41.

heroism, and decisive action are the keys to fascist leadership. Thus Sir Oswald Mosley, founder of the British Union of Fascists in 1932, criticized Britain's political system, which "by its whole structure and methods, makes action impossible; more than that, it produces a type of man to whom action and decision are impossible, even if he had the power." In contrast, Mosley asserted, "Fascism is the greatest constructive and revolutionary creed in the world ... It challenges the existing order and advances the constructive alternative of the Corporate State ... It combines the dynamic urge to change and progress, with the authority, the discipline and the order without which nothing great can be achieved."[39]

These core ideas of fascism were drawn from the Italian art movement called futurism, which flourished in the first few decades of the twentieth century and advocated a cult of violence, industry, technology, war, and speed. In his futurist manifesto, Filippo Marinetti, arguably the movement's most flamboyant spokesman, organically linked what the movement perceived as the most basic human traits and motivations (violence, patriotism, busyness, agitation, impatience, and aggression) with two essential activities, work and war ("the necessary and bloody test of a people's force"), which would facilitate the nation's most basic goals: (1) technological, commercial, and artistic progress, and (2) the concomitant domination of peoples who prove weaker on the battlefield.[40] In Marinetti's phrases: "We intend to exalt aggressive action, a feverish insomnia ... We will glorify war – the world's only hygiene – militarism, patriotism, the destructive gesture of freedom-bringers ... We will destroy the museums, libraries, academies of every kind ... We will sing of great crowds excited by work."[41] This futurist rant exhorts its followers to worship war, aggression, and industry and to move from passive contemplation to action, from slowness to speed, from the solitary individual to the crowd, and from respect for past ideas and lifestyles to a herd-like conformism with modern wisdom and ways.

---

[39] Quoted in John Stevenson and Chris Cook, *Britain in the Depression: Society and Politics, 1929–1939* (London: Longmans, 1994), pp. 222–3, 225.

[40] The goals were, in short, technological, artistic, political, and military primacy.

[41] Quoted in Mark Slouka, "Quitting the Paint Factory: On the Virtues of Idleness," *Harper's Magazine* 309, no. 1854 (November 2004), pp. 57–65 at p. 65.

At bottom, futurism's key concepts are the same ones that animate realist philosophy and theories of world politics: power, dynamism, and aggression. Realists portray the international system as a dynamic realm of perpetually rising and falling powers; the actors in this system are, by necessity, vigilant, dynamic, pro-active, and opportunistic. Prudence in an ever-dangerous environment requires the realist state to be vigilant of changes in the distribution of capabilities, to redress imbalances of power that currently threaten its security or may do so in the future, and to be ready at all times to seize opportunities to increase its power at the expense of others. And because the world is driven by fierce positional competition for scarce material and social goods, the state's domestic and foreign policies must be dynamic: if the state is not moving forward, then it is falling behind. At the very least, it must run faster just to stay in place. Thus, when aggression promises benefits that outweigh costs, prudent states unhesitatingly take to the offensive, expanding their power bases and thereby improving their relative positions within the system. Vigilance, speed, and aggressive action – these are the essential qualities of the realist state.

As can be seen from the many similarities outlined in the preceding paragraphs, fascism is similar to realism with one very important distinction: fascism created a hysterical, mass-based hyper-nationalism by means of racist ideology and propaganda that worked to energize the disillusioned masses of postwar Europe, and to whip them into a nationalist frenzy in the name of greatness and sacrifice. It was the hope of fascist leaders that, as a result of these modern psychological techniques, the entire civilian population except for the undesirable, corrosive, and impure races within the country would come to see the nation and the people's community as the highest attainment. Through the manipulation of public opinion by means of racist propaganda as well as fear, the masses would unite in passionate nationalism behind the fascist party and state; and paying no heed to the sacrifices required of them, they would support wholeheartedly the state's relentless drive for power and revenge over its enemies.

In fundamental ways, fascism is realism with a racist and social Darwinist overlay – one built on a repertory of familiar themes: "the primacy of the 'race' or the 'community' or 'the people' (the *Volk*, for Germans) over any individual rights; the right of the strongest races to fight it out for primacy; the virtue and beauty of violent action on behalf of the nation; fear of national decline and impurity; contempt for compromise; pessimism about human nature."[42] If we substitute "states" for "races," are these not familiar realist themes? And, lest we forget, is not modern realism rooted in late nineteenth-century geopolitics – a pseudo-science that evolved (no pun intended) from popular social Darwinist ideas of the time?

This conjunction of realist and fascist thought can be found in the writings of Carl Schmitt. One of the leading political theorists during the Weimar period, Schmitt decided, after the Enabling Act of March 1933, to become the self-appointed ideologue of the Nazi regime. In his famous book, *The Concept of the Political*, Schmitt attacks modern parliamentary liberalism for negating the concepts of the state and the political and for undermining state authority and power by stirring up centrifugal forces. Liberalism's greatest crime against the state is its pluralistic notion of human identity, its creation of new political spaces for subnational and supranational associations that would compete with the state for the individual's loyalty.

For Schmitt, the concept of the political turns on the fundamental distinction between friend and enemy. By this definition, Schmitt accords centrality to those who are with you and those against whom you struggle; the "high points of politics" are "the moments in which the enemy is, in concrete clarity, recognized as the enemy."[43] Along with the friend–enemy distinction, war and the possibility of death are necessary for the existence of politics. This is because, as Schmitt puts it:

Only in real combat is revealed the most extreme consequence of the political grouping of friend and enemy. From this most extreme possibility human life derives its specifically political tension ... A world in which the possibility of war is utterly eliminated, a completely pacified globe, would be a world without the distinction of friend and enemy and hence a world without politics ... War as the most extreme political means discloses the possibility which underlies every political idea, namely, the distinction of friend and enemy.[44]

Consistent with realism and its Hobbesian "state of nature" analogy, Schmitt believed that states constantly confront each other in the international arena with the ever-present possibility of war. Unlike

[42] Paxton, *Anatomy of Fascism*, p. 38.
[43] Carl Schmitt, *The Concept of the Political* (Chicago: University of Chicago Press, [1927] 1996), p. 67.
[44] Ibid., p. 35.

Hobbes, who focused on the state of war among individuals, Schmitt focused on the state of war among conflict groups, especially sovereign states. The friend–enemy grouping is not about "my" enemy or a "universal" enemy but rather "our" enemy. It is this inherent groupness or we-ness that distinguishes politics from other non-political activities. Here, Schmitt wants to excise from politics any notion of justifying actions on the basis of universal moral principles. Because everyone belongs to humanity, humanity has no enemies: "The adversary is thus no longer called an enemy but a disturber of the peace and is thereby designated to be an outlaw of humanity."[45] Liberal universalism of this kind dismisses the centrality of conflict rooted in group identities; it is, therefore, a dangerous and unrealistic negation of politics and the role of the state – a familiar realist charge against liberal idealism.

Also consistent with realism, Schmitt indivisibly linked the state and politics. Summarizing Schmitt's views on this matter, George Schwab writes: "Concretely speaking, only states, and not just any domestic or international association, are the bearers of politics. Hence only states may conduct with each other relations which in an ultimate sense are binding on their respective members ... It thus follows that in concrete circumstances it is the prerogative of the state to define the content and course of politics."[46] Accordingly, only the state has the authority to distinguish between friends and enemies of the group; and because war is the ultimate political act, only the state as sovereign has the authority to make that decision. In Schmitt's words: "The political is the most intense and extreme antagonism, and every concrete antagonism becomes that much more political the closer it approaches the extreme point, that of the friend–enemy grouping. In its entirety the state as an organized political entity decides for itself the friend–enemy distinction."[47]

Of course, Schmitt's work was not the only influence on fascist political thought. Its intellectual origins can also be traced, among many other figures, to Vilfredo Pareto, whom Mussolini made a fascist senator and whose book, *A Treatise of General Sociology* (1916), gained great fame despite its ponderous and dull style. Not lacking in scholarly ambition, Pareto sought to arrive at the essence of man,

---

[45] Ibid., p. 79.   [46] George Schwab, "Introduction," ibid., pp. 6–7.
[47] Ibid., pp. 29–30.

which he claimed was irrational and constant; this he called the "residues." The residues took on constantly changing forms according to impermanent and artificial rationalizations called "derivations." This dual conceptualization of human behavior led Pareto to formulate a doctrine of elite power. As George Mosse explains,

The main business of this elite must be to manipulate residues through controlling their derivations. Here propaganda came into its own, for the residues were irrational and thus the derivations had to appeal to the irrational in man. Only the elite, the practitioners of Pareto's system, knew that all this could be grasped scientifically and therefore manipulated ... What was the underlying motive? A longing to grasp and maintain power.[48]

Given the irrational essence of man, Pareto's elite could not rule by reason; society had to be governed by propaganda and force.

Schmitt and Pareto were not alone in their disgust for parliamentary government and party politics. "After 1918 parliamentary government, so precious to Liberals, was under attack everywhere."[49] The sin of parliamentary government was that it fragmented the people and their politicians. In so doing, it gave rise to domestic forces that "often caused states to immerse themselves in internal political struggles, and this not only weakened the state's posture vis-à-vis other states, but undermined the sovereign state in general."[50] The alternative to parliamentary government was the organic state, which "retained the class structure, but ... fused the population into a whole through the ideology of the *Volk*."[51] Unlike parliamentary government, fascist regimes would be responsive to the true nature of man: his primeval instincts to identify himself with a group, to be heroic, and to seek danger and adventure in a perpetual quest for power, which is desirable for its own ends.

This intoxication with power, which was thought to be rooted in man's primitive instincts, is compatible with realism's view of human nature and its basic premise that states relentlessly seek to maximize their relative power. Thus Hans Morgenthau, the father of modern-day realism, averred that "the selfishness of man has limits; his will to power has none. For while man's vital needs are capable of

---

[48] George L. Mosse, *The Culture of Western Europe: The Nineteenth and Twentieth Centuries*, 3rd edn (Boulder, CO: Westview, 1988), p. 299.
[49] Ibid., p. 343.   [50] Schwab, "Introduction," p. 12.
[51] Mosse, *Culture of Western Europe*, p. 345.

satisfaction, his lust for power would be satisfied only if the last man became an object of his domination, there being nobody above or beside him, that is, if he became like God."[52] If states were, in fact, human beings motivated by a natural, animal-like instinct to acquire power over others, by an *animus dominandi*, then we would see far more bids for hegemony than have occurred throughout history. Put differently, if all states were ruled by fascist regimes, offensive realism's predictions of state behavior and international politics would be more accurate than they have proven to be. States would not regularly pass up opportunities to expand. Instead, stronger states would absorb weaker ones on a regular basis. They would possess the internal unity and strength, the ruthlessness, and will to power required for expansion and empire. It is precisely these qualities, which permit (one might say, propel) powerful states to fill structural holes when they open, that are most lacking in liberal, capitalist democracies. To be sure, fascist regimes did not expand simply when opportunities arose; they expanded recklessly and with terrible consequences for their nations. But, had Hitler and Mussolini stopped their wars of conquest in 1939 or even in 1941, would not realists have applauded (even if begrudgingly) their efforts on behalf of Germany and Italy? There is no requirement that fascist states be led by insatiable dictators with unlimited revisionist aims.

Why we see so few cases of expansion in the modern world

A neoclassical realist approach to foreign expansion provides critical elements that are missing in structural realism, especially offensive realism. In the modern age, expansion requires a unified state composed of (1) elites that agree on an ambitious grand strategy, (2) a stable and effective political regime with broad authority to pursue uncertain and risky foreign policies, and (3) a compliant mass public that unreservedly supports the state's expansionist policies and is willing to make the necessary sacrifices asked of it to implement the strategy. For this type of unity among elites and the multitude, the state must possess an ideology capable of mobilizing passions into a nationalist fervor. Realism does not provide such an ideology. There is

---

[52] Hans J. Morgenthau, *Scientific Man vs. Power Politics* (Chicago: University of Chicago Press, 1946), p. 193.

nothing about the realist creed that would stir the passions of average citizens in support of the state, much less cause them to rise up as one without regard to hardship. Large-scale mobilization campaigns in pursuit of risky and aggressive expansion require a crusade of some kind, which is precisely what realism decries as a basis for foreign policy.[53]

Realism is, instead, a cynical and largely pessimistic theory or political philosophy about why things remain the same, why wars and conflict will persist, why the struggle for power and prestige among states will endure, and why, in Morgenthau's words, "man cannot hope to be good but must be content with being not too evil."[54] At its core, realism is a hollow political doctrine, as E. H. Carr asserts:

Realism, though logically overwhelming, does not provide us with the springs of action which are necessary even to the pursuit of thought ... Consistent realism excludes four things which appear to be essential ingredients of all effective political thinking: a finite goal, an emotional appeal, a right of moral judgment and a ground for action ... The necessity, recognized by all politicians, both in domestic and international affairs, for cloaking interests in the guise of moral principles is in itself a symptom of the inadequacy of realism.[55]

As a normative theory, realism does not offer much practical political advice for representative elites trying to gain or remain in power. It lacks the normative content (namely, the idealism, utopianism, moral principles, and the "ought" as opposed to "is") that would make it an effective political platform in an age of mass political participation. Indeed, realism's limitations are most evident under conditions when its prescriptions are most needed, namely, when

---

[53] Along these lines, Thomas Christensen, a neoclassical realist, develops a sophisticated two-level model that explains how elites manipulate ideology and conflict to mobilize popular support for expensive, long-term security strategies. See Thomas J. Christensen, *Useful Adversaries: Grand Strategy, Domestic Mobilization, and Sino-American Conflict, 1947–1958* (Princeton, NJ: Princeton University Press, 1996).

[54] Morgenthau, *Scientific Man vs. Power Politics*, p. 192. For realism's amoral, pessimistic nature, see Carr, *The Twenty Years' Crisis*, chap. 6; John J. Mearsheimer, "The False Promise of International Institutions," *International Security* 19, no. 3 (winter 1994/5), pp. 5–49, at p. 48; Keith L. Shimko, "Realism, Neorealism, and American Liberalism," *Review of Politics* 54, no. 2 (spring 1992), pp. 281–301; Gilpin, "No One Loves a Political Realist"; and Gilpin, "The Richness of the Tradition of Political Realism," p. 321.

[55] Carr, *Twenty Years' Crisis*, pp. 89, 92.

structural changes call for dramatic departures in current foreign policy, such as costly arms buildups to balance against rising adversaries or territorial conquests for the purposes of hegemony, empire, or eliminating dangerous power vacuums.

Small wonder that the "golden age" of the balance of power occurred from 1648 to the Napoleonic era, when: (1) the state truly was an individual, and therefore fit the realist assumption of a unitary, intentional actor, (2) the state floated above society rather than being integrated with it, and (3) war between states overlaid rather than engulfed the lives of average citizens. As Thomas Schelling observed of war during those times:

It was a contest engaged in by monarchies for stakes that were measured in territories and, occasionally, money or dynastic claims. The troops were mostly mercenaries and the motivation for war was confined to the aristocratic elite. Monarchs fought for bits of territory, but the residents of disputed terrain were more concerned with protecting their crops and their daughters from marauding troops than with whom they owed allegiance to. They were ... little concerned that the territory in which they lived had a new sovereign. Furthermore, as far as the King of Prussia and the Emperor of Austria were concerned, the loyalty and enthusiasm of the Bohemian farmer were not decisive considerations. It is an exaggeration to refer to European war during this period as a sport of kings, but not a gross exaggeration. And the military logistics of those days confined military operations to a scale that did not require the enthusiasm of a multitude.[56]

Prior to mass politics, the state truly could be considered an individual; it was embodied in and personified by the ruler. The pursuit of greedy, aggressive, and opportunistic foreign policies that promised to maximize the state's relative power did not require mass participation; it did not rely on the people's voluntary or coerced compliance. Consequently, rulers could more easily follow realist prescriptions in this period than afterwards. Monarchs could simply take their foreign policy cues from objective and material factors in their external environment, such as changes in the balance of power or the opening of power vacuums, and act on them. They did not have to couch the rationales for their actions in terms that would appeal to a "Bohemian

---

[56] Thomas C. Schelling, *Arms and Influence* (New Haven, CT: Yale University Press, 1966), pp. 27–8.

farmer," in slogans and phrases that the masses would understand and be eager to mobilize behind.

In contrast, for rulers to follow balance of power logic in the modern age, realist principles must be infused with ideological content that arouses the hearts and minds of average people. Fascism proved to be just such an ideology. This is in no way to suggest that realists are fascists; far from it. What I am saying is that, with the onset of mass political participation, fascism provided the ideological content, the "springs to action," missing from realism. Needless to say, this fusion proved disastrous for humankind. Also needless to say, realists of all stripes condemn fascism; there can be no question of their disgust for racist ideologies. And surely no realist would have advised their use to animate realist principles of state power and interests. But, in my view, this is precisely what fascism did: it posited an unrelentingly dangerous world and then sought, as a remedy for this dismal condition, to maximize the nation's power at everyone else's expense. Brutality and ruthlessness were portrayed as necessities for the victimized group's survival; and dissent within the group, whether among elites or within society, was not tolerated.

9 The limits of neoclassical realism: additive and interactive approaches to explaining foreign policy preferences

BENJAMIN O. FORDHAM

The central purpose of this volume is to evaluate the relative weight of domestic and international factors in determining the national security behavior of states. The neoclassical realist agenda that Jeffrey Taliaferro, Steven Lobell, and Norrin Ripsman lay out in their introductory essay seeks to accomplish this task by viewing domestic interests and institutions as an imperfect transmission belt that can frequently ignore or distort objective international circumstances, thereby affecting national policy. As I will argue in this chapter, however, their neoclassical assumption that domestic and international pressures are easily separable and identifiable is problematic. The nature of international threats is determined to a great extent by the interests of the domestic coalition that governs the state, and domestic political and economic interests are affected by international circumstances. Therefore, it makes little sense to treat domestic and international variables in an additive manner, by assuming an objective set of national interests and seeing how domestic political actors respond to them. Instead, I propose an interactive model that considers how the interaction between domestic interests and the international political environment determines foreign security policy choices. My model considers the interaction between subnational political actors and the international environment when theorizing about the preferences of domestic political actors, including state policy-makers. I will illustrate the explanatory advantages of this approach by examining the changing positions of domestic political factions on American national security policy during the Cold War era.

Two caveats are necessary at this point. First, an explanation for the preferences of domestic political actors, including state policy-makers, is not a complete theory of foreign policy. These preferences are only the initial inputs into the policy-making process. The final policy choice also depends on bargaining among the relevant political actors and the institutions that govern the policy-making process. Preferences are critically important, but they are not the whole story. Second, the case study presented here is intended to illustrate the advantages of an interactive approach to integrating domestic and international influences on the preferences of political actors. It is not sufficiently rigorous to qualify as a test of either the interactive approach or the substantive arguments about the case. The evidence presented suggests that some explanations for the changing positions of American domestic political factions during the Cold War are more plausible than others, but it is hardly definitive.

Integrating domestic and international factors in theories of foreign policy

Kenneth Waltz's neorealism is often said to imply that domestic politics is not an important influence on foreign policy choice. This, however, is misleading. Waltz writes, for example:

Any theory covers some matters and leaves other matters aside. Balance of power theory is a theory about the results produced by the uncoordinated actions of states. The theory makes assumptions about the interests and motives of states, rather than explaining them. What it does explain are the constraints that confine all states. The clear perception of constraints provides many clues to the expected reaction of states, but by itself the theory cannot explain those reactions.[1]

Waltz excludes unit-level considerations from his theory of international politics, but he also writes that foreign policy choice cannot be explained without them. He even indicates that using a theory of international politics to explain foreign policy choice is an error comparable to the reductionist practice of explaining international outcomes in terms of unit-level variables, though he spends much more time condemning the latter practice than the former.

A very wide range of scholars would agree with Waltz that a successful theory of foreign policy should include explanatory factors

---

[1] Kenneth N. Waltz, *Theory of International Politics* (New York: McGraw Hill, 1979), p. 122.

from both the domestic and international environments. One common way to construct such a theory is to combine systemic pressures like those described by Waltz and others with domestic considerations drawn from other theories. This is the approach Norrin Ripsman and Colin Dueck take in their contributions to this volume, though they are not alone in suggesting it. Unit-level variables enter the neoclassical realist model alongside systemic pressures on policy choice, exactly as if one were to add variables to a regression model. This approach is both simple and intuitively appealing. It makes sense to suppose that state decision-makers consider both domestic and international friends and adversaries when making foreign policy choices. For instance, the Johnson administration brought concerns about both domestic reactions to a communist victory in Vietnam, and the credibility of American international commitments to its decisions about the Vietnam War. Similar examples are not hard to find.

The distinction between domestic and international considerations is a defining feature of the additive model. Both may matter, but they are separate influences on policy choice. Separating domestic and international considerations is necessary in order to theorize about when one or the other will predominate in the decision-making process, as well as to assess their relative importance in actual cases. For example, Jack Snyder theorizes that domestic considerations will predominate in cartelized states, while international considerations are more likely to prevail in unitary or democratic states.[2] Indeed, much of the neoclassical realist agenda, which seeks to explain foreign policy choices that diverge from neorealist prescriptions, blames distinct domestic political pressures that prevent 'appropriate' responses to objective external circumstances.[3]

In spite of the intuitive appeal of this approach, additively combining arguments made at different levels of analysis into a single theory of foreign policy creates some important conceptual problems. The trouble stems from the fact that additive arguments implicitly borrow the neorealist account of state interests and motives. Whatever its advantages in constructing a theory of systemic outcomes, neorealist theory

---

[2] Jack Snyder, *Myths of Empire* (Ithaca, NY: Cornell University Press, 1991).
[3] See, for example, Randall L. Schweller, *Unanswered Threats: Political Constraints on the Balance of Power* (Ithaca, NY: Cornell University Press, 2006).

requires unrealistic assumptions about state interests and motives. These assumptions pose serious problems for explaining foreign policy choice, but the additive approach makes no sense without them.

As Waltz acknowledges, the neorealist account of the state is a set of assumed motives rather than a genuine theoretical explanation. The assumed motive Waltz proposes is very broad indeed: "I assume that states seek to ensure their survival." Waltz makes little effort to establish the plausibility of this assumption, noting that it is "a radical simplification made for the sake of constructing a theory."[4] Although the assumption is substantively defensible, it is an extremely thin and problematic basis for a theory of foreign policy. The optimal policy for ensuring survival is not always clear, and survival is not at stake in many instances where policy choices are nevertheless necessary. Assumptions of this sort may be adequate to describe systemic pressures in the broadest terms, but they are inadequate to account for the choices of any particular state, an explanatory task Waltz repeatedly (and wisely) forswears.

Assumptions about motives are necessary in order to understand international and domestic influences on policy choice separately, as the additive model does. The structural pressures neorealists identify constrain policy choice because they impinge on the state's assumed motives. States are constrained because the actions of other states in the system influence their ability to achieve their goals. The nature of these goals – the "interests and motives of states" that Waltz mentions – is thus a very important theoretical issue. In order to explain the choices of actual state decision-makers, we need to know more about their motives than the broad assumptions that systemic theories offer us. State leaders seeking to maximize their power are likely to make different decisions than those pursuing the more modest goal of national survival. These different policy goals imply different sets of threats and opportunities in the international environment. (It may be true, as Waltz and others contend, that these differences do not affect systemic outcomes, but this claim is simply irrelevant to a theory of foreign policy.) We can only know the policy implications of international events and conditions – the "international variables" to be included in the additive model – if we know the motives and interests of state policy-makers with some precision.

[4] Waltz, *Theory of International Politics*, p. 91.

As Waltz suggests, a genuine theory of foreign policy requires explaining the interests and motives of state decision-makers rather than simply making assumptions about them. Defensive realist and offensive realist assertions about the pursuit of moderate or expansionist foreign policies as the best route to security are merely alternative assumptions about state motives and the types of behavior rewarded by the international system; they are not explanations. These claims imply that state leaders' motives are universal and constant, when it is obvious that motives vary across time and space. There have been pathologically aggressive regimes, suicidally passive ones, and virtually everything in between. This variation strongly suggests that any theory of foreign policy claiming that all states share the same priorities – whatever these are said to be – is bound to fail almost any serious empirical test. This problem gets worse when one wants to explain choices about narrower policy questions, because even more precise information about interests and motives is necessary in these cases. Issues such as whether a state will choose to act alone or in concert with its allies, use force or rely on diplomatic pressure, or build conventional rather than nuclear weapons are substantively important, and require quite detailed information about state leaders' priorities. Because these priorities vary even more on these relatively narrow issues than they do on broader questions, the probability that a theory asserting fixed and universal motives will be useful diminishes as greater explanatory demands are made upon it.

Theories of foreign policy that allow state leaders' motives to vary are possible, but the effects of domestic and international considerations cannot be additive in these lines of argument. Allowing leaders' interests to vary has important consequences for what a theory of foreign policy can and cannot tell us. Unless we assume fixed and universal state motives, we will need to know enough about the domestic politics of a state to specify the interests and motives of its leaders before anything can be said about the implications of international events and conditions. International considerations thus do not enter the model additively alongside unit-level factors, but rather interactively with the domestic political process determining the interests of the faction that happens to control the state. In other words, as the chapters in this volume by Steven Lobell, Mark Brawley, and Jennifer Sterling-Folker suggest, we cannot know whether a particular international event or condition constitutes a threat, an opportunity, or an irrelevancy until we know who was selected to enter the ranks of the state leaders charged with making decisions about these matters. Explaining the foreign policy views of other domestic political factions is no different in this respect. Their preferences depend on the interaction of their interests and motives with prevailing international conditions.

The interactive model does not imply that international conditions are secondary to domestic forces in shaping foreign policy preferences. Just as one cannot deduce the response to international conditions without knowing the preferences of the political actors controlling the state, one cannot know the policy preferences of any domestic faction unless one knows the international conditions it faces. For reasons of economic interest or ideological commitment, a particular political faction may have a special concern with the domestic or foreign policies of a neighboring state. Nevertheless, the policies this faction favors will depend as much on international circumstances as on the interests that form the basis for their concern. Domestic political factions in Cuba and the United States stand in this relationship with one another. It may make sense for some such faction in the United States to advocate military action against Cuba, but the reverse is certainly not true. Although the case I will examine here will not deal extensively with these other issues, it is important to note that policy choice also depends on the outcome of bargaining among the political actors, the nature of the institutions governing the decision-making process, and perhaps other considerations.

An interactive model of foreign policy choice is preferable to an additive model for normative as well as explanatory reasons. Additive models imply that state leaders would select the optimal response to international conditions in the absence of unit-level considerations. The function of unit-level considerations in these models is to explain deviations from the correct response to systemic pressures. If international constraints and the correct means of responding to them are clear this argument implies that those who control the state always know best, and that those who oppose state leaders' interpretation of international events and conditions can only harm the interests of the state (see the discussion of 'World 1' in the Conclusion). These actors' motives for behaving in this way are puzzling, since they also suffer the harm that accrues to all the citizens of the state as a result of a suboptimal policy choice. Unless they are ignorant or irrational, they must receive some private benefit from the suboptimal policy that compensates them for this harm. Put more starkly, the additive model implies that domestic political actors who fail to support state policy are crazy, stupid, or treasonously greedy. This implication might make sense when applied to trade protectionists or defense contractors, but it is more problematic in other instances. What is one to say about the economists who lobbied against the passage of the Smoot-Hawley tariff or the large number of international relations scholars (including many realists) who signed statements opposing the Bush administration's decision to go to war in Iraq?

Because it does not imply that there is an optimal response to the international environment apart from the interests of the coalition that happens to control the state, an interactive model gives state decision-makers no special normative status. They may indeed select the optimal policy given the interests they represent, but there is no implication that these interests are universal. Arguments about the "national interest" make sense in terms of an interactive model only under very special conditions, such as when most or all political actors have identical preferences. Similarly, the interactive model implies that it makes no sense to talk about the demands of the international system in the abstract, since these are as much a function of the domestic faction in question as of the international environment.

Explaining foreign policy preferences: the case of American Cold War national security policy

The remainder of this chapter will demonstrate some of the advantages of an interactive approach to understanding foreign policy preferences by applying it to a concrete historical case: American Cold War national security policy. Beyond its considerable historical importance, this case is attractive from the standpoint of empirical research. The positions taken by major political factions in the United States are relatively easy to observe. Congressional voting data provide a window onto elite attitudes and polling data on mass public opinion are more abundant than they are in most other states. The case is also useful for testing explanations for the preferences of political factions because these attitudes changed over the course of the Cold War. In the 1940s and 1950s, Democrats, especially liberal Democrats, were more supportive of military spending and other important aspects of Cold War foreign policy than Republicans, especially conservative Republicans. During the 1970s and 1980s, these two political factions roughly switched sides on these issues, with Republicans becoming more supportive of Cold War foreign policy than Democrats. The changing position of the two parties provides a more difficult test of arguments about the sources of preferences than a case in which the preferences of each faction remained unchanged.

Changing party positions on Cold War national security policy

The change in the two parties' positions on national security policy over the course of the Cold War has been discussed extensively elsewhere,[5] but a brief review of the evidence helps to establish just what a theory of foreign policy preferences must explain in this instance. The shifting positions are easy to see in congressional roll call voting data on military spending. Figures 9.1 and 9.2 represent the annual position of each party in the Senate and House of Representatives from 1948 through 1990. The annual position is the proportion of all votes cast by members of the party in favor of greater military spending in a given year. All roll call votes on military spending were used to construct these indices. Each vote was coded according to whether it would increase or decrease the military budget. The *Congressional Quarterly Almanac* was consulted on difficult measures in order to determine how the vote was understood by its supporters and opponents. Votes on amendments concerning other issues such as the desegregation of the armed forces, projects for specific districts, or the reallocation of resources to another military use were excluded. In order to avoid confounding general attitudes toward military spending with particular wars or uses of military force, votes on spending for specific interventions, such as the Vietnam War, were also excluded. The resulting index gives a rough idea of the relative position of each party concerning the level of resources needed for American national security policy.

Both the partisan switch and a pattern of declining Democratic support for military spending are clear in the two figures. House and

---

[5] Patrick Cronin and Benjamin O. Fordham, "Timeless Principles or Today's Fashion? Testing the Stability of the Linkage between Ideology and Foreign Policy in the Senate," *Journal of Politics* 61, no. 4 (November 1999), pp. 967–98.

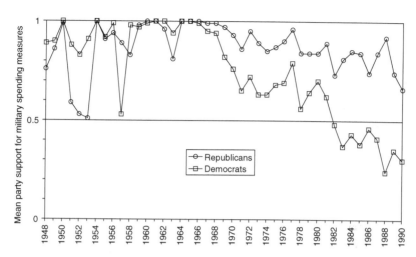

Figure 9.1 House Democratic and Republican support for Cold War military spending
Source: Congressional Quarterly, Inc. (1948–90)

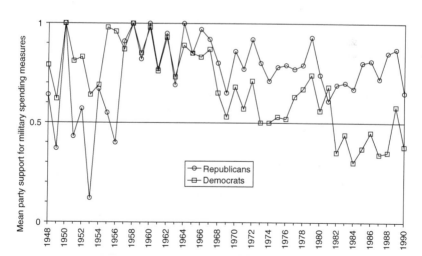

Figure 9.2 Senate Democratic and Republican support for Cold War military spending
Source: Congressional Quarterly, Inc. (1948–90)

Senate Democrats overwhelmingly supported military spending through the mid-1960s, when their support began a gradual decline that continued through the end of the Cold War. Republicans, on the other hand, were initially less supportive of military spending than Democrats, but joined them in strongly supporting it by the late 1950s. Unlike the Democrats, Republicans have maintained their position since then. The story told in figures 9.1 and 9.2 is a familiar one to students of American foreign policy. During the Vietnam War, the "Cold War consensus" gave way to a period of increasing controversy over military spending, among other issues, as party differences widened. It is worth noting that, while the partisan divergence may have begun during the Vietnam War, it continued and deepened through the 1980s.

The "key votes" on military spending identified by the *Congressional Quarterly Almanac* help confirm that the patterns in figures 9.1 and 9.2 do not stem from some anomaly in the many minor issues on which the votes took place. These votes were selected to represent issues on which there was especially great public interest or controversy. They include critical procedural questions rather than votes on final passage of a measure when those effectively decided the issue. Table 9.1 shows the average proportion of each party in the House and Senate voting in support of military spending on these measures for five-year periods beginning in 1950. The party switch is even clearer on these important measures than it is on all votes.

The patterns evident in congressional voting can also be found in public opinion data. The biennial American National Election Study (ANES) is an important source of data on public opinion that is comparable over time. Since the early 1970s, ANES respondents who identified themselves as Republicans have been more likely to support increases in military spending than Democrats. These differences are even larger among party activists.[6] Table 9.2 presents the

---

[6] In their study of changing party positions on race, Edward Carmines and James Stimson, *Issue Evolution* (Princeton, NJ: Princeton University Press, 1989), p. 93, identified party activists based on several campaign activities surveyed by the ANES. These are (1) voting; (2) attending political rallies or meetings; (3) wearing a campaign button or displaying a bumper sticker; (4) working for a party or candidate; (5) attempting to influence others; and (6) donating money. Individual ANES respondents were identified as activists if they reported engaging in four or more of these acts.

Table 9.1 *Party support on key Cold War military spending votes* (%)

Time period	House of Representatives			Senate		
	Democrats	Republicans	Number of votes	Democrats	Republicans	Number of votes
1950–54	0.710	0.200	8	0.867	0.254	6
1955–59	0.844	0.210	2	0.854	0.096	3
1960–64	n.a.	n.a.	0	n.a.	n.a.	0
1965–69	0.674	0.998	3	0.299	0.551	5
1970–74	0.343	0.752	6	0.299	0.705	13
1975–79	0.420	0.748	4	0.443	0.729	8
1980–84	0.322	0.758	12	0.391	0.740	10
1985–89	0.217	0.839	13	0.236	0.847	11

Note: The number shown is the average proportion of each party voting in favor of measures that would increase the funding or bureaucratic autonomy of the military, or against measures intended to reduce funding or autonomy. The key votes are taken from *Congressional Quarterly Almanac.*

Table 9.2 *Support for military spending among party activists and identifiers* (%)

Year	Identifiers			Activists		
	Republicans	Democrats	Difference	Republicans	Democrats	Difference
1972	64.8	51.4	13.4	68.0	10.5	57.5
1976	83.5	72.7	10.8	88.5	69.8	18.7
1980	72.7	54.7	18.0	78.0	37.5	40.5
1982	40.3	19.9	20.4	53.6	26.1	27.5
1984	42.6	22.3	20.3	50.0	12.5	37.5
1986	38.0	21.6	16.4	51.7	19.3	32.4
1988	39.9	20.5	19.4	35.0	15.2	19.8
1990	21.9	17.9	4.0	30.8	5.1	25.7

Source: American National Election Studies, The 1948–2004 ANES Cumulative Data File (machine-readable dataset) (Stanford University and the University of Michigan [producers and distributors], 2005). Respondents were coded as activists if they reported engaging in at least four of the following six activities: (1) voting; (2) attending political rallies or meetings; (3) wearing a campaign button or displaying a bumper sticker; (4) working for a party or candidate; (5) attempting to influence others; or (6) donating money. In 1972 and 1976, respondents were asked the following question: "Some people believe that our armed forces are already powerful enough and that we should spend less money for defense. Others feel that military spending should at least continue at the present level. How do you feel – should military spending be cut, or should it continue at least at the present level?" The percentages in the table are for respondents who said that military spending should continue at least at its present level. In 1980 and subsequent surveys, respondents were asked "Some people believe that we should spend much less money for defense. Others feel that defense spending should be greatly increased. Where would you place yourself on this scale or haven't you thought much about this?" Respondents were shown a seven-point scale with "great decrease defense spending" at point 1 and "greatly increase defense spending" at point 7. The percentages in the table are those who placed themselves at point 4 or higher.

party differences found in the ANES surveys. Republican identifiers consistently supported military spending more than Democrats did, although the magnitude of the difference declined as the Cold War came to an end.

Because the partisan switch in congressional voting took place before the ANES began asking respondents about military spending, the few pieces of information on the military spending attitudes of Republicans and Democrats in the mass public are especially important. Table 9.3 presents the results of a Gallup poll which asked four questions on military spending before 1970 for which responses disaggregated by party were available. In three of the four cases, Democrats were more supportive of maintaining or increasing military spending than Republicans. This evidence suggests that mass partisan alignments resembled those found in congressional voting, with Democrats supporting more military spending than Republicans before the mid-1960s.[7]

The careers of many well-known senators from both parties exemplify these patterns. Republican examples include Wallace Bennett of Utah, whose Senate career began in the eighty-second Congress (1951–2), where his military support score was 0.21. It had risen to 0.86 by the ninety-third Congress (1973–4), his last in the Senate. Everett Dirksen of Illinois, who served as minority leader throughout the 1960s, followed a similar pattern. Elected in 1950, his military support score rose from 0.25 in his first Congress to 0.90 in his last. Barry Goldwater of Arizona is another important case in point. The 1964 presidential nominee's military support score in the eighty-third Congress (1953–4), his first, was 0.25. In his final Congress, the ninety-ninth (1985–6), it was 0.88. Well-known Democratic examples are probably less surprising, since their change of heart over the war in Vietnam is well known. Their diminished support for military spending persisted after the end of the war, however. Examples include Stuart Symington of Missouri, whose score declined

---

[7] One additional piece of evidence of the partisan switch comes from the ANES question asking respondents to rate their feelings toward the military on a scale of 0 to 100. This question was first asked in 1964. Democratic activists and identifiers gave the military higher average scores than Republicans in 1964 and 1968, but lower scores in every survey afterwards. Because the military feeling thermometer scores are not correlated with support for greater military spending, though, the relevance of these responses is open to question.

Table 9.3 *Pre-1970 Gallup poll questions on military spending (%)*

Question and possible responses	Republican	Democrat
September 1950: "Some people say the United States is spending so much on national defense that the country is in danger of spending itself into bankruptcy. Do you agree or disagree?"		
Agree	67	50
Disagree	23	38
No opinion	10	12
July 1953: "Do you agree, in the main, with those people who say the defense budget has been cut so much that the nation's safety is threatened – or with those who say only waste and extravagance have been cut out of the budget?"		
Safety threatened	7	26
Waste, extravagance cut	69	44
No opinion	24	30
August 1953: "Do you think too much of the taxes you pay is being spent on defense – or is too little being spent on defense?"		
Too much	20	17
Too little	19	27
About right	48	43
No opinion	13	13
March 1960: "There is much discussion as to the amount this country should spend for national defense. How do you feel about this – do you think we are spending too little, too much, or about the right amount?"		
Too much	15	24
Too little	51	42
About right	19	20
No opinion	15	14

Source: George H. Gallup, *The Gallup Poll: Public Opinion, 1935–1971* (New York: Random House, 1972).

from 1.00 to 0.40 over the course of his time in the Senate, Frank Church of Idaho, whose score declined from 0.89 to 0.51, and Hubert Humphrey of Minnesota, whose score declined from 0.89 to 0.58.

Explaining national security policy preferences

Why did Democratic support for military spending begin to decline in the 1960s and continue to do so through the 1970s and 1980s? Why did Republicans begin to support military spending during the late 1950s when they had been reluctant to do so earlier? Useful theories of foreign policy should suggest plausible answers to these questions. Additive and interactive theories of foreign policy suggest several explanations. Additive arguments might focus on either the domestic or the international environment. Plausible arguments can be constructed employing either set of considerations. Interactive arguments focus on the relationship between international conditions and domestic actors' interests and motives. Several of these arguments are possible as well, focusing on the domestic and international costs and benefits of military spending. The evidence reviewed here is suggestive rather than con-clusive. Its purpose is to illustrate the promise and pitfalls of the additive and interactive approaches to foreign policy preferences.

Did changing international conditions cause the switch?

Because foreign and defense policy is directed at the international environment, most explanations for policy change focus on changes at the system level. For example, defensive realists such as Barry Posen and Stephen Walt use shifts in the international balance of military power or threat to explain choices about military doctrine and alli-ance formation.[8] In explaining foreign and defense policy choices in terms of efforts to anticipate or respond to other states' behavior, many diplomatic histories adopt a similar approach.[9] Those who adopt an additive approach to the inclusion of domestic politics might

[8] Barry R. Posen, *The Sources of Military Doctrine* (Ithaca, NY: Cornell University Press, 1984); and Stephen M. Walt, *The Origins of Alliances* (Ithaca, NY: Cornell University Press, 1987).

[9] See, for example, Melvyn P. Leffler, *A Preponderance of Power* (Stanford, CA: Stanford University Press, 1992); A. J. P. Taylor, *The Struggle for Mastery in Europe, 1848–1918* (Oxford: Oxford University Press, 1954).

still emphasize international sources of explanation. In principle, changes in the international environment or the behavior of other states can account for shifts in the positions of domestic political factions as well as overall policy choice.

Examining the shifting Cold War balance of power helps illustrate both the attraction and the pitfalls of international explanations for the party switch. Figure 9.3 illustrates the changing balance of power in Europe with the Correlates of War Project's composite index of national capabilities.[10] The patterns in the graph correspond to the perceptions of American policy-makers at key points. The shift against the United States in the late 1940s is the reason generally offered for the formation of the NATO alliance in 1949 and the military buildup associated with National Security Council (NSC) paper no. 68 and the Korean War.[11] The erosion of the western edge during the 1970s was the principal reason offered for the military buildup of the 1980s. Shifts of this kind can certainly influence the positions of domestic political actors.

The second of these changes in the international environment corresponds to the surge in support for military spending by both the

[10] The composite index of national capabilities is derived from the state's share of the indicators of national capabilities gathered by the correlates of War (COW) Project: military spending, military personnel, iron and steel production, energy consumption, urban population, and total population. It is generally computed by summing all observations on each of the six capability components for a given year, converting each state's absolute component to a share of the international system, and then averaging across the six components. J. David Singer, Stuart Bremer, and John Stuckey, "Capability Distribution, Uncertainty, and Major Power War, 1820–1965," in Bruce Russett, ed., *Peace, War, and Numbers* (Beverly Hills, CA: Sage, 1972), pp. 19–48; J. David Singer, "Reconstructing the Correlates of War Dataset on Material Capabilities of States, 1816–1985," *International Interactions* 14, no. 2 (1988), pp. 115–32 (See http://cow2.la.psu.edu/). In this case, alternatives employing only military spending produce very similar results. Cold War NATO members included Belgium, Canada, Denmark, France, Iceland, Italy, Luxembourg, the Netherlands, Norway, Portugal, the United Kingdom, and the United States from 1949. Greece and Turkey joined the alliance in 1952, West Germany in 1955, and Spain in 1982. The Warsaw Treaty Organization, which was formally organized in 1955, included Albania, Bulgaria, Czechoslovakia, East Germany, Hungary, Poland, Romania, and the Soviet Union.

[11] Leffler, *Preponderance of Power*, pp. 355–60; Samuel F. Wells, Jr., "Sounding the Tocsin: NSC 68 and the Soviet Threat," *International Security* 4, no. 2 (autumn 1979), pp. 116–58.

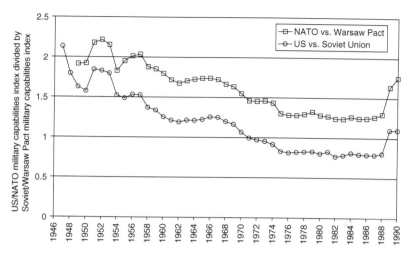

Figure 9.3 The Cold War military balance in Europe, 1947–90
Source: Correlates of War Project

public and members of both parties in Congress evident in figures 9.1 and 9.2. Larry Bartels has shown that the change in public opinion influenced congressional voting on military spending in 1981.[12] Nevertheless, it does not explain the party switch. Because both parties confront the same balance of power, this consideration cannot explain why domestic political factions might move in opposite directions, as they do in this case. Moreover, it is not simply the case that one party was more sensitive to changes in the balance of power than the other across the entire Cold War era. Democrats were more supportive of military spending during the Soviet gains of the early Cold War era. Republicans were more supportive of it when the Soviets made gains during the 1970s. In order for an international condition to explain the party switch, it must affect the two parties in different ways, as the interactive model suggests.

Similar problems confront another possible international explanation for the party switch: the Vietnam War. The Vietnam War figures prominently in explanations for the changing positions of

---

[12] Larry M. Bartels, "Constituency Opinion and Congressional Policy Making: The Reagan Defense Buildup," *American Political Science Review* 85, no. 2 (June 1991), pp. 457–74.

many individual politicians, especially Democrats who turned against the war, and there is no reason to doubt that it made a big difference in many cases. Nevertheless, even if one accepts the war as the reason for the Democrats' declining support for military spending, it does not explain the Republican side of the party switch. After all, Republicans might have argued that the war vindicated their earlier suspicion of Cold War foreign policy, especially since a Democratic president committed American troops. Even as an explanation for the Democratic switch, the war leaves some unanswered questions. If a bloody and unpopular war was enough to shake their support for military spending, then events in Korea between 1950 and 1953 should have sufficed. In spite of the relative lack of street protests, public opinion polls suggest that it was just as unpopular, and the rate of American casualties was even higher.[13] Moreover, the Vietnam War cannot explain why Democratic support for military spending continued to decline for more than a decade after the last Americans had fled Saigon. The trouble once again is that both parties confronted the same war, but moved in opposite directions. If the Vietnam War is to play a role in explaining the party switch, it will have to do so interactively with some explanation for the different reactions it produced in the two parties.

Could an exclusively domestic condition have caused the party switch?

If one adopts an additive approach to the explanation of foreign policy preferences, domestic as well as international factors might cause change. Political actors operate in an environment where military spending is only one of many issues they face. Indeed, issues that had little to do with foreign and defense policy dominated the political agenda during much of the Cold War. To the extent that other issues brought about changes in the composition of the two parties, they might have been indirectly responsible for the shift in their positions on military spending. If so, the party switch on military spending might have been the result of an exclusively domestic political process.

---

[13] John E. Mueller, "Trends in Popular Support for the Wars in Korea and Vietnam," *American Political Science Review* 65, no. 2 (June 1971), pp. 358–75.

This line of argument is more plausible than those emphasizing international factors alone, because domestic processes could have affected the two parties in different ways. Perhaps the most obvious candidate explanation of this sort here concerns the two parties' changing views on race, which Edward Carmines and James Stimson document in great detail.[14] This change might well have indirectly affected party positions on military spending. The changing positions of the two parties on racial issues eventually changed the South from a region controlled almost exclusively by Democrats to one dominated by Republicans. The process took many years, and Republicans were not truly ascendant in the South until perhaps 1994, or even later.[15] Because the Southern congressional delegation has always been relatively conservative, its gradual shift from an exclusively Democratic to a largely Republican Party affiliation increased the ideological homogeneity of both parties. If Southerners were the principal hawks in the Democratic Party during the early Cold War era, then their move to the Republican Party might explain the party switch.

While this line of argument is plausible, an examination of data from the Senate does not support it. Figure 9.4 depicts the mean level of support for military spending among Southern senators and among Democratic and Republican senators from other regions of the country. Two features of the graph are especially worth noting. First, Southerners were not very different from other Democrats during the early Cold War era or Republicans during the latter part of this period. They do not appear to have been any more hawkish than members of these two parties from other regions on the appropriate side of the party switch. Second, the shift in the attitude of the two parties toward military spending is at least as clear when Southerners are treated separately as it is when they are included. The changing party affiliation of the Southern congressional delegation is not a very promising explanation for the parties' changing positions on military spending.

Explanations that focus on either domestic or international considerations are additive if they treat the influence of these variables as

[14] Carmines and Stimson, *Issue Evolution.*
[15] Earl Black and Merle Black, *The Rise of Southern Republicans* (Cambridge, MA: Harvard University Press, 2002).

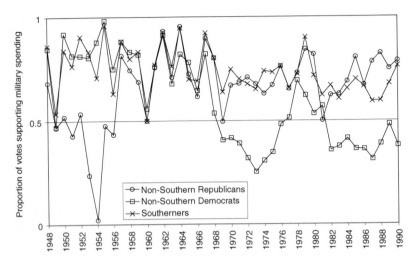

Figure 9.4 Party, region, and support for military spending in the Senate
Source: Congressional Quarterly, Inc. (1948–90)

analytically separable, even if they may both have effects in practice. The explanations discussed thus far are examples. They embody claims that some international or domestic factor is behind foreign policy preferences. Though each one focuses on a particular causal path, they do not imply that other considerations might not have independent, additive effects. An interactive approach differs in that it suggests that the effects of domestic and international variables depend on one another. Several explanations for foreign policy preferences of this sort are possible.

Why would the policy implications of military spending have differed for the two parties?

The two parties' differences over Cold War priorities are one possible reason for their different responses to changes in the international environment during the 1950s and 1960s. During the early 1950s, military spending served several complementary purposes for the Democratic policy-makers in the Truman administration. Although the Korean War was a critical source of political support for the military buildup, most of the additional resources were not intended for the conflict there.[16] Instead, the expanded military forces were used to underscore the American commitment to western Europe and Japan, the areas Truman administration policy-makers viewed as most important. They hoped the military commitment would not only deter potential Soviet aggression, but also psychologically reassure American allies.[17] Military spending also served economic policy goals. The military buildup entailed basing American forces in western Europe and Japan, and procuring a substantial amount of military equipment there, so it provided a source of foreign exchange that assisted in the economic recovery of these war-ravaged areas. Both western Europe and Japan were experiencing large balance of payments deficits with the United States, the so-called "dollar gap." This situation put pressure on these states to devalue their currencies, endangering their commitment to the new international monetary system established at Bretton Woods.[18]

The Democratic policy-makers who proposed and implemented the military buildup of the early 1950s were also very concerned about postwar economic arrangements. Important policy-makers like Paul Nitze and Averell Harriman had backgrounds in international finance, and were well aware of the implications of the "dollar gap" during the immediate postwar era. Nitze recalled that, as the writing of NSC 68 began, "almost all of our policy initiatives had been economic and political: little attention had been given to our or anyone else's military capabilities."[19] When Averell Harriman was brought into the White House staff from his position implementing the Marshall Plan in Europe, his tasks were "to take over the dollar gap problem ... and to interest himself in coordinating the implementation of

---

[16] Doris M. Condit, *History of the Office of the Secretary of Defense*, vol. II (Washington, DC: Historical Office, Office of the Secretary of Defense, 1988), pp. 224–40; Samuel P. Huntington, *The Common Defense* (New York: Columbia University Press, 1963), p. 55.

[17] John L. Gaddis, *Strategies of Containment* (New York: Oxford University Press, 1982), pp. 90–5; Leffler, *A Preponderance of Power*, pp. 383–90.

[18] Fred L. Block, *The Origins of International Economic Disorder* (Berkeley: University of California Press, 1977); Fred L. Block, "Economic Instability and Military Strength: The Paradoxes of the 1950 Rearmament Decision," *Politics and Society* 10, no. 1 (1980), pp. 35–58.

[19] John Lewis Gaddis and Paul H. Nitze, "NSC-68 and the Soviet Threat Reconsidered," *International Security* 4, no. 4 (spring 1980), pp. 164–80, at p. 171.

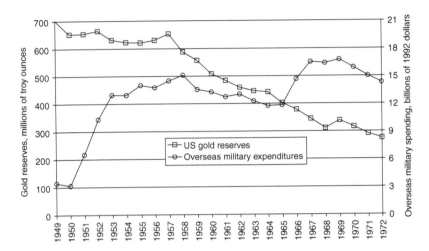

Figure 9.5 Overseas military spending and gold reserves
Sources: US gold reserves – international monetary fund; overseas military spending – US Department of Commerce

NSC 68."[20] The backgrounds of Nitze and Harriman were not unusual. Bankers and lawyers from New York and Washington who helped make foreign policy under Harry Truman included Dean Acheson, James V. Forrestal, Robert A. Lovett, and John McCloy, among others.[21]

American military spending overseas had helped alleviate the balance of payments problem in western Europe and Japan during the early 1950s. By the early 1960s, however, the "dollar gap" of the earlier period was only a memory, and overseas military spending was adding to the American balance of payments problem. Figure 9.5 shows the growth in American overseas military expenditures during the 1950s and US gold reserves, which declined as a consequence of the American balance of payments position. The decline in overseas military expenditures after 1958 reflects American policy-makers' response to these declining gold reserves, which threatened the Bretton Woods system. As the graph indicates, the Vietnam War made the

[20] Souers memorandum for the file, 8 June 1950, Souers Papers, Box 1, Harry S. Truman Presidential Library, Independence, MO.
[21] Philip H. Burch, *Elites in American History*, vol. III (New York: Holmes and Meier Publishers, Inc, 1980).

problem worse. While overseas military expenditures rose, American gold stocks fell steadily until Lyndon Johnson was forced to suspend gold payments in 1968. The balance of payments problem was a major preoccupation for American policy-makers during the Vietnam War. Indeed, there is evidence that it was one of the factors that led the so-called "wise men," an advisory group of senior policy-makers that included key Truman administration officials such as former Secretary of State Dean Acheson, to advise Lyndon Johnson against escalation in Vietnam in March 1968.[22]

Because Democratic policy-makers had been the strongest supporters of the military spending to protect western Europe and handle the dollar gap during the 1940s and early 1950s, it makes sense to suppose that changes in the implications of military spending for these issues would influence their attitude toward it. The same group of policy-makers that sought higher military spending around 1950 had good reasons to question its continuing economic usefulness by the mid-1960s. Because Republican policy-makers did not control the executive branch when these multilateral institutions were established, the impact of military spending on these institutions may have been less important to them. At any rate, Republicans have generally been more skeptical of such multilateral institutions than Democrats.

Not only was military spending undermining international economic arrangements the Democrats had worked to establish, but actual American military action was no longer playing the role many had anticipated during the early Cold War era. As figure 9.6 indicates, the regional focus of American military action shifted away from Europe and Japan, the big prizes identified by Democratic policy-makers during the early Cold War era, and toward less-developed parts of the world. By the 1960s, the emergence of anti-American regimes in some less-developed states and the growth of movements that threatened to establish more of them in others, suggested that this trend was likely to continue. Whether because of the interests of their constituents or the strategic culture of their national security elite, prominent Republicans had long argued for a stronger military posture in these areas, particularly toward China during the late 1940s and

---

[22] Robert M. Collins, "The Economic Crisis of 1968 and the Waning of the 'American Century,'" *American Historical Review* 101, no. 2 (April 1996), pp. 396–422, at p. 415.

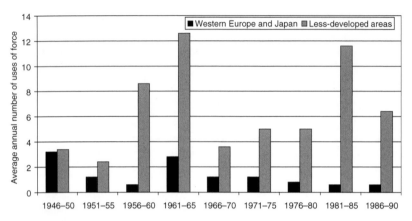

Figure 9.6 Regional emphasis of US military action, 1946–90
Source: Benjamin O. Fordham and Christopher C. Sarver, "The Militarized Interstate Disputes Data Set and United States Uses of Force," *International Studies Quarterly* 45, no. 2 (September 2001), pp. 455–66.

early 1950s. The American military role in less-developed parts of the world, ranging from Vietnam to Angola to Nicaragua, remained a partisan bone of contention throughout the remainder of the Cold War.

Other considerations may have magnified the Republican shift toward support for Cold War national security policy. Given their traditional commitment to a relatively smaller government role in the economy, the fiscal, regulatory, and tax policy implications of military spending may have loomed larger for Republicans. By the end of the Korean War, the United States devoted 14.2 percent of GDP to military spending. Although this was far less than had been the case during World War II, it still required government wage and price controls to prevent inflation, as well as the rationing of some commodities required for military production. Higher taxes were also necessary.[23] These considerations reduced business support for military spending, even during the Korean War.[24] The views of conservative Republican

---

[23] Michael Hogan, *A Cross of Iron* (New York: Cambridge University Press, 1998), pp. 315–65; Paul G. Pierpaoli, *Truman and Korea* (Columbia: University of Missouri Press, 1999).

[24] Clarence Y. H. Lo, "Theories of the State and Business Opposition to Increased Military Spending," *Social Problems* 29, no. 4 (April 1982), pp. 424–38.

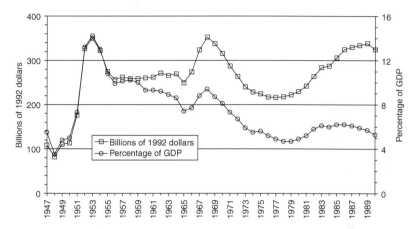

Figure 9.7 United States Cold War military spending
Source: US Department of Commerce

politicians on military spending during this period reflected their distaste for high taxes and government regulation.

As the US economy grew, military spending posed a smaller inflation risk and required correspondingly lower tax rates and less regulation. Figure 9.7 shows military spending in both real 1992 dollars and as a proportion of GDP. Even though the military buildups associated with the Vietnam War and the Reagan administration reached roughly the same level of spending in real dollars as the buildup associated with the Korean War, they were much smaller in terms of the entire economy. Indeed, as a percentage of GDP, the high point of the Reagan buildup was substantially less than the low point of the budget-conscious Eisenhower administration. Although spending as a proportion of GDP provides a misleading indicator of actual military strength, it offers a good approximation of its impact on other economic activities. It helps explain why Republican political leaders could support the Reagan buildup when they had remained concerned about the much lower levels of military spending that had prevailed during the Eisenhower administration.

A similar interactive argument could be made concerning international trade. Many scholars point to the establishment and maintenance of a relatively open international economic order as one of the principal international public goods provided by American military and economic hegemony.[25] Such an international order was one of the principal goals of American policy-makers during the early Cold War era.[26] As NSC 68 pointed out, the goal of containing the Soviet Union was closely related to the goal of establishing a prosperous and healthy international community.[27] The trade implications of Cold War foreign policy were politically important, influencing congressional support for the Truman administration's national security program.[28]

Expanding international trade is a potential explanation for the party switch on military spending because it had different political implications for the Democratic and Republican parties. Republicans had long preferred greater trade protection than Democrats, so it is not surprising that they were less likely to support the Truman administration's expensive effort to establish and maintain an international environment where free trade could flourish.[29] The Republican Party had begun to abandon its commitment to protectionism by the late 1940s, but only about half of congressional Republicans supported the 1949 renewal of the Reciprocal Trade Agreements Act (RTAA).[30] Congressional Democrats had been consistent supporters of the RTAA since the 1930s.

By the late 1960s, the two parties had begun to shift their positions on trade protection. Unionized industries in the northeast were facing greater import competition by the late 1960s, and organized labor, one of the mainstays of the Democratic Party, began to

[25] See, for example, Robert O. Keohane, *After Hegemony* (Princeton, NJ: Princeton University Press, 1984); Charles P. Kindleberger, *The World in Depression* (Berkeley: University of California Press, 1973); Stephen D. Krasner, "State Power and the Structure of International Trade," *World Politics* 28, no. 3 (April 1976), pp. 317–47.

[26] See, for example, Robert A. Pollard, *Economic Security and the Origins of the Cold War, 1945–1950* (New York: Columbia University Press, 1985).

[27] Block, "Economic Instability and Military Strength," pp. 38–9.

[28] Benjamin O. Fordham, "Economic Interests, Party, and Ideology in Early Cold War Era US Foreign Policy," *International Organization* 52, no. 2 (spring 1998), pp. 359–96.

[29] On the trade preferences of the two parties, see Barry R. Weingast, Judith Goldstein, and Michael A. Bailey, "The Institutional Roots of American Trade Policy: Politics, Coalitions, and International Trade," *World Politics* 49, no. 3 (April 1997), pp. 309–38.

[30] Douglas A. Irwin and Randall S. Kroszner, "Interests, Institutions, and Ideology in Securing Policy Change: The Republican Conversion to Trade Liberalization after Smoot-Hawley," *Journal of Law and Economics* 42, no. 2 (October 1999), pp. 643–73.

support trade protection. At the same time, areas in which the Republican Party was especially strong, particularly the southwest, were among the most important winners from free trade.[31] As was the case with the Truman administration's military buildup in the early 1950s, members of Congress from states less threatened by import competition were more likely to support the Reagan administration's military buildup.[32] Like the balance of payments problems created by overseas military spending, the changing implications of international trade helped create a political environment in which the implications of military spending were quite different than they had been in the early 1950s.

What makes these lines of argument plausible is that they all rest on the interaction between international conditions and the interests and motives of different domestic political factions. Most of the possible explanations reviewed here trace the differences between the two parties' perspectives on national security policy to the economic interests of their constituents. Alternative explanations based on other sources of political cleavage, such as political ideology or ethnic identity, could easily be constructed, however. The point of presenting these examples here is to demonstrate the usefulness of an interactive approach. Additive approaches are only useful for explaining foreign policy preferences when all domestic factions share the same interests and motives, and thus respond to international events and conditions in the same way. There are certainly times and places where this happens, but constructing a theory of foreign policy on the assumption that it always does seems unwise as well as unnecessary.

Conclusion

Before reviewing the pros and cons of additive and interactive approaches for explaining foreign policy preferences, it is important to recall one of the caveats that opened this chapter: the explanation of foreign policy preferences and the explanation of foreign policy

---

[31] Peter Trubowitz, *Defining the National Interest* (Chicago: University of Chicago Press, 1998); Peter Trubowitz, "Sectionalism and American Foreign Policy: The Political Geography of Consensus and Conflict," *International Studies Quarterly* 36, no. 2 (June 1992), pp. 173–90.
[32] Trubowitz, *Defining the National Interest*, pp. 229–32.

outcomes are not synonymous. An account of the preferences of relevant political actors is a necessary component of a theory of foreign policy, but it is only the beginning of the policy-making process. The outcome will rest on institutions, bargaining between political actors, and perhaps other considerations as well. Because the purpose of this chapter is to consider some problems in one aspect of a theory of foreign policy, it made sense to set these other issues aside. Any attempt to build a theory useful for predicting policy choice will have to return to them, however.

Interactive accounts of policy preferences have several important advantages over additive accounts. First, interactive models can explain cases in which international events produce conflicting responses among domestic political actors. In the case examined here, only arguments about conditions affecting Democrats and Republicans differently can explain their evolving views on Cold War national security policy. Because the impact of international events does not vary across domestic factions in additive models, such cases pose serious problems for them. Interactive approaches are common in the study of foreign economic policy. The redistributive effects of trade and trade protection are at the core of most analyses of the politics of trade policy. In these accounts, domestic actors are commonly distinguished based on the competitiveness of the economic activity in which they are engaged or the factors of production they own.[33] As even the most casual observer of contemporary American politics must be aware, questions of war and peace also produce domestic political divisions. The ability to explain these divisions is a considerable asset for interactive accounts of foreign policy.

Interactive accounts of foreign policy point to more fruitful areas of research than additive accounts. Interactive models invite scholarly research into the sources of motives and interests across states and domestic political factions. The construction of a genuine theory of foreign policy requires judgments about whether economic interests, ideology, or other political differences are more important in shaping

---

[33] Benjamin O. Fordham and Timothy J. McKeown, "Selection and Influence: Interest Groups and Congressional Voting on Trade Policy," *International Organization* 57, no. 3 (summer 2003), pp. 519–49; Michael J. Hiscox, *International Trade and Political Conflict* (Princeton, NJ: Princeton University Press, 2002); Ronald Rogowski, *Commerce and Coalitions* (Princeton, NJ: Princeton University Press, 1989).

preferences. Theoretical arguments along any of these lines will have testable implications about variation in preferences on a wide range of issues. By contrast, additive models force assumptions about unitary state motives. Even Waltz, no critic of unitary actor models in general, acknowledged that this approach was inadequate for constructing a theory of foreign policy. Unless these assumptions are extremely detailed – and thus increasingly unrealistic – they will apply to only a limited range of policy questions. Moreover, because they are simply assumptions, testing them is not a useful enterprise. To the extent that these tests are conducted, simple assertions about the universal motives of states are not likely to find much empirical support anyway.

For all their advantages, interactive accounts of foreign policy preferences come at a price. They sever the linkage between neorealist accounts of international political outcomes and theories of foreign policy. This may put them beyond the purview of neoclassical realism as it is understood in this volume, since, as Taliaferro, Lobell, and Ripsman indicate in their introductory chapter, for neoclassical realists domestic interests and coalitions merely act as rather imperfect transmission belts of rather clear objective international stimuli. Moreover, many of the concepts and arguments commonly deployed in everyday discourse about foreign policy choices also make little sense in light of an interactive understanding of foreign policy. Casual use of notions like "national interest" or "international threat" makes no sense apart from an explanation of where these interests come from or what exactly is being threatened. Because policy-makers are not likely to stop using these old chestnuts, however, interactive theories of foreign policy may increase the gulf between academics and practitioners. This may be a price any successful theory of foreign policy will have to pay.

10 Conclusion: The state of neoclassical realism

NORRIN M. RIPSMAN, JEFFREY W. TALIAFERRO, AND STEVEN E. LOBELL

Despite important differences between the chapters, most of the contributors to this volume have expressed strong preferences for an approach to international politics that stresses the primacy of the international system, but that also acknowledges the importance of domestic political arrangements and the perceptions of leaders in the selection and implementation of foreign policy responses to the international environment. The question remains, however, how important this enterprise of neoclassical realism is as a research agenda and whether, in practical terms, it truly represents an improvement on existing theoretical approaches. In order to place our discussion in a broader context, therefore, our purpose in this chapter is threefold: (1) to map out the scope of neoclassical realism as understood in this volume; (2) to compare its performance in the cases covered in this volume to other popular approaches to international politics and foreign policy (principally neorealism, liberal theory, and other *Innenpolitik* approaches); and (3) to identify directions for future research.

The scope of neoclassical realism

A central theme of this volume has been that neoclassical realism is a more coherent approach to foreign policy than has been previously appreciated. In particular, we have articulated a common conception of the state that underlies disparate neoclassical realist theories, uniting them into a single, coherent body of theory. For neoclassical realists, the state exists as a potentially autonomous actor that is distinct from any societal group. In the foreign policy realm, the state consists of the foreign policy executive, principally the head of government and key ministers and officials charged with the conduct of foreign policy. The foreign policy executive has privileged access to information about international threats, opportunities, and national capabilities. Consequently, it is best positioned to respond to international exigencies as the relative distribution of power in the international system requires. For this reason, although the members of the foreign policy executive may be drawn from a particular class or societal coalition, their interests and preferences will differ from those of their cohorts out of government. Executive preferences reflect a distinct *raison d'état* focus. Yet, depending on domestic political arrangements, society can affect the ease with which state leaders are able to enact policy, or extract or mobilize societal resources to implement foreign policy. Consequently, the foreign policy executive must frequently bargain with legislatures, societal actors, and interest groups. Neoclassical realists, therefore, expect policy to deviate from the requirements of systemic imperatives when the state has limited authority to conduct foreign policy, when there are many domestic veto players in the policy process, when domestic opposition to the government's policy is high, or under other domestic political circumstances that impede policy flexibility. This conception of the state differs equally from the pluralist image of a state captured or hijacked by domestic interest groups, the Marxist state that represents only the interests of a particular domestic class, and the neorealist image of an autonomous state that responds to international threats and opportunities without reference to the domestic political environment.

A second theme of this volume has been that neoclassical realism is more broadly applicable than is typically assumed. Rather than explaining merely surprising deviations from structural realist expectations, as Randall Schweller suggests, we contend that it is a useful approach for understanding foreign policy, more generally.[1] The domestic political variables that the school's proponents identify can explain not only why states occasionally fail to balance against

---

[1] Randall L. Schweller, "The Progressiveness of Neoclassical Realism," in Colin Elman and Miriam Fendius Elman, eds., *Progress in International Relations Theory: Appraising the Field* (Cambridge, MA: MIT Press, 2003), pp. 311–47; and Schweller, *Unanswered Threats: Political Constraints on the Balance of Power* (Ithaca, NY: Cornell University Press, 2006).

hostile powers, but also why they select particular balancing strategies from a range of acceptable alternatives (e.g. alliance versus rearmament) and the timing and style of their foreign policy. Mark Brawley's chapter, for example, illustrated that because of their unique domestic circumstances Great Britain, France, and the Soviet Union pursued different long-term balancing strategies against the expected rise of Germany, beginning in the 1920s. Colin Dueck's chapter demonstrated that public pressure in the United States affected the timing and style of American military intervention in Korea and Vietnam, but not the core of the strategy itself. Neoclassical realist theories, therefore, can elucidate, among other things, the conditions under which national foreign policy is likely to deviate from systemic requirements, the conditions under which states will prefer a grand strategy of alliances over internal balancing or economic engagement over deterrence, as well as the style of foreign policies that are likely to emerge from different domestic political circumstances.

Since neoclassical realists assert the primacy of the international system, however, its utility as an approach to foreign policy will vary depending on the clarity of the systemic imperatives that states face. We can thus generalize more broadly about the applicability of neoclassical realism and the relative importance of systemic versus domestic and individual-level variables. We can imagine four possible worlds that states might inhabit, varying along two dimensions: the clarity of the international system regarding threats, opportunities, and the national interest; and the degree of information it provides on how best to respond to these structural conditions (see table 10.1). These are the operative dimensions for neoclassical realists, who argue that international imperatives play the dominant role in shaping national security strategies. To the extent that international constraints are clear and the proper policies to respond to them are clear, we can infer the likelihood that societal actors should influence foreign policy and the type of impact they are likely to have according to neoclassical realists. In World 1, the international system provides concrete and unambiguous incentives and constraints, and provides clear information on how to respond to them. A prototypical example of this situation would be Israel in May–June of 1967. With the Straits of Tiran blockaded, Egypt's call for the removal of the United Nations Emergency Force (UNEF), and Egyptian troops concentrated in Sinai, the threat was clear and the most appropriate

Table 10.1 *Neoclassical realism and the four worlds*

	Clear information on threats	Unclear information on threats
Clear information on policy responses	*World 1* Consistent with realism. Domestic actors normally affect only the style or timing of policy. Neoclassical realism is useful only to explain dysfunctional behavior. (Schweller, Dueck, Lobell, Ripsman, Taliaferro)	*World 4* Inconsistent with realism. Domestic actors can help determine national interests, but policy responses are largely determined by international institutions. Neoclassical realism is not useful for explaining the behavior of states.
Unclear information on policy responses	*World 2* Consistent with realism. Domestic actors can affect not only the style or timing of policy, but also the nature of policy responses to international challenges. Neoclassical realism is useful to explain foreign policy choices of states. (Brawley, Dueck, Lobell, Ripsman, Sterling-Folker, Taliaferro)	*World 3* Inconsistent with realism. Domestic actors help determine national interests and policy responses to them. *Innenpolitik* theories are more useful than neoclassical realism in explaining the behavior of states. (Fordham)

response – a preemptive strike – was reasonably self-evident.[2] Despite this clarity, however, on occasion states may fail to discern the situation correctly or may be unable to respond appropriately due to domestic constraints. Thus, in World 1, neoclassical realist

[2] Jack S. Levy and Joseph R. Gochal, "When Do Democracies Fight Preventive Wars?" Paper presented to the annual meeting of the International Studies Association, Montreal, Canada, March 17–20, 2004.

theories may explain why some states occasionally choose suboptimal strategies despite the clarity of systemic incentives. Indeed, one of the big enterprises of neoclassical realist scholars has been to explain the failure of Britain and France to balance against the clear and present danger of Germany in the 1930s in terms of domestic politics.[3] In this volume, Randall Schweller's argument that fascist states are better equipped to mobilize national resources to respond to systemic opportunities for hegemonic expansion that offensive structural realists identify is a World 1 approach. Indeed, by setting up his analysis as an explanation of "under-expansion" and "under-aggression," he is explicitly acknowledging that the international system provides sufficient information about the optimal policy; in Schweller's view, domestic political arrangements are useful merely in explaining suboptimality.

In World 2, the system provides unambiguous information about the types of threats and opportunities – principally information about shifts in the relative balance of power – but it offers little information about the optimal types of strategies states should pursue to respond to these constraints and incentives. In other words, national interests are determined by the international system, but it is not clear what policies would maximize the national interests or, as Steven Lobell suggests in his chapter, whether different policy responses could suffice. Therefore domestic political factors, such as coalition politics, institutional preferences, cultural proclivities, etc., determine the foreign security policy response. An example might be the United States responding to the rise of China in the 1990s. Clearly the growth in Chinese power represents a threat to American interests in Asia and a constraint on US foreign policy more broadly; yet since China does

---

[3] See, for example, Schweller, *Unanswered Threats*; Randall L. Schweller, "Unanswered Threats: A Neoclassical Realist Theory of Underbalancing," *International Security* 29, no. 2 (fall 2004), pp. 159–201; Mark L. Haas, *The Ideological Origins of Great Power Politics, 1789–1989* (Ithaca, NY: Cornell University Press, 2005); and Kevin Narizny, "Both Guns and Butter, or Neither: Class Interests in the Political Economy of Rearmament," *American Political Science Review* 97, no. 2 (May 2003), pp. 203–20. For a contrary perspective, see Norrin M. Ripsman and Jack S. Levy, "The Preventive War that Never Happened: Britain, France, and the Rise of Germany in the 1930s," *Security Studies* 16, no. 1 (January 2007), pp. 32–67; and Norrin M. Ripsman and Jack S. Levy, "Wishful Thinking or Buying Time? A Reinterpretation of British Appeasement in the 1930s," *International Security* 33, no. 2 (fall 2008).

not pose a clear and present danger to the US, it is not clear how Washington should respond. Therefore, societal interests can contest the relative merits of engagement versus containment, and thereby help to shape and tailor the policy response.[4] Moreover, beyond these programmatic debates, societal actors can weigh in on every single policy as well. Thus there is even less structural determinism in World 2 than in World 1.

Mark Brawley's chapter fits squarely into World 2. Brawley describes the international system of the 1920s as a "permissive environment," in which the source of threat was clear to all European powers, but foreign policy executives were provided with little information on the optimal means of balancing against Germany. Consequently, domestic political and economic coalitions could shape national foreign policy responses to a common challenge. Jennifer Sterling-Folker's chapter suggests that, while the international system provides incentives for reduced military competition between economically interdependent states, the domestic politics of national identity frequently intervene, which can result in persistent military spending and aggressive foreign policy rhetoric between growing trading partners.

Several of the contributions to this volume straddle Worlds 1 and 2, reflecting our view that neoclassical realism is both a framework for explaining suboptimal policy choices by states and a useful approach to the study of foreign policy. Steven Lobell's chapter argues that domestic political constraints can lead to "inappropriate balancing" – a concept that fits well in World 1, where the international system requires clear policy responses, but states are not always able to meet those requirements for domestic political reasons. When the balance of power provides insufficient cues to the foreign policy executive, Lobell argues that societal opposition can also affect the style and speed of balancing. Colin Dueck claims that states intervene in military conflicts on the basis of the national interest, which is determined by the balance of power. Leaders will often tailor the type of intervention, its magnitude, and its timing to secure domestic political

---

[4] See John W. Dietrich, "Interest Groups and Foreign Policy: Clinton and the MFN Debates," *Presidential Studies Quarterly* 29, no. 2 (June 1999), pp. 280–96; and Tohishiro Nakayama, "Politics of US Policy toward China: Analysis of Domestic Factors," *Brookings Institution – CNAPS Working Paper Series* (September 2006), available at: www.brook.edu/fp/cnaps/papers/nakayama2006.htm.

approval, which occasionally leads to suboptimal strategies. Norrin Ripsman's chapter contends that when security in the international system is scarce, national foreign policy options tend to be clearer and domestic political and economic interest groups have only limited opportunities to influence policy. In contrast, when the security environment is more stable, domestic interests have greater latitude to shape the content of foreign policy. Finally, Jeffrey Taliaferro's resource extraction model also straddles Worlds 1 and 2. In Taliaferro's model, anarchy and competition within the international system provide states with incentives to emulate the political, military and technological practices of the leading states, but do not provide clear information on exactly which practices of which great powers to emulate. Whether and how effectively states are able to emulate the successful strategies of others and which states they seek to copy are determined by second-image factors, such as the ideology of the state and its extractive capacity.

In World 3, the international system is not really all that informative about constraints and opportunities. The national interests of states and appropriate foreign policies to maximize them, therefore, are almost entirely determined by unit-level factors. In this 'bottom-up' world, domestic actors have the greatest influence and can actually help define the foreign security goals of the state, rather than merely shaping the response to a clearly defined set of international constraints. Nonetheless, unlike the other two worlds, by circumscribing the role of the international system so much, World 3 is not consistent with realism, and instead is more consonant with liberal or constructivist explanations of foreign security policy. In our volume, only Benjamin Fordham's chapter inhabits World 3. In fact, the essence of his critique of the neoclassical realist agenda is that it is impossible to separate the influences of the international and domestic imperatives precisely because he doubts that the international system sends clear signals to states about threats, opportunities, and the proper strategies to navigate them. Instead, he contends that states understand the international environment in terms of the interaction between international signals and the interests of the social coalition that controls the state.

Finally, to complete the matrix, there should be a fourth world, in which threats and opportunities are unclear, but policy responses are clear. In other words, international politics in World 4 is completely regulated by some other imperative, perhaps the demands of international regimes, which condition the foreign policies of individual states.[5] Once again, as the national interest in this world is completely determined by domestic groups, it is not at all consistent with realism, and therefore bears little relevance to our discussion.

As table 10.1 indicates, the impact of domestic actors is more limited, and therefore the scope of neoclassical realism is quite restricted in World 1. As the international system provides tremendous clarity for states, domestic interests do not typically contribute to a definition of national interests and have a meaningful impact on policy choices only in exceptional circumstances, when they derail the ship of state and cause suboptimal choices to be made. Beyond that, domestic groups may frequently be able to affect the style of foreign policy responses without altering its thrust. In World 2, however, domestic interests have a much greater role in the making of national security policy and thus frequently help determine not only the style of foreign policy, but also the means used to respond to systemic challenges. Thus, in World 2, neoclassical realism becomes an appropriate paradigm to construct theories of foreign policy, rather than merely suboptimal deviations. Only rarely in these two realist worlds can domestic actors actually shape the interpretation of the national interest, which can result in dysfunctional policy responses, as international constraints are ignored or misinterpreted.

Having identified the scope of neoclassical realist theory as understood in this volume, the next section will consider the value added of neoclassical realist theory by comparing the cases covered in this volume with the expectations of other leading approaches to international politics and foreign policy.

Neoclassical realism versus other theoretical approaches

Throughout this volume, neoclassical realism has been advanced principally as an alternative to structural realist theory. It is not sufficient merely to identify the theoretical disagreements between these approaches; we must consider whether there is any explanatory payoff to treating the domestic decision-making environment as an intervening variable between the international system and foreign policy. To this end, we shall consider the implications of case study evidence

[5] We thank Michael Lipson for bringing this World to our attention.

presented in this volume for the debate between structural and neo-classical realism.

The case studies and anecdotal examples presented in this volume challenge the neorealist image of the national security state as lib-erated from domestic considerations. Neorealists expect states to emulate the successful practices of other states in order to survive. Yet Taliaferro's chapter illustrates that states vary significantly in their ability to copy successful states. He shows that domestic poli-tical differences can have a considerable impact on the ability of different states to mobilize domestic resources in response to similar challenges. Thus the Qing dynasty in China was unable to restruc-ture the Chinese defense culture along European lines in order to counter the threat of western imperialism, while the Meiji oligarchs in Japan could respond effectively by emulating the German army and state bureaucracy, as well as the British Royal Navy. Schweller's chapter asserts that offensive structural realist theories cannot account for the timidity of states such as the United States, India, and Brazil in the mid-twentieth century, and their unwillingness or inability to seek regional or global hegemony. Instead, he argues that the difficulty of mobilizing domestic resources makes some states ill-equipped for expansion, whereas fascist states can mobilize resources with considerable ease. Ripsman's example of the Canadian government bowing to domestic opposition to the 2003 Gulf War, thereby forsaking its primary ally, principal trading partner, and the global hegemon, is clear evidence that neorealists pay insufficient attention to domestic politics. Even though Fordham is critical of the neoclassical realist agenda as well, his example of American attitudes to military spending and internal balancing against the Soviet Union cannot be explained by systemic constraints alone; party affiliations and interests determined how Congress viewed and responded to Soviet challenges. Thus evidence abounds that neo-realism overestimates the fluidity with which states react to changes in the international system.

Neoclassical realism's attention to domestic politics also distin-guishes it from rationalist approaches that explain foreign policy in terms of governmental responses to external stimuli. Bruce Bueno de Mesquita's expected utility theory posits that leaders make decisions of war and peace on the basis of the expected utility of their actions, determined by calculations of systemic factors such as, inter alia, relative capability, the power of allies, and geographical distance.[6] The bargaining model of war is another rationalist approach, which assumes that states prefer to avoid costly wars, and therefore reach agreements based on the distribution of power in the international system that privilege the stronger in proportion to its strength. According to this model, war occurs only in the event that the stronger state is declining in power, and consequently would rationally expect any agreement reached to be violated by the rising challenger once its power transition was complete.[7] Neoclassical realists would take issue with the implicit assumptions of both these models that state leaders have automatic access to all national resources, that they do not have to bargain with societal groups to enact or implement policy, and that they can, therefore, respond to shifts in the balance of power in a fluid and flexible manner.

Empirical evidence presented in this volume supports this theoretical challenge to rationalist theories. For example, Lobell indicates that, although Britain faced clear systemic incentives to engage in internal balancing against Germany, it was difficult for British leaders in the late 1930s to raise the necessary resources for a serious and rapid rearmament effort because internationalist elites in the City of London believed that balancing would harm their interests. Given their power within the government, these business elites were able to slow down British rearmament considerably. Dueck similarly points out that public aversion to war in Vietnam led President Lyndon Johnson to pursue a suboptimal incremental escalation so as to sustain domestic support for his Great Society project.

Although neoclassical realism incorporates domestic political variables in its explanatory framework, it also offers a distinct alternative to liberal approaches to foreign policy, most of which assume a considerable societal input into policy-making. Democratic peace theory, for example, assumes that some key strategic alternatives – principally, the use of force against other democratic states, but also, presumably, arms racing with or alliance formation against fellow democracies – are denied to democratic leaders by the public and the

---

[6] See Bruce Bueno de Mesquita, *The War Trap* (New Haven, CT: Yale University Press, 1981); and Bruce Bueno de Mesquita and David Lalman, *War and Reason* (New Haven, CT: Yale University Press, 1992).

[7] See James D. Fearon, "Rationalist Explanations for War," *International Organization* 49, no. 3 (1995), pp. 379–414.

legislature.[8] Thus the distinction between these schools is that for democratic peace theorists, domestic politics and not the international system determines the broad parameters of alternative foreign policies. Similarly, commercial liberalism posits that domestic economic interests will restrain states from aggressive foreign policy directed at significant trading partners.[9] These liberal approaches are qualitatively different from neoclassical realism in that they do not assume that states respond, in the first instance, to international imperatives. As Sterling-Folker observed elsewhere, the debate between liberalism and realism (in general) boils down to a debate between whether actors' preferences are determined by their external environment or whether they are shaped by the process by which they are formed.[10] Neoclassical realists could imagine a situation where states view erstwhile trading partners as strategic rivals or where democratic states view a powerful and rising democracy as their primary strategic threat. In contrast, these liberal alternatives maintain that domestic politics would make such threat identification impossible. Thus neither democratic peace theorists nor commercial liberals would consider it likely for today's western democracies to balance against American primacy, but neoclassical realists might.

In practical terms, the cases discussed in this book provide little evidence against these liberal *Innenpolitik* theories. The Sterling-Folker chapter does directly address commercial liberalism, but she

---

[8] The classic statements of democratic peace literature remain Michael Doyle, "Kant, Liberal Legacies, and Foreign Affairs, part 1," *Philosophy and Public Affairs*, 12, no. 3 (1983), pp. 205–35; "Kant, Liberal Legacies, and Foreign Affairs, part 2," *Philosophy and Public Affairs*. 12, no. 4 (1983), pp. 323–53; and Bruce M. Russett, *Grasping the Democratic Peace* (Princeton, NJ: Princeton University Press, 1993). On the argument that democracies eschew so-called "hard balancing" strategies against other democracies, see John M. Owen IV, "Transnational Liberalism and US Primacy," *International Security* 26, no. 3 (winter 2001/2), pp. 117–52; and T. V. Paul, "Soft Balancing in the Age of US Primacy," *International Security* 30, no. 1 (summer 2005), pp. 46–71.

[9] The term "commercial liberalism" is used by Robert O. Keohane, "International Liberalism Revisited," in John Dunn, ed., *The Economic Limits to Modern Politics* (Cambridge: Cambridge University Press, 1990), pp. 186–7. See also Geoffrey Blainey, *The Causes of War*, 3rd edn (New York: The Free Press, 1988), chap. 2, and Michael W. Doyle, *Ways of War and Peace: Realism, Liberalism, and Socialism* (New York: Norton, 1997), pp. 230–50.

[10] Jennifer Sterling-Folker, "Realist Environment, Liberal Process, and Domestic-Level Variables," *International Studies Quarterly* 41, no. 1 (March 1997), pp. 1–25, at p. 6.

challenges the structural aspect of it (i.e. that economic interdependence serves as an external constraint against defense spending and the use of force between trading partners) by introducing the domestic politics of identity as an intervening factor. Thus Sterling-Folker finds that, although China and Taiwan are increasing their economic interaction, defense competition and nationalist rhetoric between them has escalated. She does not, however, make the converse claim that geostrategic concerns override calls from domestic economic interests for foreign policy restraint.[11] Nor does this volume offer any concrete evidence that balance of power considerations trump democratic procedural or normative restraints on the use of force against other democracies.[12]

Because neoclassical realism contends that the international system is the dominant influence on foreign policy, it also distinguishes itself from other so-called *Innenpolitik* approaches that view foreign policy as the product of domestic political pressures. Pluralist approaches view policy as the product of competition between interest groups for the control of the state. The successful coalition of interests is able to tailor policy to maximize its own interests.[13] State capture approaches, such as Marxist theories of foreign policy, similarly assume that the dominant classes or ruling coalitions control the state and enact policies that advance their group interests, often at the expense of rival groups.[14] Neoclassical realists would take issue with

---

[11] For an article that does provide evidence that systemic imperatives override the constraints of interdependence, see Norrin M. Ripsman and Jean-Marc F. Blanchard, "Commercial Liberalism under Fire: Evidence from 1914 and 1936," *Security Studies* 6, no. 2 (winter 1996–7), pp. 4–50.

[12] Such an argument is made and supported by Christopher Layne, "Kant or Cant: The Myth of the Democratic Peace," *International Security*, 19, no. 2 (fall 1994), pp. 5–49; and Errol Henderson, *Democracy and War: The End of an Illusion?* (Boulder, CO: Lynne Rienner, 2002).

[13] See, for example, Martin J. Smith, *Pressure, Power, and Policy: State Autonomy and Policy Networks in Britain and the United States* (Pittsburgh, PA: University of Pittsburgh Press, 1993); and John M. Hobson, *The State and International Relations* (Cambridge: Cambridge University Press, 2000), chap. 3.

[14] See, for example, Rosa Luxemburg, "Militarism as a Province of Accumulation," in Daniela Gioseffi, ed., *Women on War: An International Anthology of Women's Writings from Antiquity to the Present* (New York: Feminist Press at the City University of New York, 2003), pp. 5–6; Harry Magdoff, *The Age of Imperialism: The Economics of US Foreign Policy* (New York: Monthly Review Press, 1969); and Gabriel Kolko, *The Roots of American Foreign Policy* (Boston: Beacon Press, 1969).

the idea that policy could be made independently of international circumstances. Indeed, neoclassical realists would expect that in many situations widely varying coalitions of interests in different countries would choose similar foreign policies when faced with comparable international threats. Thus, as Mark Brawley's chapter indicates, the governments of Great Britain, France, and the Soviet Union all identified the rise of German power as the key threat in the early 1930s, despite different political systems and governing coalitions. Domestic political considerations affected the strategies state leaders employed to balance against the German challenge, but not the basic parameters of foreign policy. In a similar fashion, Colin Dueck's chapter demonstrates that domestic preferences did not drive American intervention in Korea or Vietnam. These were driven by international pressures, although public and legislative opinion helped determine the parameters of intervention and its timing.

Overall, then, the evidence discussed in this book supports our claims that neoclassical realism provides a rich understanding of the determinants of foreign policy and the way that states respond to international challenges. Since this volume was intended primarily for theoretical development and refinement of the neoclassical realist conception of the state rather than rigorous testing, though, we leave for future research systematic attempts to test neoclassical realism against these other bodies of theory. The next section discusses these plans in greater detail.

Avenues for future research

Now that we have added more conceptual flesh to the skeleton of neoclassical realism and, in particular, elucidated the view of the state that unites its diverse strands, we believe that the next phase of the neoclassical realist research agenda should be to test the explanatory power of neoclassical realism systematically against other approaches to foreign and national security policy. This entails several different research agendas.

First, we look forward to systematic tests of neoclassical realism against other leading approaches to foreign policy, including liberal and constructivist *Innenpolitik* theories and neorealist systemic approaches. To evaluate the relative merits of these different schools, it would be helpful to evaluate empirically which approach provides the most satisfying explanations of the major foreign policy decisions of states with different domestic political contexts and different positions in the international system.

Consider, for example, the burgeoning literature on military effectiveness, broadly defined as the study of states' relative ability to translate basic material and human resources into military power at the strategic, operational, and tactical levels.[15] This area of research goes to the heart of the international relations field. Furthermore, it has clear policy implications, especially in light of the United States' efforts to train and equip new national armies and security forces in Iraq and Afghanistan, as well as the fierce competition between the US, the European Union, Russia, and China to sell conventional weapons to developing countries.

Proponents of democratic peace theories argue that liberal democracies are more likely to win wars for two reasons. First, there is the so-called selection effect. Democracies are simply better at picking the wars they fight, choosing to initiate or enter ongoing hostilities where the prospects of victory are relative good. Second, once at war, democracies are better able to harness the material and human resources necessary for victory because of popular support and leaders' accountability to the electorate. This is the military effectiveness argument.[16] Constructivists and cultural theorists, conversely, attribute

---

[15] Much of the recent international relations literature on military effectiveness tends to focus on the tactical level of warfare or tactical effectiveness. See Risa A. Brooks, "Making Military Might: Why Do States Succeed or Fail?" *International Security* 28, no. 2 (fall 2003), pp. 49–91, at p. 153; and Stephen D. Biddle, *Military Power: Explaining Victory and Defeat in Modern Battle* (Princeton, NJ: Princeton University Press, 2004). However, the concept of military effectiveness can also apply to the operational and strategic levels of warfare. See Allan R. Millet, Williamson Murray, and Kenneth W. Watman, "The Effectiveness of Military Organizations," in Millet and Murray, eds., *Military Effectiveness*, vol. I: *The First World War* (Boston: Allen and Unwin, 1988), pp. 1–30.

[16] Examples of these two lines of the democratic peace literature include: David A. Lake, "Powerful Pacifists: Democratic States and War," *American Political Science Review* 86, no. 1 (March 1992), pp. 24–37; Dan Reiter and Allan C. Stam III, "Democracy and Battlefield Military Effectiveness," *Journal of Conflict Resolution* 42, no. 3 (June 1998), pp. 259–77; Reiter and Stam, "Democracy, War Initiation, and Victory," *American Political Science Review* 92, no. 2 (June 1998), pp. 377–89; Reiter and Stam, *Democracies at War* (Princeton, NJ: Princeton University Press, 2002); William Reed and David H. Clark, "War Initiators and War Winners: The Consequences of Linking

variation in military effectiveness to either preexisting cultures within military bureaucracies and national elites or broader social divisions within society (whether based upon class, ethnicity, religion, or some other immutable characteristic).[17] Still other scholars have looked at how patterns of civil–military relations affect states' ability to absorb new technologies and by extension the battlefield effectiveness of forces.[18] However, very few of these works systematically examine how unit-level factors such as regime type, nationalism, civil–military relations, or societal cleavages might interact with systemic-level factors, such as the international distribution of power and power trends, in explaining variation in states' ability to generate military power. Here neoclassical realism might add some insights that purely *Innenpolitik* or systemic approaches cannot. Although much of the neoclassical realist literature has thus far focused on the grand strategic level, there is no reason why one cannot derive hypotheses about the implications of international threat assessment and strategic adjustment on the effectiveness of armed forces.

Second, it would be useful to test neoclassical realism against the interactive model that Benjamin Fordham develops in this volume to evaluate: (1) whether we really can separate international and domestic influences on foreign policy, as neoclassical realists assume; and (2) whether making this assumption yields more efficient and accurate explanations of major foreign policy events than Fordham's model. Such an endeavor may be hampered by the lack of precision in Fordham's model, which may make it difficult to generate a priori predictions of

---

Theories of Democratic War Success," *Journal of Conflict Resolution*, 44, no. 3 (June 2000), pp. 378–95. For criticisms of this literature see Brooks, "Making Military Might"; Michael C. Desch, "Democracy and Victory: Why Regime Type Hardly Matters," *International Security* 27, no. 2 (fall 2002), pp. 5–47.

[17] See, for example, Stephen P. Rosen, *Societies and Military Power: India and its Armies* (Ithaca, NY: Cornell University Press, 1996); Kenneth M. Pollack, *Arabs at War: Military Effectiveness, 1948–1991* (Lincoln: University of Nebraska Press, 2002); and Christopher S. Parker, "New Weapons for Old Problems: Conventional Proliferation and Military Effectiveness in Developing States," *International Security* 23, no. 4 (spring 1999), pp. 119–47.

[18] Stephen D. Biddle and Robert Zirkle, "Technology, Civil–Military Relations, and Warfare in the Developing World: Conventional Proliferation and Military Effectiveness in Developing States," *Journal of Strategic Studies* 19, no. 2 (June 1996), pp. 171–212.

domestic group preferences within different international circumstances. Nonetheless, it will be important to verify whether this neoclassical realist simplification, justified in Ripsman's chapter, is truly warranted.

Future neoclassical realist work might also examine how realist arguments about polarity and war, shifts in power, and balancing behavior explain the foreign policy, grand strategy, or military doctrine of a particular leading state such as the United States, Germany (or the European Union), Russia, India, Brazil, and China or a specific historical event. A realist foreign policy model requires the inclusion of unit-level intervening variables to understand the domestic policy process. For instance, the current unipolar system is unique. The Soviet Union's demise and the lack of international constraints on the United States mean that the system sets only broad parameters on its foreign policy. Washington might exploit the situation and opt for unilateralism, interventionism, and expansionism because it can, since there is little risk of the formation of a counterbalancing coalition. Washington might also adopt a more lackadaisical and disengaged global attitude because it can, since there is no threat on the immediate horizon.[19] Given this environment, neoclassical realists might look to executive–legislative competition (especially a reaction to the notion of an "imperial presidency"), the influence of business elites, the advisory process, domestic audiences, strategic culture, or leadership style to speculate on the specific course of action from America's foreign policy menu.

Future research might also examine how secondary states will respond to the United States in this new unipolar environment. How will they assess and adapt to exogenous shifts in the international environment? Specifically, will China act like erstwhile emerging great powers with aspirations of regional hegemony, and thereby expand its geographic reach, military capability, and influence to reflect its growing power and position?[20] For neoclassical realists this path is not

---

[19] Barry R. Posen, "European Union Security and Defense Policy: Response to Unipolarity?" *Security Studies* 15, no. 2 (April–June 2006), pp. 149–86.

[20] The recent literature on the future of Chinese grand strategy and the implications of China's rise for East Asian security and US grand strategy is enormous. For a good overview of the debates among international relations theorists and academic and non-academic East Asia specialists, see Aaron L. Friedberg, "The Future of US–China Relations: Is Conflict Inevitable?" *International Security*, 30, no. 2 (fall 2005), pp. 7–45, and Robert S. Ross and Zhu Feng, eds., *Rising China: Theoretical and Policy Perspectives* (Ithaca, NY: Cornell University Press, 2008).

inevitable. Will Japan acquire the maritime and air capabilities necessary to project power beyond its home waters – war-making capabilities clearly in violation of the country's pacifist (and American-written) 1947 constitution and its self-imposed 1 percent of gross domestic product (GDP) limit on defense spending?[21] Will Germany seek to 'slip its leash' from the control of the European Union and NATO?[22] Instead, will an enlarged EU become a vehicle for Germany and other European powers to challenge the United States' six-decades-long hegemonic role, if not in terms of military capabilities, then in terms of economic might?[23] Alternatively, have norms of peaceful conflict resolution, domestic institutions, and multilateral regimes tempered these trad-itional tendencies?[24] Will secondary powers balance against the United States through traditional military and economic methods or will domestic and unit-level forces constrain and dampen these 'law-like' tendencies, resulting in a wide variation in responses ranging from hard and soft balancing to bandwagoning or even hedging?[25]

[21] For arguments that this is precisely what Japan is doing, see Richard J. Samuels, "New Fighting Power! Japan's Growing Maritime Capabilities and East Asian Security," *International Security*, 32, no. 3 (winter 2007/8), pp. 84–112; and Samuels, *Securing Japan: Tokyo's Grand Strategy and the Future of East Asia* (Ithaca, NY: Cornell University Press, 2007).

[22] On the strategy of leash-slipping, see Christopher Layne, "The Unipolar Illusion Revisited: The Coming End of the United States' Unipolar Moment," *International Security* 31, no. 2 (fall 2006), pp. 7–41.

[23] For example, see Charles A. Kupchan, *The End of the American Era: US Foreign Policy and the Geopolitics of the Twenty-First Century* (New York: Alfred A. Knopf, 2002); and Kenneth N. Waltz, "Structural Realism after the Cold War," in G. John Ikenberry, ed., *America Unrivaled: The Future of the Balance of Power* (Ithaca, NY: Cornell University Press, 2003).

[24] See Thomas U. Berger, *Cultures of Antimilitarism: National Security in Germany and Japan* (Baltimore, MD: Johns Hopkins University Press, 2003).

[25] On soft balancing, see Robert A. Pape, "Soft Balancing against the United States," *International Security* 30, no. 1 (summer 2005), pp. 7–45, and Paul, "Soft Balancing." For rejoinders, see Stephen G. Brooks, William C. Wohlforth, "Hard Times for Soft Balancing," *International Security* 30, no. 1 (summer 2005), pp. 72–108; Keir A. Lieber and Gerard Alexander, "Waiting for Balancing: Why the World is Not Pushing Back," *International Security* 30, no. 1 (summer 2005), pp. 109–39; Robert J. Art, Stephen G. Brooks, William C. Wohlforth, Keir A. Lieber, and Gerard Alexander, "Correspondence: Striking the Balance," *International Security* 30, no. 3 (winter 2005/6), pp. 177–96. On hedging, see Thomas J. Christensen, "Fostering Stability or Creating a Monster? The Rise of China and US Policy toward East Asia," *International Security* 31, no. 1 (summer 2006), pp. 81–126.

Are power shifts between the leading states likely to lead to war even among democratic and interdependent dyads or do different kinds of states allow for peaceful transitions? These questions cannot adequately be addressed with reference solely to the position these states occupy in the contemporary international system. Nor, we contend, should internal approaches that ignore the constraints of US hegemony be helpful.

Another area of research that neoclassical realists have started to address is questions about power – what is it and how do we measure it, how can state leaders extract and mobilize it, and how can they use it? For realists power is defined as material power (i.e. geography, natural resources, population, trade and industrial capacity, technology, etc.) and military power (i.e. expenditure, size and quality of military, training, organization, leadership, power projection, etc.). But power cannot be calculated solely on the basis of material factors. Other elements of power include individual leadership (whether dominated by charismatic statesmen or trouble-makers), the quality of government, the competence of its administrators, and a government's reputation or track record in world politics.[26] These variables all contribute to internal extraction capacity, as resources without the political means to extract them are virtually useless.

Fareed Zakaria differentiates between state power and national power to highlight that resource extraction and mobilization is not as seamless and fluid as many realists portray.[27] William Wohlforth and Aaron Friedberg examine elite perceptions of the international distribution of power, including the relative extractive and mobilization capacities of states, as determinants of grand strategic choices.[28]

[26] See, for example, Hans J. Morgenthau, *Politics among Nations*, 3rd edn (New York: Alfred A. Knopf, 1964), pp. 110–48; and Steven L. Spiegel, *Dominance and Diversity: The International Hierarchy* (Boston: Little, Brown, 1972), pp. 39–91.

[27] Fareed Zakaria, *From Wealth to Power: The Unusual Origins of America's World Role* (Princeton, NJ: Princeton University Press, 1997), esp. pp. 30–7 and 90–127. Also see Aaron L. Friedberg, *In the Shadow of the Garrison State: America's Anti-Statism and its Cold War Grand Strategy* (Princeton, NJ: Princeton University Press, 2000), pp. 9–33.

[28] William Curti Wohlforth, *Elusive Balance: Power and Perceptions during the Cold War* (Ithaca: Cornell University Press, 1993), esp. pp. 10–17, 179–81, and 293–307; Aaron L. Friedberg, *Weary Titan: Britain and the Experience of Relative Decline, 1895–1905* (Princeton, NJ: Princeton University Press, 1988), esp. pp. 279–91. See also Stephen G. Brooks and William C. Wohlforth,

Other important constraints on extraction and mobilization include the level of political and social cohesion, and public support for foreign policy objectives.

We began this volume by posing a set of questions about the different ways in which the state – that is, the central apparatus or institutions of government – inhibits or facilitates the ability to assess international threats and opportunities; to undertake grand strategic adjustments; and to implement specific military, diplomatic, and foreign economic policies. Our critique of the existing international relations literature is twofold. First, theoretical approaches that look only to the international system cannot explain much of the variation in the types of foreign and security strategies that states actually pursue. Second, theoretical approaches that focus only on societal actors, downplay the potentially autonomous role of the foreign policy executive in determining the national interest, and ignore the constraints imposed on all states by the international system, are also sorely deficient.

We believe neoclassical realism improves upon other schools of international relations theory precisely because it both gives causal primacy to systemic variables and posits an important intervening role for domestic variables. This volume has sought to build upon and expand the scope of neoclassical realism by better specifying how, why, and under what conditions domestic political institutions, and the relationship between those institutions and various societal groups, filter international systemic pressures on states. The contributors have presented a variety of neoclassical realist hypotheses on, or models of, the politics of grand strategy – from threat assessment to the actual implementation of diplomatic, military, and economic strategies. Some of the contributors have also sought to test the limits of neoclassical realism and to suggest avenues for dialogue with other theoretical approaches.

Overall, then, neoclassical realism is quite broad and can address the most significant questions studied by scholars of international politics and foreign policy. Some critics will always deride neoclassical realism for lacking parsimony or for layering systemic and unit-level

"Power, Globalization, and the End of the Cold War: Reevaluating the Landmark Case for Ideas," *International Security* 25, no. 2 (winter 2000/1), pp. 5–53.

variables to improve explanatory and predictive accuracy and range. Yet, as Schweller observes about the study of international politics and foreign policy: "To be sure, the political process is messy, but it is the subject matter we have chosen to study and theorize about ... It seems that, as the discipline becomes more self-conscious about its status as a science, it produces less interesting and more apolitical work."[29] Most of the contributors to this volume would concur with Schweller's assessment. Rigid adherence to parsimony, mono-causality, and metatheoretical orthodoxy should not inhibit political scientists from asking and seeking to answer big and important questions. We believe neoclassical realism will continue to flourish as a research program precisely because its proponents have not lost sight of the "political" in the study of international politics, foreign policy, and grand strategy.

[29] Randall L. Schweller, "The Progressive Power of Neoclassical Realism," in Colin Elman and Miriam Fendius Elman, eds., *Progress in International Relations Theory: Appraising the Field* (Cambridge, MA: MIT Press, 2003), p. 347.

Index